THE SHAKESPEAREAN STAGE 1574–1642

For almost forty years *The Shakespearean Stage* has been considered the liveliest, most reliable and most entertaining overview of Shakespearean theatre in its own time. It is the only authoritative book that describes all the main features of the original staging of Shakespearean drama in one volume: the acting companies and their practices, the playhouses, the staging and the audiences. Thoroughly revised and updated, this fourth edition contains fresh materials about how specific plays by Shakespeare were first staged, and provides new information about the companies that staged them and their playhouses. The book incorporates everything that has been discovered in recent years about the early modern stage, including the archaeology of the Rose and the Globe. Also included is an invaluable appendix, listing all the plays known to have been performed at particular playhouses and by specific companies.

ANDREW GURR is Emeritus Professor of English at the University of Reading. As chief academic advisor, he was a key figure in the project to rebuild Shakespeare's Globe Theatre in London. His many publications include *Playgoing in Shakespeare's London* (Cambridge, third edition 2004) and *The Shakespearean Playing Companies* (1996). Professor Gurr regularly contributes articles on Shakespeare to publications ranging from *Shakespeare Survey* to the *Times Literary Supplement*.

THE SHAKESPEAREAN STAGE
1574–1642

FOURTH EDITION

ANDREW GURR

Professor of English Emeritus
University of Reading

CAMBRIDGE
UNIVERSITY PRESS

CAMBRIDGE
UNIVERSITY PRESS

University Printing House, Cambridge CB2 8BS, United Kingdom

One Liberty Plaza, 20th Floor, New York, NY 10006, USA

477 Williamstown Road, Port Melbourne, VIC 3207, Australia

4843/24, 2nd Floor, Ansari Road, Daryaganj, Delhi - 110002, India

79 Anson Road, #06-04/06, Singapore 079906

Cambridge University Press is part of the University of Cambridge.

It furthers the University's mission by disseminating knowledge in the pursuit of
education, learning and research at the highest international levels of excellence.

www.cambridge.org
Information on this title: www.cambridge.org/9780521729666

© Andrew Gurr 2009

First published 2009
5th printing 2014

A catalogue record for this publication is available from the British Library

Library of Congress Cataloging in Publication data
Gurr, Andrew.
The Shakespearean stage, 1574–1642 / Andrew Gurr. – 4th ed.
p.   cm.
Includes bibliographical references and index.
ISBN 978-0-521-50981-7
1. Shakespeare, William, 1564–1616 – Stage history – To 1625.   2. Shakespeare, William,
1564–1616 –
Stage history – 1625–1800.   3. Shakespeare, William, 1564–1616 – Stage history –
England.
4. Theater – England – History – 16th century.   5. Theater – England – History –
17th century.   I. Title.
PR3095.G865   2008
792'.0942–dc22
2008049137

ISBN 978-0-521-72966-6 Paperback

Contents

Illustrations

Preface

The term 'Shakespearean' is used to cover what are normally called the Elizabethan, Jacobean and Caroline periods – that is, the latter half of Elizabeth's reign, from the 1570s to 1603, the whole of the reign of James I, 1603–25, and the period of rule (as distinct from reign) of Charles I, 1625–42. Shakespeare's own contact with the London theatre world extended only from about 1590 to 1616, but he stands on its highest peak, and his name if anyone's has to be given to the period. The theatre conditions that supplied Shakespeare with the venue for his plays came into existence in the 1570s, and disappeared abruptly in 1642. The first official recognition of the London-based commercial acting companies was given in 1574; a total ban on playing was imposed in 1642, and was thoroughly enforced for the next eighteen years, long enough to destroy almost all traces of Shakespearean theatre conditions and traditions. The seventy years of play-acting in which Shakespeare's career was embedded needs to be seen as a whole, and the best single word for it is Shakespearean.

A number of the variables of the Shakespearean period have been regularised for convenience. The old-style system of dating, which began the calendar year in March instead of on 1 January, has been silently adjusted to the modern dating. The titles of plays and the names of players, which were spelt in various ways even by their owners, have been regularised in the forms adopted by Chambers and Bentley. On the other hand money is recorded in the old form of pounds, shillings and pence. That is, the 'penny' mentioned in this book is one two-hundred-and-fortieth part of a pound, one-twelfth of a shilling, not the one-hundredth part of a pound that is the modern value for a penny. The quotations use the old denotation of the penny as 'd.', not the modern 'p.'. In accordance with the same principle of supplying an authentic picture of the Shakespearean background, quotations are given wherever possible in the original spelling, except that the Elizabethan typographical conventions of i for j, initial v and medial u have been altered to the modern usage. And to be consistent in the same principle, actors are normally called players, theatres are playhouses, playwrights (a term which crept into favour along with 'actors' in the 1630s) are given their own name for themselves, poets. Their product is the unserious business of playing.

FROM THE NOTE FOR THE THIRD EDITION

In this third edition some, though small, account has been taken of the shifts in priorities which have appeared in the last decade, under the pressure of new theories about the heuristic and self-reflexive nature of this game of studying Shakespeare's working conditions. The Appendix listing the plays and their circumstances of performance, for instance, is now arranged in the alphabetical order of the plays themselves, not their dead authors. But for the most part the revision simply seeks to incorporate the new evidence that has appeared since 1980. The groundplan of the Rose playhouse and a few of its implications, the Globe's entrance lobby, a better translation of Orazio Busino's Italian, some recent conjectures about the staging of the plays, revised datings and related information about particular plays, these and other details have been inserted in the relevant chapters. There is even a small attempt in Chapter 2 at humanising the old picture of Philip Henslowe as a tight-fisted theatre impresario. Chapter 4, on the design of the different kinds of playhouse, has had the most additions. For different reasons Chapter 6, on the audiences, has had the least. Subheadings have been added to each chapter to clarify the organisation of the material.

A FOURTH PREFACE

It is now forty years since as a junior university teacher I felt the need to provide my students with an accessible summary of useful information about Shakespearean theatre. Having struggled through the eleven packed volumes of Chambers and Bentley, I felt attracted to their hard-nosed pursuit of material evidence but appalled at the sheer quantity of minutiae they accumulated. To pick out exemplary events and anecdotal stories long before New Historicism's elevation of the anecdote as good history and to focus them on the plays seemed like a good idea at the time. The result was the first rather tentative version of this book. Since then I have returned again and again to the book's subject-matter, making several of its chapters whole books, and for one a physical reconstruction of the original playhouse. Revising and augmenting all the bits of evidence now, for this fourth and probably final edition, it seems only a little surprising that so many of the 'hard' facts and anecdotes still stand up from the fog of theory that has clouded the subject so intensely in recent years.

For this revision I have stuck by most of the earlier principles, such as reproducing all quotations in the original spelling and relying very largely on illustrations from the time. It is regrettably true that the preference for modernised spelling still dominates reading texts – in, for instance, almost all editions of the plays and even in scholarly source books like *English Professional Theatre, 1530–1660*, which reprints many of the documents quoted here, but all in modernised spelling. When we modernise the original spelling we all too readily conceal the differences between then and now, and those differences are the basic subtext of this book.

Its essential justification stays the same: to provide a material basis for understanding what evoked that unique florescence of plays created through those years. Materialism of this kind can produce some intriguingly fresh insights into what went on in the Shakespearean theatre. I am still teased, for instance, by the nature of the actor–audience relationship that provoked one extraordinary simile set down in a Shakespeare play of 1596. In *1 Henry IV*, 1.3.186–91, Worcester tries to tell the furious Harry Hotspur about the plot to take the crown from King Henry. It is, he says, 'a secret book', its 'matter deep and dangerous, / As full of peril and adventurous spirit / As to o'erwalk a current roaring loud / On the unsteadfast footing of a spear'. Spears were for throwing at boars or deer when hunting. Their handles were round, light in weight and flexible, unlike the heavy square or bevelled fixity of a pikestaff. To use such a fragile rod for a bridge would undoubtedly be perilous. Editors link the simile to medieval chronicles such as *Erec and Enid*, where a gleaming sword appears as a bridge over troubled waters. A spear bridging a gulf would certainly make an 'unsteadfast footing'. But why a spear rather than a sword, the symbolic bridge of the romances? We might remember that when Shakespeare's company first set his name to his plays, in 1598 with *Richard II* and *Richard III*, and a year later for *1 Henry IV*, in each case they presented his name with a hyphen, as 'William Shake-speare'. Knowing this little joke about the author as an actor playing huntsman or soldier enhances the likelihood that Worcester's peculiar simile was set down as an in-joke among the players, perhaps even that the speaker of the lines about the shaky spear was the author himself. Such a reading tells us a lot about the quality of intimacy shared not only by the players amongst themselves but with their regular audiences, and the expectation on both sides that even the tensest or most portentous moment in a play could be broken easily and harmlessly with a metatheatrical in-joke. What was in Shakespeare's mind when he composed the joke? Was he saying that his company could not trust him to carry them over their obstacles? Perhaps the simile was a quiet admission of the lack of trust between them. Some failure of confidence certainly led the company to revise his second sequel to *1 Henry IV*, as the first quarto in 1600 of *Henry V* shows, a point made in Chapter 3 of this edition. Such features of early playing brighten the complex and collaborative business of staging that our modern reverence for Shakespeare all too readily obscures.

Acknowledgements

The author and publisher would like to thank the following for permission to reproduce the illustrations: the Marquess of Tavistock and the Trustees of the Bedford Estates (for Nos. 1 and 43); the British Library (2, 3, 4, 5, 11, 16, 17, 19, 22, 37, 41); the Photographic Survey, Courtauld Institute of Art (6, 8); the Governors of Dulwich College (7, 9, 10, 12, 13, 20); the Folger Shakespeare Library (14); the Master and Fellows of Magdalene College, Cambridge (15); the Ashmolean Museum (18); the Herzog Anton Ulrich Museum, Braunsweig (21); Andrew Fulgoni Photography (23); the Bibliotheek der Rijksuniversiteit, Utrecht (26); the Mellon Foundation (27); Richard Hosley (31); the Guildhall Library, City of London (32, 38); the Museum of London (24, 28, 29); Jon Greenfield (25); Shakespeare's Globe (30); the Provost and Fellows of Worcester College, Oxford (33, 34, 36); the Department of the Environment (35); the Victoria and Albert Museum (39); the Marquess of Bath (40); the Duke of Devonshire and the Trustees of the Chatsworth Settlement (42).

CHAPTER I

Introduction

I. THEN AND NOW

Hamlet, like any other Shakespearean nobleman, wore his hat indoors. When the foppish and murderous Osric came flourishing his headgear with the invitation to fight Laertes, Hamlet undoubtedly doffed his bonnet in reply to Osric's flourish, and then put it back on. Osric's failure to follow suit led to Hamlet's reproof ('Put your bonnet to his right use, 'tis for the head'). The unbonneted Hamlet familiar to modern audiences is a creation of the indoor theatre and fourth-wall staging, where every scene is a room unless it is specified otherwise, and where everyone goes hatless accordingly. Hamlet in 1601 walked under the sky in an open amphitheatre, on a platform that felt out-of-doors in comparison with modern theatres but indifferently represented indoors or out to the Elizabethans. There was a wall at the back of the platform, fronting the 'tiring-house' or room where the players changed, the offstage area. It gave access to the playing area by two or more doors and a balcony. These places of entry could equally well provide the imagination with the exterior doors and balcony of a house or the interior doors and gallery of a great hall. Hamlet's headgear was worn with equal indifference to the imagined scene.

The wearing of hats on stage is a minor matter in comparison with, say, Hamlet's use of a 'nighted colour' in his clothes, so far as the play's general concerns go. But unless we know Hamlet is himself bonneted the point of his verbal fencing with Osric may be missed. Hats are useful either to guard the wearer's face against the sun, or to keep the head warm. Hamlet's request that Osric should put his bonnet to its right use is taken by Osric to be made out of concern for the hot sun ('I thank your lordship, it is very hot'). Hamlet, having been too much 'in the "son"', denies this ('No, believe me, 'tis very cold, the wind is northerly'), an equally good reason for keeping his own hat on; and when Osric hastens to agree, catches him up on it ('But yet, methinks, it is very sultry and hot for my complexion'). He

Illustration 1. Giles Brydges, the third Lord Chandos, wearing the kind of hat that Osric flourished. From a portrait by the Dutch painter Hieronimo Custodis, painted in 1589 and now at Woburn Abbey. Most hats made in England before 1600 were of leather, with a narrow brim and a seam across the flat crown. The Museum of London has an example. Osric's headgear, the most fashionable kind of wear, would have come from France or the Netherlands. Horatio's image of him as a lapwing with the eggshell he was born from still on his head suggests a hat like Lord Chandos's.

keeps his hat on with both reasons. Hamlet is not just making Osric look a fool. Hats were doffed (put off) as a gesture of respect. At the end of the gesture they went back on the head. Only a courtier in the presence of the king would keep his hat in his hand. For Osric to keep his hat off in Hamlet's presence was excessively deferential, especially in a creature of the usurping King addressing that King's victim, and Hamlet ensures that the excess is made apparent. Shakespeare made stage business out of similar by-play with hats in *Love's Labours Lost*, 5.1, *A Midsummer Night's Dream*, 4.2, and *As You Like It*, 3.3. Unless we know that Hamlet kept his hat on while Osric continued to flourish his, we miss the real point of the incident. It also helps to know that a typical Elizabethan 'bonnet' in 1600 had a high crown, a narrow brim and a round dome – a kind of elongated bowler hat – in order to visualise Horatio's image of Osric running off like a baby lapwing 'with the shell on his head'.

Hamlet makes highly sophisticated use of the theatre conditions of its time. The company of players who arrive in 2.2 were real, not the caricatures of players found in *A Midsummer Night's Dream* or Marston's *Histriomastix*, and the specimen of their work that the leading player offers is a genuine if deliberately archaic set speech, an audition piece, not a parody. Despite Polonius's interruptions, the player delivers his 'passionate speech' about rugged Pyrrhus with such good inward accompaniment to his outward appearance of passion that he changes colour and tears come into his eyes. And all this, as Hamlet bitterly tells himself afterwards, is monstrously for a fiction, a 'dream of passion':

> what would he do,
> Had he the motive and the cue for passion
> That I have?

All that is really monstrous, of course, is that Hamlet has no more motive or cue for passion than the player; he himself is as much a fiction as the player. What Shakespeare is doing in this scene is to refine the familiar Elizabethan paradox of 'tragedy played in jest', the view that sees murders done for entertainment, and appearances pretending to be reality. The fictitious Hamlet rails at the fiction of the player. Shakespeare's refinement is to make this paradoxical situation not a joke but an emphatic assertion of Hamlet's reality.

Many other details of the play's staging depend on life in Shakespeare's own time. The disposition of the stage for the play-within-the-play, for instance, which has exercised the ingenuity of some commentators, must have followed the pattern for plays at Court. The performers of the play stand at the back of the stage by the largest opening in the tiring-house wall (the so-called discovery-space), King Claudius and Queen Gertrude sit on the 'state' or throne at the front of the stage in the middle of the amphitheatre yard, facing the tiring-house, Hamlet and Ophelia to one side with a view of both.[1] Another example is the dumb-show, the mimed plot-summary with which the play within the play begins. By the time *Hamlet* was written dumb-shows were still not so archaic that Shakespeare's contemporaries hesitated to use them. Nor were they such rare devices that Hamlet should not have foreseen the players using one. The mistake in prematurely revealing the mousetrap through the dumb-show is partly due to Hamlet's lack of foresight, and his failure to allow for the players' stupidity is a component in the savagery with which he greets them when they come out to start the play itself. Again, when Polonius is stabbed through, as the Second Quarto and the schoolboy joke have it, the arras, it is worth knowing that the cloth behind which Polonius hid hung in front of the 'discovery-space', an alcove or similar structure deep enough to conceal quite substantial properties. The player of Polonius could have called out from the back of the alcove, leaving room for the player of Hamlet to make a full-blooded lunge through the curtain without fear of actually running his fellow through. Polonius could then lie down as a corpse before Hamlet drew the cloth back to reveal him. The duel at the climax in 5.2 must have been similarly full-blooded. Fencing displays were a feature of the entertainment the stages offered to the Elizabethan public, and at least one player (Richard Tarlton the clown) was a Master of Fence. Though Hamlet claims in his opening soliloquy to be utterly unlike Hercules (the archetypal man of action), he would certainly have been required to belie his words when it came to the duel with Laertes.

One feature of the headgear used in the original *Hamlet* was the difference between Hamlet's bonnet and Claudius's crown. On stage a gilded crown was the most obvious mark of authority. Crowns and coronets along with earl's bonnets have an absolutely central function in *King Lear*, where they signify the decline of authority through the play. *Lear* opens with the king wearing his crown and announcing that he will hand his authority over to the two dukes (wearing smaller coronets) who are husbands to his two elder daughters. A third coronet is on hand to be given to the suitor who chooses the third and youngest daughter as his wife. When she refuses the test he sets her, he banishes her and hands the third coronet, an unbreakable ring of gold, to the two dukes, ordering them to split it between them, a small mark of how impossible it should be to divide a kingdom. As his loss of authority becomes obvious Lear acquires a coronet of flowers instead of his golden crown, which never appears on stage again. At the end, with one of the two dukes and the youngest daughter dead, the surviving duke tries to hand rule over to two earls, Kent and Gloucester, asking them to 'sustain' the gored state of ancient Britain. The earls have no golden headgear, and their response is ambiguous (it differs in the two extant versions of the play). That the last surviving wearer of a golden headpiece should offer it further down the social scale marks how far Lear's utopian control has degenerated into a dystopia.[2]

King Lear has another major feature that we ignore today, perhaps rightly, though in recent years it has acquired an oddly fresh resonance: the union of England and Scotland. The idea of Britain as a united kingdom began as an issue when King James of Scotland became king of England at Elizabeth's death in 1603. James wanted to unite his two crowns and rule over a single kingdom. By 1605 when Shakespeare wrote his play the union of his two kingdoms was an issue being fought out in both parliaments. The play begins with the Earls of Gloucester and Kent speculating over who the King might prefer as his successor, the Duke of Cornwall or the Duke of Albany, or perhaps divide the kingdom. To us Cornwall and Albany are just names, but the first Jacobeans who heard this in 1605 would have reared up in alarm, because in that year James, whose younger son had been made Duke of Albany when he was still in Scotland, made his elder son and heir Henry into the Duke of Cornwall, the title that went with being Prince of Wales. So the first audiences would have recognised that the play was about the disunion of the two kingdoms. But there would have been a double take. James was the Shakespeare company's patron, so the play must have been recognised as the company's propaganda on their patron's behalf to satisfy his desire for a single united kingdom. Utopia would be a united Britain, dystopia a realm divided into three, the west (Cornwall and Wales), the north (Albany and Scotland) and the south, England, where Lear says he hopes to end his days with his youngest and most beloved daughter.

The government's censor of plays, the Master of the Revels, would not normally have allowed any reference to naming living people on stage. He had closed down a play the Shakespeare company set up when James first came to the English throne, about the so-called Gowrie conspiracy. Although it echoed James's own account of the attempt to assassinate him, it was banned because it dealt with living people, notably the king himself. Shakespeare changed the names from his source play, *King Leir*, into Albany and Cornwall and announced them at the very outset. So the first audiences would have thought first, how could those names be used, and secondly they must have official permission to use them. So as propaganda for the king's policy of a united kingdom the play's descent into anarchy and dystopia must have seemed a trick the players had been licensed to use.

Other plays have similar features that were aimed just for their time. Othello's colour is one of the most obvious, though its immediate reason is long lost. In 1601 Edward Alleyn, leader of the Admiral's Men at the new Fortune playhouse, restaged one of his old favourites, *The Battle of Alcazar*. Alleyn played the leading villain, Muly Mahamet, who in the play opposed the virtuous Moor Abelmelec. As Muly Mahamet Alleyn made himself like what the play calls 'a Negro Moor' in blackface, while Abdelmelec was white-faced. It was a simple use of Christian imagery, white for virtue and black for devilry. Reginald Scot in his *Discoverie of Witchcraft* (1584) noted that the devil was thought capable of appearing to humans in the shape of a blackamoor: '[Bodin] sometimes alloweth the divell the shape of a blacke Moore.' (sig. H5). Alleyn's black make-up used the standard assumptions of his time. When Shakespeare wrote *Othello* a year later he used two standard ideas which had served routinely on the stages of the time, one the devilish blackamoor, the other the simple soldier. But he reversed them, making black Othello a simple soldier and soldier-like Iago a black-hearted manipulator for his own devilish ends.

2. ORIGINAL STAGING PRACTICES

Awareness of the original staging can tell us a lot about Shakespeare's times, and the complex games he played with his audiences. His plays throw up many features that seem anomalous to us today, Shylock's forced conversion to Christianity in Act 4 being only one such case. We can too easily forget that even *Romeo and Juliet* was radical in its own time, setting young love above what has in the last few years become known in British law as 'forced marriage'. If there is any Shakespeare work that can be seen as directly prompting a total reversal in social attitudes it is there. But we always rewrite Shakespeare into our own image, and in the process lose much that originally enriched the plays. *The Taming of the Shrew* has had a hard time for a century now because of its ostensible misanthropy, the image it sets up of an independent-minded wife as a hawk to be forced into obedience. We lose sight of the play's ingenuity and originality in shifting attention from the romantic wooing that anticipates marriage to life after marriage. Most modern viewers of the play find it hard to take Baptista Minola's two daughters as a pair of opposites, the elder shrewish because the younger and prettier is her father's favourite, while the younger relishes her pretence of being submissive while she is wooed and won but turns wilful shrew as soon as she is married. The elder by contrast fights her way into a bargain with her enforced husband, and ends with the prospect of an energetic and lively marriage as a result. Awareness of the social preconditions for such stories is a major help if we are to draw on their truly Shakespearean strengths.

Shakespeare's language is always in need of translation. Historical shifts are a feature of Shakespeare and his contemporaries that we have to translate for ourselves. A basic adjustment is also needed to our idea of what theatre can and should do. The Shakespeareans were against illusionism. We need only to look at the lamentable comedy of Pyramus and Thisbe in *A Midsummer Night's Dream* to see that the moonlight, the lion and the wall were quite implausible illusions. Bottom says that his company will need to protect the audience from too much belief in what they are to be shown. The ladies must not be made to tremble at the sight of the lion. That concern was expressed in joke many years before the most famous stage direction of all appeared, '*Exit pursued by a bear*', when stage realism was similarly made an occasion for comedy. We now tend to think of Shakespeare, thanks to Olivier, Branagh and Al Pacino, as a would-be maker of film scripts. Cinematic realism, however, is almost antithetical to Shakespeare's idea of what theatre can do. It was not only Bottom who was afraid of too much realism in Tudor times.

The hatred of plays and playgoing that boiled up out of English churches from the 1570s onwards was far more positive and considered than we think it now. It was much more than a knee-jerk reaction by puritans to ordinary people getting pleasure. Behind their diatribes sat a real fear of illusion, a revulsion against the deliberate dishonesty and pretence that theatre is based on. Stephen Poliakoff applied the term 'Breaking the illusion' to one of his plays, reflecting the high value we now give illusion. Such a valuation terrified many Elizabethans because it used the work of the devil. William Perkins, the sharpest reasoner of the late Elizabethan church, put the case against any form of deception succinctly. 'An illusion,' he declared, 'is the work of Satan, whereby he deludeth or deceiveth man. And it is two-fold: either of the outward senses or of the minde.'[3] The sermon in which he made this statement was aimed at witchcraft, the most overtly Satanic of the various trickster professions that used the arts of illusion. Like witchcraft, play-acting was a deliberately deceptive business, and so must be the Devil's work. When what we call Elizabethan drama got going in the 1580s and 1590s excessive realism was a constant concern. It shows itself in everything the playwrights created. Metadrama, the explicit acknowledgement that

Illustration 2. A vignette from the titlepage of *Roxana* (1632) by William Alabaster. It shows hangings (a cloth of 'arras') behind the players. Audience are on both sides of the players, some above them on the balcony, and more sit on the pit benches below. The rail round the flanks of the stage suggests it was a hall playhouse, though it is doubtful whether the engraving was meant to portray any specific venue. Note the audience on both sides of the players, as well as in the galleries to each side, which are not shown. For the doubtful reliability of this picture, see John H. Astington, 'The Origins of the *Roxana* and *Messallina* Illustrations', *ShS* 43 (1991), 149–69.

a stage-play was a work of illusion, where boys played girls who dressed as boys, is only the cream on the many-layered cake the players fed to their audiences. They were rarely allowed to forget that they were engaged in a con-game in which they were willing participants.

The lies inherent in illusionism were visible on stage immediately, in the players' clothing. Dress bespoke the person, and stood out as the most obvious form of deception. The Tudor sumptuary laws dictating what kind of dress and fabrics should be confined to which social classes grew out of the view that clothes ought to depict the wearer's social status, if not character. Concern that outward appearance should reflect the inward person became a weapon in the case that playing was a devilish deception, and there were nearly as many attacks on players for their misuse of dress as for their bawdry. The poet and courtier Sir John Harington once offered an ironic defence of what he called 'dissimulation' through dress in his defensive *Treatise on Play* written in 1597, the decade when professional playing got its first official recognition as a legitimate recreation for Londoners. To Harington 'play' included all forms of recreation, from dicing to theatre, and he took care to give a summary of the range of the games of outward deceit used in everyday life.

Wee goe brave in apparell that wee may be taken for better men then wee bee; we use much bumbastings and quiltings to seeme better formed, better showlderd, smaller wasted, and fuller thyght, then wee are; wee barbe and shave oft, to seeme yownger then wee are; we use perfumes both inward and outward to seeme sweeter then wee be; corkt shooes to seeme taller then wee bee; wee use cowrtuows salutations to seem kinder then wee be; lowly obaysances to seeme humbler then we bee; and sometyme grave and godly communications to seem wiser or devowter then wee bee.[4]

To which, as the exhibitionistic charmer he was, he added that the potential gain from such deceits was that the users might actually become what they pretended to be. Players posing on stage as kings or great lords in the velvets and satins that the sumptuary laws preserved for noble status offered clear examples of the misuse of dress in public to claim a non-existent eminence.

Metatheatricality was the stage custom, and it manifested itself in many ways. Two in particular should illustrate how pervasive was the suspicion of illusionism. The first was, in the absence of any of the modern trappings of illusion such as an invisible audience, the obviousness of the location's identity as a theatre, in full daylight with instead of a scenic backdrop half the audience visible beyond the actors, and frequent addresses made from the stage directly to the visible audience, the folk standing around the stage who Hamlet with lordly contempt called groundlings, small fish with big mouths. Secondly was applause, which might be prompted at any point in the play, not just at the end. And with the ending's applause for the performers went comic song-and-dance jigs, even at the close of a tragedy.

Many theatrical benefits came from the avoidance of illusionism on stage. One was games exploiting transparent disguise, recognisable to the audience but not to the characters in the play. Once there were only two companies entertaining all Londoners in the 1590s the eight or ten speakers in each play became instantly recognisable in their human as well as their player shape to the many habitual playgoers. An uncrowned and therefore unkingly Henry V wrapped in Erpingham's cloak, the boy playing Rosalind playing the boy Ganymede, Bottom in his ass's head before he turned up at court as Pyramus were all immediately recognisable to the audience despite their disguises. Another feature of non-realism was the noble or serious characters speaking in verse. When Laurence Olivier started his career as a film director with the 1944 *Henry V* he found the verse a big impediment to cinematic realism, and cut out two-thirds of it. He also started the film tradition of speaking soliloquies to camera mute-faced with a voice-over. To Elizabethans spoken soliloquies and asides were of a piece with the overtly non-realistic rhythms that verse entails, addressed directly at the wholly visible audience. Prologues and choruses compering the story along with commentating characters speaking asides directly to the audience like Richard III, Edmund in *Lear* and Iago who keep the audience informed of their acts of deception were all components in the apparatus of anti-realistic staging.

This non-realism was part of the pretence, of course, and at times it created its own problems. A bare stage with no curtains or lighting to put the scene into darkness for instance could make getting rid of on-stage corpses awkward. The murdered soldier-hostage in Brendan Behan's *The Hostage* gets up and sings at the end of the farce, but we might well wonder what happens to the three corpses left onstage at the end of the tragedy of *Hamlet* when there was no obvious means or order to remove them. Funeral processions were used as closing spectacles, and orders were given to carry off most bodies, but *Hamlet* was an exception to this rule. After Hamlet himself has been carried off 'like a soldier', as Fortinbras orders, King Claudius is left lying there by his throne with his crown, his Queen Gertrude nearby, and bloodied Laertes is left on stage too. Nothing in any of the three texts of the play says what happens to them. Getting to their feet and walking off was one option, but there was another, which is worth conjecturing about once we know a little more about how plays routinely ended.

Contemporary comments refer to 'plaudities' at the end of a performance, but nothing says that the whole cast, dead or alive, appeared to take a bow. Dudley Carleton, an enthusiastic playgoer, wrote in a letter in 1603 about 'all the actors being together (as use is at the end of a play)',[5] but he may have been simply referring to the practice in comedies and other plays of ensuring that the whole cast is there for the finale. Curtain-calls only became a practice after 1660 with proscenium-arch staging and its concealing curtains. Epilogues do certify that it was customary for one player to ask for applause, as Puck does in *A Midsummer Night's Dream*, Rosalind in *As You Like It* and Prospero in *The Tempest*. Most of these figures, however, make their request when alone on stage. Moreover applause was not confined to the close. Michael Drayton wrote of sitting at a play he had written and hearing 'Showts and Claps at ev'ry little pawse, / When the proud Round on ev'ry side hath rung.' In *The Scourge of Villainy* Marston confirmed that applause by enthusiasts among his fellow law-students greeted specific lines when they heard *Romeo and Juliet* at the Curtain playhouse in 1598. Audiences accustomed to shouting and clapping throughout the two hours' traffic of the stage would not have been content with just a bit more applause to confirm their sense of an ending. The closure of a performance was generally marked by something much more substantial.

In another letter a year after the one cited above Dudley Carleton gives us a clue. He follows a story about someone's death with a joke, calling it 'a jig after this tragedy' (p. 65). We know what he meant from an account by a German-speaking Swiss tourist, Thomas Platter, who went by ferry to the Globe on 21 September 1599 to see *Julius Caesar*. His diary reports that he admired it, although his English was tenuous. He specified that it had fifteen players, which suggests that he survived a play with over thirty characters entering and leaving by watching more closely than he listened. He especially liked the ending when, as he wrote 'they danced together admirably and exceedingly gracefully, according to their custom, two in each group dressed in men's and two in women's apparel.'[6] Even at the end of a tragedy it seems the custom was to dance a comic jig. The players moved straight from the funeral procession for the noblest Roman of them all to a bawdy song-and-dance act.

Endings to the plays themselves routinely involved the players moving offstage in harmony. During the struggles of the play itself oppositional sides would come onstage each by one of the pair of doors on the flanks of the tiring-house front. The groups of Montague and Capulet servants or Oberon when he first confronts Titania entered from each of the flanking doors and meet centre stage for their encounters with their enemies. *Romeo and Juliet*'s brawling servants from each side of the stage were stopped only by the Duke's arrival through the broader central opening, the locus of authority.[7] At the end of a play all pairs, whether of lovers and their followers in comedies or the mourning groups in tragedies, made their exits in procession through the locus of harmony, the central opening. Such a shape to the stage dictated where authority lay and where the opposing discords that challenged it stood. That structure made the play's closure simple when as it normally did it involved a procession heading offstage, whether for a wedding or a funeral. It is *Hamlet's* closing procession that was left so oddly incomplete.

Most of Shakespeare's tragedies make explicit provision to get the principal bodies off through the central opening. In *Titus Andronicus* Lucius gives orders for each body to be taken away. Coriolanus is given a soldier's funeral ('Take him up. / Help three of' th' chiefest soldiers; I'll be one,' says Aufidius). *Julius Caesar* closes with a similar procession when Octavius says 'Within my tent his bones tonight shall lie, / Most like a soldier, ordered honourably.' In *Othello* the two principals lie dead together on Desdemona's bed, with only the other murdered wife, Iago's Emilia, lying somewhere there untouched. We must assume that she was carried off with her husband as part of the evidence against him, or perhaps that she was put on the bed with the other two, though that would spoil the symmetry of the black and the white bodies on the one bed. In *Antony and Cleopatra*, after Antony has conveniently been cleared away in Act 4, Cleopatra in her regal finery and her two maids are carried off together at Caesar's order 'Take up her bed, / And bear her women from the monument.' In the Folio text of *King Lear* Albany orders the bodies of Goneril and Regan to be brought onstage so they join those of Lear and their sister Cordelia. Edmund is reported as dead offstage, so the Lear family is together in death onstage. Nine lines from the end Albany orders 'Bear them from hence', the family finally reunited as corpses. All these tidy endings are in stark contrast to the disjunctive closure of *Hamlet*.

Hamlet's ending raises many questions, not the least of which is whether it originally ended with a jig. Fortinbras's orders at the end award only Hamlet himself a dead soldier's procession. Fortinbras's appearance in the finale is a peculiar form of the classical *deus ex machina*, because as leader of the Norwegian forces he would have worn exactly the accoutrements of the dead King Hamlet at the play's beginning, full armour with a beaver on his helmet, and carrying the marshal's truncheon of an army general. The ghost would have been pleased to see his son honoured by such a familiar figure (we might ask whether originally old Hamlet and young Fortinbras doubled their roles as well as their armour). But what happened to the ignored bodies of King Claudius, Hamlet's mother and Laertes? Either they got up and walked off, or stage hands came on to carry them off, or else, as I think most likely, they got up and started to dance the closing jig. Editors and commentators all assume that the players invariably took one of the first two choices. In the absence of more tangible evidence it seems a real possibility that they did otherwise. Hamlet himself had mocked Polonius for liking jigs, so perhaps he came back to life to join the others in the dance. Or possibly Ophelia joined Gertrude to make the dance that Platter noted as two men dressed as women along with a male pair (if Osric, who probably doubled her, had time to shed his male garments after slipping away to avoid the onstage massacre). A closing jig would go with the basic need of every play's conclusion, restoring the sense of reality, that vital awareness of the falsity of the illusion, that we today have lost but that Shakespeareans could never forget.

Shakespeare does give us one hint of his own sense of what theatre should be. In the final act of *A Midsummer Night's Dream* Hippolita, puzzling out her answer to Theseus's scorn at lunatics, lovers and poets for their excess of 'imagination', says that the real mystery about the story of the four lovers and their night in the forest is that they all had the identical dream.

> But all the story of the night told over,
> And all their minds transfigured so together,
> More witnesseth than fancy's images
> And grows to something of great constancy;
> But howsoever, strange and admirable.

Strange, meaning abnormal or alien, and a matter for wonder and admiration. That is the best metaphor Shakespeare gives us for the experience of undergoing a play in a theatre. A dream that lots of people share, 'of great constancy', memorable and faithful within itself, and yet unreal. As Stephen Greenblatt says, 'the theatre elicits from us complicity rather than belief'.[8]

3. THE LONDON FOCUS

Inevitably, given the fact that with roughly 200,000 people in 1600 London had by far the largest concentration of England's population, ten times the number in Norwich or Bristol and easily England's largest port for foreign travellers, it became the prime and prize target of the professional playing companies and the leading playwrights. My purpose in writing this book is not so much to identify individual contributions but rather with the shape of the wood than single trees, in the hope that knowing the shape of the wood might help to make better sense of the shapes the trees took. Or, to change one inexact metaphor for another, to sketch in a deeper background in order to sharpen the focus of the foreground.

The contextual features of Shakespearean drama are vital to our understanding of the plays for many reasons, not least because the salient features were at the same time thoroughly distinctive and thoroughly transient. Except for a few of the poets nobody gave a thought to posterity. The players were there to give immediate entertainment and to take money. There was no reason to make the product durable or to record it for future generations. So the plays lived in a medium as ephemeral as the sounds through which they were brought to life. So far as we can tell, far fewer than one in ten of the total number of plays staged have come down to us in print or manuscript.

Even for the majority of the poets it was entertainment they were creating, not art, and the poets accordingly wrote for their age, not for all time. Their paymasters were players, not printers. In *Hamlet* the travelling players turn up because they were fetched to divert Hamlet's attention and distract him from his melancholy. They were a casual diversion from serious affairs. The poets merely supplied the raw material for such diversions, material for the most part as transient as the performances that gave it life. The publisher of Jasper Mayne's *The City Match* (1639) claimed that the poet, a clergyman, held the belief 'that works of this light nature ... be things which need an apology for being written at all, not esteeming otherwise of them, whose abilities in this kind are most passable, than of masquers who spangle and glitter for a time, but 'tis thoroughly tinsel'. Shakespeare and Jonson's plays were no more substantial than Christmas decorations. It follows from this attitude – a widespread orthodoxy – that plays were dependent on the conditions of performance as few written works have ever been. They were working playscripts before they became written texts. Print was at some remove from the event for which they were created. Not many objects in the foreground of literature have been so dependent on their immediate background to give them form and identity. By their nature plays were thoroughly occasional events.

Another consideration shaping this book is the commercial motive of the players, which directed them to London. Almost the whole of Shakespearean drama was written for companies that used their play-books solely for the purpose of making their living, and by far the best living was to be made in the metropolis. Almost no poets whose work later got into print were writing with anything but the London companies in mind. From 1594, as we shall see, London was where the players were officially licensed by the Privy Council to perform in their own custom-built playhouses, week after week and year after year. Everywhere else they had to use town halls, market-places, schools and churches, or if they were lucky the great halls in the manor-houses of the nobility. Although Bristol and a couple of other small towns acquired their own playhouses in the early years of the seventeenth century,[9] no poet wrote expressly for them, or for the companies that passed through Norwich or Newcastle or York or even Stratford. In London there were regular venues, regular audiences, regular incomes. Every player's ambition was to belong to a company securely resident in London. And equally, the only place where a play could be profitably marketed was with the companies working in London. With few exceptions most players were London born and bred.[10] Since London was the peak of the mountain of entertainment thrown up in the seventy or so years of Shakespearean theatre, this book economises by confining itself to the conditions that existed for the performance of plays only in that one fortunate city.

Playhouses were places of impure art, and in many eyes they were not even places of legitimate entertainment. William Harrison commented when the first playhouses were built in 1576 that 'It is an evident token of a wicked time when players were so riche that they can build such houses.'[11] To Harrison the entertainment they offered was no better than that of 'houses of baudrie'. They certainly occupied the same neighborhoods, as Prynne, the Puritan author of a massive attack on playing, wrote in 1633.

our Theaters if they are not Bawdy-houses, (as they may easily be, since many Players, *if reports be true, are common Panders,*) yet they are Cosin-germanes, at *leastwise neighbours to them*: Witnesse the *Cock-pit*, and *Drury-lane: Black-friers Play-house*, and *Duke-humfries*; the *Red-bull*, and *Turnball-street*: the *Globe*, and *Bank-side Brothel-houses*, with others of this nature.[12]

The poet and epigrammatist John Davies sketched the day of a typical playgoer, an idle gallant, in terms that openly acknowledged the equivalent status of brothels and playhouses ('In Fuscum': *Epigrammes*, 39):

> *Fuscus* is free, and hath the world at will,
> Yet in the course of life that he doth leade,
> He's like a horse which turning rounde a mill,
> Doth alwaies in the selfe same circle treade:
> First he doth rise at 10. and at eleven
> He goes to *Gyls*, where he doth eate till one,
> Then sees a play til sixe, and sups at seaven,

And after supper, straight to bed is gone,
And there till tenne next day he doth remaine,
And then he dines, then sees a commedy,
And then he suppes, and goes to bed againe.
Thus rounde he runs without variety:
Save that sometimes he comes not to the play
But falls into a whore-house by the way.

Such ideas about playgoing were hardly likely to sponsor a devotional attitude to their art in the players. Playing was deplored by the authorities, in 1574 when innyards were the venues and the crowds were largely artisans and apprentices just as it was deplored in 1633 when playhouses were in great halls in the heart of London, and the trouble was caused more by the coaches of the great than by tumultuous apprentices. In 1574 the city authorities described the scene in these words:

the inordynate hauntyinge of greate multitudes of people, speciallye youthe, to playes, enterludes, and shewes, namelye occasyon of Frayes and quarrelles, eavell practizes of incontinencye in greate Innes, having chambers and secrete places adjoyninge to their open stagies and gallyries, inveglynge and alleurynge of maides, speciallye orphanes and good Cityzens Children under Age, to previe and unmete Contractes, the publishinge of unchaste uncomelye and unshamefaste speeches and doynges, withdrawinge of the Queenes Majesties Subjects from dyvyne service on Sonndaies and hollydayes, at which Tymes suche playes weare Chefelye used, unthriftye waste of the moneye of the poore and fond persons, sondrye robberies by pyckinge and Cuttinge of purses, utteringe of popular busye and sedycious matters, and manie other Corruptions of youthe and other enormyties, besydes that allso soundrye slaughters and mayheminges of the Quenes Subjectes have happened by ruines of Skaffoldes, Frames and Stagies, and by engynes, weapons, and powder used in plaies.[13]

The inns were in the City's jurisdiction, and in 1594 the City Fathers managed to close them all to the players. The playhouses designed and built as playhouses were located just outside the City's jurisdiction, and in 1633 it was the Privy Council, the executive instrument of the King's government, that had to intervene to impose traffic regulations in the vicinity of London's leading playhouse. They declared that

Whereas y⁰ Board hath taken consideration of the great inconveniencs that growe by reason of the resort to the Play house of y⁰ Blackffryars in Coaches, whereby the streets neare thereunto, are at the Playtime so stopped that his Majesties Subjects going about their necessarie affayres can hardly finde passage and are oftentymes endangered: Their lordships remembring that there is an easie passage by water unto that playhouse w^{th}out troubling the streets, and that it is much more fit and reasonable that those wch goe thither should goe thither by water or else on foote rather than the necessarie businesses of all others, and the publique Commerce should be disturbed by their pleasure, doe therefore Order, that if anie p[er]son man or woman of what Condicion soever repaire to the aforesayd Playhouse in Coach so soone as they are gone out of their Coaches the Coach men shall departe thence and not retourne till the ende of the play, nor shall stay or retourne to fetch those whome they carryed anie nearer wth their Coaches then the farther parte of St Paules Church yarde on the one syde, and Fleet-Conduite on the other syde, and in ye tyme betweene their departure and returne shall either returne home or else abide in some other streets lesse frequented with passengers and so range their Coaches in those places that the way be not stopped, wch Order if anie Coachman disobey, the next Constable or Officer is hereby charged to commit him presently to Ludgate or Newgate; And the Lo: Mayor of ye Citie of London is required to see this carefully performed by the Conestables and Officers to whom it apperteyneth and to punish every such Conestable or officer as shall be found negligent therein. And to the ende that none may p^{r}etende ignorance hereof, it is lastly ordered that Copies of this Order, shallbe set up at Paules Chaine, by direction of the Lorde Mayor, as also at the west ende of St Paules Church, at Ludgate and the Blackfryers Gate and Fleete Conduite.[14]

A contemporary noted that these regulations were duly enforced, but that, human flesh being what it is, they were not effective for more than two or three weeks.

The official records of course are chiefly concerned with the troubles the players made. The other side of the story is suggested by the awed wonder with which foreign travellers described what they saw on the London stages, and the declarations of much-travelled Englishmen like Fynes Moryson, who said in his *Itinerary* (p. 476) written in 1617, that

The Citty of London alone hath foure or five Companyes of players with their peculiar Theaters Capable of many thousands, wherein they all play every day in the weeke but Sunday, with most strang concourse of people, besydes many strange toyes and fances exposed by signes to be seene in private houses, to which and to many musterings and other frequent spectacles, the people flocke in great nombers, being naturally more newefangled then the Athenians to heare newes and gaze upon every toye, as there be, in my opinion, more Playes in London then in all the partes of the worlde I have seene, so doe these players or Comedians excell all other in the worlde. Whereof I have seene some stragling broken Companyes that passed into Netherland and Germany, followed by the people from one towne to another, though they understoode not their wordes, only to see theire action, yea marchants at Fayres bragged more to have seene them, then of the good marketts they made.[15]

In the sixteenth century life for the playing companies was a constant battle to keep a foot-hold in London in the teeth of the City Fathers and the Puritan preachers. According to the preachers most apprentices were

seduced away into idleness by the temptations of the players, and as everyone knows the Devil finds work for idle hands. The City Fathers, most of
whom employed apprentices, understandably felt themselves to be better
employers than the Devil. The Court however, lacking the financial interest
in the matter that the City Fathers had, held no such objections to playing.
In 1572 and 1574 the Privy Council more or less openly took the leading
companies of players under its wing. Only with such protection could the
players afford to invest in permanent playhouses. Between 1575 and 1577
two open amphitheatres and two indoor halls opened as commercial venues
for playing. The outdoor pair, for safety, were located in the suburban
spaces just outside the City's jurisdiction. The indoor venues occupied
spaces in the precincts of the City called 'liberties', free from the Lord
Mayor's authority. This gave them an immunity the inns could not have,
and with royal help they proved sound and lasting investments. Not until
the political balance of power was reversed nearly seventy years later did
the City finally get its way over the Court and the players. In the early
seventeenth century, when all the leading London companies basked in the
warmth of royal patronage, the City's hostility was necessarily quiescent.
For nearly forty years London never had fewer than six playhouses with four
regular companies performing daily except on Sundays and for most of
Lent, or when the plague set everyone apart from their fellows. Only in
1642, when the King's impoverishment forced him to put himself at
Parliament's mercy, did the City and Parliament gain the power to close
the haunts of idleness.

The players performed their own small part in the downfall. Their aims
and objects changed drastically through the period, reflecting the shifts in
social structure that brought about the revolution in society at large. Under
Elizabeth the players might be summoned to Court to make a contribution
to the Christmas festivities, and they might more often be called on to
entertain a noble or gentleman's friends at his private house. But the plays
that were performed on such occasions were not different from the fare the
players gave to the citizenry who could not afford such expensive exclusive-
ness. The idle artisan's admission fee was a minimal penny. For this he had
equally the choice of Shakespeare or the baiting of bulls and bears, the same
choice as the Queen. The Queen sent for the players or her bear-warden, the
apprentices were enticed with printed or hand-written playbills posted
up around the town on which they might read where plays were available.
One of the few handbills that have survived shows what the rival kind of
entertainment for the apprentices was. It is an undated advertisement for

an afternoon at the Beargarden, probably from early in the reign of James. Written in a large, plain hand, it says

Tomorrowe beinge Thursdaie shalbe seen at the Beargardin on the banckside a great Mach plaid by the gamstirs of Essex who hath chalenged all comers what soever to plaie v dogges at the single beare for v pounds and also to wearie a bull dead at the stake and for your better content shall have plasant sport with the horse and ape and whiping of the blind beare (Vivat Rex.)[16]

This kind of show or its theatrical equivalents was available to high and low alike in the sixteenth century. Except for what the intermittently active boy companies provided, it could be said that the basic penny fee bought the apprentice as much as Elizabeth herself could buy, and entertainment moreover of exactly the same kind.

In the seventeenth century under the Stuarts the process changed. The 'citizen' amphitheatres continued to offer a pennyworth of bear-baiting or playgoing throughout the period, but the upper end of the market expanded and altered radically. Just before 1600 two hall playhouses reopened inside the city walls. By 1629 London had three indoor halls and three open-air playhouses, and most of the new plays were being written for the companies occupying the halls and their wealthier patrons. The smaller capacity of the auditoria at the hall playhouses was more than compensated for by their higher prices. The cheapest admission fee to the Blackfriars only gained you a place on the rearmost bench in the upper gallery. The same fee would buy you the luxury of a lord's room at the Globe. With a price range between sixpence and two shillings and sixpence as against the one to sixpenny range of the amphitheatres, the halls automatically catered for the wealthier levels of London society. Besides their roofs, and their central location close to the wealthier residential areas, the Blackfriars and its kin also catered for the wealthy with such practices as allowing a dozen or more spectators to sit on the stage itself to view the play. For a young gallant anxious to parade his newest clothes, the chance to sit in full view alongside the players must have been irresistible. It took an order from the king in person to ban sitting on the stage at the smallest of the hall playhouses in 1639. As it became acceptable for fashionable ladies to occupy the boxes alongside the stage the social advantage of parading oneself at the Blackfriars or the Cockpit came second only to an appearance at the Court itself. By 1642, even though the open amphitheatres were still running citizen fare, the hall playhouses had become closely identified with Court circles and Court tastes. Their closure by Parliament in that year was the clearest measure of the Court's loss of power.

Illustration 3. A triumphal arch depicting London, built for King James's entry
into London in March 1603. This arch, designed by Ben Jonson and the first in the
sequence James was carried through, depicted the City of London. On it sat the
City musicians, shown in the galleries on each side. In the central niche stood
Edward Alleyn as 'the Genius of the City', personified thinly clad and shown with
a torch in his hand, arm raised. When James reached the arch Alleyn made a
speech written for the occasion by Thomas Dekker. Dekker's speech was later
published in his *The Wonderful Year*. Engravings of each arch were published
in 1604 in Stephen Harrison's *Arches of Triumph*, from which this
illustration is taken.

Illustration 4. Alleyn gesturing from the Londinium arch as the 'Genius of the City'.
A detail from the Arch of London set up in 1604.

4. LIFE IN LONDON

It is worth emphasising that the single penny gaining an apprentice admission to the Bel Savage or the Theatre in the 1570s was still the basic price at the Fortune, the Red Bull and the Globe in 1642. The hall playhouses expanded their price range with more costly seats and boxes, and their minimum sixpenny charge must have excluded most apprentices. This was an extension of the market, though, not a change. The basic penny lost some of its value through inflation, and while most prices rose artisan wages remained steady. And so did playhouse prices. Amphitheatres, baiting-houses, prize-fights and whorehouses were always within reach for the great majority of the working population as well as the wealthy.

Throughout the period the industrious artisan earned about six shillings a week (6s. 5d. for masons, 6s. 2d. for carpenters), less than a third of a pound.[17] Apprentices earned very considerably less than that, though board and lodging were provided in the terms of their indentures. Handicraft apprentices did not in fact officially earn anything at all until they could produce work good enough to be sold in the citizen owner's shop. To such artisans a good food diet cost as much as half the weekly wage in Tudor times. The Tudor soldier's daily food allowance was 24 ounces of wheat bread and two-thirds of a gallon of beer, each costing a penny; 2 pounds of beef or mutton (cod or herring on fish days), at a cost of twopence, half a pound of butter and a pound of cheese. The cost of this diet under Elizabeth was about sixpence, but food prices never recovered from the seven successive bad harvests at the end of the century, and rose by about 25 per cent in the early seventeenth century. By the mid-century beef was as much as fivepence a pound. Bread and circuses went together in price throughout the period, but the quantity of bread that could be bought for the price of admission to the playhouse steadily declined.

As always in a predominantly subsistence economy the price of manufactured articles was markedly higher than the cost of food. It is difficult to be specific about prices because they were likely to fluctuate more according to quality than by the type of commodity, and because prices also shifted according to the social status of the purchaser. A pair of silk stockings might cost £2 or £4 depending on quality and purchaser. A woman's gown might cost anything from £7 to £20 or more. The Earl of Leicester paid £543 for seven doublets and two cloaks, at an average cost for each item rather higher than the price Shakespeare paid for a house in Stratford. The same Earl's funeral cost £3,000, five times what it cost to construct the second Blackfriars playhouse. The tendency of the better playing companies to cater for the higher income brackets is understandable.

It is difficult to generalise about the distribution of income through the country and the social patterns to which it relates, and even more difficult to locate typical playhouse audiences amongst those social patterns. Statistics are inadequate and potentially misleading. None the less a broad picture does appear, suggesting that while the poor, and particularly the London artisan poor, grew poorer, the number of the rich grew markedly, and especially in London. Large numbers of the seventeenth-century gentry, chiefly those based in the cities, drew wealth both from the relatively few very rich noblemen of the sixteenth century and from the poor through the inflation of prices and stability of wages. Trade was prosperous for the London merchant. The East India Company, floated in 1600 with a capital of £72,000, brought its investors a minimum return of 121 per cent on each voyage.[18] In that year, 1600, there were estimated to be in the country as a whole 60,000 landed yeomen and gentry with annual incomes of £40 to £100, well above the artisan and schoolmaster level of £15. As many as 10,000 had incomes of £300 to £500. The average income of nobles was £2,000 to £3,000, which was about what a prosperous merchant could rise to. From that date a good deal of the wealth turned up in the form of money, not land, which was the traditional form that wealth took until the sixteenth century. Drake's bullion ships indirectly helped the players, because the more that wealth came to hand in the readily exchangeable form of money, the more idle gallants, hangers-on at Court and Inns-of-Court lawyers were created to seek the entertainment the players were selling. In *The Alchemist* 3.4 the trickster Face urges the gullible young country gentleman Kastril to turn his land into cash, on the grounds that 'men of spirit hate to keep earth long'. Spending power was cash, not property.[19] It was inevitable that in the course of the seventeenth century the moneyed and therefore leisured audiences came to override the penny-paying apprentices in the eyes of the players.

The government, being comprised entirely of nobles and gentry, went to great lengths to ensure that the distinction of gentle from commoner was firmly maintained, and not only in dress. You qualified as a gentleman so long as you had land bringing you £40 a year, the minimum thought necessary for such status. Land, however, was not portable, and by the mid-century the conversion of land into cash was a constant temptation, one that Jonson openly derided, especially in his depiction of young Kastril (kestrel, the smallest of the hawks). As well as dressing in velvet and satin gentleman status gave you the right to wear a sword, and it tended to presume literacy. It also meant that you could not work at any formal occupation. University graduates, lawyers and army captains could claim gentle status by their professions, but only commoners worked for a wage. Most of the playwrights when they were named on titlepages called themselves 'Gent.'. Even Shakespeare, who married young and so disqualified himself from ever going to university, bought himself the claim to be gentle by purchasing for his father the rank of armiger he had tried to get years before, a status he finally gained when his son could afford it in 1596.

Land did not always bring money unless it was sold, but trade did. A constant tension in Elizabethan society divided the landed nobility and gentry, with their country wealth, from the merchants of the City with their industry. The plays are full of penniless younger sons of landed gentry whom the law of primogeniture, inheritance by the oldest son, gave no hope of future prosperity. Being unemployable unless they forsook their gentle status, they had to seek wealth by making rich marriages, usually to the daughters of rich merchants. In *The Merry Wives of Windsor* the ostensibly gentle Falstaff makes unsuccessful attempts to milk two citizen wives of their money, although being Falstaff he offers them sex rather than marriage. By contrast the penniless young Fenton, gentleman and friend of the Prince, succeeds in wooing and winning the Pages' daughter Anne against her citizen parents' wishes. Dekker's *Shoemaker's Holiday* at the Rose in 1599 begins with a similar plot, where the Earl of Lincoln's gentleman nephew woos the Lord Mayor's citizen daughter against the will of both representatives of the older generation, and like Fenton wins through true love. The plays of the boy company at Blackfriars are full of similarly penniless gentlemen, who like Falstaff have to pursue money, though more often through sex than marriage. The idle and industrious apprentices of *Eastward Ho!* (1605) share the same need.

5. SOCIAL DIVISIONS

The different kinds of repertory that were maintained at the different playhouses confirm the evidence of these economic changes. In the seventeenth century the so-called 'citizen' playhouses, the amphitheatres in the suburbs on the eastern and northern sides of the city – chiefly the Fortune and the Red Bull – went on with a staple list of plays made up from the favourites of the end of the previous century. Marlowe's plays ran at these playhouses until the closure. Heywood became the Red Bull's leading playwright, and his lavishly staged plays, or displays, of the Four Ages mark a high point of achievement for the companies who catered for citizen audiences. There was only one interruption to this pattern, when Christopher Beeston, the player of the early Red Bull company who ran its finances, set up a hall playhouse in Drury Lane and stocked it with players and plays from the amphitheatre. On the two following Shrove Tuesday holidays gangs of apprentices tried to mob the new hall playhouse and destroy it, presumably in protest at having their plays taken away from the penny playhouse and transferred to a sixpenny venue.

Beeston built his new playhouse, the Cockpit, in Westminster's Drury Lane in 1616. The next apprentice holiday was Shrove Tuesday at the beginning of Lent in 1617. A contemporary gives a vivid account of what happened:

The Prentizes on Shrove Tewsday last, to the nomber of 3. or 4000 comitted extreame insolencies; part of this number, taking their course for Wapping, did there pull downe to the grownd 4 houses, spoiled all the goods therein, defaced many others, & a Justice of the Peace coming to appease them, while he was reading a Proclamation, had his head broken with a brick batt. Th' other part, making for Drury Lane, where lately a newe playhouse is erected, they besett the house round, broke in, wounded divers of the players, broke open their trunckes, & whatt apparrell, bookes, or other things they found, they burnt & cutt in peeces; & not content herewith, gott on the top of the house, & untiled it, & had not the Justices of Peace & Sherife levied an aide, & hindred their purpose, they would have laid that house likewise even with the grownd. In this skyrmishe one prentise was slaine, being shott throughe the head with a pistoll, & many other of their fellowes were sore hurt, & such of them as are taken his Majestie hath commaunded shal be executed for example sake.[20]

In the following year the apprentices planned to try again, assembling at the Fortune to attack both the Cockpit and the Red Bull. The Privy Council had notice this time though and stopped them. Having rebuilt his Drury Lane playhouse (it was sometimes called the Phoenix, because of its instant rebirth from the flames of 1617), Beeston often took plays from the Red Bull's repertory for staging at his hall playhouse. It is not quite clear how much it was the apprentice patrons or how much it was their favourite plays that gave the Red Bull its reputation as a 'citizen' playhouse in distinction to the hall playhouses, since the Cockpit often ran Red Bull plays for its privileged audiences.[21]

The plays available for a penny included the heroics of fantasy romances like Heywood's *Four Prentices of London*. Its heroes are four apprentices, nobles in disguise ('all high borne, / Yet of the Citty-Trades they have no scorne'), who march across Europe and Asia performing the incredible feats of knight-errantry that were the staple fare of the chivalric romances long popular with the sixteenth-century reading public.[22] Beaumont burlesqued the citizen taste for this kind of romantic heroics in *The Knight of the Burning Pestle*, written for the sixpenny private playhouse repertory in 1607. Beaumont's burlesque is very much in the manner of *Don Quixote*, which was almost contemporary with it. The play shows a citizen Grocer and his wife being fooled by a sophisticated boy company at the Blackfriars into exposing their taste for *Don Quixote*-like feats of improbable valour. At each pause in the play the Grocer and his wife lay new demands on the players for feats of arms from their apprentice, whom they have thrust on the players to take the leading part. At the beginning of Act 4, for instance, they confer over what they would like to follow:

CITIZEN. What shall we have *Rafe* do now boy?
BOY. You shall have what you will sir.

CITIZEN. Why so sir, go and fetch me him then, and let the Sophy of *Persia* come and christen him a childe.

BOY. Beleeve me sir, that will not doe so well, 'tis stale, it has beene had before at the red Bull.

WIFE. *George* let *Rafe* travell over great hils, and let him be very weary, and come to the King of *Cracovia's* house, covered with blacke velvet, and there let the Kings daughter stand in her window all in beaten gold, combing her golden locks with a combe of Ivory, and let her spy *Rafe*, and fall in love with him, and come downe to him, and carry him into her fathers house, and then let *Rafe* talke with her.

CITIZEN. Well said *Nell*, it shal be so: boy let's ha't done quickly.

BOY. Sir, if you will imagine all this to be done already, you shall heare them talke together: but wee cannot present a house covered with blacke velvet, and a Lady in beaten gold.

CITIZEN. Sir boy, lets ha't as you can then.

BOY. Besides it will shew ill-favouredly to have a Grocers prentice to court a kings daughter.

CITIZEN. Will it so sir? you are well read in Histories: I pray you what was sir *Dagonet*? was not he prentice to a Grocer in London? read the play of the *Foure Prentices of London*, where they tosse their pikes so: I pray you fetch him in sir, fetch him in.

So the boy goes off to prepare Rafe, apologising on the way to the 'gentlemen' on their stools on stage for this fresh affront to their tastes. The incident with the Sophy of Persia was in *The Travels of the Three English Brothers*, by Day and Wilkins, performed at the Red Bull in 1607. Sir Dagonet was actually King Arthur's jester.

In the first decade of the century several of the hall playhouse plays had what Beaumont called 'girds at citizens'. Two or three years after Beaumont's play Nathan Field, who probably acted in it, wrote a play of his own for the company, *A Woman is a Weathercock*, in which one player says to another (2.1):

> Ile thinke
> As abjectly of thee, as any Mongrill
> Bred in the Citty; Such a Cittizen
> As the Playes flout still.

The boy company at the Blackfriars provided witty and satirical comedies for their 'gentlemen' audiences. When they disappeared from the forefront of the scene after 1609 there seems to have followed a period of uncertainty in which girds at citizens were muted. Shakespeare's company had taken over the Blackfriars, and their repertory had never been anti-citizen (*The Merry Wives of Windsor* is a neat example of a citizen play, ending as it does with a penniless young gentleman marrying a wealthy merchant's daughter). In fact even the audience at the Blackfriars in 1607 for the boy company's performance of Beaumont's play seem not to have appreciated his satire on the Red Bull's citizen repertoire, since the play was not a success at its first appearance. Beaumont may have been premature in thinking that the sixpenny-payers in 1607 would relish an anti-citizen satire.

Later on, however, the taste of the indoor playhouse audiences for wit and satire reasserted itself, and by Caroline times the distance between the repertories favoured by the citizens at the northern public playhouses and those favoured by the gallants and Inns-of-Court men at the private playhouses in the city was fairly distinct. The wealthier taste was for wit, salacity ('sallets'), a closer fidelity to the unities of time and place and more complex emotional patterns in romance and tragedy alike. Art, in playwriting as in the visual forms, became more self-conscious and Mannerist.[23] In tragedy the world frequently appears as pervasively corrupt and corrupting, all motives expedient, and evil brings about the downfall of everyone, as in Middleton's *Women Beware Women*, or Massinger's *The Roman Actor*. In romances the milieu has a pastoral element, the golden world of Sidney's *Arcadia*, especially in the Beaumont and Fletcher plays. Love and politics mix when kings use their power tyrannically to force their subjects into sexual submission. Fashions changed in the more aristocratic repertories, and it is the changeability more than the principles embodied in the plays that marks the difference from citizen repertories.[24]

In looking at the repertories and the social divisions they may reflect, as everywhere else in the picture, we must beware of oversimplification. The representation of contemporary life in thoroughly prejudicial forms was not a feature only of the more gentlemanly plays. A letter of 1601 from the Privy Council condemned a company performing at the Curtain for doing just that. 'We do understand,' they wrote,

that certaine players that use to recyte their playes at the Curtaine in Moore-feildes do represent upon the stage in their interludes the persons of some gentlemen of good desert and quallity that are yet alive under obscure manner, but yet in such sorte as all the hearers may take notice both of the matter and the persons that are meant thereby.[25]

The Curtain players shortly after this became the Red Bull players. It was not only gentlemen of good desert that became their targets either. In 1638 the Red Bull company found itself in trouble for a play that lampooned one of the most notorious of the monopolist merchants, Sir William Abell, a City Alderman.[26] The identification of 'citizen' playhouses does not mean they shared the interests of the City's magnates.

6. THE POETS

In describing the general outlines of a picture of the period, it remains now to take some notice of the suppliers to the playing companies, the poets themselves. The largest body of playwriting in the Shakespearean period was what is commonly regarded as hack-work, much of it written in collaboration. In the commercial conditions of the time, when all that was asked of the playwrights was to supply an entertainment industry, it could hardly have been anything else. What has survived into this century is probably not a large proportion of the total output, though it is likely to include most of the cream. Certainly what is read today is only the cream, and being so it can mislead us about the rest.

The grammar schools set up in the sixteenth century were producing scholars for whom there was no work. Graduating from university made them gentlemen, and so prohibited them from any normal craft occupation. They were expected never to be anything other than landowners or parsons. The theatre's appetite for plays was the most obvious source of income for anyone who lacked income and did not want to enter the church, talented dramatist or not. Although the demand for plays was great, the number of hack-writers able to supply them was greater still. So it was a buyer's market for plays. Poets were the servants of the players, in economic servitude to them. The Cambridge scholars who wrote the Parnassus plays said so from the safety of their university (2 *Return from Parnassus*):

> And must the basest trade yeeld us reliefe?
> Must we be practis'd to those leaden spouts,
> That nought downe vent but what they do receive? (4.4)

For would-be writers players were mere drainpipes. There was more money in playing than in playwriting:

> With mouthing words that better wits have framed,
> They purchase lands, and now Esquiers are made. (5.1)

That Shakespeare died better off than many of his fellow dramatists is probably more due to his share in his company of players and in their property than to his pen.

Of Shakespeare we really know almost nothing substantial, except that besides being a poet faithful to his company he was an exceptionally good businessman. In his early years, before 1594, when he joined the Chamberlain's Men and made his fortune with them, he dallied with aristocratic patronage as well as playing, and no doubt received good money for it. But the survival of his plays dating from 1594 and earlier is significant. When they were incorporated in the First Folio in 1623 they were the property of the Chamberlain's Men's successors, the King's Men. Plays were mostly the property of the company that bought them from the playwright. That the King's Men should own the pre-1594 plays seems to show that Shakespeare had somehow kept in his own possession the ownership of his early plays and that he did not sell them to the companies that first performed them. Through the early years when fortune's wheel was spinning with uncomfortable speed for the companies it was obviously wise to keep playbooks as financial assets, and take them from company to company. That may be how they ended up with the Chamberlain's Men. Indeed, they may well have been the capital with which Shakespeare bought himself a share in the company. The profits his player share brought him and his investments as a Stratford property-owner are well known. Otherwise we have to assume that in 1594 some prescient mind with the authority to do so seized the early Shakespeare plays and gave them to the Chamberlain's while at the same time giving all of Marlowe's to the Admiral's. That is an equally plausible conclusion in the absence of more tangible evidence. What it really says is that both companies' organisers were well aware of the value of a good play.

As both writer and player Shakespeare became in effect the Chamberlain's Men's resident poet. The plays surviving in the First Folio and such accurate dating as can be made for them suggest that he wrote one serious play and one light play a year, more or less, throughout his active writing career. Another player-poet, Heywood, worked with the Admiral's and then Queen Anne's Men, the Red Bull company of 1605–19, and later for other companies. In 1633 he claimed to have had '*either an entire hand, or at the least a maine finger*' in the writing of 220 plays.[27] He started work as one of a group of writers paid for their plays by Philip Henslowe at the Rose, while also like Shakespeare serving as a player. The usual system followed by such writers was for one of them to compose an outline or scenario for a play. The actual wordage of each scene was then written out by himself with two or three colleagues who would turn their scenes into whatever the scenario demanded. Henslowe's *Diary* suggests that the full process of composition of a play usually took about two months. Henslowe paid each writer individually on production of each section of the script, depending on how large a part their contribution was, the scenario-writer usually getting only an equal share. Often the chief writer would read out the scenario one evening at a tavern before the company, the Admiral's Men, who would then decide whether to buy it or not. Shakespeare, himself a player in his company, was fairly distinctive in writing most of his plays without any collaborators, although a number of his earlier plays such as *Titus Andronicus* and *1 Henry VI*, both performed at the Rose before 1594, probably emerged from such a process of collaboration. In his last years he wrote *Henry VIII*, *The Two Noble Kinsmen* and the (probably) lost *Cardenio* in collaboration with John Fletcher.

From 1594 once the two dominant companies were settled to work at the Rose and the Theatre London's massive appetite for plays and the commercial incentive to produce in quantity led to a good deal of collaborative writing. For the Admiral's Men if not for the Chamberlain's as many as four or five authors might contribute to the text of a single play. Henslowe, one of the best-known and most prosperous of theatre impresarios, kept in close touch with at least eight different writers, assorted groups of them teaming up for each new play. He would additionally employ individual writers from the groups such as Dekker to patch on additions or alterations to plays he had bought for his companies, or to old plays that needed freshening up. He paid Ben Jonson to write additions to Thomas Kyd's *Spanish Tragedy* (*Henslowe's Diary*, pp. 182, 203), and others to augment *Dr Faustus*, for instance. Some authors shopped around with their services, others stayed more or less literally indebted to one impresario. Jonson soon proved incapable of maintaining good relations with any one employer for long. He moved from Henslowe to the Chamberlain's Men, from them to the boys of Blackfriars, then to and fro between Shakespeare's Men and the boys for a decade, and to other companies thereafter.

Of the twenty-five or more poets who made a living or part of a living by writing for the playing companies, probably not more than eight had regular contracts.[28] Shakespeare seems to have led the way in this as in so many other of his activities. His liaison with the Chamberlain's Men from 1594 was subsequently copied by Heywood, who signed a two-year contract as a player with Henslowe in 1598. They were followed on varying terms by Dekker, William Rowley, also a player (a 'fat foole'), Fletcher, Massinger, Shirley and Richard Brome. To judge from a comparison of what Henslowe was paying at the turn of the century (about £5) with what Brome commanded in the 1630s (at least £20, or £54 per annum on the promise of three plays a year), it increasingly became a lucrative business.

The greatest demand for new plays is well recorded in Henslowe's *Diary*, much of which records what was done between 1594 and 1600. In those years only two companies shared the exclusive right to perform for Londoners. Thanks to Henslowe's records we know that the Admiral's Men bought and performed on average over thirty plays a year in each of those fertile years. We must assume that its companion company, the Chamberlain's Men, through that period bought far more than the fifteen or so plays by Shakespeare and others that have survived.

As the number of plays bought for the repertories increased, of course, the demand for new plays dropped off. New fashions became an increasingly self-conscious development out of the familiar and popular species of established plays. The King's Men, outstandingly the leading company in the 1630s, once they had the most socially reputable playhouse at Black-friars, seem to have commissioned barely four new plays a year. Under Charles sixty-four out of the eighty-eight known plays distinguished by being staged at Court were old, some of them by twenty years or more. This lowering of the priority for novelty coincided with a rise in the status of plays to the level of poetic 'works', worthy of publication in folio along with graver matter. The fact that most of the plays that got into print were the product of solo authorship (and their getting to the press largely a result of author interest) makes it easy to forget how dominant was the collaborative process in playwriting.

By the later years Charles himself read plays that got into print, and marked his copies with appreciative comments. Through his years of rule courtiers and gallants began to figure amongst the writers of plays. There was less collaborative writing, with its aura of hack-work, and a greater readiness to publish plays for reasons of pride instead of money. John Ford was a gentleman resident at the Middle Temple, an Inn of Court which prided itself on its literary talents. He spent nearly twenty years writing laborious poems on the one hand, but on the other collaborating with Dekker and others to write plays for the citizen repertories. Only under Charles did he start writing plays on his own for the new and privileged market, first the Blackfriars and later Beeston's Cockpit. Some of his late plays he published under an anagram of his name, 'Fide Honor'.

Only one contract between a poet and a playing company has survived in any detail, and then only because the contract was broken and as a result came into the lawcourts.[29] Richard Brome, who was once Jonson's assistant and started playwriting for the King's Men at the Globe, signed a contract in July 1635 with Queen Henrietta's Men who were then playing at the Salisbury Court hall playhouse. For them for the next three years he was to write three plays a year. This was a higher level of production than the two plays annually that most poets managed when not writing in collaboration, and part of the dispute became a question whether Brome had firmly promised nine plays in all over the three years, or simply said he would do his best. He actually completed five. In return he was to receive 15 shillings a week throughout the term of the contract, plus one day's profit from each play. The practice of giving poets a day's takings seems to have operated since before 1611.[30] We do not know how standard the weekly wage might have been.

What basically caused the trouble between Brome and his employers was the plague. It interrupted playing drastically in 1636, and altogether prevented the players from gaining any London income for a good half of the three years of Brome's contract. The weekly wage therefore became intermittent, though by the end of the period the company claimed they were only £5 or less than eight weeks behind in their payments. In that time Brome had supplied only five plays, and moreover had sold one of them to a rival impresario, William Beeston, when he was short of ready cash.

Despite these shortfalls on both sides of the contract, Brome and the company entered on a new contract in 1638. The terms offered Brome now were more generous – £1 weekly, plus the profits from one day of each new play – but the demands were still for three plays yearly, and for the poet's exclusive services for seven years. Also the plays still owing from the previous contract were not forgotten. Two were to be delivered in the first year, and a third at any time during the contract. If Brome fell behind again half of his wage would be forfeit.

Predictably Brome did not manage such a rate of production. After less than a year he was seduced away once again by Beeston, who now had a new company at the Cockpit to find plays for. The contract itself could not be found, and the affair sank into the arms of the law, where the depositions of both parties in the dispute are preserved. They make it clear that whether or not a contracted poet received a weekly wage from the company employing him he was expected to write only for his employers, to provide a fixed number of plays each year, and not to publish any of them for at least the term of his contract. The players do not seem to have held copyright in the modern sense – Shirley published all the plays he wrote for Queen Henrietta's Men after he left them, although they still used his plays in their repertory.[31] Occasionally the players may have given permission for a play to appear in print while the poet was still under contract. Jonson and Webster both published their plays, including '*more than hath been Publickely Spoken or Acted*' as Jonson put it on the titlepage of *Every Man out of his Humour*, in the years after their first staging.

It seems likely that the practice of benefit days, when the poet took the profits of his new play, gradually became the standard method of payment for all poets, whether they were contracted to the players or not. The eight or so poets who had a steady working relationship with a single company presumably had not only this specific reward but also the security of a written contract and a steady wage. They were all evidently happy enough with this system. Some freelanced, like Jonson. Others must have signed long-term contracts, like Shakespeare, Fletcher and Shirley. The fundamental principle they all held, which underlies all consideration of the body of literature they produced, is that their works were written for the stage, for the playing companies, and that the durability of print was a secondary consideration, the sort of bonus that would normally only come in the wake of a successful presentation in the company repertoire. Shakespeare never tried to get his plays published for readers in his lifetime. The half of his extant body of plays that appeared while he was alive were issued by his company, not by the author himself.[32]

7. THE CITY AND THE COURT

Most of the other matters relating to the poets are too near the foreground to be dealt with in a study of the background. Two questions, though, or rather one question with two aspects, does have to be given some consideration. That is, firstly, the social allegiances of the poets and their engagement with their audiences, and, secondly, their engagement with the Court.

Social tensions were latent amongst all the playhouse audiences, and the record of the poets exploiting those tensions with satire is considerable. Censorship held down comments on the government's foreign policy except for the spectacular eruption of anti-Spanish feeling in Middleton's *A Game at Chess* in 1624, and the censor also reacted to satire on living personages. But the anti-bishop Marprelate uproar of the late 1580s, mockery of Scotsmen by the boy companies in the early years under James, attacks on the Lord Mayor in *Hog hath Lost his Pearl* (1613), on Mompesson in *A New Way to Pay Old Debts* and on Alderman Abell at the Red Bull in 1638, along with attacks on royal policy by Massinger and others under Charles, all got under the fence of censorship. The examples of satire that drew the censor's attention are only the peaks of a mountain of contemporary allusions. In a city lacking newspapers and dependent on gossip amongst the crowds for their news, they were a very marketable commodity.

Social tensions showed up in different forms at different kinds of venue. At the citizen amphitheatres under the Stuarts the union of City Fathers and Puritans against playing was offset by the continuing patronage of the northern playhouses, the Fortune and Red Bull, by citizens and apprentices. On the Bankside and especially in the hall playhouses both poets and audiences had the Court much more in their minds. The reasons for this are complex, and the evidence open to a wide range of interpretation. Throughout the period the best companies might expect to be summoned to entertain the Court with their plays. Every Christmas as many as a dozen plays would be presented before the monarch and assembled courtiers and ambassadors. To be summoned was an acknowledgement of status. Only the best of the companies performing in London were ever called for. So in a sense playing at Court was the ultimate goal of all the players, the final accolade for their success. What is not clear is whether the existence of this goal had any influence on their professional habits.

The records of the Revels Office and the Works accounts show how much time and money went into the preparation of the Court festivities, and the Court would in any case have been the top of the market so far as the players were concerned. The difficulty is in ascertaining how much they deliberately catered for that end of their market, and therefore how much influence the Court venues might have had on the day-to-day presentations around the city. Richard Hosley has gone so far as to suggest that the public playhouses' tiring-house façades, such as the Swan with its two broad entry doors and gallery above, were modelled on the screens in the halls of great houses.[33] When players performed in a great hall, whether at Court or on their travels, they might have used the floor of the hall as their stage and the screen at one end as their means of entry and exit. Hall screens might therefore have provided a model for the tiring-house fronts in the commercial playhouses, though we should not forget that the street theatres of the sixteenth century, where travelling players erected a platform with a curtained booth at the back for their tiring-house, provided a broadly similar set of facilities.[34] Two kinds of venue, two traditions, came together in the course of the Shakespearean period. One was the popular theatre of the street and the market-place, the home of the nomadic travelling mummers, tumblers and players. The other was the great halls, used for the entertainment of the household whenever a company of travelling players came by. Both traditions, I suspect, merged in the permanent London playhouses, where the stability of a good income and audiences consistent both in attendance and taste created a kind of central, normative venue different from either the street booth or the great hall.

The Court did of course provide one potentially very powerful influence in the form of the masques by which most of the major events, especially royal marriages, were celebrated. Under James and Charles players took speaking parts in these lavishly presented shows of verse, music and dance, and at the very least must have seen in them evidence of what the Court liked. The principle of masquing was a banquet of all the senses. Hence not only did orchestras play, choristers sing and courtiers dance, ladies as well as gentlemen donning the most colourful costumes for the occasion, but the eye was dazzled by the *trompe l'oeil* effects of Inigo Jones's perspective scenery. The stories of the masques were entirely allegorical, whereas the great majority of plays based themselves on forms of realism. But music, dancing and the speaking of verse did also feature in the plays, especially those staged at the hall playhouses, and the temptation to imitate the feast of the other senses, especially the eye, must have gripped the players when they saw what the Court was able to do. Costume (apparel) was a major feature on the commercial stage, and the masquers' dress was both enviable and capable of being copied in the playhouses.

Beyond that, however, the players' resources in both time and money were limited. It took days to set up a Court venue for a masque, to fix the perspective scenery and the sort of machines that could fly boys in on an angle or, as in Campion's masque for Lord Hay's wedding in 1607, to contrive a House of Darkness through which bats and owls could flit on wires. It was dazzlingly clever but it was very costly, and none of the professional players ever used changeable scenery on their stages. Throughout the whole period the audiences they confronted daily on their home ground went away feasted with much less, or with a markedly different fare, than the Court enjoyed when it banqueted on its masques. Only with the Restoration did visual feasts of perspective scenery arrive to transform English staging.

There is room for disagreement over how much Court fashions might have influenced what the players and their poets offered on the common stages, and disagreement there is. The advantage to the players of pleasing the Court was straightforward. Financially they gained little. The fee for taking a play to Court was £10, comparable to the income they would get from a good day in their common playhouse. What they did gain from royal patronage was prestige and more tangibly some protection against the wolves of Guildhall who prowled round the London folds throughout the sixteenth century. When James gave his name to Shakespeare's company and his wife's and son's names to the two other leading groups of London-based players, he gave them security as well as prestige. How far in return they consciously shaped their stage presentations to match what they understood to be the Court fashion remains an open question.

It is hard to see how Court preferences would have had a really radical effect on common staging. Appearances at Court were infrequent, at best not more than half-a-dozen a year by the leading companies compared with their daily appearances in the common playhouses. The Court's love of masques involved big spending on stage effects, which the common players could never dream of imitating in their plays. The two forms of spectacle were entirely different from each other. It was not the players so much as the poets who seem to have responded to the pressures of Court fashions, and even then much more in masques than in their plays.

The poets saw their work in plays and in masques as distinct. Both forms, according to Jonson, who wrote a good many of both, should combine instruction with the pleasure they gave. As he declared in the prefatory note to his masque *Love's Triumph*,

all Representations, especially those of this nature in court, publique Spectacles, eyther have bene, or ought to be the mirrors of mans life, whose ends, for the excellence of their exhibiters (as being the donatives, of great Princes, to their people) ought always to carry a mixture of profit, with them, no lesse then delight.[35]

But the audience at Court, the home of the ruler, was different from the audience at Blackfriars. So the masques written for the Court defined virtue in the abstract instead of evoking pity or laughter over a simulacrum of reality. Muriel Bradbrook has pointed out that Jonson's masque *Hymenaei* which launched the great era of Jacobean masques with its vision of the ideals of courtly conduct, needs to be set against his play *Sejanus*, which heralded James's reign by an account of the disastrous vices of a Roman court ruled by a homosexual.[36] Under the Stuarts masques were designed to show the ideal world, with the comic grotesques of anti-masques an incidental reflection of how important the ideal world was by contrast with the ordinary world of the plays. Charles on at least one occasion looked over his censor's shoulder and ordered a passage in one of Massinger's plays to be struck out because it was 'insolent'. The distance of what was written for the Court from what appeared on the popular stages makes it clear that poets and players alike led their own lives and saw no need to imitate Court fashions in the process of earning their daily bread.

Jonson was far more openly opinionated than most of his fellow writers. Quite apart from *Sejanus*, his *Catiline* of 1611 is almost certainly a fictitious presentation of the Gunpowder Plot and a defence of his own dubious part in it (like Marlowe before him he seems to have found one source of finance in spying for the government). He was a violent controversialist against several of his fellow poets in his contributions to the so-called Poetomachia, or War of the Theatres, in 1601–2.[37] With all this, however, he was also and always a passionate moralist, a running commentary on the follies of his times. Whatever the players made out of what he sold them, his masques were also statements of opinion, moral and political. The man who could write under a Stuart that 'A *good King* is a publike Servant'[38] was brave as well as outspoken, and no acquiescent royalist. Jonson was imprisoned in 1597 for writing a seditious play, in 1598 for killing a man (a player) in a duel, and in 1605 for another play, *Eastward Ho!*, which he wrote along with Chapman and Marston for the boys of Blackfriars, in which they satirised the King and his Scottish entourage.

Other playwrights were less loudly opinionated than Jonson, but not much less forthright. Massinger, who wrote for several companies, including the King's Men between 1613 and 1639, on the whole wrote plays like *The City Madam* (for the King's Men at Blackfriars in about 1632). This play (the title is an antonym for 'Court lady') has a curiously ambivalent attitude to its citizen characters. It begins with a situation like those of the satires, showing up citizen greed and folly, but it ends with citizen values triumphant. The same author's *The Roman Actor*, however, written in 1625–6 at the beginning of the second Stuart's reign, is a veritable mirror for magistrates, a trenchant sermon to the new ruler and a playwright's manifesto.[39] On the political front it sets out the dangers of wrong rule, displayed in the conveniently distant setting of ancient Rome, where the chronic and increasingly disregarded question of the divine right of kings was irrelevant. It puts up a spirited case for players and playing. Players are necessary members of the commonwealth, says the title character at the beginning of the play,

> That with delight joyne profit and endeavour
> To build their mindes up faire, and on the Stage
> Decipher to the life what honours waite
> On good, and glorious actions, and the shame
> That treads upon the heeles of vice.

The profit of course was moral and educational for audiences, not financial for poets. Before the end the Emperor kills the leading player who makes this speech.

The chapters that follow in this book present the background to the plays in the fullest practicable detail. First, a history of the playing companies provides the essential story of what happened through the seventy years between 1572 and the closure in 1642. The next chapter describes the players themselves, their social backgrounds and their play-acting system. The playhouses that they built for themselves once they had royal protection, and the staging of plays in the playhouses are described next; and finally a look at the audiences for the plays, the system's beneficiaries, fills in more of the main features in this general picture.

CHAPTER 2

The Companies

I. THE LAWS OF PLAYING

One of the many but rarely noted features of playgoing in the years up to
and including Shakespeare's arrival on the scene was the English government's determination to control it. With the onset of the Reformation
Thomas Cromwell's Tudor regime under Henry VIII faced a massive
challenge to secure an authority to govern that was independent of the
church and the Pope. In 1578 the Privy Council gave the Master of the
Revels, the Lord Chamberlain's executive officer who spent five months
planning and supervising the plays staged at Court each winter, authority to
control playing throughout the whole country. Centralised government
under the Tudors of course lacked the resources that modern governments
have to control civil and civic activities, and long after that date local mayors
and magistrates continued to take it into their own hands to determine what
their local populace might be allowed to enjoy. Nobles continued to run
their own playing companies in spite of the Acts of Parliament that
recurrently restricted who could run his own travelling company to higher
and higher levels of the aristocracy. Even under the Stuarts, who made a
great effort in 1615 to check and restrict the licences to play, many more
companies toured the country than government wanted. The Privy
Council's most severe control was understandably exercised where they
lived, in London. Nonetheless, the very strictness of the laws cited in this
chapter is an indication of how easy players could find it to avoid the
regulations imposed on them.

The 'Acte for the punishment of Vacabondes' of 1572 served the companies of players much as it was designed to serve the commonwealth of
England as a whole. It authorised the better members of the profession to
pursue their trade and turned the idle and poor members to higher things. It
was an early step in the progress of the professional players from peripatetic
entertainers who never performed in the same place twice running to

permanently established repertory companies, with enormous financial investments backing them and a position in London guaranteed by the King himself. The statute of 1572 required each travelling company to be licensed by one noble or two judicial dignitaries of the realm:

All and everye persone and persones beynge whole and mightye in Body and able to labour, havinge not Land or Maister, nor using any lawfull Marchaundize Crafte or Mysterye whereby hee or shee might get his or her Lyvinge, and can gyve no reckninge howe he or shee dothe lawfully get his or her Lyvinge; & all Fencers Bearewardes Common Players in Enterludes & Minstrels, not belonging to any Baron of this Realme or towardes any other honorable Personage of greater Degree; all Juglers Pedlars Tynkers and Petye Chapmen; whiche seid Fencers Bearewardes Comon Players in Enterludes Mynstrels Juglers Pedlers Tynkers & Petye Chapmen, shall wander abroade and have not Lycense of two Justices of the Peace at the leaste, whereof one to be of the Quorum, when and in what Shier they shall happen to wander … shalbee taken adjudged and deemed Roges Vacaboundes and Sturdy Beggers.[1]

Ordinary gentlemen who wished to support a company of entertainers now ran the risk of losing them as vagabonds. A further statute of 1598 took away the licensing power from the magistrates too, leaving only great nobles with the authority to lend their names to the players. And when James came to the throne in 1603 he took the patronage of the London companies into his own family – one for himself, the second for the heir apparent, Prince Henry, and the third for the Queen.[2]

Players were a royal pleasure, and to please royalty had to be a major aim of the companies. The story of the companies between 1572 and 1642 is one of increasing royal favour and protection, from the first statute which gave warrant to their quality through the accolade of direct royal patronage after 1603 to the final period, when royal protection ceased to be meaningful. There is, none the less, despite the royal favours and the various origins of the companies in employment as entertainers – adult mummers or boy choristers[3] – no question but that for the players the profit motive was totally predominant. The companies were independent commercial organ- isations, not doing what pleasure-bent lord or royalty commanded but going where and doing what brought most money and best audiences.

The relations of the various acting companies to the great, and to the specific patrons who gave them their names, was always complex. The Earl of Leicester kept a travelling company of high renown but seems never to have used them for his own entertainment. Instead he used them to circulate his colours and his name through the country in order to advertise his fame. Relations of the Privy Council with individual noble patrons of the professional companies changed radically as they became an established feature of London life. In 1583, when Elizabeth gave order to form a company under her own name, two powerful reasons probably dictated her decision. One was the way great lords such as Leicester and Oxford were using their playing companies in the Christmas festivities at Court as emblems of their own power. The other was the sustained attack on plays in London fostered by the Lord Mayor and Corporation. Elizabeth's abstraction of the leading players out of every major company to make the Queen's Men checked the rivalry among the great nobles and at the same time gave powerful backing to the continued presence of the players in London. The Queen's Men could carry the royal livery throughout the country, advertising her power and presence everywhere to the public mind. In London the mayoralty was persuaded to give them leave to play at specific inns inside the City. When James took over the patronage of the Chamberlain's Men in 1603 and later made his son and his wife patrons of the other leading companies he was renewing and systematising Elizabeth's early tactic. Under Charles, the first monarch to take a personal interest in plays, royal patronage continued but the players now divided themselves between the theatres that performed for the privileged and the Court, and the 'citizen' playhouses catering for London's masses.

However wide the divergence of social allegiances, all the playing companies were driven by the need to make a living. Company organisation was commercial, a core of shareholders and decision-makers and a periphery of hired hands, backed in many cases by a theatre- and property-owning impresario who supplied ready cash in return for a share of the takings. Success meant working in London, where the biggest audiences were and where there might be the accolade of performing in the Christmas season of festivities at Court. For the players, most of whom were Londoners themselves, playing in London meant living in one place instead of travelling and, more important, enjoying a steady income. The impresario with his playhouse would also have a store of properties and plays to help expand the repertoire. From 1594, as we shall see, London offered the two essentials for success, financial backing and a permanent playing place. The honey was in London, and the bees proved tenacious in clinging to it. Usually what dislodged them was a total prohibition on London playing because of the plague, when they had to resume travelling. Or it might be an impresario who broke them up to form new combinations of players more amenable to his financial terms. There were always new combinations ready to swarm in.

As the quality of the common players grew in the course of the sixteenth century, and as they developed from mumming and tumbling to acting, so their recognition by government increased, and so likewise the hostility to them in London from the City Fathers. Their status was a matter for hostilities between the Crown and the Lord Mayor and aldermen for nearly a whole century before 1642. The threat to the common players from the statute of 1572 was a very real one, since London's City Fathers had long before given notice of their willingness to enforce it. Primarily it was a renewal of the old series of statutes about retainers, which restricted the number of liveried servants that a noble might employ to those of his immediate household. Technically therefore the companies, if they were to protect themselves against the municipalities, had to enroll themselves in such a household and carry their patron's livery as his personal retainers; though of course they would not, except for specific services in entertaining him, receive any wage for their position. James Burbage, writing on behalf of his company to their patron, the Earl of Leicester in 1572, made this very clear:

To the right honorable Earle of Lecester, their good lord and master.

Maye yt please your honour to understande that forasmuche as there is a certayne Proclamation out for the revivinge of a Statute as touchinge retayners, as youre Lordshippe knoweth better than we can enforme you thereof: We therfore, your humble Servaunts and daylye Oratours your players, for avoydinge all inconvenients that maye growe by reason of the saide Statute, are bold to trouble your Lordshippe with this our Suite, humblie desiringe your honor that (as you have bene alwayes our good Lord and Master) you will now vouchsaffe to reteyne us at this present as your houshold Servaunts and daylie wayters, not that we meane to crave any further stipend or benefite at your Lordshippes hands but our lyveries as we have had, and also your honors License to certifye that we are your houshold Servaunts when we shall have occasion to travayle amongst our frendes as we do usuallye once a yere, and as other noblemens Players do and have done in tyme past, Wherebie we maye enjoye our facultie in your Lordshippes name as we have done heretofore.[4]

The protection of a patron, especially one so powerful, accommodating, and ready to get them opportunities to play at Court as Leicester was, clearly had enormous value. Still more so was the explicit royal protection that the same company was offered, unprecedentedly, two years later, in their patent of 10 May 1574, which gives this book its starting date. This was the first ever royal patent for a company of adult players. It specified the permissible scope of the company in unambiguous terms, and came to serve as a model for all patents granted subsequently under the early Stuarts.

Elizabeth by the grace of God quene of England, &c. To all Justices, Mayors, Sheriffes, Baylyffes, head Constables, under Constables, and all other our officers and mynisters gretinge. Knowe ye that we of oure especiall grace, certen knowledge, and mere mocion have licenced and auctorised, and by these presentes do licence and auctorise, oure lovinge Subjectes, James Burbage, John Perkyn, John Lanham, William Johnson, and Roberte Wilson, servauntes to oure trustie and welbeloved Cosen and Counseyllor the Earle of Leycester, to use, exercise, and occupie the arte and facultye of playenge Commedies, Tragedies, Enterludes, stage playes, and such other like as they have alredie used and studied, or hereafter shall use and studie, aswell for the recreacion of oure loving subjectes, as for oure solace and pleasure when we shall thincke good to see them, as also to use and occupie all such Instrumentes as they have alreadie practised, or hereafter shall practise, for and during our pleasure. And the said Commedies, Tragedies, Enterludes, and stage playes, to gether with their musicke, to shewe, publishe, exercise, and occupie to their best commoditie during all the terme aforesaide, aswell within oure Citie of London and liberties of the same, as also within the liberties and fredomes of anye oure Cities, townes, Bouroughes &c whatsoever as without the same, thoroughte oure Realme of England. Willynge and commaundinge yow and everie of yowe, as ye tender our pleasure, to permytte and suffer them herein withoute anye yowre lettes, hynder-aunce, or molestacion duringe the terme aforesaid, anye acte, statute, proclamacion, or commaundement heretofore made, or hereafter to be made, to the contrarie notwithstandinge. Provyded that the said Commedies, Tragedies, enterludes, and stage playes be by the master of oure Revells for the tyme beynge before sene & allowed, and that the same be not published or shewen in the tyme of common prayer, or in the tyme of great and common plague in oure said Citye of London. In wytnes whereof &c. wytnes oure selfe at Westminster the xth daye of Maye.[5]

The players in all probability gave their thanks to Elizabeth when Leicester laid on his famous entertainment at Kenilworth in the following year, and they performed at Court over Christmas in both 1574 and 1575.

They had other business in London too. Through family links Burbage had already established himself in the suburbs with an early playhouse in Stepney. His brother-in-law John Brayne built an amphitheatre consisting of a scaffold of galleries and a large stage in a yard called the Red Lion in 1567.[6] It does not seem to have been a great success, and may have been constructed too soon to be securely profitable as a regular venue for a playing company. By 1576, though, the new legislation and the Leicester's 1574 patent prompted Burbage to take another step towards real security, the establishment of his own permanent playing headquarters in London. With his brother-in-law as co-financier in 1576 he used his status as a member of the Carpenters' guild and built the Theatre. On land leased for twenty-one years, with a special proviso in the lease that he could dismantle and remove the construction if need be, he set up the framework that was later to be reused for the Globe, and gave it a grand Roman name, one normally then used as the name for the great printed atlases by Mercator and others, as the first of its kind in London. His stage came from the name for a world atlas (all the world's a *theatrum*). He was probably still sceptical about the security of playing in London, because the proviso he tried to build into the lease was in part an attempt to preserve his investment in building materials from the usual fate of structures put up on leasehold land, which reverted to the owner when the lease expired.

He need not have worried, at least for the duration of his lease. The Theatre was in regular use by early in 1577, and a near neighbour, the Curtain, was set up soon after. Both were located in the suburb of Shoreditch on the main road north outside the jurisdiction of the City Fathers, whose opposition was soon in evidence. It was intensified by the launching of a pamphlet campaign against playing and playhouses once the Theatre was in use. This campaign did not stop until the Queen gave playing her patronage in 1583. Outside the City limits but inside the royal patronage, from 1583 the players' London foot-hold and the corollary London profits became secure.

For the next few years Leicester's Men and the other companies able to reach London, Sussex's (then the Lord Chamberlain), Warwick's, Essex's and Oxford's continued the pattern of playing in London while they could and travelling each summer. They played at first only once or twice a week, but the Puritans were soon complaining of a greater frequency.[7] Puritan preachers and City Fathers alike renewed their attacks in 1582–3, and were given ammunition by an Act of God on 13 January 1583, a Sunday, at Paris Garden when some scaffolding collapsed, killing eight spectators and injuring many more.[8] This was at a bear-baiting but all forms of entertainment were branded alike in City eyes. It may have been this event and the outcry it caused as much as the scramble of players around London that led Sir Francis Walsingham on behalf of the government to depute the Master of the Revels in 1583 to cream off the current acting talent and form one predominant company which would have the Queen's own name and patronage. As Edmond Howes later described it,

Comedians and stage-players of former time were very poor and ignorant in respect of these of this time: but being now grown very skilful and exquisite actors for all matters, they were entertained into the service of divers great lords: out of which companies there were twelve of the best chosen, and, at the request of Sir Francis Walsingham, they were sworn the queens servants and were allowed wages and liveries as grooms of the chamber: and until this yeare 1583, the queene had no players. Among these twelve players were two rare men, viz. Thomas [i.e. Robert] Wilson, for a quicke, delicate, refined, extemporall witt, and Richard Tarleton, for a wondrous plentifull pleasant extemporall wit, he was the wonder of his time.[9]

The Queen's Company, possessing as it then did all the most famous players – Wilson, John Laneham, and probably Tarlton taken from Leicester's, John

Dutton from Oxford's, John Bentley and John Singer – held its predominance for the next five years. Its existence under the royal protection may well have helped the City Fathers to mollify their attitude to the players. Having to grant access to the one royally supported company gave them the right to refuse access to all the lesser stars in the circuit. In 1585 they produced a relatively modest list of requirements for the 'toleration' of players, including restrictions on playing during time of plague and restrictions in the authorisation of companies. They summed up their requests as follows:

That they hold them content with playeing in private houses at weddings etc without publike assemblies.

If more be thought good to be tolerated: that then they be restrained to the orders in the act of common Counsell tempore Hawes.

That they play not openly till the whole [plague] death in London have been by xx daies under 50 a weke, nor longer than it shal so continue.

That no playes be on the sabbat.

That no playeing be on holydaies but after evening prayer: nor any received into the auditorie till after evening prayer.

That no playeing be in the dark, nor continue any such time but as any of the auditorie may returne to their dwellings in London before sonne set, or at least before it be dark.

That the Quenes players only be tolerated, and of them their number and certaine names to be notified in your Lordships lettres to the L. Maior and to the Justices of Middlesex and Surrey. And those her players not to divide themselves into several companies.

That for breaking any of the orders, their toleration cesse.[10]

With this on paper, the Queen's Men could rule in the City, and the relations of City and Court government remained unaltered for the next few years.

Gaining the right to play in the City did not do anything to stop the professional companies continuing their tradition of touring the country. Summer was a good time to travel, and even the strong companies with a permanent base in London continued to tour in most years. Taking a company on its travels might even have been a holiday of sorts, a break from the daily grind in London of performing a different play every day. But getting money was always a consideration, and the Admiral's for one used to travel in mid-winter through the official closure time of Lent's forty days.

Travelling, with a waggon for the properties and costumes and the younger players and the leaders on horseback, lasted for two months or more, and took the London companies all over the country. The leading groups went as far from London as York and Newcastle in the north and Cornwall and Shropshire in the west. They might well have developed the habit, living in England's largest port as they did, of starting their tours by using coastal shipping, since many of their known stops recorded in the many *Records of Early English Drama* volumes took them to ports such as Dover, Rye, Folkestone, Southampton, Bristol, Exeter, Bridgewater and Newcastle, as well as to towns accessible from the sea by river such as York and Carlisle. One player in particular, Martin Slater, who was in the Admiral's up to 1597, seems to have had permanently itchy feet. He was in Edinburgh in 1599, and although he worked briefly in London from 1608 as a senior member of the King's Revels Children at Whitefriars he took travelling companies all over the country between 1600 and 1625. For all his travels he is on record in London in 1609 as having ten dependents there.

The Puritan attacks on the stage were aimed fairly precisely at all the purveyors of entertainments such as bull- and bear-baiting, tumbling, fencing displays and plays ('Theaters, Curtines, Heaving houses, Rifling boothes, Bowling alleyes, and such places').[11] They saw no difference between bear-baiting, fencing matches, plays and prostitution. Nor did they entirely exclude the boy players attached to the singing schools of St Paul's and the Chapel Royal at Windsor, and at such schools as the Merchant Taylors'. There are records of Puritan attacks specifically aimed at them. Even in the academic exercise of playing the profit motive reared its ugly head, and in 1573 plays were banned at Merchant Taylors' because of the rowdyism of the audience. They had become commercial shows open to the public. Therefore they were on a par with and in competition with the adult companies, not only at Court, where they had traditionally enter-tained the Crown with plays, but also in London.[12]

2. THE EARLY BOY COMPANIES

In 1576, the year the first adult players' theatre was built, the Chapel Children moved into the City to a playhouse in the Blackfriars precinct, which was at that time in a 'liberty' free of the City's jurisdiction. This first Blackfriars playhouse was owned by Richard Farrant, deputy to William Hunnis as Master of the Chapel Children. He appears to have taken over Hunnis's duties in 1576 largely in order to run the Children at the playhouse as a commercial enterprise. He can have taken up the lease of the Blackfriars property in that year for no other reason. In 1578 his company was listed along with the adults in a Privy Council protection order.[13] In 1580 he died and his company was eventually taken in hand by Henry Evans, a scrivener, along with John Lyly the playwright, presumably for similarly commercial purposes. Not long after, in 1582, the Paul's Children lost their Master,

Sebastian Westcott, under whom the commercial aspects of their playing had not been predominant. After Westcott's death the Paul's boys seem to have joined forces with the Blackfriars company, as they had done for Court performances on occasions in the past.

In the course of 1584 the joint company was deprived of the Blackfriars playhouse, and consequently disappeared from the commercial stage. The Paul's Children resumed activities under their own identity in the same year, under a new Master, Thomas Giles, with the services of Lyly as their poet. They performed regularly at Court up to 1590. In that year Lyly's part in the Martin Marprelate religious controversies with his company, who had helped to publicise his contributions, were officially disowned and all the playing companies for a time were suppressed. The adult companies, also involved in the Marprelate mudslinging, were considerably dampened by the experience, and the boy companies did not resurface for several years.

The early boy companies had an air of respectability which set them in contrast to the adult companies. Ostensibly still schoolboys and choristers receiving prized education in singing, the much smaller audiences at their indoor playhouses regarded them as having a much higher social standing than the common players. There is a story here still to be told about why boy players were seen, particularly by the nobility, as superior to adult performers. One possibility, to be considered further in Chapter 3, is the likelihood that what Heywood called their 'juniority' made them more readily acceptable as play-actors than could adults, who might all too easily be seen as truly the figures that they only pretended to be and whose dress they wore. Besides the tradition of performing on stage as part of their education, a tradition maintained in some of the colleges at Oxford and Cambridge, their smaller size made it impossible for them to be seen as truly simulating the language and garb of their social superiors. That must have comforted the superiors who watched them perform.

The boy companies' better status socially than adult players appeared for instance in the frequency with which they were summoned to perform for the Court. Their performances at Court continued in a longstanding tradtion of plays staged by boys. As such groups of players they were quite distinct from the boys who acted with the adult companies as women or boy pages. For such boys, whatever their social origin, their career prospects were to play the women's parts until their voices broke, after which if they were lucky or particularly skilled they might be kept on, ostensibly as apprentices tied to specific players, who would house them as before and let them play junior roles until they might have earned enough to buy a share in the adult company.

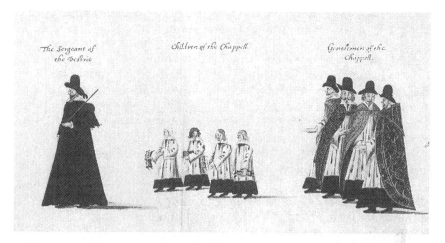

Illustration 5. A manuscript drawing of the Children of the Chapel Royal in Queen Elizabeth's funeral procession, 1603, British Library MS.35 324 fol. 31v. Chorister garb has been slow to change.

3. THE EARLY ADULT COMPANIES

After the establishment of the Queen's Men in 1583 the adult companies still rose and fell regularly. The Queen's Men were depressed after the death of their famous clown Tarlton in 1588, and suffered a number of desertions. Worcester's were their closest rivals through the five years they were on top, and it was from Worcester's rather than the Queen's that the leading actors of the next decade, and in particular one, Edward Alleyn, emerged. Alleyn wore the livery of Charles Howard, who was made Lord Admiral in 1584 and raised his own company of players with Alleyn as their leader. They performed the first Marlowe plays, *Tamburlaine* with its sequel and *Faustus*, in 1587–88. From 1588 two years of rapidly changing fortunes reshuffled company membership until in 1590 two companies merged to take the predominant position on the London scene. This was uniquely a joint enterprise between Alleyn of the Admiral's and Strange's Men. Strange's owed their allegiance to Ferdinand Stanley, Lord Strange of the Earl of Derby's family, while Alleyn, who led them, retained his livery as a servant of Charles Howard, the Lord Admiral. This united company lasted until the last of the major reshuffles following a massive outbreak of plague in 1593, out of which in 1594 emerged the two most successful companies of all, Shakespeare's with most of the former Lord Strange's under the Lord Chamberlain's patronage, and a new company with one ex-Strange's man led by Alleyn with the Lord Admiral as its patron.

Henry Carey
Lord Hunsdon
BY MARK GERARDS.

ÆTATIS SVÆ 66
AN 1591

Illustration 6. Henry Carey, the first Lord Hunsdon, painted by Marcus Gheerhaerts the Younger at the age of sixty-six in 1591. He carries the white rod that signified his role as the Lord Chamherlain. A son of Mary Boleyn, Carey was a cousin to Queen Elizabeth through her mother, Mary's sister Anne. As the queen's first cousin (and conceivably, if that is the right word, her half-brother as a possible bastard son of Henry VIII) he worked for her at first as a soldier, a name he always held high. His daughter Katherine was the queen's closest friend and wife to Charles Howard, the Lord Admiral. When Katherine Carey died in March 1603, the queen was said to have lost the will to live, and died only a few days later. A blunt and boisterous man, Carey was patron in the 1590s to Emilia Lanier, a poet and musician from a family of exiled Italian musicians at Court. She has sometimes been identified as Shakespeare's 'dark lady'. Carey's patronage of her was more intimate than official. She bore

The membership of Shakespeare's company and the company that shared a monopoly of London playing with it after 1594 seems largely to have been drawn from the Strange's company of 1590–3 along with individual players from the old Admiral's which had been travelling round the country since 1591 and a few from the Queen's Men and other travelling groups. This process seems to have reproduced in duplicate the original procedure of setting up the Queen's Men in 1583. The years preceding this new set-up in 1594 had been strained and frenetic. Marlowe and his university fellows were producing radically new and hugely popular plays. The Queen's Men had lost their predominance. There was a massive new appetite to cater for. And yet times were hard again – the plague restricted opportunities to perform massively through 1593 and as a result companies were breaking and their members reverting to travel. The turnover of company membership was faster between 1588 and 1594 than ever before or after. Just how precarious and changeable an existence it was we can see by following what is known of the chief players through these years.

We can pick up the trail at Elsinore, of all places, in June 1586, where three players, the clown Will Kemp, George Bryan and Thomas Pope, are recorded as playing for Danish royalty, probably after serving in the Earl of Leicester's company accompanying his army fighting in the Netherlands. In September Kemp returned to England while Bryan and Pope went to play for the Elector of Saxony. In 1590 the latter two reappear in the records of Strange's with Alleyn at the Theatre. Their names are among the actors named in the plot of the second part of *The Seven Deadly Sins*, which survives among other Alleyn papers at Dulwich College and is thought to have been prepared for Strange's Men in that year.[14] Of Bryan and Pope's fellow actors in this play two (Richard Cowley and Augustine Phillips) stayed with them in Strange's until it was dissolved at its patron's death in 1593, after which the four of them went to help form the Chamberlain's Men. Will Kemp rejoined his former fellows some time before 1593, since he is recorded on the titlepage of *A Knack to Know a Knave* (of 1593 or earlier) as having performed his 'merrimentes' in it along with Alleyn for Strange's. A warrant from the Privy Council of 6 May 1593 permitting the company to travel names Alleyn as the Lord Admiral's Man,

---

Illustration 6 (*cont.*)

him a son, also called Henry, in 1593, when he was sixty-eight. Along with his son-in-law he was responsible for the two companies that dominated London and Court performances from 1594 till 1600. When he died in July 1596, his son George, the second Lord Hunsdon, took over as the company's patron and a few months later became the new Lord Chamberlain.

with Bryan, Pope, Kemp, Phillips and John Heminges as the leading Strange's
Men's sharers.[15] Nothing of Heminges's earlier history is known except that he
might have been a Queen's Man; he could have been a long-term member of
Strange's, his name not appearing in the *Seven Deadly Sins* plot because he
played one of the two major roles for which no player is named. A letter of
Alleyn's written from Bristol to his wife in London during a Strange's tour
mentions Richard Cowley as another member. All of these except for Alleyn
moved into the Chamberlain's Men when it was formed in 1594.

Strange's was a curious kind of company organisation even in a period of
such sharply fluctuating fortunes as the companies suffered over these years.
Alleyn had been a Worcester's man for four or more years up to 1587, when he
seems to have joined a newish grouping calling itself the Admiral's. Uniquely
while working with Strange's Alleyn retained the personal status as the Lord
Admiral's servant that he secured after leaving Worcester's and joining
Charles Howard's new company some time after 1584. A Strange's company
had performed at Court in the winter of 1588–9, and must have suffered with
the Admiral's in the cold official winds of the Marprelate displeasure in 1590,
when the surviving boy company was suppressed altogether.

Alleyn's group seems to have staged Marlowe's plays at James Burbage's
playhouse, the Theatre, in 1590–1. The plot of *2 Seven Deadly Sins* is usually
thought to date from this period because in addition to naming all the major
players of Strange's with the single exception of Alleyn himself it included
among the lesser parts the name of James Burbage's son Richard. The plot
of *The Dead Man's Fortune*, another Dulwich manuscript, also has Richard
Burbage's name in it, and probably dates from the same time for the same
reason.[16] In May 1591 however there was some sort of quarrel between the
company and old Burbage over his retention of some playhouse receipts.
John Alleyn, Edward's brother, subsequently testified in a lawsuit brought
by the widow of a former gatherer against Burbage for a similar reason that
in May 1591, shortly after a fracas with the widow's relatives,

when [Alleyn] … came to [Burbage] for certen money which he deteyned from
[Alleyn] and his fellowes, of some of the dyvydent money betwene him & them,
growinge also by the use of the said Theater, he denyed to pay the same. [Alleyn] told
him that belike he ment to deale with them, as he did with the poore wydowe …
wishing him he wold not do so, for yf he did, they wold compleyne to ther lorde &
M[r] the lord Admyrall, and then he in a rage, litle reverencing his honour & estate,
sayd by a great othe, that he cared not for iii of the best lordes of them all.[17]

Strange's company with Alleyn consequently abandoned the Theatre,
moving early in 1592 to a new home, Philip Henslowe's Rose playhouse,

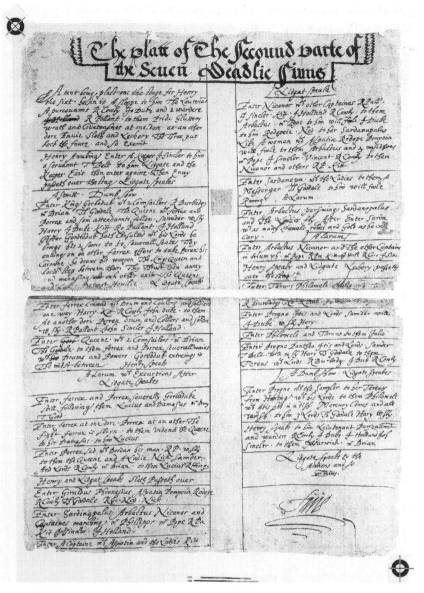

Illustration 7. Part of '*The Platt of the Secound parte of the Seven Deadlie Sinns*'.

then five years old. When this new and eminent company arrived Henslowe promptly enlarged his Rose, stretching its formerly regular polygon into an irregular cup shape by rebuilding the stage and its gallery scaffolding a few feet further back, increasing the audience capacity by four or five hundred extra customers.[18] Presumably this was for the purpose of utilising the evident skills of the new company. They certainly found a warm welcome. Alleyn's long and profitable association with the Henslowe enterprises was well fixed by this new arrangement, since in October 1592 he married Henslowe's only stepdaughter. From this time, as the company's chief player with his personal warrant from the Lord Admiral, he began to take a share in financing and running the company along with Henslowe. The Henslowe records show the Admiral's–Strange's company performing for him regularly from early in 1592 until the plague prohibitions of 1593 forced the company back to its travels. Then from May 1594, still under the Lord Admiral's livery, Alleyn led a new company that played exclusively at the same playhouse for the next six years.

The two companies formed in May 1594 and allocated to play exclusively at the two suburban playhouses, the Theatre and the Rose, were a distinctly new mix of players. Five of the former Strange's Men, Pope, Bryan, Heminges, Phillips and Cowley, all travelling with Alleyn as Strange's Men in 1593, went into the new Chamberlain's. Others whose names are on the list for the *Seven Deadly Sins* are not mentioned, their names turning up instead among the debris of a Pembroke's company that is in the records as travelling through Leicester near the end of 1592, at Court that Christmas and in the country again at York, Rye, Ludlow (their patron's territory in the Welsh Marches), Shrewsbury, Coventry, Bath and Ipswich through the summer of 1593. Pembroke's seems to have been set up in 1591 as a travelling company mixing some of Strange's Men with some of the 'flag-fallen' Queen's Men.

Even travelling though was difficult throughout this gloomy plague-ridden time. Henslowe wrote to Alleyn during the Admiral's–Strange's tour in September 1593 that Pembroke's 'had broken' while on tour and had been forced to sell their costumes (*Henslowe Papers*, p. 40). A will of one of them, Simon Jewell, tells us that the value to the six sharers of the costumes they sold was £80.[19] They also evidently sold their playbooks, because Marlowe's *Edward II* was entered on the Stationers' Register in July as a Pembroke's play, and a little later *The Taming of a Shrew*, a version of Shakespeare's play. *Edward I*, published in 1594, was probably another of their texts, and the early versions of *2* and *3 Henry VI* were certainly theirs, apparently printed from a transcript made up by some members of the company. The longer text of

2 Henry VI as printed in the Shakespeare First Folio names John Holland as an actor at 4.2.1, and John Sincler is named both in *3 Henry VI* (at 3.1.1) and in *The Taming of the Shrew* (Induction 1.88). He was later named as a Chamberlain's man in *2 Henry IV*. Both Holland and Sincler appear in the *Seven Deadly Sins* list. There is also a 'Nicke' in that list who may be the same as the 'Nicke' named in the Cade scene in the Pembroke's text of *2 Henry VI* and in *The Taming of the Shrew* (3.1.82). It would perhaps be stretching coincidence too far to identify these Nicks with Nicholas Tooley, who was to become a sharer in Shakespeare's company and who was once Richard Burbage's boy,[20] but it is at least possible that the Nicks were the same person and that Tooley moved with Sincler and Holland from Strange's company in 1591 to Pembroke's in 1592–3 and thence to the Chamberlain's company of 1594 along with the plays in which all these names appear. The possibility that it was Tooley is strengthened by the likelihood that his master Burbage did the same. We can infer that Burbage's break with the Strange's company must have come when the Alleyns quarrelled with his father in 1591. He is noted in the lawsuit that describes the quarrel as vigorously defending his father's property and profits.[21] He may have formed a new company to play at his father's abandoned Theatre along with Sincler and Holland plus perhaps Tooley, and others, and taken up with the Earl of Pembroke as a new master. The Earl's son William described the player as his 'old acquaintance' in 1619 when Burbage died. Shakespeare may have been another Pembroke's man if their possession of his plays is any indication of where his early allegiance lay.[22]

Most of the changes in personnel seem to have happened when a company 'broke and went into the country', as Henslowe put it of the Queen's, or perhaps when they returned to a foot-hold in London. Pay in the provinces was markedly less than in London – Henslowe paid hired men five shillings weekly when they were travelling as against ten in London – and any player who could join a well-placed London company when his own was forced out of town would presumably have done so. Alleyn as an Admiral's man joining Strange's must have been one such regrouping, as we learn from the company's plea to the Privy Council of 1592 or 1593,[23] which pointed out that 'oure Companie is greate, and thearbie our chardge intolerable, in travellinge the Countrie, and the Contynuaunce thereof wilbe a meane to bringe us to division and seperacion'. When the company went on its travels it does seem sometimes to have divided into its constituent parts – the *Records of Early English Drama* evidence shows a joint tour of Strange's and the Admiral's in the summer of 1593 and separate tours in 1592 and the spring of 1594.[24]

We can see, then, a shifting population amongst the companies up to 1594, players moving from group to group as each company's financial circumstances pushed them. If the *Seven Deadly Sins* dating of 1591 is to be trusted we can recognise among the Admiral's–Strange's combination at that time the following players: Edward and John Alleyn, George Attewell, James Tunstall, Pope, Bryan, Phillips, Cowley, Burbage, Sincler, Holland, Will Sly, John Duke, the boys Robert Gough and Thomas Belte, and a 'Harry', 'Nicke', 'Kit' and 'Sander', who may or may not have been Henry Condell, Nicholas Tooley, Christopher Beeston and Alexander Cooke respectively, all of whom turn up later in the Chamberlain's. Kemp and Heminges had joined the allied company by 1593, and were company sharers along with Alleyn, Pope, Bryan and Phillips. Cowley and Thomas Downton were also with them in 1593, while Attewell and Tunstall, who reappear in the Admiral's in 1595, may have been members of the earlier Admiral's on tour throughout the period too. We have no record of John Alleyn playing after 1591, but there is no reason for him to have left his brother's company for any other.

Of Burbage, Holland, Sincler, Sly, Duke, Gough, Condell, Tooley and Beeston there is no positive record until they reappear in the Chamberlain's Men after the reshuffle of 1594. They may have helped found Pembroke's when John Alleyn and the Strange's company quarrelled with old Burbage. The 'Bevis' who appears in *2 Henry VI* with John Holland was certainly a member of the Pembroke's that printed the play (the shorter quarto version has a gratuitous reference to 'Bevys of South-hampton'), and two other players named by Shakespeare, 'Humfrey' (along with Sincler in *3 Henry VI*, 3.1.1) and 'Gabriel' (*3 Henry VI*, 1.2.48, and *Taming of the Shrew* with 'Nicke' at 3.1.82), are likely to have been the Humphrey Jeffes and Gabriel Spencer who turn up in the later Pembroke's of 1595–7 before it merged with the Admiral's. The presence of Shakespeare's histories along with *The Taming of the Shrew* and others of his plays in the repertory of the Pembroke's players seems to indicate that either Shakespeare himself or a player such as Burbage able to afford his playbooks, or both, were in the company in 1593 until they broke that summer.[25] Eventually either or both moved to the Chamberlain's Men, who were the later owners of the plays. Strange's had none of Shakespeare's plays in 1592 except perhaps for *1 Henry VI*, so far as we can tell from Henslowe's records of their repertory.[26] Performances of *Titus Andronicus* at the Rose early in 1594 by Sussex's Men may give us the name of a new company formed to replace Pembroke's. On the quarto's titlepage in 1594 Pembroke's were credited with playing it in between Strange's and Sussex's. The play's second quarto of 1599 added the Chamberlain's name to these three preceding companies.

With the possible exception of 'harey the vj' (*1 Henry VI*, in the *Diary*, pp. 16–20), *Titus Andronicus* is the only Shakespeare play that can be positively identified from Henslowe's lists. He noted it as performed by Sussex's for the first time on 23 January 1594. This was well after Pembroke's had broken. If the sequence of companies performing the play listed on the titlepage of the 1594 quarto is correct it went from Derby's (i.e. Strange's), to Pembroke's and thence to Sussex's. This may reflect the changing allegiances either of Shakespeare himself or of Burbage if he bought the play from its author, probably along with some others of their fellows, some time between the play's composition in about 1590 and 1594, when it was staged at the Rose and printed. Sussex's were travelling through the summer of 1593 but came to London for the winter, including a six-week season with Henslowe for which they may well have needed reinforcement from the better remnants of the broken Pembroke's.

4. THE STRONG COMPANIES

The Queen's Men broke in May 1594, and mergers were obviously then desirable, but none of the Queen's Men except the clown John Singer who joined the new Admiral's, seems to have been involved in the last and greatest reshuffle. The membership of the Admiral's and Chamberlain's, the two new companies that from this date came to bestride the London scene like the monopolistic colossi they were, is known in reasonable detail. They appeared together for Henslowe between 5 and 15 June 1594, probably playing separately on alternate days, and after that settled in their different homes for good. Alleyn's new Admiral's stayed on with father-in-law Henslowe at the Rose and Burbage's new Chamberlain's went to father Burbage at the Theatre.[27] Alleyn along with Attewell, Tunstall and Downton of the old Admiral's were joined in the new company by Richard Jones, who had been a fellow of Alleyn and Tunstall in Worcester's in 1583–9 and who had spent 1592–3 travelling on the continent, and Singer from the Queen's, together with Thomas Towne, Martin Slater and Edward Juby, whose names are all recorded in Henslowe's *Diary* amongst memoranda for 1594–6 (pp. 87, 136). Other Henslowe entries and additional evidence such as the 1597 plot of *Frederick and Basilea* identify the new names of Edward Dutton, Richard Allen (not as sometimes assumed a relative of the Alleyns), Thomas Hunt, Robert Ledbetter and a number of boys, some of whom ('Sam', 'Pyk' and 'Will') can perhaps be traced back to the earlier Admiral's.

The monopolising of London playing that started in May 1594 seems to have been a fresh concept set up by two Privy Councillors, one of whom, the

Illustration 8. The Lord Admiral and Lord Chamberlain preceding the queen in 1597–8, from a painting (School of Robert Peake), known as the 'Procession Portrait' of Queen Elizabeth (the Photographic Survey, Courtauld Institute of Art).The portrait, now at Sherborne Castle in Dorset, is thought to represent Elizabeth's visit to the Blackfriars precinct in about 1597. The two figures on the left leading the queen are Charles Howard, the Lord Admiral, patron of the Admiral's Men, and George Carey, the second Lord Hunsdon, second patron of the Lord Chamberlain's Men. The grey-bearded Howard is looking back at Elizabeth while Carey has his left hand on his sword and in his right holds the white rod of the Lord Chamberlain, the Court official responsible for all the queen's public appearances.

Lord Chamberlain, was the queen's officer on the Privy Council responsible for playing. Modelled on the prior establishment of the Queen's Men eleven years before, the deal the two nobles set up insured against a repeat of that company's decline by having two companies instead of the one. The two companies were allocated the best current players and the best current plays. The Admiral's acquired all of Marlowe's plays while the Chamberlain's took all of Shakespeare's along with the man himself as a player. A significant feature of the deal was that Alleyn at the Rose had already been a servant, first in his own company and later in Strange's, to Charles Howard the Lord Admiral for the past ten years, and James Burbage had similarly worn the Lord Chamberlain Henry Carey's livery for the same period. That must have helped to fix the allocation of the two playhouses for the two companies. In part the new set-up was organized to appease the Lord Mayor, since it meant stopping all playing at inns or innyards inside the City. Instead it licensed them to perform only at their named playhouses out in the suburbs, where the Mayor had no power. It was a clever deal not only because it checked the Lord Mayor's flood of complaints about players in London but because the Chamberlain's led by Richard Burbage were allocated to his father's playhouse the Theatre while the Admiral's under Alleyn's leadership were allocated to the Rose, owned by Alleyn's father-in-law.

Although one of the two companies soon tried to evade the deal's refusal to give them access to play indoors at an inn through London's hard winters, it did give both companies for the first time a permanent place to perform in and a site where they could store their rapidly growing resource of costumes and playbooks. The six years the 'duopoly' lasted gave Londoners the richest theatre imaginable, in almost every sense. Given the choice of only the two venues playgoers became utterly familiar with the players and the thirty and more plays each of them staged every year. The Admiral's were soon inventing tricks to exploit their audience's familiarity with them. They developed games with disguise, for instance, that depended on the familiar face of each player being recognisable whatever his disguise. In their brilliant farce *Look About You* for instance at one point or another eight characters adopt different disguises, sometimes dressed as one another. In Munday's highly popular play of 1595 about two competing magicians, one of them meets the other while each is disguised as his opponent. In Chapman's first comedy, *The Blind Beggar of Alexandria*, Alleyn himself took on not only the main part but appeared in three disguises, each of them parodying one or other of his famous Marlowe roles. When actors and audiences were so familiar to each other metatheatrical games became wonderfully exploitable.

For the reborn companies the six years of their 'duopoly' were exceptionally stable in comparison with the flux caused by the prohibitions of the previous five. According to Henslowe's records the Admiral's were able to play from the outset through six days a week continuously for forty-nine weeks, breaking only for thirty-seven days of Lent during which the Rose was renovated. A summer tour of eight weeks or so in 1595 was again followed by forty-two weeks of playing broken only by Lent (*Henslowe's Diary*, pp. 21–37). Such unprecedentedly trouble-free runs in London, shared as they were by only the two companies, provided a stability of conditions in which they laid down the basis for their mutual prosperity and predominance for the rest of the reign. This joint predominance, affirmed by Privy Council decrees limiting the number of permitted

Illustration 9. Edward Alleyn, the official portrait at his foundation, Dulwich College.

London companies to the two of them, was not challenged till after the turn of the century.

The Privy Council's deal was not kept entirely secure through these six wonderful years. One intrusion on the monopoly is worth noting for the light it throws on the companies' financial organisation and problems, as well as their profitability, and also of the government's not entirely consistent attitude to playing in London. A new Pembroke's company had appeared in the country in 1595–6, and near the end of February 1597 Francis Langley, owner of the recently built Swan playhouse, made an agreement with a group calling themselves Pembroke's Servants to play for twelve months at the Swan. They included Gabriel Spencer (probably the 'Gabriel' of *2 Henry VI*), probably Humphrey Jeffes (the 'Humfrey' of the previous Pembroke's *3 Henry VI*), Robert Shaw or Shaa and William Bird (also known as Borne), together with Jones and Downton, who up to then had been with the Admiral's. The Rose was left unoccupied by the Admiral's for three weeks from 12 February, an occurrence that should have been a routine closure for Lent but may be connected with the departure of Jones and Downton, either as cause or effect. Each of the named Pembroke's Men gave Langley a surety of £100 to guarantee their staying with him for three years. That July, however, the Privy Council produced a drastic and probably unexpected prohibition. It issued an order not only for all playing to stop but that all the suburban playhouses should be pulled down. Langley was a special target, perhaps the only real target of the order, most likely as a result of his dubious dealings over a large diamond that the Privy Council had reason to suspect he had illegally in his possession (he claimed to be a goldsmith or financier, and was probably a fence).[28]

Even so Langley might have escaped – the two other companies were relicensed in October 1597, and carried on as prosperously as before. But that same July Pembroke's Men at the Swan staged *The Isle of Dogs*, possibly even giving new offence by mounting it after the Privy Council's prohibition was announced. It was declared to be 'seditious', and one of its authors, Ben Jonson (who probably also acted in it), was put in prison, along with Spencer and Shaw from the company. Whether the Privy Council was conducting a personal vendetta against Langley or merely trying to maintain its restriction on the number of London-based companies, either way the result was the destruction of Langley's attempt to set up a third London-based company. In August Jones fled back to Henslowe, followed by Shaw and Spencer on their release, then Bird, and in October Downton. Humphrey Jeffes and his brother Anthony also turn up in Henslowe's books for the first time after this date. Alleyn took the opportunity of the new arrivals to retire from playing for the Admiral's, and went off into the country with his wife. The refugees from Pembroke's seem to have taken their playbooks with them to Henslowe, though a renewed Pembroke's did start touring again at the end of 1597. Subsequently Langley was unable to get a licence for playing at the Swan and began to sue the departed players for their £100 bonds. Henslowe records loans made to Bird to reach a settlement with Langley (*Diary*, p. 76).

What is most illuminating about these varied fortunes is the relationship it reveals between Langley as theatre impresario and his player tenants. After 1594 length of tenure had become as important a financial matter to the playhouse owner as it was to the players. It was valued by Langley for insurance purposes at 5 × £100 for a three-year contract. The agreement specifically laid it down that the company was to perform only at the Swan when within five miles of London, except for performances 'in private places', a proviso that Henslowe adopted later with his new Admiral's Men. In the litigation Langley claimed to have spent £300 on apparel for the players and on preparing the playhouse, and in return was to receive half of the gallery takings and in addition was to be repaid for his expenditure on apparel out of the players' half. Langley's expenditure was considerable, though of course he expected his returns would be too. All these arrange-ments are very like Henslowe's dealings with his companies, and on the evidence of the 1591 lawsuit also like James Burbage's with his (*Henslowe's Diary*, p. xxxii), except that Henslowe and Alleyn were involved to the extent of owning a number of playbooks themselves. Some plays, such as *Friar Bacon* and *The Jew of Malta*, keep on appearing in Henslowe's lists whatever the company performing at the Rose. He also took out individual bonds with his players to guarantee their continued service. Richard Jones, for instance, was bound on these terms:

Memorandom that the 6 Aguste 1597 I bownd Richard Jones by & a sumsett of ii^{d} to contenew & playe with the companye of my lord Admeralles players frome Mihelmase next after the daye a bowe written untell the eand & tearme of iii yeares emediatly followinge & to play in my howsse only known by the name of the Rosse & in no other howse a bowt London publicke & yf restraynte be granted then to go for the tyme into the contrey & after to retorne agayne to London yf he breacke this a sumsett then to forfett unto me for the same a hundreth markes of lafull money of Ingland wittnes to this E. Alleyn & John Midelton.[29]

In return for such bonds Henslowe offered security and side benefits such as his moneylending business, which helped Bird extricate himself from Langley. There seems to have been a rather blurred line drawn between loans made to the company, for which Henslowe repaid himself out of the players' half of the gallery takings, and loans to individuals. With the personnel of the company likely to fluctuate as it did, this is understandable.

On the company side, the distinction between sharers, those players with a direct financial interest in the company who shared profits and expenses alike, and hired men, paid on a weekly basis, seems to have been clear-cut. It is usually and I think rightly assumed that a prefatory 'mr' in Henslowe's accounts denotes a sharer as distinct from a hireling.[30] There were probably ten or so sharers in the full-size London companies through the 1590s. Those of the Admiral's after 1597 were Jones, Downton, Singer, Juby, Towne, Shaw, Bird, Spencer and the two Jeffes.[31] Alleyn, who retired from acting late in 1597 after the Pembroke refugees had been re-enlisted, returning to play at his new Fortune in 1600, lived more or less as Henslowe's partner in his theatrical and bull- and bear-baiting affairs. His taking a share in the financial side probably explains why Henslowe's own records are so much more sparse for this period than they are before 1597 or in 1600–3, when Alleyn returned to the stage.

The sharers of the Chamberlain's Men by 1596 seem at first to have been eight in number: Burbage, Shakespeare, Kemp, Pope, Bryan, Phillips, Sly and Heminges. Bryan dropped out soon after 1596, and Pope was dying by 1603; they were replaced by Condell and Cowley. Kemp left in 1599 to dance his famous morris to Norwich and was replaced by Robert Armin from Lord Chandos's Men. In 1603, once they had become the King's Men, the number was increased to twelve with the elevation of Alexander Cooke and Nicholas Tooley, the addition of John Lowin from Worcester's and Laurence Fletcher, who had been favoured by James when he took a company touring in Scotland and whose addition to the King's Men in 1603 may have been a further mark of royal favour. His name does not recur in the company's actor-lists, and it is not clear who may have replaced him. The number of sharers remained at between ten and twelve for the rest of the company's long life.[32]

The Chamberlain's Men's relationship with the owner of their playhouse was probably at first similar to that of the Admiral's with Henslowe and Pembroke's with Langley. The Chamberlain's leading player Richard Burbage was the son of the company financier, as the Admiral's Alleyn was son-in-law to Henslowe. But when James Burbage died in February 1597 he bequeathed his son and the company not a stable home for their playing but a disastrous financial mess. Knowing that the lease of the Theatre was due to expire in April 1597 and that the landlord was loudly hostile to its use for playing, the ageing Burbage had ventured all his capital to build a new playhouse in the Blackfriars. The use of halls at City inns for

Illustration 10. Richard Burbage, from the portrait in the Dulwich Gallery, DPG 395. It has long been assumed to be a self-portrait, since he was known as a painter, but no tangible evidence upholds that idea.

playing had been stopped in 1594, and a memory of the first Blackfriars theatre, used by the Children of the Revels for several years up to 1584, may have set his mind on a novel course. The company had got their patron, the Lord Chamberlain, to ask in October 1594 if the Lord Mayor would allow them to use the Cross Keys for their performances through the winter. The company did not want to lose the roofed venues which the inns had provided up to then. After what we must assume to be the Lord Mayor's denial of this bold request, in 1596 Burbage bought the upper frater of the old Blackfriars monastery in its exclusive precinct close to where the Revels Office lodged, and converted it into a hall playhouse. It was inside the City but safe from the Lord Mayor in a 'liberty' where, as in the suburb of Shoreditch, mayoral authority did not run. Unfortunately, though, old Burbage had not allowed for the attitude of the wealthy and influential residents in that central west-end enclave. The dignitaries who occupied the precinct petitioned the Privy Council to ban the performance of plays at the new playhouse. George Carey, a Privy Councillor, was resident in the Blackfriars himself as well as the company's new patron (son to Henry Carey, who had supported the company's purchase of the Blackfriars property). He added his signature to the petition. Burbage died two months later, shortly before the Theatre's lease expired, with all his cash tied up in a now-unusable playhouse.

The company, faced by the loss both of the Blackfriars and the Theatre when its lease expired, struggled for the next two years, renting other playhouses such as the Curtain near the Theatre, which stood empty. The older Burbage son, Cuthbert, whose inheritance it was (Richard got the Blackfriars), spent nearly two years trying fruitlessly to negotiate a renewal of the lease. In the end, probably in some sort of despair, he and his brother took out a thirty-one year lease on a new plot of land fifty yards from the Rose in Southwark and hired a builder to secretly dismantle the Theatre and use its frame timbers as the basis for a new amphitheatre, which they called the Globe. The decision to rebuild the old amphitheatre as well as the theft of the old timbers marks how desperate their financial situation was.[33] Using the Theatre's framing timbers was simply an economy, since they became a contribution as part of the price of putting up a new playhouse elsewhere. The landlord promptly took them to court over their theft and the trespass on his land to steal the timbers, and the case struggled on for years with profit to nobody but the lawyers.

Another measure of the young Burbages' desperation is the novel decision they took to help finance the new construction by bringing in five of the other sharers in the company to raise the cash for their new home. The two Burbages put up fifty per cent between them, including the framing timbers, and five sharers, Heminges, Kemp, Phillips, Pope and Shakespeare, each put up another ten per cent. By this device six company sharers became not only 'sharers' in the company's fortunes but 'housekeepers' in their playhouse, entitled to a share in the owner's traditional half of the gallery takings. Shakespeare's housekeeper share, which soon increased when Kemp sold out to the other contributing sharers, in the long run proved to be one of his most profitable investments.

This novel arrangement whereby members of the playing company, the tenants, also became the company's landlords was a unique invention forced on them by the desperate straits the company went through in the years between November 1596, when the petition of Blackfriars residents was granted by the Privy Council, and mid-1599, when they began to use the Globe. Viewed in strictly commercial terms it was the company's salvation. Almost certainly this fortuitous underwriting of their finances was what made them the richest and most durable playing company that English theatre has seen. And yet all the events in the story seem to have happened by chance rather than design. Richard Burbage made some money from the lost Blackfriars playhouse by leasing it out in 1599, when cash was urgently needed to build the Globe. He gave it to an impresario, who used it to house a new boy company. These 'little eyases', as Burbage playing Hamlet called them a year or two later on the Globe stage, did not attract the hostility of the local gentry as did the adult players, and they helped the Burbages to recoup some of their father's investment. More to the point, in the long run the boys renewed the habit of performing plays in the Blackfriars precinct as a routine activity. Consequently by 1608, when the boy company was in deep trouble and their impresario surrendered the lease back to the Burbages, they proved to have cleared the way for the adult company at long last to start acting at Blackfriars. The Shakespeare company, now the King's Men, could perform in the hall playhouse that old Burbage had built for them twelve years before so that they could now for the first time since 1593 perform through the long London winters with a roof over their heads.

On re-acquiring the Blackfriars tn 1608 Richard Burbage sensibly extended the ownership arrangements he and his brother had set up for the Globe, cutting in the Globe's housekeeper-sharers to become house-keepers of the Blackfriars as well. From then on the company ran the two playhouses exclusively, alternating between them season by season. This arrangement was not unlike the early practice, blocked in 1594, of using the amphitheatres most of the time but turning to the great rooms of City inns when the weather did not encourage trudges through the mud to the suburban playhouses for outdoor viewing. Extravagant in resources though it was, this new system of alternating between the amphitheatre and the hall evidently suited them, because when they lost the Globe by fire in 1613 they promptly rebuilt it at great expense. From then on they could have gone on playing throughout the year just at the Blackfriars, but the outdoor play-house was evidently a feature of their activities a majority of them decided they should not dispense with. So they dug deep into their pockets and rebuilt it, in order to continue the alternating pattern of summer and winter seasons at different venues.[34]

The year 1599 was important for the Chamberlain's Men because it secured their new venue and started their new system of company management and financing. It was also important for their new neighbour Henslowe and his company. Once they knew the Globe was to become a close neighbour Henslowe and Alleyn wasted no time. Although the land on which the Rose stood had six years of its lease still to run, they reversed the relative locations of the two companies by taking the Admiral's to the northern suburbs now deserted by the Chamberlain's Men and built the Fortune a little to the west of the old Theatre site. The year 1600 was particularly important for them. Not only did their new playhouse, the Fortune, enable them to move from the Bankside to the north-western boundary of the city, but Alleyn returned to play in the company, at the wish, so their backer Charles Howard claimed, of the Queen herself.[35] The times were still favourable to playing, and there does not seem to have been any more travelling until after the Queen's death in 1603. Henslowe's accounts over these years reveal mainly such minor matters as ten shillings paid in May 1601 'to geatte the boye into the ospetalle which was hurt at the fortewne', twenty-four shillings in July to buy 8 pounds of copper lace, in November 6s. 7d. to mend a tawny coat 'which was eatten with the Rattes', and on Christmas Day hose for a boy 'to tumbell in be fore the quen' (*Diary*, pp. 169, 177, 184, 186). The repertory gained thirty-one new plays between 1600 and 1603, a lower number than in the three years up to 1597, partly because of the extremely large number of new plays bought immediately before 1600, and partly (one would assume) because Alleyn, back in the company, was content to revive his old favourites. This he certainly did, along with a set of new plays telling stories from the Bible. He may already have been thinking of his long-term ambition to set up the foundation which he was to call 'God's Gift', now Dulwich College.

Meanwhile another company, Worcester's, came under Henslowe's spreading wing, because with the Admiral's move to the Fortune his old playhouse, the Rose, was going vacant. Worcester's Men can be traced around the country throughout the decade or so after 1587, when Alleyn, Tunstall and Jones left them to become Admiral's Men. Their patron was ambitious to show himself at Court, and his Rose-based company performed there in January 1602 and in March were admitted by the Privy Council as a third London company together with Oxford's, 'being joyned by agrement togeather in on companie'.[36] They appear in Henslowe's *Diary* in August 1602, receiving advances for playbooks and apparel. Henslowe, who often did business over food (there are frequent entries in the summer the Fortune was being built for meals with the builder), records that the supper at the famous Mermaid Tavern when he reached his agreement with Worcester's cost him nine shillings, a sum he characteristically debited to his new company (*Diary*, p. 214). The Admiral's were now permanently at the Fortune, and Worcester's moved into the Rose.

The Worcester's company may have been new to London, but its membership was not. Players who authorised payments for Henslowe were Kemp, John Duke and Christopher Beeston, all former Chamberlain's Men, Robert Pallant, once of Strange's and probably subsequently of the Admiral's, John Lowin, who was soon to join the Chamberlain's, and Thomas Heywood, who was an Admiral's man as player and poet in 1597. Richard Perkins had joined by the time Elizabeth died, and Heywood and Perkins together formed the core of the company, as leading poet and player, from the time Worcester's became Queen Anne's Men early in James's reign. By the middle of the decade they were occupying the new Red Bull playhouse. In 1609 their licence to play was drafted on the familiar Leicester's model with the now standard addition of their customary playing place, as follows:

Knowe yee that wee of our especiall grace certayne knowledge and meere mocion have lycenced and aucthorised and by these presents doe lycence and aucthorize Thomas Greene, Christofer Beeston, Thomas Haywood, Richard Pirkyns, Richard Pallant, Thomas Swinnerton, John Duke, Robert Lee, James Haulte, and Roberte Beeston, Servantes to our moste deerely beloved wiefe Queen Anne, and the reste of theire Associates, to use and exercise the arte and faculty of playinge Comedies, Tragedies, historyes, Enterludes, Moralles, Pastoralles, Stageplayes and suche other like, as they have already studied or hereafter shall use or studye, aswell for the recreacion of our loving Subjectes as for our solace and pleasure when wee shall thinke good to see them, during our pleasure. And the said Comedies, Tragedies, histories, Enterludes, Moralles, Pastoralles, Stageplayes and suche like to shewe and exercise publiquely and openly to theire beste commoditye, aswell within theire nowe usuall houses called the Redd Bull in Clarkenwell and the Curtayne in Hallowell, as alsoe within anye Towne halles, Mouthalles and other convenient places within the libertye and freedome of any other Citty, universitye, Towne or Boroughe whatsoever within our Realmes and Domynions.[37]

5. THE LATER BOY COMPANIES

The position the Privy Council had spasmodically struggled to maintain from 1594, of keeping only the two pre-eminent adult companies, was complicated in the new decade not only by the arrival of the third adult company, and at the end of the decade a fourth, the Duke of York's with Prince Charles as their patron, but also by the return of two boy companies. A new company of Paul's Boys was back in operation by 1599 and in 1600 Henry Evans the scrivener established a new Chapel Children boy company in Blackfriars. It does seem that for the first few years the new boy companies maintained the pretence that they were giving only 'private' performances, and that they did not therefore have to submit to being controlled by the Master of the Revels as the adult companies at their 'public' playhouses did. When King James gave patronage of the Blackfriars boy company to his wife, Samuel Daniel the poet and playwright was assigned as their 'Master' and censor. But he soon lost that job, so for the next few years the Blackfriars boys ran unchecked by any government censorship, to their own eventual cost.

To some extent the size of the part that the boy companies played in this decade has been exaggerated, at least so far as the history of the companies is concerned. Rosencrantz's claim that the 'little eyases' were carrying it away, even 'Hercules and his load', that is, the Globe's patronage, has promoted this idea, even though its mention in *Hamlet* was giving a boost to the company of which Richard Burbage himself, playing Hamlet, was landlord. Because more of the boy company repertory is extant than there is from the adult companies through the first years of the new century their work, radical as it was, and full of the work of new writers, has received a lot of special attention. But as a radically fresh theatrical fashion they lasted less than a decade, one of the two companies only till 1606, the other till 1608, when James decided, as Elizabeth had before him, that their services must be dispensed with. They really carried it away mostly in the first of the three phases of their career up to the death of Elizabeth, at which time Henry Evans was on the point of giving up his venture altogether. By 1608 there was only one company, now no longer boys but young adult players, their leaders aged about twenty. Boy companies as such never reappeared. The company known as 'Beeston's Boys' in the late 1630s had six adult players playing in it and mentoring the boys in the group. The boy companies' chief mark of distinction was that they secured the services of the three most ambitious and opinionated poets of the day – Jonson, Chapman and Marston – and that they were well placed to carry out the tasks these three laid on them. Jonson for one obviously valued the children because he could order them to do what he wanted more easily than he could his adult employers. Beaumont, Fletcher, Middleton and Dekker also wrote for them.

Paul's were the first to return to the surface, as they had been the last to sink beneath it. Theirs was a smallish enterprise – they seem to have begun by charging only a hesitant twopence, whereas when they closed in 1590 they had been charging four or sixpence.[38] Their playhouse was a small one and they performed only on Sundays and Mondays. They may have begun in a small way over Christmas 1597–8. By 1599, though, Marston had written *Antonio and Mellida* for them, a piece strikingly self-conscious about its venue and its presentation, as if it was their first overt venture into the openly commercial playing world of the adult groups.[39] Jonson wrote a similarly introductory play, *Cynthia's Revels*, for the second boy company located at the Burbage playhouse in Blackfriars and reminding Londoners of recent history by calling itself the Chapel Children.

The nature of this enterprise of reviving the boy actors is shown by the membership of the backers for this second company. The manager was Evans, former associate of Lyly at the old Blackfriars company. He enlisted to help him two men: Nathaniel Giles, who had been appointed Master of the Chapel Children at Windsor three years before, and Edward Kirkham, the Yeoman of the Revels. Giles had the authority necessary for getting the acting personnel, the power to 'take up' children for service in his choir school, and Kirkham as officer in charge of the Revels wardrobe had all the necessary materials for acting at his disposal. A fourth associate was Evans's son-in-law Alexander Hawkins. Evans clearly believed in the familiar Elizabethan practice of keeping business affairs in family hands, and the subsequent wrangles over the company's finances give point to his faith in family loyalty.

Of the original four associates Giles seems to have dropped out with some haste. His authority was to take up boys for singing, not acting, and was clearly going to be abused. A complaint brought against him by one Henry Clifton shows that it was. Clifton alleged that his son had been abducted while on his way to school and forced to 'exercyse the base trade of a mercynary enterlude player, to his utter losse of tyme, ruyne and disparagment'. When the case was heard in 1602 Giles was not summoned and may already have made his peace with the authorities. His powers of taking up boys were renewed with all the other renewals of the new reign in 1604, but somebody had evidently remembered the Clifton case by 1606, for in that year he lost those powers for good.[40] He remained Master of the Chapel Children at Windsor until his death at the rare age of seventy-five in 1634, but seems never again to have meddled with playing.

The brunt of the censure over the Clifton abduction fell on Evans, who temporarily dropped out of the company's management in 1602, after making over his lease of the Blackfriars to his son-in-law. According to a later lawsuit he subsequently enlisted two more backers, William Rastell and Thomas Kendall, to join Kirkham. Between them they apparently paid out £200 for apparel and other playing materials, and spent £400 on the premises. Evans in return made a verbal promise to transfer half the lease to them, but of course did not do so; it was already in Hawkins's name. The associates drew up articles on 20 April 1602 whereby the three financiers gave Hawkins, as front man for Evans, a bond of £200 to guarantee their payment of half the rent and repairs to the premises, in return for which they would get half the profits of the company. It does seem a little odd that the financiers were satisfied, as Kirkham testified in 1612, with a verbal understanding over the lease when they were drawing up articles for the company's finances, especially since they seem to have been already on difficult terms with Evans. At the same time as they drew up the company articles they agreed to pay Evans eight shillings for every week the company performed, apparently to stay out of the way. Perhaps they thought that would be enough to leave them in charge.

But Evans did not stay out of the way, for during the prohibition on playing in 1603 he took the pessimistic initiative of discussing with the Burbages, from whom he had a twenty-one-year lease for the playhouse, whether to give up the lease. In December 1604 he was in the way enough to lock up the 'Chamber called the Schoolhouse' on the premises in order to keep Kirkham and the others out, because they had not paid their share of a £10 repair bill.

The company restarted after the plague-driven distractions of 1603, and in February 1604 James gave them a new patent as the Children of the Queen's Revels, naming Kirkham, Hawkins and Kendall along with a new man, Robert Payne, in place of Rastell. An additional feature of the new patent made Samuel Daniel, the poet, their licenser of plays. This was a unique arrangement which may have had something to do with the boy company insisting that they were a 'private' company, not a 'public' company like the adults, for whom the Master of the Revels acted as censor and licenser. It is possible that the 'private' companies at the 'private' playhouses were left free of this control by the fiction that they were not the sort of commercial operation that the adult companies were. The appointment of Daniel to be master of the revels for this one company may have been a device to accompany the fiction of their private performances.

Daniel did not enjoy this distinction for long because his own play *Philotas*, which the boys performed in 1604, got him into trouble for its reflection of the Essex rebellion, and cost him the job. Despite this warning the boys seem to have continued to play without licence or control, and in the next year another of their plays, *Eastward Ho!*, got two of its authors into prison. The third writer, Marston, who had a financial interest in the company, had to flee for safety. In February 1606 John Day's *Isle of Gulls* got them into trouble again for a more extreme version of the same offence, satire against James and the long tail of Scotsmen who had followed him to the English Court. A contemporary account reported that 'all men's parts were acted of two divers nations', presumably using English and Scottish accents.[41] That lost the company the patronage of Queen Anne, and they had to drop her name from their title. Whereas over *Eastward Ho!* it had been the poets whom the government pursued, in this case the leading boys of the company were put in Bridewell prison. The management was reconstructed. Evans still kept himself in the background, and Robert Keysar, another financier-goldsmith, moved in to take control. Under his rule the company's title shrank to the Children of the Blackfriars, and the system of impressment originally employed on Giles's authority seems to have been replaced with an indenture system rather more like that followed by the adult companies with their boys.[42] At about this time the Paul's company found it expedient to retire from playing altogether, and it is possible that the changes in the Blackfriars company system may have been partly designed to allow for the admission of some members from Paul's.

It is not really clear whether, at this late point in the Blackfriars boys' career, the Master of the Revels had now taken over control of their 'private' activities, and put them under the same constraints as the 'public' players.[43] Possibly he had not, because it was not long before the troubles of 1606 were repeated. In March 1608 the French Ambassador took offence over one or both of Chapman's *Byron* plays. He took particular exception to a scene (not in the surviving texts) where the French King's mistress slaps the Queen's face. To sharpen his complaint he added that 'a day or two before, they had slandered their king, his mine in Scotland, and all his favourites in a most pointed fashion; for having made him rail against heaven over the flight of a bird and have a gentleman beaten for calling off his dogs, they portrayed him drunk at least once a day'.[44] The result of this was that James 'vowed they should never play more, but should first begg their bread ...' and gave orders 'to dissolve them, and to punish the maker besides'.[45] Chapman escaped, but Marston, involved over a related offence, and several of the players in the now almost adult company were imprisoned. Evans then surrendered the residue of his twenty-one-year lease of the Blackfriars playhouse to Richard Burbage, apparently without consulting Keysar.

The company was not entirely destroyed. It performed at Court the next Christmas for the first time in four years, a striking mark of royal forgiveness or forgetfulness, and soon found a new indoor playhouse just outside the City walls in Whitefriars. In 1610 Keysar allied himself with Phillip Rosseter the lutenist and several adult players including Richard Jones, once of the Admiral's, to organise a new company which he was allowed once again to call the Children of the Queen's Revels. By this time of course some of the 'boys' were not even youths. Nathan Field, who had been the company's leading actor since 1600, was twenty-two. Two others, William Ostler and John Underwood, left after 1608 for the King's Men, where they had full adult status. In the very earliest days the boys had performed only weekly compared with the daily performances of the adults. After 1610 their practices in this as in all other respects cannot be distinguished from the adults. By then the King's Men even had the same kind of indoor playhouse, because they moved into the Blackfriars once the children relinquished it. As a 'Children's' company the ex-Blackfriars group at Whitefriars may have had a larger proportion of boys than usual, but it included at least six full adults, some of them with decades of acting behind them.

Apart from the age of the players, and their use of indoor playhouses located inside the City walls, the chief distinctions the boy companies enjoyed came from the more radical plays in their repertory. A large proportion of what the Blackfriars boys staged, after a few unsuccessful attempts to revive their pre-1590 repertory, were satirical comedies of a kind likely to give enjoyment above all to the courtiers and gallants who sat on the Blackfriars stage by their mockery not only of citizen values but also of the King and his Scottish followers. Such scandalous girds purveyed from the theoretical safety of 'their juniority', as the offended Heywood put it, were the staple diet at Blackfriars from early on, when the so-called War of the Theatres was fought out between their poets.[46] It was the poets who had, in all probability, a much larger say in the company's repertory and a freer hand than the poets of the adult companies ever enjoyed so long as the Master of the Revels had to sign his licence onto each play manuscript before it could be put on stage. It seems very likely that the Blackfriars plays written between 1601 and 1607 were the most radical ever staged in London between 1574 and 1642.

6. THE LATER ADULT COMPANIES

Once the Burbages had reclaimed their Blackfriars playhouse for their own adult company the boy companies' biggest achievement proved chiefly to be returning adult players to the City, restoring their right to play in the comfort of the centre which they had lost when the inns were finally closed to them in 1594. The inhabitants of the Blackfriars precinct stopped the Burbages in 1596 by petitioning the Privy Council, but no protest was raised twelve years later when they and their adult company took the playhouse over from the boys. In 1608 the whole Blackfriars precinct, which had for centuries been exempt from City jurisdiction although inside the City walls, came at long last under the scope of City government, and yet nothing was done to prevent the adults from starting to play there.

It was an unparalleled stroke of good fortune for the King's Men, for which they must have owed their royal patron a lot. They could revive their preferred practice of separate winter and summer venues, this time with not an inn for the bad-weather season but an already well-patronised indoor theatre. The King's Men's predominant position was never again to be seriously challenged so long as the theatres lasted, even when the indoor Cockpit and Salisbury Court were used by other adult companies with a similar object. From 1609 the picture becomes pyramid-shaped, with the King's Men at the Globe for five months of the summer and Blackfriars for the rest of the year standing at the apex, and the companies of the Fortune and Red Bull maintaining a fairly constant position along the base line. The Cockpit companies rivalled the King's Men in later years, but generally floated somewhere between the apex and the base line occupied by the outdoor playhouse companies.

The story for the last thirty years of playing is basically one of consistent tenure and prosperity, though the prosperity came more to the managers than the companies themselves, and, with the exception of the King's Men, the only company to last unaltered throughout, there was a fairly regular turnover. Apart from two disastrous fires, at the Globe in 1613, which the King's Men were able to survive, and at the Fortune in 1621, which the Palsgrave's, descendants of the Admiral's, were not,[47] the chief disturbances were in litigation over company finances, and in the relations of companies with their theatre-owners and impresario-backers.

Needless to say the King's Men had secured the primary role for play-goers well before the turn of the century. Even as the company lost its main base, the Theatre, in 1597 Falstaff made himself the prize example of what theatre could then do. He marched with *Romeo and Juliet* as the prize conversation piece that year. He stayed popular until the closure, and was hailed in 1660 as a feature of all that England had lost for the eighteen years the playhouses were closed. John Lowin, an experienced player who joined the Shakespeare company in 1602, as he grew older and fatter started playing Falstaff, a part he took regularly till 1642, when he was sixty-five years old.

The Queen Anne's company's story is characteristic of the decade after 1609. The last eleven years of their existence, 1612–23, began with the death of one of the company's leading sharers, Thomas Greene, who left his widow his share in the company, valued at £80, and a credit of £37 it owed him. After some argument the widow and her next husband, James Baskervile, agreed with the company in 1615 to give them an investment of a further £57 10s. in return for a pension of one shilling and eightpence every playing day for the couple's lifetime. A year later the company, not

Illustration 11. Falstaff, probably John Lowin on stage as remembered by an unknown engraver, most likely John Chantry. 'Clause' is a character from Fletcher's *The Beggars' Bush*, a later King's Men's play. The footlights are an innovation of the Restoration, post-1660. A detail from a picture first appearing on the frontispiece of Francis Kirkman's book of drolls, *The Wits* (1661). Drolls were short excerpts from plays staged surreptitiously at the Red Bull and Cockpit during the Interregnum.

having honoured its agreement and still short of ready money, managed to get another £38 from Mrs Baskervile for a further pension of two shillings for her and her son's lifetime. The agreement was revised again a year later for the widow and another of her sons, who was a player with the company and had not been paid his wages. At length, in 1623, Mrs Baskervile took the three players who still survived in the company since the time of the original agreements to the court of Chancery in order to enforce payment of their bonds, and the company had to break.

The Chancery records contain a number of revealing depositions about the company's affairs at the time the bonds were made. In the first place they show that the original £80 the company admitted they owed the widow of their former fellow was the value of a current share, and their payment to her was to cover the value, not to buy back the share. This automatically remained with the company. The price of a share of course depended entirely on the state of the company's health, and their difficulties grew largely because they were committed to repay a healthy value in time of sickness. As C. J. Sisson has described it,

> The accepted and agreed value of a share was a safeguard of the interests of the individual sharer and of his family, being part of a body of assets, including goodwill as well as properties, playbooks and costumes, to which he had contributed either in money or by his skill, or both. But it was also a pawn or hostage by which the whole body of sharers safeguarded the general interests of the company. The actual and real value of a share depended upon the condition of the company and of the trade in which it was engaged. It seems pretty clear that it was not an asset likely to justify itself in a Court of Law. It was very different, of course, with a share by lease in a playhouse building or ground.[48]

The villain of this particular piece and the only player to come out of it with any profit was Christopher Beeston, the former Chamberlain's man, who had been a member of the company since its arrival on the London scene and increasingly through the second decade of the century its financier. He rose to power as James Burbage and Alleyn had done before him by supplying his fellows with money for playbooks and properties, and by renting other properties to them. At times, judging by the depositions in the Baskervile case, it looks as if Beeston rented them properties which he had in fact bought with company funds. Considering the fluctuating condition of company membership, the verbal nature of many of the agreements and the secretive nature of the accounting this is not unlikely. One might attribute some of the success of the King's Men to the patent honesty of the man who did their paperwork, John Heminges. It seems to have been Beeston who was instrumental in milking Mrs Baskervile's funds, and his adroitness in departing from the company without himself being bound to answer for repaying her is of a piece with the other indications of his character. The depositions of the players in 1623 allege that Beeston, upon whom the players 'at that tyme and long before and since did put the managing of their whole businesses and affaires belonging unto them joyntly as they were players in trust',[49] had been bribed by Mrs Baskervile to commit the company in her favour.

In 1619 Queen Anne died, and the company was broken up. Perkins and others remained at the Red Bull while Beeston, by then owner of the second indoor playhouse, the Cockpit, went to Prince Charles's Men as manager and landlord. An otherwise unknown mercer by the name of John Smith promptly took them all to court to get payment for 'tinsell stuffes and other stuffe' delivered on Beeston's instructions to the company between 1612 and 1617. The other players charged Beeston in the same lawsuit with consistently looking after himself before he served the company, while he 'much enriched himself', and falsely billed the company for £400. Furthermore he had taken all the company's property with him when he left the Red Bull. He may even have taken a whole playhouse with him, for the recently constructed Cockpit, at which the Red Bull company played for a while in 1617, remained at Beeston's disposal. But of the financing of the Cockpit we know nothing except that the lease taken out in 1616 was in Beeston's name. In this case, as with the 1623 suit, the players were all too anxious to rid themselves of the burden of bills that they felt Beeston had unfairly left them with, and were certainly interested in shifting the onus on to him.

Beeston was unlikely to have been the only unscrupulous mismanager of company finances at this time. Henslowe's records of his operations at the Rose and the Fortune mainly concern his financial dealings with his companies, and show little evidence of his feelings for his business. In the 1590s, the period when he maintained the records of his day-to-day dealings in his so-called *Diary*, he evidently worked closely with the players and had consistently good relations with them. He kept careful records of the material possessions, playbooks, apparel and other properties acquired for the companies. He scrupulously recorded the income from his gallery rents as well as the outgoings and the loans he made to the companies while they built up their resources for playing. The pawnbroking and moneylending side of his business made him technically a usurer, since he made loans at more than ten per cent interest, but on occasions he lent money to the players without charging any interest at all. Lending money to get a player out of debtor's prison was good business, of course, since a player could not play his parts while he was incarcerated, but the fact that Henslowe's records are all about his financial transactions does not mean that he took a narrowly commercial view of his activities. There are quite a few hints that he indulged in this relatively novel sport of sponsoring plays out of a genuine enthusiasm for playgoing.[50]

As time went on, however, Alleyn took over more and more of the running of the companies. Henslowe became a dignitary at Court in the 1590s and perhaps more distanced from playing. Under James he became Gentleman Sewer of the Chamber, and in 1607 he was made a vestryman in the Southwark parish of St Saviour. In management he seems to have become gradually more distanced from his players and more autocratic.[51]

The Dulwich papers left by Alleyn include a pungent document, dating from 1615, drawn up by the Lady Elizabeth's Men and entitled 'Articles of Grievance and Oppression against Philip Henslowe'. Lady Elizabeth's, the fifth company to receive a member of the royal family as patron, had come to London in the Christmas season of 1612–13 and merged with Phillip Rosseter's Queen's Revels, the former Blackfriars children. Nathan Field was their star player, along with other old boys from the Blackfriars company and Joseph Taylor and William Ecclestone, all three later to become King's Men. Field seems to have had very good relations with Henslowe. He addressed one letter to him as 'Father Hinchlow', and signed several as his 'loving son'. But he must have shared at least some of the anger voiced in the company's paper of 1615. It reads like a catalogue of long accumulated grievances. Overstated though they are, they make a compendium of everything that the players thought could be said against Henslowe as a manager, a victim's critique of his increasingly autocratic dealings after twenty-eight years as the first of London's great theatre impresarios (*Henslowe Papers*, pp. 86–90):

Imprimis in March 1612 uppon m^r: Hynchlowes Joyninge Companes with m^r: Rosseter ye Companie borrowed £80 of one m^r: Griffin and the same was put into m^r: Hinchlowes debt; which made itt sixteene score poundes whoe [a]fter the receipt of the same or most parte thereof in March 1613 hee broke the saide Comp[any a]gaine and Ceazed all the stocke; under Culler to satisfie what remayned due to [him]; yet perswaded M^r: Griffyne afterwardes to arest the Companie for his £80: whoe are still in daunger for the same; Soe nowe there was in equitie due to the Companie £80

   Item m^r Hinchlowe having lent one Taylor £30: and £20 to one Baxter fellowes of the Companie Cunninglie put theire said privat debts into the generall accompt by which meanes hee is in Conscience to allowe them £50

   Item havinge the stock of Apparell in his handes to secure his debt he sould tenn poundes worth of ould apparrell out of the same with out accomptinge or abatinge for the same; heare growes due to the Companie £10

   Also upon the departure of one Eglestone a Fellowe of the Companie hee recovered of him £14: towardes his debt which is in Conscience likewise to bee allowed to the Companie £14

   In March 1613 hee makes upp a Companie and buies apparrell of one Rosseter to the value of £63: and valued the ould stocke that remayned in his handes at £63: likewise they uppon his word acceptinge the same at that rate, which being prized by M^r: Daborne justlie, betweene his partner Meade and him Came but to £40: soe heare growes due to the Companie £23

   Item hee agrees with the said Companie that they should enter bond to plaie with him for three yeares att such house and houses as hee shall appointe and to allowe him halfe galleries for the said house and houses; and the other halfe galleries towardes his debt of £126: and other such moneys as hee should laie out for playe apparrell duringe the space of the said 3 yeares, agreeinge with them; in Consideracion theareof to seale each of them a bond of £200: to find them a Convenient house and houses; and to laie out such moneies as fower of the sharers should think fitt for theire use in apparrell which att the 3 yeares, being paid for: to be delivered to the sharers; whoe accordinglie entered the said bondes; but M^r: Henchlowe and M^r: Mead deferred the same; an in Conclusion utterly denied to seale att all.

Item M^r: Hinchlowe havinge promised in Consideracion of the Companies lying still one daie in forteene for his baytinge to give them £50: hee havinge denied to bee bound as aforesaid gave them onlie £40 and for that M^r: Feild would not consent thereunto hee gave him soe much as his share out of £50: would have Come unto; by which meanes hee is dulie indebted to ye Companie £10

In June followinge the said agreement, hee brought in M^r: Pallant and shortle after M^r: dawes into the said Companie; promisinge one 12^s a weeke out of his part of the galleries; and the other 6 a weeke out of his parte of the galleries; and because M^r: Feild was thought not to bee drawne thereunto; hee promissed him six shillings weekelie alsoe; which in one moneth after unwilling to beare soe greate a Charge; he Called the Companie together; and told them that this 24^s was to bee Charged uppon them; threatninge those which would not Consent thereunto to breake the Companie and make upp a newe with out the[m] Wheareuppon knowinge hee was not bound; the threequarters sharers advauncinge them selves to whole shares Consented thereunto by which meanes they are out of purse £30 and his parte of the galleries bettred twise as much £30

Item havinge 9 gatherers more then his due itt Comes to this yeare from the Companie £10

Item the Companie paid for [Arra]s and other properties £40 which Mr: Henchlow deteyneth £40

In Februarie last 1614 perceav[ing]e the Companie drew out of his debt and Called uppon him for his accompts hee brooke the Companie againe; by with drawinge the hired men from them: and selles theire stocke (in his hands) for £400 givinge under his owne hand that hee had receaved towardes his debt £300: Which with the juste and Conscionable allowances before named made to the Companie which Comes to £267: makes £567

Articles of oppression against M^r: Hinchlowe./

Hee Chargeth the stocke with £600 and odd; towardes which hee hath receaved as aforesaid £567 of us; yet selles the stocke to strangers for fower hundred poundes; and makes us no satisfaction./

Hee hath taken all boundes of our hired men in his owne name whose wages though wee have truly paid yet att his pleasure hee hath taken them a waye; and turned them over to others to the breaking of our Companie./

For lendinge of £6 to p[ay] them theire wages; hee made us enter bond to give him the profitt of a warraunt of tenn poundes due to us att Court./

Alsoe hee hath taken right gould and silver lace of divers garmentes to his owne use with out accompt to us or abatement./

Illustration 12. Nathan Field, from the portrait in the Dulwich Gallery, DPG 385.

Uppon everie breach of the Companie hee takes newe bondes for his stocke; and our securitie for playing with him Soe that he hath in his handes, bondes of ours to the value of £5000 and his stocke to; which hee denies to deliver and threatens to oppresse us with.

Alsoe havinge apointed a man to the seeinge of his accomptes in byinge of Clothes (hee beinge to have vi^s. a weeke; hee takes ye meanes away and turnes the man out./

The reason of his often breakinge with us; hee gave in these wordes should these fellowes Come out of my debt, I should have noe rule with them

Alsoe wee have paid him for plaie bookes £200 or thereaboutes and yet hee denies to give us the Coppies of any one of them./

Also with in 3 yeares hee hath broken and dissmembred five Companies./

Henslowe died at the end of the year, probably not of a broken heart, and Alleyn then amalgamated the two companies into one under the name of Prince Charles's Men. The membership was reshuffled considerably. Field left and became a King's sharer, possibly buying Shakespeare's share, while Taylor and Robert Pallant moved to the new company. It then took up the third place in eminence behind the always predominant King's and the Fortune company, the Palsgrave's Men. From about this time four companies were consistently licensed to play in London, and it seems to have been in the brief of the Revels Office to maintain that number. In January 1618 the Revels records carry a note of the payment of 44s. by Heminges 'in the name of the four companys, for toleration in the holdy-days'.[52] Further references to 'the four companys' appear in 1623 and 1636, when the Master of the Revels noted that warrants were sent ordering 'the four companys of players' to stop playing because the plague bill had risen to fifty-four deaths a week. Other companies (including in 1629 and 1635 a celebrated French troupe) might visit, but no more than four were in residence. In 1618 the four were the King's at the Globe and Blackfriars, Palsgrave's at the Fortune, Queen Anne's at the Cockpit and Prince Charles's, who had probably replaced the Queen's at the Red Bull when they left for the Cockpit, and then succeeded them at the Cockpit when Beeston left Queen Anne's to join them.[53]

The next important year for change was 1619. For the King's it was a difficult time: Burbage died in March, and the citizens of Blackfriars renewed their protest about the presence of the theatre and the effect of the carriages that thronged the streets around the playhouse and blocked trade:

there is daylie such resort of people, and such multitudes of Coaches (whereof many are Hackney Coaches, bringinge people of all sortes) That sometymes all our streetes cannott containe them, But that they Clogg upp Ludgate alsoe, in such sort, that both they endanger the one the other breake downe stalles, throwe downe mens goodes from their shopps, And the inhabitantes there cannott come to their howses, nor bringe in their necessary provisions of beere, wood, coale or haye, nor the Tradesmen or shopkeep[er]s utter their wares, nor the passenger goe to the comon water staires without danger of ther lives and lymmes, whereby alsoe many times, quarrelles and effusion of blood hath followed; and what further danger may bee occacioned by the broyles plottes or practises of such an unrulie multitude of people yf they should gett head, your wisedomes cann conceave; Theise inconveniences fallinge out almost everie daie in the winter tyme (not forbearinge the tyme of Lent) from one or twoe of the clock till six att night, which beinge the tyme alsoe most usuall for Christeninges and burialls and afternoones service, wee cannot have passage to the Church for performance of those necessary duties, the ordinary passage for a great part of the precinct aforesaid beinge close by the play house dore.[54]

Illustration 13. Richard Perkins, from the portrait in Dulwich Gallery, DPG 423.

This move was eventually checked by a renewal of the company's patent of 1604 in which the name of the Blackfriars theatre was at last added to the Globe as their licensed playing places. They sailed on as before. Burbage's place was filled by the acquisition of Joseph Taylor from Prince Charles's, and this in turn seems to have led the Prince's to welcome Beeston from the flag-fallen Queen Anne's, who were reorganised when their patron died, also in March 1619. Beeston's transfer in the long run proved to be a major event in company history since he gave the Prince's Men the Cockpit, the first indoor playhouse to offer a chance of rivalling Blackfriars as the moneyed section of the London audiences's most favoured playhouse.

The change understandably proved more to Beeston's advantage than his company's. As property owner and theatre manager Beeston's practice seems to have been like Henslowe's in his later years, to run a company for only so long as it remained amenable to his dealings – usually three years – then deliberately break it, as the Lady Elizabeth's Men accused Henslowe of doing, reforming it later with a few survivors from the old company and a large infusion of new blood. One can only speculate darkly on his motives. The Prince's Men lasted until 1622, when they were supplanted by a new group called the Lady Elizabeth's Men, drawing Andrew Cane, destined to be one of the leading Caroline clowns, from Palsgrave's, Joseph Moore from the original Lady Elizabeth's, and William Sherlock and Anthony Turner from unknown groups. The year 1625 brought not only the death of James but the worst visitation of plague in London's history, with an eight-month closure for all theatres. Subsequently Beeston reopened with a company patronised by the new Queen, Henrietta Maria. It was headed by Richard Perkins, perhaps the most famous actor of his day, formerly of the Red Bull and since then briefly a King's man, and others from the Red Bull, together with Sherlock and Turner from the old company.

The new Cockpit company rose steadily in prosperity and reputation for the next ten years, the only company to stay at Beeston's Cockpit for longer than three. The Master of the Revels signalled his judgement of their success in the winter season 1629–30 by giving them ten Court performances compared with twelve by the King's Men, who up to then had given as much entertainment to the Court as all the other companies put together. Shirley was the dramatist for Beeston, and more popular than Davenant or the other young courtier-wits currently providing for the Blackfriars. In the 1630–1 season they gave sixteen plays at Court, and were the only company besides the King's to receive the grant of royal liveries.

Royal protection helped both of the indoor playhouse companies. In 1637 for instance the Lord Chamberlain forbade the printing of any plays without

some Certificate in writeing under the handes of John Lowen & Joseph Taylor for the Kings servantes & of Christopher Bieston for y^e. Kings & Queenes young Company.[55]

This 'young Company' was Beeston's latest. In 1636 during a nine-month-plagued interruption of playing Beeston deliberately broke Queen Henrietta's company and in 1637 reopened with a new group chiefly made up of young actors. As the Master of the Revels noted:

At the increase of the plague to 4 within the citty and 54 in all – This day the 12 May, 1636, I received a warrant from my Lord Chamberlin for the suppressing of playes and shews, and at the same time delivered my severall warrants to George Wilson for the four companys of players, to be served upon them.

On Thursday morning 23^d feb: the Bill of the Plague made the number at 44 upon which decrease the king gave the players ther liberty & they began 24 feb: 1636 [1637].

The plague encreasinge the players laye still untill the 2 of Oct. 1637 when they had leave to play.

Mr Beeston was commanded to make a company of boyes, and began to play at the Cockpitt with them the same day.

I disposed of Perkins, Sumner, Sherlock and Turner, to Salisbury Court, and joynd them with the best of that company.[56]

The old company was broken, though it later came together again playing at the indoor Salisbury Court. As that theatre's manager, Richard Heton, noted,

When her Majesties servants were at the Cockpit, beinge all at liberty, they disperst themselves to severall Companies, soe that had not my lord of Dorsett taken care to make up a new Company for the Queene, she had not had any at all.[57]

Perkins, Sherlock and Turner went to Salisbury Court with the revived company, five others went to the King's Men, and at least six returned to Beeston. The new company became known to the Revels Office as Beeston's Boys, and seems to have consisted of a much larger than usual ratio of boys to adults,[58] rather like the Queen's Revels Children after 1609. There were enough adults for five to be summoned before the Privy Council in 1637 and three to be committed to Marshalsea prison in 1640. They managed their own affairs in a sufficiently adult way for Beeston to bequeath them two of the six company shares, half his own holding, when he died in 1638. In addition to the adults retained from the old Queen Henrietta's Men, two came from the King's Revels and two had been in Prince Charles's as early as 1631–2. Of the other recruits two had been boys with the King's Men.

Beeston's Boys may have been modelled on a new company first put together by Richard Gunnell when he built the Salisbury Court playhouse in 1629. This was a group of fourteen youngsters, trainee players, who were given bed and board while they were being fattened for the market. The object was, ostensibly,

to train and bring up certain boys in the quality of playing not only with intent to be a supply of able actors to his Majest's servants of the Black Friars when there should be occasion … but the solace of his Royal Majesty when his Majesty should please to see them and also for the recreation of his Majesty's loving subjects.[59]

Apart from the idea of a school to train boys for the King's Company this sounds very like the formula for the boy companies of the first decade of the century. The training school may have been something of a pretext to gain the company an entrée into London playing. One or two of the boys do seem to have gone on to the King's Company. Stephen Hammerton, who was playing girl's parts for them in 1633[60] and later became the idol of the women in the audiences for his young romantic leads, was bought by Gunnell's partner in 1629 from his apprenticeship to a merchant tailor for the sum of £30.[61] But the primary return from such investments was in playing, and the boys appear to have been supplemented soon after they got started with six adult players, who became sharers with Gunnell in the enterprise. Boys were an investment, and were cheaper to maintain than adults. A lawsuit in 1632 claimed that after the long closure through plague the fourteen boys only had seven shirts between them, and that one had died because of their poor diet. Beeston might well have seen the financial advantages of mixing boys with adults when he set up Beeston's Boys in 1637.

When Beeston died in 1638 his son William took over management of the company's affairs. William was a less adroit diplomat than his father, who is recorded by Henry Herbert, the opinionated and self-satisfied Master of the Revels, as on one occasion giving 'my wife a payre of gloves, that cost him at least twenty shillings'.[62] Beeston no doubt found it money well spent. In the spring of 1640 William fell, like his father before him more than once, into trouble with Herbert for failing to consult him over a play that contained political matters. The play was almost certainly Richard Brome's *The Court Beggar*, which satirised the courtier and wit of the Queen's circle John Suckling, his friend Davenant and several other members of the circle. The times were getting warmer as they moved nearer the explosions of the 1640s, and William was unable to mollify Herbert for his audacity as his father had done. He was visited with a total prohibition:

Wheras William Bieston and the Company of Playerrs of the Cockpitt in Drury Lane have lately Acted a new play without any Licence from the M^r of his Ma^{tes} Revells & beeing commaunded to forbeare playing or Acting of the same play by the sayd M^r of the Revells & commaunded likewise to forbeare all manner of playing have notwith-standing ... Acted the sayd Play & others ... Theis are therfore in his Ma^{tes} name, & signification of his royall pleasure to commaund the sayd William Bieston & the rest of that Company of the Cockpitt Players from henceforth & upon sight heerof to forbeare to Act any Playes whatsoever untill they shall bee restored by the sayd-M^r of the Revells unto their former Liberty. Wherof all partyes concernable are to take notice & to conforme accordingly as they and every of them will answere it.[63]

Furthermore William lost his position as 'Governor & Instructe' to the company, and with two of his players was put in the Marshalsea. Ironically he was replaced by Davenant himself, the putative son of Shakespeare, former King's poet, current Court masque-writer and Poet Laureate, and founder of the most ambitious theatre project to date, one that had been squashed (ironically again with Herbert's connivance) only a year or so before. Planned for a site on the Strand, it was meant to have a huge indoor stage suitable for singing and dancing, the first attempt at operatic staging in London. Davenant had little time to work as manager because he was soon away to the so-called Bishops' Wars against the Scots, and after the collapse of the second campaign it was obvious that he along with all he stood for were on the losing side in a conflict that was more and more quickly coming into the open. In May 1641 Suckling was summoned before the House of Lords about a band of soldiers he had gathered together in London, supposedly to rescue the King's strong man, Strafford, from the Tower, where Parliament, with mortal intent, had put him. Suckling gained time by declaring with characteristic smoothness that he was raising a force for service in the Portuguese army, and by the time Parliament had obtained a denial from the Portuguese Ambassador Suckling and his fellow-conspirators in what became known as the Army Plot were on their way out of the country. Four of the five named by Parliament escaped; Davenant, with an ostentation as characteristic as Suckling's smoothness, managed to get himself captured in Kent. His famous 'saddleback' nose perhaps made him easily recognisable. He was held until Parliament realised it could not decide what to do with him and allowed him to depart into exile.[64] Beeston meanwhile seems to have slipped back into his managership – his mother still had the lease of the playhouse and a one-third holding in the company – but in any case the end was too near for either profit or delight, and at the beginning of September 1642 Parliament put a stop to both.

The authority the Master of the Revels had over the theatre impresarios is signalled by Herbert's part in the transfer from Beeston to Davenant. His degree of control and the extent to which the impresarios had taken over a directly managerial role are shown in a document drawn up in 1639 by Richard Heton for the Salisbury Court company, the revived Queen Henrietta's. According to this document Heton was to have the sole patent for the company, and he stipulated moreover

That such of the company as will not be ordered and governed by me as of their governor, or shall not by the M[r] of his M[ts] Revells and my selfe bee thought fitt Comedians for her M[ts] service, I may have power to discharge from the Company, and, with the advice of the M[r] of the Revells, to putt new ones in their places; and those who shalbe soe descharged not to have the honor to be her M[ts] servants, but only those who shall continew at the aforesaid playhouse.

And the said Company not to play at any tyme in any other place but the forsaid playhouse without my consent under my hand in wryting, (lest his M[ts] service might be neglected) except by speciall comand from one of the Lo. Chamberlaines, or the M[r] of his M[ts] Revells, &c.[65]

Illustration 14. William Davenant with his famous nose, from the engraving
on the frontispiece of the 1673 edition of his *Works*.

7. COMPANY STRUCTURE

Recognition of what the patterns of change were in the history of the
London companies is necessary before any meaningful generalisation
about their organisation and practices sufficient to apply to the whole
seventy years can be identified. Subject to the conditions of perpetual

change, some picture can be made of the primary features, that is, the management of company finances and the pattern of governmental regulations by which the companies were bound. Between these more tangible matters some filling in of the human company affairs, the customs, corporate tastes and traditions is worth attempting.

The chief distinction of the London companies from travelling groups was their growing size and resources. These in turn made their financial organisation different from that of the travelling groups, which at least in the early days had no more than six or eight players, few properties other than costumes, and were usually led by a player who was at once leading man, manager, financier and warrant-holder. After about 1580 the London-based companies consisted of a core of between eight and twelve co-owning players, 'sharers', who divided between them both profits and costs such as properties and apparel, rent, and the wages of the hired extras. Most plays required casts of at least fifteen with a lot of doubling, and in London the companies had the additional costs of buying many more plays than were needed for the earlier groups touring to different towns, plus the stagekeepers, tiremen, the gatherers who took money at the London play-house doors, musicians and other assistants needed for each playhouse's operation. The Admiral's *1 Tamar Cam* of 1596 ended with a procession of twelve pairs representing a number of different races and made up from the players not already on the stage. *Frederick and Basilea*'s 'plot' summons even a number of the gatherers to augment the procession that ended the play. The biggest London companies in the seventeenth century had a total personnel of forty or more, of whom thirty were hirelings of one kind or another. Sometimes, as happened with that peak of stage spectacle Heywood's *Ages*, two companies might join forces for a particular production. Heywood noted in his preface to *The Iron Age* that the *Ages* were 'often … Publikely Acted by two Companies, uppon one Stage at once'. The cast-list of *The Silver Age* has forty-one named parts, with additional 'servingmen, swaines, Theban ladies, the seven Planets and the Furies'. But such amalgamations were extremely rare. It was quite costly enough in terms of extras to perform an ordinary play. Even with the maximum doubling of parts a 'normal' London company would need to employ, in addition to the eight, ten or twelve sharers, four boys or more for the women's and page's parts, and six or more hired players, plus stage hands and musicians. To be a shareholder in a London company was to be involved in a commercial enterprise with a substantial turnover in expenditure as well as income.

In a normal situation a company sharer would be expected to buy his way into the company, and if the company remained a going concern he could sell his share when he left, providing he left with the agreement of his fellow sharers.[66] A share in the Admiral's Men with ten sharers in 1597 or 1602 was worth £50; in its successor in 1613 with twelve sharers it was worth £70. A Queen Anne's company share in 1612 was valued at £80. The former Blackfriars boy company in 1610 had fewer than an adult company, six shares, but they were valued at £100 each, a total of £600 against the £840 of the Palsgrave's in 1613. Against that investment valuation the income on a King's Company share in 1634 was £180 for the year.[67] If a sharer died the company reimbursed his widow for the value of her husband's share and resold the share to a new active member of the company. It was an essential feature of the share system that it should operate not only as an investment for the sharer but as a commitment binding its owner to play for the company and to keep their interests his own. If a sharer left without his fellows' consent he was not reimbursed for his share. A begging letter from Charles Massey to Henslowe in 1613 describes the traditional sharers' agreement (*Henslowe Papers*, p. 64):

I know [you] und[er]stande th[at ther] is [the] composisions betwene oure compenye that if [any] one gi[ve] over with consent of his fellowes, he is to r[ece]ve thr[ee] score and ten poundes (antony Jefes hath had so mu[ch]) if any on dye his wi[dow] or frendes whome he appoyntes it tow reseve fyfte poundes (m^{r}es pavic, and m^{r}es round hath had the lyke) be sides that lytt[ell] moete I have in the play housses, which I would willing[ly] pas over unto you by dede of gifte or any course you [w]ould set doune for your securete, and that you sho[ul]d be sure I dow it not with oute my wiffes consenn[te] she wilbe willinge to set her hand to any thinge that myght secure it to you, Ser fifte poundes would pay my detes, which for on hole twelve month I would take up and pay the intreste, and that I myght the better pay it in at the yeares ende, I would get m^r Jube to reseve my gallery mony, and my qua[r]ter of the house mony for a yeare to pay it in with all, and if in [six] monthes I sawe the gallerye mony would not dow [then in] the other six monthes he should reseve [my whole] share, only reservinge a marke a wekke to furnish my house with all.

In the later years, when verbal agreements were supplemented by written articles, the bonds committed the sharer to stay with the company for a specified number of years, usually three, and gave financial penalties for such uncooperative actions as missing performances or rehearsals or being drunk. This at least is what Henslowe got Robert Dawes to agree to when he joined the Henslowe enterprises in 1614:

the said Robert Dawes shall and will plaie with such company, as the said Phillipp Henslowe and Jacob Meade shall appoynte, for and during the tyme and space of three yeares from the date hereof for and at the rate of one whole share, accordinge to the custome of players; and that he the said Robert Dawes shall and will at all tymes during the said terme duly attend all suche rehearsall, which shall the night before the rehearsall be given publickly out; and if that he the saide Robert Dawes shall at any tyme faile to come at the hower appoynted, then he shall and will pay to the said Phillipp Henslowe and Jacob Meade, their executors or assignes, Twelve pence; and if he come not before the saide rehearsall is ended, then the said Robert Dawes is contented to pay Twoe shillings; and further that if the said Robert Dawes shall not every daie, whereon any play is or ought to be played, be ready apparrelled and – to begyn the play at the hower of three of the clock in the afternoone, unles by sixe of the same company he shall be lycenced to the contrary, that then he, the saide Robert Dawes, shall and will pay unto the said Phillipp and Jacob or their assignes Three [shillings]; and if that he, the saide Robert Dawes, happen to be overcome with drinck at the tyme when he [ought to] play, by the judgment of Fower of the said company, he shall and will pay Tenne shillings; and if he, [the said Robert Dawes], shall [faile to come] during any plaie, having noe lycence or just excuse of sicknes, he is contented to pay Twenty shillings … And further the said Robert Dawes doth covenant, [promise, and graunt to and with the said Phillip Henslowe and Jacob Meade, that if he, the said Robert Dawes], shall at any time after the play is ended depart or goe out of the [howse] with any [of their] apparell on his body, or if the said Robert Dawes [shall carry away any propertie] belonging to the said company, or shal be consentinge [or privy to any other of the said company going out of the howse with any of their apparell on his or their bodies, he, the said] Robert Dawes, shall and will forfeit and pay unto the said Phillip and Jacob, or their administrators or assignes, the some of Fortie pounds of lawfull [money of England][68]

The sharers had to pay for the rental of their playhouse, the purchase of costumes and other playing materials, the wages of all their hirelings, and the various fees exacted by the Revels Office. It was also usual, at least in the early days, to show good-neighbourliness by making regular payments to the parish poor. The burlesqued company Sir Oliver Owlet's Men in *Histriomastix* (*c.* 1598) were accosted by the local constable for their 'taxe mony, / To releeve the poore'. The rent for the playhouse was traditionally half of the gallery takings. If the playhouse-owner was loaning the company money to buy properties he took his repayments from the other half of the gallery takings, the gathering of which was usually his concern rather than the company's. Much of the function of impresarios such as James Burbage, Henslowe, Langley and Beeston lay in financing the purchase of such properties. It was an exceptionally stable company that could afford its own, and apart from the King's Men not many seem to have done so. They usually began with a loan from the impresario to buy playbooks and apparel, and never got out of his debt. It was in the interests of the Henslowes and Beestons to maintain a turnover of companies since each fresh company needed fresh finance to renew its apparel and repertory.

The system whereby several sharers of a company bypassed the impresario and themselves became playhouse owners or house-keepers began when Shakespeare and some of his fellows were called in by the Burbages, who needed capital for their new Globe in 1599. It was copied by some other companies – Queen Anne's Men at the Red Bull and the Palsgrave's at the Fortune after 1615 are the chief examples – but it was less common than single managerial ownership, and it frequently led to difficulties. A share in a playhouse, being an item of material property, was more durable than a share in a company and could easily pass out of a company sharer's possession. When that happened it almost always led to trouble and often litigation in order to secure for the householder his proportion of the rent, or for the company or other householders the part of the cost of repairs and maintenance that went with a property share.

It was a litigious age, of course, and the opportunities for human backsliding and inhuman sharp practice were omnipresent. The valuation of a company share was a subjective consideration, depending on the appearance of the company's health and prospects. The proportion of a householder's obligation for payment of a small repair bill was difficult to assess as well as to collect if, as not infrequently happened, a share had been passed on by inheritance and the original holding split into several fractions. The opportunities for a single financier to play on the fallible memories of verbal agreements made by a corporate organisation over several years amongst a changing membership were numerous. Even the gatherers might prove less than reliable, if a reference in 1643 to gatherers who 'seeme to scratch their heads where they itch not, and drop shillings and half croune-pieces in at their collars'[69] is any guide.

The sums of money involved were enormous by the standards of the time in comparison with the social class of those involved. Henslowe is reckoned to have spent £1,317 between 1597 and 1603 directly on the Admiral's Men's properties, of which playbooks took a half.[70] This, on a unit of comparison of a normal working-man's wage as one shilling a day[71] is equivalent to the wages of thirteen or fourteen such men over the whole six years. In 1631 a committee studying the Blackfriars property in an attempt to get the playhouse removed noted that the players had presented an itemised account valuing the property at £21,990. The committee's own valuation, covering loss of rent and interest in the site, was £2,900 13s. 4d.[72] The householders' price was understandably high and the committee's understandably low, but even the lower figure is impressive for just the estimated rental value of a single playhouse through the fourteen years that remained of the lease.

On the day-to-day level we have detailed records of Henslowe's gallery receipts for six years near the turn of the century, and more fragmentary records of other enterprises. The Admiral's Men's half-gallery takings were averaging £20 a week in 1597 (*Diary*, p. xxxv), to which they could add another £20 or so from the yard. To build the Fortune, possibly on the framework of an existing building, cost £520; to rebuild the Globe from ground level in 1614 cost about £1,400. Ground-rent was £16 a year for the Fortune, £14 10s. for the Globe. The Revels licensing fee for playhouses rose from 10s. a week in 1596 to £3 a week in 1600 for the new Fortune. A King's Company housekeeper in 1615 took £20 for one-fourteenth of the Globe and a similar amount for one-seventh of the Blackfriars, the total takings from half the galleries of both houses therefore amounting to £420 in the year. By 1635 the Blackfriars was yielding £700–£800 a year and the Globe rather less, though it was still worth twice as much as the Rose in the 1590s.[73] A single performance at Court brought the company £10.

At the lowest level the pay of a player was little different from a journeyman's daily shilling. Henslowe in 1597 contracted to pay William Kendall 10 shillings weekly for playing in London, and 5 'in ye Cuntrie' (*Diary*, p. 269), while *Ratsey's Ghost* (anon., 1606) claimed that 'the very best' of provincial actors 'have sometimes beene content to go home with fifteene pence share apiece' (A4). A reference in 1620 to 'twelve-penny hirelings' at the Fortune suggests that even Kendall was lucky while playing in London (John Melton, *Astrologaster*, E4). Richard Jones wrote to Alleyn in 1592 asking to borrow £3 to get his clothes out of pawn, so that he could join a company about to travel in Germany. He complained that 'some tymes I have a shillinge a day, and some tymes nothing, so that I leve in great poverty' (*Henslowe Papers*, p. 33). Hired men nonetheless had the promise of shareholding in their future, and some were even prepared to furnish bonds of £40 to guarantee their stay with their company (*Henslowe's Diary*, p. 242).

Boys were paid even less than hired men. Henslowe charged the company 'a Ratte of iii s A wecke' in 1600 for their use of his boy James Bristow (*Diary*, p. 167). The *Articles of Oppression against Mr Hinchlowe* record six shillings weekly for the man responsible for 'bying of Clothes', which compares with the wages of the hired players. The other hirelings would hardly have been paid more, unless perhaps the 'book-keeper' was regarded as especially responsible. Musicians were more generously rewarded, but in any case often existed in a separate organisation; they had to be licensed separately by the Revels Office. In every case, of course, the wage would have to vary according to the company's takings and general prosperity. Nobody was paid during inhibitions. Roger Clarke joined the Red Bull company for a six shilling weekly wage, as was 'sett downe in their booke', but in the hard times that followed his income went down to a half-crown or two shillings a week.[74] Even the hired men were sharers in a company's misfortunes.

The Red Bull appears to have found even cheaper labour on occasions. Pepys records how he heard of

Thos. Killigrew's way of getting to see plays when he was a boy. He would go to the Red Bull, and when the man cried to the boys, 'Who will go and be a devil, and he shall see the play for nothing?' then would he go in, and be a devil upon the stage, and so get to see plays.[75]

One other matter of company finances is of interest. Poets were often directly employed by Henslowe, and their products were a regular and major drain on company finances. Thomas Dekker in 1598 had a busy year during which he shared in the writing of sixteen plays. His total payment from Henslowe for them was £30, representing a weekly income of a little over twelve shillings. Henslowe at this time was paying about £5 for a play purchased outright. By 1615 his prices had been pushed up to £20. The Court was paying £50 for masques. In later years the Restoration practice of giving its poets benefit afternoons seems to have been used in some cases to pay them, on the basis of payment by results.[76] Companies had a necessary appetite for new plays. The Admiral's absorbed roughly one a fortnight in the years up to 1600. With far fewer plays daily the boys at Blackfriars after their initial period seem to have taken about four a year. In the last twenty years of playing the incomplete records of the Revels Office suggest a rather lower rate of consumption by each of the four companies.

8. GOVERNMENT CONTROL

Government regulation of the companies grew up as a natural concomitant of both the government's and the companies' interests. The government gained by its power to limit plays, players and playhouses in what was spoken and by whom, and by the more incidental command of the quality of the players who entertained the Court. Playing companies gained above all protection from hostile local authorities. From 1583 and still more from 1594 they profited by the security of the artificially monopolistic situation maintained under the Revels Office, and later still by such protection as the Master of the Revels could offer in preventing unauthorised performing or printing of the various companies' repertories.

The Crown's interest was exercised through the Privy Council, with the Lord Chamberlain as the Council's officer delegated to watch over plays and playing matters. His executive came to be the Revels Office, originally run intermittently under Henry VIII to organise Court shows, with a Master in the managerial role, one and a half clerks and a Yeoman, who in the early days was a tailor concerned to maintain the extensive Revels Office wardrobe.[77] Under the Stuarts he seems to have become more of a stage manager. Once the adult theatres were permanently established in London it became expedient to extend the powers of the Office, and in 1581 the Master was granted wide powers, including the censorship of plays staged anywhere in the country. The licensing of plays for performance had been required by proclamations of as early as 1559, when licences were to be issued 'within any Citie or towne corporate, by the Maior or other chiefe officers of the same, and within any shyre, by suche as shalbe Lieuetenauntes for the Quenes Majestie in the same shyre, or by two of the Justices of peax inhabyting within that part of the shire where any shalbe played'.[78] The royal patent to Leicester's Men in 1574 noted above specified that their plays should be 'sene & allowed' only by the Master of the Revels. The 1581 commission to the Master, after specifying his rights to employ 'propertie makers and conninge artificers and laborers' and to buy materials for Court shows, laid it down that he was to take over all licensing authority:

we have and do by these presents authorize and command our said servant, Edmunde Tilney, Master of our said Revels, by himself, or his sufficient deputy or deputies, to warn, command, and appoint in all places within this our realm of England, as well within franchises and liberties as without, all and every player or players, with their playmakers, either belonging to any nobleman, or otherwise, bearing the name or names or using the faculty of playmakers, or players of comedies, tragedies, interludes, or what other showes soever, from time to time, and at all times, to appear before him with all such plays, tragedies, comedies, or shows, as they shall have in readiness, or mean to set forth, and them to present and recite before our said servant, or his sufficient deputy, whom we ordain, appoint, and authorise by these presents, of all such shows, plays, players, and playmakers, together with their playing places, to order and reform, authorize and put down, as shall be thought meet or unmeet unto himself, or his said deputy in that behalf.

And also likewise we have by these presents authorized and commanded the said Edmunde Tilney that in case if any of them, whatsoever they be, will obstinately refuse upon warning unto them given by the said Edmunde, or his sufficient deputy, to accomplish and obey our commandment in this behalf, then it shall be lawful to the said Edmunde, or his sufficient deputy, to attach the party or parties so offending, and him or them to commit to ward, to remain without bail or mainprise until such time as the same Edmunde Tilney, or his sufficient deputy, shall think the time of his or their imprisonment to be punishment sufficient for his or their said offences in that behalf; and that done, to enlarge him or them so being imprisoned at their plain liberty, without any loss, penalty, forfeiture, or other danger in this behalf to be sustained or borne by the said Edmunde Tilney or his deputy, any act, statute, ordinance, or provision heretofore had or made to the contrary hereof in any wise notwithstanding.[79]

This commission formally extended Tilney's powers from the arrangement of all royal entertainments to the regulation of all the playing companies. It proved an effective form of control. The Privy Council edicts of the 1590s that affirmed the limit of two for the number of London-based companies strengthened the Master's position. Subsequent commissions in 1603 and 1622 simply renewed these terms. Later Masters extended their functions, taking on the licensing of plays for printing as well as performance, but that seems to have been more for the additional revenue than for tighter control.

On the whole, the system was beneficial to both controller and controlled. Tilney prospered as Master of the Court's entertainments largely because he supported the playing companies. More and more from the 1570s he invited the players to Court to perform through the long Christmas season instead of mounting masques. This was to their mutual advantage because plays were much cheaper for the Revels Office than masques. The three masques in the 1573–4 season cost £75 each. In 1579–80 Tilney put up nine plays at £25 each.[80] Increasingly too, as the players began to bring their own costumes and properties, plays drew less and less on the coffers of the Revels Office. The chosen companies gained from this a healthy reputation and Court favour, while the Office improved its financial health. It was a hard but a profitable collaboration. George Buc's bill for four months' work in 1615 specified 'for his owne attendaunce and his fower men viz from and for the laste day of Oct 1615 untill and for the xiiijth of Febr following for Rehearsalles and making choice of playes & Comedies and reforming them by the space of Cvij daies and xix nightes ...'[81] Choosing, rehearsing and reforming plays kept the Master, his Yeoman, his groom and two secretaries well occupied through each winter.

With Tilney's appointment censorship was now centralised, and the censor had close contact with the London companies. Not only did he read the manuscript of every play before signing the last page to make it an 'allowed book', but from 1594 he licensed the companies and their playhouses as well. Each royal patent for a playing company was issued through the Revels Office and specified the Master's control. His exercise of his function is indicated in a warrant of 1616, which was evidently sent round the country and has survived because the local authorities in Norwich copied it into their records:

Whereas Thomas Swynnerton and Martin Slaughter beinge two of the Queens Ma[rs] company of Playors havinge sep[ar]ated themselves from their said Company, have each of them taken forth a severall exemplification or duplicate of his ma^{ts} Letters patente graunted to the whole Company and by vertue thereof they severally in two Companies with vagabonds and such like idle p[er]sons, have and doe use and exercise the quallitie of playinge in div[er]se places of this Realme to the great abuse and wronge of his Ma^{ts} Sub^{ts} in generall and contrary to the true intent and meaninge of his Matie to the said Company And whereas William Perrie haveinge likewise gotten a warrant whereby he and a certaine Company of idle p[er] sons with him doe travel and play under the name and title of the Children of his Ma^{ts} Revels, to the great abuse of his Ma^{ts} srvice And whereas also Gilberte Reason one of the prince his highnes Playor^s having likewise sep[ar]ated himselfe from his Company hath also taken forth another exemplification or duplicate of the patent granted to that Company and lives in the same kinde & abuse And likewise one Charles Marshall, Homfrey Jeffes and Willm Parr: three of Prince Palatynes Company of Playo^{rs} haveinge also taken forthe an exemplification or duplicate of the patent graunted to the said Company and by vertue thereof live after the like kinde and abuse Wherefore to the and [*sic*] such idle p[er]sons may not be suffered to continewe in this course of life These are therefore to pray, and neatheless in his Ma^{ts} name to will and require you upon notice given of aine of the said p[er]sons by the bearer herof Joseph More whome I have speciallye directed for that purpose that you call the said p[ar]ties offendo^{rs} before you and thereupon take the said sev[er]all exemplifications or duplicats or other ther warrants by which they use ther saide quallitie from them, And forthwith to send the same to me.[82]

It was all too easy to make a copy and forge the Master's signature on it if a company split into two groups, one travelling and the other staying in London, while the second group took a copy of the first licence to authorize them on their travels. Slater, Gilbert Reason and Charles Marshall were more or less permanently on the road with fake licences. Slater used a copy of the patent for Queen Anne's Red Bull company to travel with even after her death in 1619. He may even have altered it after her death became known, because in 1623 he was noted at Coventry as travelling with a patent from Queen Elizabeth.

From early in James's reign the Master began to license plays for printing as well as performing. This may have been a natural extension of the main point of licensing companies and playhouses, which was not so much the control it established as the revenue it gave the Master. Every extra duty brought him extra income. Up till then licensing plays had officially been in the hands of the Bishop of London, who never took much interest. By the time of Henry Herbert, the last and most eager fulfiller of the office, the playhouse fee and the company fee were lumped together in a single annual payment, either from a benefit performance or as a lump sum. The King's Men gave him one day's takings each from the Blackfriars and Globe up to 1633, when they replaced them with a lump sum of £10 every Christmas and

Midsummer. Beeston seems to have made a single annual payment.[83] Herbert's predecessor, George Buc, noted in 1613 a payment of £20 for licensing the Whitefriars playhouse, but this was a rare windfall, and in contrast we should note at least two occasions when the Master had to prevent a playhouse going up. Buc stopped Rosseter from building in Blackfriars in 1615, and Herbert stopped Davenant from building a large indoor playhouse in the Strand in 1639.

The 'allowing' of plays was also profitable for the Master, but in this case the ostensible object, censorship, was also a very real one and the Master's labours were a serious duty taken seriously. The ordinance of 1559 had specified censorship of 'matters of religion or of the governance of the estate of the common weale'.[84] The hand of the censor can be seen descending on such matters in four extant manuscripts, *Sir Thomas More* (1594? 1601?), *The Second Maiden's Tragedy* (1613), *Sir John van Olden Barnavelt* (1619) and *Believe as you List* (1628). The deposition scene in Shakespeare's *Richard II* is missing from the early quartos, evidently for censorship reasons, and the extant texts of *The Isle of Gulls*, Chapman's *Byron* plays and conceivably many others are obviously censored.

It is not certain what degree of control the Master of the Revels exercised over the 'private' boy companies in the first years of the seventeenth century. The likelihood that he did not control them as he did the adult companies has already been mentioned. He may have authorised the censorship cuts showing in the printed texts of their plays, but this may have been a retrospective action after spectators at the plays in performance complained of them. The trouble that *Eastward Ho!*, *The Isle of Gulls* and the Byron plays roused may well have been what led the Master to take over responsibility for licensing all plays for printing. Certainly the years from 1605 to 1608 produced enough scandals to warrant an intensified concern for official control of plays, whether it was to restrain satires about Scottish behaviour at Court or to curb more general offensiveness, against either the state or the church.

In 1606 an Act 'to Restraine Abuses of Players' ordered the censorship of profane oaths:

If ... any person or persons doe or shall in any Stage play, Interlude, Shewe, Maygame, or Pageant jestingly or prophanely speake or use the holy name of God or of Christ Jesus, or of the Holy Ghoste or of the Trinitie ... shall forfeite for everie such Offence by him or them committed Tenne pounds.[85]

This is one reason why the pagan gods begin to be called on with more frequency in the drama after this date. Herbert, the censor whose judgements we have most record of, in 1634 clarified the interpretation of the statute of oaths as a result of a tiff with his royal master. As he noted,

This morning, being the 9th of January, 1633 [i.e. 1634], the kinge was pleasd to call mee into his withdrawinge chamber to the windowe, wher he went over all that I had croste in Davenants play-booke [*The Wits*], and allowing of *faith* and *slight* to bee asseverations only, and no oathes, markt them to stande, and some other few things, but in the greater part allowed of my reformations. This was done upon a complaint of Mr Endymion Porters in December.

The kinge is pleasd to take *faith, death, slight*, for asseverations, and no oaths, to which I doe humbly submit as my masters judgment; but under favour conceive them to be oaths, and enter them here, to declare my opinion and submission.[86]

Herbert's basic concerns are revealed in a few of the opinions he recorded, such as these:

For the king's players. An olde playe called Winter's Tale, formerly allowed of by Sir George Bucke, and likewyse by mee on Mr. Hemmings his worde that there was nothing profane added or reformed, thogh the allowed booke was missinge; and therefore I returned it without a fee, this 19 of August, 1623.

For the Palsgraves Company. January [1624] The history of the Dutchess of Suffolk by M[r]. Drewe being full of dangerous matter was much reformed & for my paines this 2[d] Jan. 1623 I had 2li [£2].

18 Nov. 1632. In the play of The Ball, written by Sherley, and acted by the Queens players, ther were divers personated so naturally, both of lords and others of the court, that I took it ill, and would have forbidden the play, but that Biston promiste many things which I found faulte withall should be left out, and that he would not suffer it to be done by the poett any more, who deserves to be punisht; and the first that offends in this kind, of poets or players, shall be sure of publique punishment.[87]

His one detailed note on the reforming of matters of governance of the commonwealth again followed his master's voice. On 5 June 1638 he quoted the problematic lines:

> Monys? Wee'le rayse supplies what ways we please,
> And force you to subscribe to blanks, in which
> We'le mulct you as wee shall thinke fitt. The Caesars
> In Rome were wise, acknowledginge no lawes
> But what their swords did ratifye, the wives
> And daughters of the senators bowinge to
> Their wills, as deities, &c.

and added

This is a peece taken out of Phillip Messingers play, called The King and the Subject, and entered here for ever to bee remembered by my son and those that cast their eyes

on it, in honour of Kinge Charles, my master, who, readinge over the play at Newmarket, set his marke upon the place with his owne hande, and in thes words:
This is too insolent, and to bee changed.
Note, that the poett makes it the speech of a king, Don Pedro king of Spayne, and spoken to his sujects.[88]

Don Pedro was only slightly exaggerating King Charles's practices over money through the 1630s.

The payment for 'allowing' a play was seven shillings under Edmund Tilney, the first regular Master of the Revels. His successor, George Buc, started licensing plays for printing in 1606, and added that duty to his licences for performing when he took over the Mastership at Tilney's death in 1610. He charged £1 for both a licence to perform and a licence to print. Henry Herbert, who bought the reversion of the office in 1622, charged the same, doubling it for plays needing a lot of correction, and charging £2 regularly after 1632. Herbert paid £150 a year for the privilege of fulfilling the Master's duties, so his total income must have amounted altogether to substantially more than that.

The companies were not obliged to the Revels Office only for the licences which regulated and protected them. The Master also safeguarded public health by enforcing the plague regulations, and safeguarded religion by enforcing prohibitions on playing through Lent, though in later years Mammon was worshipped as well, in the form of profitable Lenten dispensations to play that Herbert issued.

Plague regulations so far as the theatres were concerned followed simply from the general requirement that places of public assembly should be closed in time of infection. The City made the point as early as 1569:

Forasmuch as thoroughe the greate resort, accesse and assembles of great multitudes of people unto diverse and severall Innes and other places of this Citie, and the liberties & suburbes of the same, to thentent to here and see certayne stage playes, enterludes, and other disguisinges, on the Saboth dayes and other solempne feastes commaunded by the church to be kept holy, and there being close pestered together in small romes, specially in this tyme of sommer, all not being and voyd of infeccions and diseases, whereby great infeccion with the plague, or some other infeccious diseases, may rise and growe, to the great hynderaunce of the comon wealth of this citty, and perill and daunger of the quenes majesties people, the inhabitantes thereof, and all others repayrying thether, about there necessary affares.[89]

The battles between City and Court in the 1570s and 1580s inevitably included the need to close places of public assembly such as playhouses in time of plague. The Leicester's patent of 1574 forbade playing 'in the tyme of common prayer, or in the tyme of great and common plague'. The clashes ten years later that produced the Queen's Men and the City's 'Remedyes' over playing concluded that playhouses should not open until the weekly bill of plague victims had been below fifty for three weeks. In 1604 the Privy Council brought this down to thirty a week. The King's Men's patents of 1619 and 1625 specify forty. The limits were not always very exactly enforced, but the visitations of plague nonetheless were by far the most severely limiting phenomenon the players encountered. Prolonged closures in the really bad years, 1581–2, 1592–3, 1603–4, 1608–9, 1609–10, 1625, 1630, 1636–7, 1640 and 1641, never failed to endanger the companies and usually caused major reshuffles of membership. All the companies, even the boy groups, would try to keep themselves solvent by travelling to wherever there was no plague. But that was always likely to be a doubtful resort, and in times of plague any sort of travelling was known to be dangerous, since the plague could easily accompany new arrivals at any town, as indeed it often did. Because the London catchment area was much wider than the territory under the Lord Mayor's control it was always the Privy Council that ordered the closures. Often its orders closed larger parts of the country to travel of any kind, though the effect on carters who had to take food and the shippers shipping timber and coal down the North Sea into London was always difficult.

Worship of God was less disruptive than visitations of plague. The Privy Council ordered that all theatres must be closed through Lent in 1579, and Henslowe's records show an obedient closure in 1595 and 1596. In 1597, however, the Admiral's Men played through twelve days of Lent and observed the closure for less than the whole period again in the following year. At Lent in other years they went on tour, despite the weather, hoping that provincial mayors would observe Lent less rigorously than London's priests. In 1600, 1601 and 1604 the Privy Council renewed its orders about Lenten playing yet in 1605, although Lent began on 13 February, the Prince's Men played before royalty at Whitehall on the 19th. In 1607 the King's Men similarly played before James nine days after Lent had begun. In 1615 there were substantial violations of the closure order, and there is little evidence in later Revels Office records of any very strict enforcement.[90] On occasions throughout this period the outdoor playhouses were rented out for prize fights with swords, even during the Lenten closures. There is also some evidence to suggest that the Master of the Revels took a fee for a 'Lenten dispensation', allowing playing throughout Lent excepting only 'sermon days', that is, Wednesdays and Fridays, and Holy Week. The performances are often noted as being displays of fencing or acrobatics rather than the more directly provocative stage-plays.[91] Dispensations of this kind make it readily understandable that in 1642 the whole business of playing should be taken out of the Privy Council's and its deputy's hands by Parliament's firm pronouncement that

Whereas the distressed Estate of Ireland, steeped in her own Blood, and the distracted Estate of England, threatned with a Cloud of Blood, by a Civill Warre, call for all possible meanes to appease and avert the Wrath of God appearing in these Judgements; amongst which, Fasting and Prayer having bin often tryed to be very effectuall, have bin lately, and are still enjoyned; and whereas publike Sports doe not well agree with publike Calamities, nor publike Stage-playes with the Seasons of Humiliation, this being an Exercise of sad and pious solemnity, and the other being Spectacles of pleasure, too commonly expressing lacivious Mirth and Levitie: It is therefore thought fit, and Ordeined by the Lords and Commons in this Parliament Assembled, that while these sad Causes and set times of Humiliation doe continue, publike Stage-Playes shall cease, and bee forborne.[92]

This was Parliament's first intervention about playing. The only previous record of its interest in playgoing seems to be a proposal made back in 1604 by Lord Say and Sele, an early member of a notably eccentric family. On 30 October 1604 he proposed to the Lord Treasurer in Parliament a variety of means by which he might raise money for the new king. One good source of revenue, he argued, would be to tax every playgoer one penny for their access to a playhouse.[93] Quite apart from the fact that this would have doubled the cost of a place in the yard at the open-air playhouses the Lord Treasurer evidently felt that it was impractical, and the proposal went no further. It stands as witness to the great wealth that the players were by then thought to be amassing for themselves, and the even greater strength of the playgoing market.

CHAPTER 3

The Players

I. THE SOCIAL STATUS OF PLAYERS

In an epigram to Robert Armin, a King's player, John Davies of Hereford wrote:

> Wee all (that's Kings and all) but Players are
> Upon this earthly Stage.   *The Scourge of Folly* (1610), Q2v.

Kings might well be compared to players. Comparing players to kings, however, was a very different matter. The more usual attitude to players was that put by an anonymous author in the mouth of the highwayman Gamaliel Ratsey, whose execution in 1605 was the occasion for the publication of several pamphlets about his life and opinions. One anecdote involved how he exploited a company of travelling players (*Ratsey's Ghost* A3v–B1v). Ratsey, according to the pamphleteer, came to an inn where

that night there harbored a company of Players: and Ratsey framing himselfe to an humor of merriment, caused one or two of the chiefest of them to be sent for up into his chamber, where hee demanded whose men they were, and they answered they served such an honorable Personage. I pray you (quoth Ratsey) let me heare your musicke, for I have often gone to plaies more for musicke sake, then for action. For some of you not content to do well, but striving to over-doe and go beyond your selves, oftentimes (by S. George) mar all; yet your Poets take great paines to make your parts fit for your mouthes, though you gape never so wide. Othersome I must needs confesse, are very wel deserving both for true action and faire deliverie of speech, and yet I warrant you the very best have sometimes beene content to goe home at night with fifteene pence share apiece.

Others there are whom Fortune hath so wel favored, that what by penny-sparing and long practise of playing, are growne so wealthy, that they have expected to be knighted, or at least to be conjunct in authority, and to sit with men of great worship, on the Bench of Justice.

Evidently for this playgoing highwayman the idea of a player becoming a knight or a magistrate was deplorable (Ratsey himself was the son of a wealthy Lincolnshire gentleman). This last jibe seems to be a direct allusion to Edward Alleyn, since the reference to 'Others .... whom Fortune hath so wel favoured' would fit his return to the stage of the new Fortune playhouse in 1600 and the social ambitions that began to appear after his subsequent retirement.

Having patronised his guests Hamlet-fashion and sympathised with their hard lot, Ratsey rewards them for listening to him and goes his way. A week later, still in his humour of merriment, he meets them again in a different disguise, like the players themselves, who were now masquerading under another name:

lying as they did before in one Inne together, hee was desirous they should play a private play before him, which they did not in the name of the former Noblemans servants. For like Camelions they had changed that colour; but in the name of another, (whose indeede they were) although afterwardes when he heard of their abuse, hee discharged them, and tooke away his warrant. For being far off, (for their more countenance) they would pretend to be protected by such an honourable man, denying their Lord and Master; and comming within ten or twenty miles of him againe, they would shrowd themselves under their owne Lords favour.

Ratsey heard their Play, and seemed to like that, though he disliked the rest, and verie liberally out with his purse, and gave them fortie shillings, with which they held themselves very richly satisfied, for they scarce had twentie shillings audience at any time for a Play in the Countrey.

Ratsey has other ideas of what they deserved, of course, and they become targets for his Robin Hood-like rough justice. The next day he overtakes them on the road and retrieves his bounty, taking the opportunity to reprove them for their 'idle profession'. The leader he singles out for gratuitous good counsel:

And for you (sirra saies hee to the chiefest of them) thou hast a good presence upon a stage, me thinks thou darkenst they merite by playing in the country: Get thee to London, for if one man were dead, they will have much neede of such a one as thou art. There would be none in my opinion, fitter then thy selfe to play his parts: my conceit is such of thee, that I durst venture all the mony in my purse on thy head, to play Hamlet with him for a wager. There thou shalt learne to be frugall (for Players were never so thriftie as they are now about London) & to feed upon all men, to let none feede upon thee; to make thy hand a stranger to thy pocket, thy hart slow to performe thy tongues promise: and when thou feelest thy purse well lined, buy thee some place or Lordship in the Country, that growing weary of playing, thy mony may there bring thee to dignitie and reputation: then thou needest care for no man, nor not for them that before made thee prowd, with speaking their words upon the Stage. Sir, I thanke you (quoth the Player) for this good counsell, I promise you I will make use of it; for I have heard indeede, of some that have gone to London very meanly, and have come in time to be exceeding wealthy. And in this presage and propheticall humor of mine, (says Ratsey) kneele downe, Rise up Sir Simon two shares and a halfe: Thou art now of my Knights, and the first Knight that ever was Player in England. The next time I meete thee, I must share with thee againe for playing under my warrant, and so for this time adiew.

How ill hee brooked this new knighthood, which hee durst not but accept of, or liked his late counsell, which he lost his coine for, is easie to be imagined. But whether he met with them againe after the senights space, that he charged them to play in his name, I have not heard it reported.

The Ratsey anecdote provides a common view of the common player in his own times, though the pamphleteer evidently had a special antipathy to players, which might be explained by his fellow-feeling with 'them that before made thee prowd, with speaking their words upon the Stage'. The poets knew how generously the players treated them; Heywood's company paid out more for the heroine's dress in *A Woman Killed with Kindness* than for the play itself.[1]

The social standing of players, or more precisely the range of social attitudes to them, can be seen in a comparison of the Theophrastan characterisation 'A Common Player' of 1615 with its counter 'An Excellent Actor'. The first was written by a law student called John Cocke from Lincoln's Inn. It claimed that

The Statute hath done wisely to acknowledg him a Rogue, for his chiefe essence is, *A daily Counterfeit*: He hath beene familiar so long with out-sides, that he professes himselfe, (being unknowne) to be an apparent Gentleman. But his thinne Felt, and his silke Stockings, or his foule Linnen, and faire Doublet, doe (in him) bodily reveale the Broker: So beeing not sutable, hee proves a *Motley*.[2]

The Player Cocke characterised was not necessarily so common either; he might be a King's or Queen's Man. But he would be, none the less, a rogue:

howsoever hee pretends to have a royall Master or Mistresse, his wages and dependance prove him to be the servant of the people. The cautions of his judging humor (if hee dares undertake it) be a certaine number of sawcie rude jests against the common lawyer; hansome conceits against the fine Courtiers; delicate quirkes against the rich Cuckold a Cittizen; shadowed glaunces for good innocent Ladies and Gentlewomen; with a nipping scoffe for some honest Justice, who hath imprisoned him: or some thriftie Tradesman, who hath allowed him no credit.

Such an imputation was too much for one company with a royal master, and a reply soon appeared in print, probably written by Webster, whose *Duchess of Malfi* had recently been performed by the King's Men. It describes in conventional terms the qualities of a good actor as Heywood had set them down in his *Apology for Actors*, stressing their educational value:

By his action he fortifies morall precepts with example; for what we see him personate, we thinke truely done before us: a man of a deepe thought might apprehend, the Ghosts of our Ancient *Heroes* walk't againe, and take him (at severall times) for many of them. Hee is much affected to painting, and tis a question whether that make him an excellent Plaier, or his playing an exquisite painter.[3]

The last reference is meant to remind us of Richard Burbage, still the leading King's player, who was well enough known as a painter to have been commissioned in 1613 and 1616 to paint escutcheons for the Earl of Rutland.[4] Cocke was being unwarrantably snobbish.

The imitating Characterist was extreame idle in calling them Rogues. His Muse it seemes, with all his loud invocation, could not be wak't to light him a snuffe to read the Statute: for I would let his malicious ignorance understand, that Rogues are not to be imploide as maine ornaments to his Majesties Revels.

Cocke subsequently backpedalled, overlooking his explicit reference to the King's and Queen's companies, and protested that he meant only common players. He was let off a good deal more lightly than a later opponent of the theatre, William Prynne, whose *Histrio-mastix* of 1633 was one of the more trenchant and certainly the longest of the Puritan blasts against plays and players. It attacked such decadences as women appearing in Court presentations. Henrietta Maria herself had recently graced a masque with her participation, so Prynne was taken up by the Star Chamber (the Privy Council in its judicial role), who stripped him of his academic degrees, fined him, pilloried him, cropped his ears and sentenced him to the Tower for life.

The descriptions of Cocke and Ratsey were probably not entirely inaccurate with regard to the great majority of professional players who travelled for their living and whose fifteen pence or two shillings were rarely as ready to hand as the craftsman's shilling. It was an exceptional player who could profess himself to be even an apparent gentleman and conceal his dyer's hand in a courtier's glove. Shakespeare purchased a coat of arms for his father, but he earned a dig from Jonson in the process. In *Every Man Out of his Humour* Jonson parodied the Shakespeare motto 'Non Sans Droict' as '*Not without mustard*', a suitable phrase for an escutcheon showing a boar's head. A more intimate sign of status, or rather of the player's consciousness of where his way of life put him, is in Shakespeare's Sonnet 29. One of a group written to his aristocratic patron and friend and expressing his awareness of the distance between a playhouse and a great house (27 and 28 were written while he was travelling), it describes how he can move from misery to joy simply by shifting his thoughts from his own 'state' to his friend. It ends

> For thy sweet love remember'd such wealth brings
> That then I scorn to change my state with kings.

This final couplet is not so simple an assertion as it looks. The poet's 'state', he says at the beginning of the poem, is 'outcast'. A 'state' of course was not just a condition of mind but also a throne, a 'chair of state'. As a player-king Shakespeare's state was 'outcast' in the sense that like all players he was kept away by a socially unbridgeable gulf from the 'lord of my love' (Sonnet 26), a particular irony if many of his playing roles entailed pretending to be a king, as Davies of Hereford said in one of his sonnets addressed to Shakespeare. He could accept the fact that his 'state' was so low like that of a player-king only by the assurance of his lord's love. Love alone can span the gulf between the player-king's and a real king's 'state'. Every sonnet written to the young aristocrat shows Shakespeare's awareness of how wide that gulf truly was.

Ratsey's gibe at the aspiration of prosperous players to knighthoods or at least to the 'Bench of Justice' would probably have been taken as an allusion to Alleyn, Burbage's peer and easily the wealthiest of the famous London players at the turn of the century. The Ratsey reference to Hamlet must apply to Burbage, so it is not unlikely that the player favoured by 'Fortune' should be Alleyn. In 1605 he was Master of the Royal Game (or Bear-warden), a post that Henslowe's father had held before him, and he was already laying plans for the foundation of his great benefaction, Dulwich College. Alleyn failed in his ambition for a knighthood,[5] though in 1610 he did become a churchwarden, a position carrying with it some judicial functions. His past as a player did not prevent him making his second marriage in 1623 to a daughter of the Dean of St Paul's. The fifty-two-year-old Dean, who in his days as Jack Donne had seen *Tamburlaine* and therefore presumably Alleyn on the London stage (in *The Calme*, line 33, he speaks of seeing Bajazeth in his cage), was less than amiable to his sixty-year-old son-in-law, but the quarrels were built on financial grounds rather than social.

James's fund-raising with such devices as his notorious £30 knighthoods at the beginning of his reign had confirmed the extent to which money was a major determinant of status. In 1630 Charles found a new source of income by fining those subjects with annual incomes of £40 a year who had not taken up knighthoods at the time of his coronation in 1625. One subject reluctant to have honour thrust upon him in such a fashion was a Cuthbert Burbage, almost certainly Richard's brother and still a proprietor of the Blackfriars and Globe.[6] If your source of income was from plays, under Charles it was no barrier to the purchase of gentility.

2. FAMOUS CLOWNS

To locate players in the well-defined strata of Elizabethan and Jacobean society we should look first at the relationships of the great players to great nobles. Phillip Sidney was not ashamed to be godfather to the son of Richard Tarlton, the clown, and when Burbage died in 1619 the Earl of Pembroke wrote to the Earl of Carlisle that he had stayed away from a play at Court 'which I being tender-harted could not endure to see so soone after the loss of my old acquaintance Burbadg'.[7] On the other hand one of the signatories to the petition of residents that prevented the Burbages and their company from moving into the Blackfriars playhouse in 1596 was their own patron, Lord Hunsdon, shortly to become the Lord Chamberlain himself.[8] Some at least of the lords of society were not prepared to tolerate the antics and dispositions of the public players except at a distance from home, and there is no evidence that many common players ever rose beyond their immediate circumstances in the tiring-houses and taverns of London and the provinces. It is probably not an overstatement to say that to the aristocracy they were at best befriended parasites, and servants in more than just their official name.

Something of the history of acting as well as actors can be found in the careers of the famous players. The first great names of the 1580s were the clowns of extempore, Tarlton and Robert Wilson, whose fame far exceeded that of their contemporary straight actors in the Queen's Men, Bentley and Knell. By 1600 the position was reversed, and the reputations as tragedians of Alleyn and Burbage dominated the theatre world. In 1599 Kemp jigged his way out of the 'world',[9] and his successor Armin was renowned as a playwright as much as a clown. Subsequently fame fell not so much on the tragedians who inherited Alleyn's and Burbage's famous roles, Perkins, Fowler or Taylor, as on the actor-managers like Beeston or actor-playwrights like Nathan Field. First the witty entertainers, next the great tragedians, lastly the impresarios. Like gentility, fame increasingly proved to be a commercial consideration.

Tarlton was not only a stage clown but a man of many parts, a maker of plays and ballads, a drummer, tumbler and qualified Master of Fencing.[10] He became famous in the 1570s, a byword in the 1580s, and a popular legend for a century after his death with his extemporised jests. Howes's additions to Stowe's *Annales* in 1615 characterise his facility as 'a wondrous plentifull pleasant extemporall wit' as distinct from that of his fellow member of the Queen's and fellow playwright Robert Wilson, whose wit was 'quicke delicate refined extemporall' (p. 697). Tarlton's 1585 play, *The Seven Deadly Sins*,

Illustration 15. Richard Tarlton, dressed in a clown's rustic apparel, carrying his pipe
and tabor. From a sepia wash drawing in the Pepysian Library, Cambridge.

enormously popular though it was, has not survived in print (we have only
the 'plot' of the second part), and the bulk of the evidence for his facility
appears in the numerous jestbooks published after his death and purporting
to record the witticisms of his life. Jestbooks were extremely popular reading
fare in the sixteenth century, and since the usual practice of fathering comic
tales on semi-legendary wits like Skelton was also applied to Tarlton few of
the anecdotes can be relied on. Fortunately some of his jokes were distinctive
enough to be repeated by more reputable authorities than the jestbook
writers. John Manningham noted one he heard, in his *Diary*, (1602):

Tarlton called Burley House gate in the Strand towardes the Savoy, the Lord
Treasurers Almes gate, because it was seldom or never opened.[11]

This was very likely heard at second or third hand, if not at a further remove, since Manningham noted it fourteen years after Tarlton's death. Henry Peacham (*Truth of our Times* (1638)) told one at first hand:

I remember when I was a schoolboy in *London, Tarlton* acted a third son's part ... His father being a very rich man, and lying upon his death-bed, called his three sonnes about him ... To the third, which was *Tarlton* (who came like a rogue in a foule shirt without a band, and in a blew coat with one sleeve, his stockings out at the heeles, and his head full of straw and feathers), as for you, Sirrah, quoth he, you know how often I have fetched you out of *Moorgate* and *Bridwell*, you have beene an ungracious villaine. I have nothing to bequeath to you but the gallowes and a rope. *Tarlton* weeping, and sobbing upon his knees (as his brothers) said, O Father, I doe not desire it, I trust in God you shall live to enjoy it your selfe.[12]

The reply may or may not have been extempore; certainly Tarlton's reputation did not entirely rest on his ability to extemporise. He is described as having a squint eye and a flat nose, and his very appearance, as Peacham also noted, was often funny enough:

Tarlton when his head was onely seene,
The Tire-house dore and Tapistrie betweene,
Set all the multitude in such a laughter,
They could not hold for scarse an houre after.[13]

As early as 1592 Nashe in *Pierce Penilesse* had described a similar reaction and its consequences when the Queen's company was in the country;

A tale of a wise Justice. Amongst other cholericke wise Justices, he was one, that having a play presented before him and his Towneship by *Tarlton* and the rest of his fellowes, her Majesties servants, and they were now entring into their first merriment (as they call it), the people began exceedingly to laugh, when *Tarlton* first peept out his head. Whereat the Justice, not a little moved, and seeing with his beckes and nods hee could not make them cease, he went with his staffe, and beat them round about unmercifully on the bare pates, in that they, being but Farmers & poore countrey Hyndes, would presume to laugh at the Queenes men, and make no more account of her cloath in his presence.[14]

Tarlton's compeer, Wilson, a more scholarly wit, played in the same company with him.[15] Evidently the value of having extemporising wits and versifiers in the group was sufficient to justify two such performers sharing the same performance. Wilson also spent some time with Leicester's Men, touring the Netherlands with them in 1585–6, when he shared his work with 'my lord of Lesters jesting plaier', as Sidney described him, Will Kemp, the clown who later became the resident extemporising comedian in Shakespeare's company and probably the first actor of Falstaff.[16]

Illustration 16. Will Kemp jigging his way to Norwich in 1599 dressed as a morris dancer, with his accompanist. From the titlepage of *Kempes Nine Daies Wonder*, 1600.

Kemp was the last of the famous Elizabethan clowns. He was better known for harlequinade and jigs than wit, and probably served his turn mainly for the dances and jigging sketches that normally followed performances on the public stages. He is rightly or wrongly thought to have been the culprit charged by Hamlet with speaking more than was set down for him, and it has even been suggested that his departure from the Chamberlain's Men in 1599 was because he took a hand in the illicit publication of the last Falstaff play, *The Merry Wives of Windsor*.[17] What is clear is that the role of the clown in adult company plays had diminished markedly in value as plays began to offer more scope for the tragic actors. Hamlet's reprimand reflects an aristocratic impatience with knockabout and extempore. Kemp's duties as a clown with a role in almost every play of his company's repertory probably did not decline, but his occupancy of the stage during the performance proper may have shrunk. The parts we know he played include Peter in *Romeo and Juliet* and Dogberry in *Much Ado*, where he was given no more than a couple of scenes in which to indulge himself. If he played Falstaff, it was a distinct and major development in his repertoire of parts.

His successor in the company had markedly different talents. Robert Armin was a playwright as Tarlton and Wilson had been, but much less an extemporiser. He was known for his singing rather than his wit. Where Shakespeare had written Falstaff and Dogberry with Kemp in mind, for Armin he produced Feste and Lear's Fool.[18] Feste's song that closes *Twelfth*

Illustration 17. Robert Armin, from the titlepage of his *The Two Maids of More-clacke*, 1609.

Night was his radically softer version of the jigs that Kemp was famous for and which he had sung and danced for the finale of the company's performances. Both Kemp and Armin claimed descent from Tarlton, but between 1580 and 1600 the inheritance had dropped sharply in value. Alleyn's Tamburlaine now bestrode the stage.

3. FAMOUS TRAGEDIANS

Alleyn was born in 1566, the son of a London 'innholder'. Possibly his father's occupation brought him into early contact with the players, for he was already with a leading company, Worcester's, when he was sixteen. By 1592 he was the outstanding player of his day. As Henslowe's son-in-law and business partner both in theatrical affairs and in their bull- and bear-baiting business he rose to an unparalleled prosperity, not only for himself but for the reputation of the stage as a whole. He became famous as Tamburlaine, Faustus and Barabbas in Marlowe's plays, as Orlando in *Orlando Furioso*, Muly Mahamet in *The Battle of Alcazar* and Tamar Cam in the play of that name.[19] His 'stalking Tamburlaine' drew similes from several pamphleteers at the end of the century. His own self-mocking name for himself in a family letter was 'the fustian king'.[20] Fuller remembered him as 'the Roscius of our age, so acting to the life, that he made any part (especially a majestick one) to become him' (*Worthies*, 1662, Fff2v). He made a speech as Genius standing on the Londinium arch for King James's triumphal parade through London in 1604. Dekker records that 'his gratulatory speech was delivered with excellent Action, and a well tun'de, audible voyce' (*The Magnificent Entertainment*, 1604, C1). Early in the new century Alleyn gave himself up wholly to his business interests, retaining his share in the Admiral's Men but as manager rather than player. In about 1605, the year of Ratsey's anecdote when he was thirty-nine, he began negotiations to purchase the manor of Dulwich and in 1613 as a work of piety started to establish the school and hospital which have since become Dulwich College. The property cost £10,000 initially, and subsequent expenditure was about £1,700 a year, all of which derived in the first instance from Alleyn's theatrical and bear-baiting interests.[21] He and his College were the age's highwater mark for both the commercial and the more pietistic respectability of his first profession.

The name linked with Alleyn's by the early historians of the Elizabethan stage as the greatest of its players was of course Richard Burbage. Richard Baker's *Chronicle* (1674) celebrates '*Richard Bourbidge* and *Edward Allen*, two such Actors as no age must ever look to see the like'.[22] Two years younger than Alleyn, Burbage was a son of the impresario who built the Theatre in 1576, and first appears at the age of twenty-three, named in a lawsuit as defending his father's takings. He protected them with a broomstick when the deponents came to collect their share in accordance with a Chancery Court order, and

scornfully and disdainfully playing with this deponent's nose, said that if he dealt in the matter, he would beat him also, and did challenge the field of him at that time.[23]

Most likely he was then in Alleyn's company with the Strange's group of 1590. He probably left them for Pembroke's after this, as we have seen, and reappeared with the new Chamberlain's Men in 1594 as their leading actor and a major shareholder.[24] When James Burbage died in 1597 he left his empty Blackfriars property to Richard and the forlorn Theatre to his elder brother Cuthbert.

Burbage seems to have been far less commercially minded than Alleyn. He avoided the temptations of managership and remained in acting until his death in 1619, when he left his wife according to contemporary rumour 'better than £300 land',[25] which though considerable for his day hardly compares with Alleyn's holdings or even with those of his fellow player Shakespeare in Stratford. He was fifty when he died, by which time he had made famous such roles as Richard III, Hamlet, Lear, Othello and Ferdinand in Webster's *Duchess of Malfi*. His name appears in all the King's Men's plays for which lists of players survive between 1599 and 1618. He was Ratsey's Hamlet as Alleyn was the one hoping to be knighted.

In the second decade of the seventeenth century Nathan Field came to rival Burbage in fame. Jonson linked the two names in *Bartholomew Fair* in 1613, and Richard Flecknoe in a retrospective comment in 1664 spoke of them as the leading players at the time when Jonson, Shakespeare and Beaumont and Fletcher were the leading playwrights. 'It was the happiness of the Actors of those Times to have such Poets as these to instruct them and write for them; and no less of those Poets, to have such docile and excellent Actors to Act their Playes, as a *Field* and *Burbidge*.'[26] Field, the son of a major churchman who spoke out strongly against playing, was a contemporary of Burbage in the King's Men for the last four years of his life, and died only a few months after him. His fame was not entirely for playing. He died a bachelor with a considerable reputation, of the kind not uncommon among players, for success with women. A story circulating in 1619 reckoned that the Earl of Argyll had paid 'for the nourseing of a childe which the worlde says is a daughter to my lady and N. Feild the Player'.[27]

After Burbage and Field died the names that became most prominent in theatre affairs were those of such men as Beeston and Richard Gunnell, who was a leading player with Palsgrave's in 1622 – Alleyn leased the rebuilt Fortune to the company with Gunnell and Charles Massey as the chief sharers – and who built the third of the indoor playhouses, the Salisbury Court, in 1629. In their years as impresarios Gunnell and Beeston did not involve themselves in playing, so far as we know. Joseph Taylor, who did, and who took over Burbage's roles in the King's Men, became celebrated for his good relationships especially with Henrietta Maria, Charles's queen. It was even rumoured that he might get a knighthood for his work for royalty, although it never happened.

The chief fame of the last years was mainly reserved first of all for the King's Men's trio of Taylor, Lowin and Swanston, and then for the clowns of the leading companies – John Shanks at the Blackfriars, Timothy Reade at Salisbury Court and Andrew Cane at the Fortune. In a number of ways the notes we have on them curiously echo the praise given to the clowns of the 1580s. Shanks's fame was for his knockabout and dancing, as was Cane's. The latter was remembered for his closing jigs as late as 1673, when Henry Chapman excused the presence of an appendix in his pamphlet by saying it was the fashion, 'Without which a Pamphlet now a dayes, finds as small

Illustration 18. John Lowin, from a portrait in the Ashmolean Museum. His age is
marked as sixty-three, which indicates that the portrait was painted in 1639–40, about
the time he was playing Falstaff along with serious and soldierly characters such
as King Henry in *Henry VIII* and Melantius in *The Maid's Tragedy*.

acceptance as a Comedy did formerly, at the *Fortune* Play-house, without
a Jig of *Andrew Kein's* into the bargain'.[28] Reade is linked with Cane in
a pamphlet of 1641, *'The Stage-Players Complaint*, in a Pleasant Dialogue
between Cane of the *Fortune* and Reed of the *Friers* [i.e. Whitefriars, or
Salisbury Court]'. In the pamphlet Cane is called *'Quick'* and described as
able to 'outstrip facetious Mercury in your tongue', while Reade is *'Light'*,
and described as nimble-footed, with heels 'as light as a *Finches* Feather'.
Reade seems to have used the trick of poking his head through the hangings
that covered the central opening and making faces that Tarlton used
according to Nashe's anecdote. In Goffe's *The Careless Shepherdess* (1656)
a character reminisces

> I never saw *Rheade* peeping through the Curtain,
> But ravishing joy enter'd into my heart

and claims to have preferred Reade's 'Craps and Quibbles' to 'the gravest speech in all the *Play*'.[29]

In noting the memories of the last decade of the Shakespearean tradition of acting it is also worth remembering the French actors whom Beeston entertained as part of his flattery of Henrietta Maria in 1629 and 1635. Their acting struck their London audiences as exaggerated. In Glapthorne's *The Lady's Privilege* (1640), a character describes them as inclined to affectation:

> Very ayry people, who participate
> More fire than earth; yet generally good,
> And nobly disposition'd, something inclining
> To overweening fancy.

The same character then demonstrates their playing by mimicking a 'Comick scene', in which he '*Acts furiously*' (2.1).

4. STYLES OF ACTING

We have already taken note of the metatheatrical games that grew out of the anxious self-consciousness of players acting roles that did not match their social status as 'common' players. The forms of such stage realism as there was exploited spectacle more than voice or gesture. Even Alleyn's 'strutting and bellowing' evoked comments on his swaggering style in his own time. So the question of degrees of affectation or 'furious' exaggeration in acting raises another matter in our consideration of players and playing, how the boy companies acted, and what difference may have existed between their playing and that of the adults.

To begin with we must distinguish between the boys of the boy companies and the boy trainees of the adult companies. Originally the backgrounds of the two kinds of boy player were quite different. The boys bound to adult players were committed for a period of several years' training in their profession before graduating at seventeen or so and apprenticed to such sharers as were 'free of the City' as members of a guild like John Hemminges, and then hired men, and eventually perhaps sharers in their company. They entered their bonds between the ages of ten and thirteen, usually playing the women's parts which their small stature and unbroken voices equipped them for. The most positive instances we have show that one boy carried on playing women's parts until he was at least twenty-one, while another had changed to men's parts by nineteen. There was no set pattern, and nothing quite like the seven-year apprenticeships that youths in the guilds went through from the age of seventeen before rising to the status of journeyman.[30] According to his brother's account Richard Burbage must have been acting male parts by the time he was that age,[31] and Alleyn was already outstanding by sixteen.

The boys of the children's companies on the other hand acted only with their own age group and were trained and directed not by their fellow players but by the managers for whose profit they worked. In 1599 and 1600 they came into existence as a venture backed by a tradition of boy playing in the choir-school companies older and far more respectable than that which the professional adult players had behind them. In actual fact by 1576, when Farrant started the Chapel Children at the first Blackfriars, their contribution to the Court Revels had already diminished and the once predominant chorister function had been separated off altogether from the playing. They were already frankly commercial, though the bland pretence to be rehearsing for her majesty's pleasure was retained as an obvious bulwark against hostile local authorities.

Between the boy company actors and the boy players in the adult companies there was no difference of interest, though there was some difference of organisation, since instead of being bound to individual sharers as in the adult companies the boy company players were all bound to their manager.[32] The major difference lay in their educational backgrounds. The descendants of the chorister groups gave performances normally less than twice a week, and some at least of the remaining time not given to rehearsing was given over to formal education. When Paul's discreetly closed down in 1606 the boys who did not join the other company returned to their nominal occupations without great difficulty. The production of plays by boy actors had always been a schoolmaster's art, and the pupils of the best schoolmasters were anxiously sought after by the managers; in some cases too anxiously, as we know from the case of the kidnapped Thomas Clifton, who was a pupil at Christ Church school in London. Most of Evans's boys probably came from St Paul's Grammar School, where Nathan Field was certainly a pupil. He was then thirteen, and evidently already an expertly trained player. The Master of St Paul's School was Richard Mulcaster, celebrated for several decades for the shows his boys produced at Court and elsewhere. The Citizen's Wife in *The Knight of the Burning Pestle* asks one of the boy players (of the Blackfriars company) if he is not one of 'Maister *Monkesters* scholars' evidently a matter for some pride. Richard Brinsley, another schoolmaster, wrote a book in 1612 called *Ludus Literarius*, praising the value of playing in the education of schoolchildren.

The background of even the post-1599 boy companies was therefore more academic than that of the professional adult players, and their training accordingly was probably not so much in pure acting practice as in the declamatory arts of rhetoric, specifically pronunciation and gesture. Acting in plays was customary in many schools in the sixteenth century as a tail on the necessary dog of their practice in oratory. The growth of commercial interests made the acting tail wag the educational dog but the link between the two was not entirely severed in the process.[33] Heywood in his *Apology for Actors* (1612) cited his own experience at Cambridge as a major argument of his lengthy justification of his profession.

In the time of my residence in *Cambridge*, I have seen Tragedyes, Comedyes, Historyes, Pastorals and Shewes, publicly acted, in which Graduates of good place and reputation, have bene specially parted: this is held necessary for the embolden-ing of their Junior schollers, to arme them with audacity, against they come to bee imployed in any publicke exercise, as in the reading of Dialectike, Rhetoricke, Ethicke, Mathematicke, the Physicke, or Metaphysicke Lectures. It teacheth audac-ity to the bashfull Grammarian, beeing newly admitted into the private Colledge, and after matriculated and entred as a member of the University, and makes him a bold Sophister, to argue *pro et contra*, to compose his Sillogismes, Cathegoricke, or Hypotheticke (simple or compound) to reason and frame a sufficient argument to prove his questions, or to defend any *axioma*, to distinguish of any Dilemma & be able to moderate in any Argumentation whatsoever. (C3v)

Readers of the *Parnassus* plays put on by Cambridge students at the turn of the century might feel Heywood's argument to be improbably pious; but this background of formal education in the decorums of speech and its attendant gestures must have had its effect on the theatrical foreground.[34]

We cannot be sure how rare was the transition that brought Nathan Field, Underwood and Ostler into the leading adult companies, but Field at least was outstanding among his adult brethren, in part for his learning. His four years with the King's Men were put to use not only as an actor but as a playwright. His educational background was far ahead of such professional players as copied out playbooks in the 1590s.[35] The classical learning even of players competent enough at writing to transcribe a playbook was so deficient that they cannot be assumed to have had much schooling of any kind, let alone training in rhetoric, which usually started fairly well on in the Elizabethan school curriculum. One of Alleyn's wryer protests to his father-in-law, Dr Donne, claimed that his education had not been in sophistry:

Before this violence brake forth you called me a plain man. I desire always to be so for I thank God I could never disguise in my life and I am too old now to learn rhetoric of the curiousest school in Christendom.[36]

By 'disguise' of course he meant dishonest misrepresentation or dissimulation, not the sort of disguise he had exploited in 1595 in plays like *The Blind Beggar of Alexandria*.

Many playgoers must have been aware of the distinction between the unschooled professionals on the one hand, whose traditions descended from the poor players touring and tumbling for a living only slightly better than vagabondage, and the academically tutored schoolchildren on the other, trained as they were in the long tradition of Quintilian's rhetoric with its emphasis on careful speech and studied gesture. The social and educational difference provides one reason why the playwrights who produced material for the boy companies in the years after 1600, particularly Marston and Chapman, regularly gave their little eyasses lines to belabour the common players with. Marston gave Paul's Boys in 1600 a chance to demand (in *Antonio's Revenge* 1.5):

> Would'st have me turn rank mad,
> Or wring my face with mimick action;
> Stampe, curse, weepe, rage, & then my bosome strike?
> Away tis apish action, player-like.

And again in 1605 (*Sophonisba* 4.1, acted by the Blackfriars Boys):

> I should now curse the Gods
> Call on the furies: stampe the patient earth
> cleave my streachd cheeks with sound speake from all sense
> But *loud and full* of players eloquence
> No, no, What shall we eate.

Loud speeches full of player's eloquence were what Alleyn had only recently stopped producing at the Fortune. Chapman similarly gave the boys an attack on exaggerated acting in his comedy *The Widow's Tears* in about 1605, also acted by the Blackfriars Children.

This straine of mourning with Sepulcher, like an over-doing Actor, affects grosly, and is indeede so farr forct from the life, that it bewraies it selfe to be altogether artificiall. (4.1.)

Given the open metatheatricality of playing where the audience surrounded the players and at the indoor theatres even sat on the stage with them, acting 'to the life' was of course intrinsically a more 'artificiall' business for boys acting men's parts than it was for the men themselves. It would be understandable for the boys to bolster their own performances by using the academically approved conceptions of what was natural, and by that yardstick to criticise the acting of the adults that exceeded their capacities. Equally,

of course, there may be a hint of sour grapes in their distaste for the adult fustian
kings and for the excesses of the 'stalking-stamping Player, that will raise a
tempest with his toung, and thunder with his heeles' (*The Puritan*, 1607, 3.4,
acted by Paul's). At the least the Blackfriars Boys seem to have developed a very
emphatic preference for satirical prose comedy over the fustian verse plays with
which in their earliest days they tried to match the adults.

Cynthia's Revels, the first play the Blackfriars boys commissioned from
Jonson in 1600, contains a large number of instructions to the boys how they
should act, and offers as good a guide as any to what a judicious bystander
such as Jonson felt they could do. They are advised to 'studie to be like cracks
[i.e. crackropes, boy players]; practise … language, and behaviours, and not
with a dead imitation: act freely, carelessly, and capriciously, as if our veines
ranne with quick-silver.' Amorphus, probably played by Field, at one point
(2.3) demonstrates to his fellows 'the particular, and distinct face of every your
most noted *species* of persons, as your marchant, your scholer, your souldier,
your lawyer, courtier, &c. and each of these so truly, as you would sweare,
but that your eye shal see the variation of the lineament, it were my most
proper, and genuine aspect'. In the same play 3.5 becomes a full-scale rehearsal
scene, a coaching session in acting run by Amorphus. Jonson's opinion of
the capacities of the player of Amorphus was evidently high and of a kind
to suggest that the boy company strictures on 'player' acting as 'stalking-
stamping' were easily justified condemnations of exaggeration.

Condemnations of exaggerated acting, however, were not confined to the
boys of 1600–8. Shakespeare gave Burbage as Hamlet the most famous
condemnation of all in 1600, when the eyasses were beginning to carry it
away. He followed that up with Ulysses's speech in *Troilus and Cressida* about
the 'strutting player whose conceit / Lies in his hamstring, and doth think it
rich / To hear the wooden dialogue and sound, / Twixt his stretched footing
and the scaffoldage' (1.3.153–6), which might be construed as stalking-stamping.
Shakespeare had produced a detailed account of over-acting much earlier than
this in *Richard III*, where Buckingham says contemptuously (3.5.5–11):

> Tut, I can counterfeit the deep tragedian,
> Speak and look back, and pry on every side,
> Tremble and start at wagging of a straw:
> Intending deep suspicion, ghastly looks
> Are at my service, like enforced smiles;
> And both are ready in their offices,
> At any time, to grace my strategems.

We might of course suspect that as always in theatre the academic teaching
of pronunciation and gesture was less useful to either the boys or the adults

than a direct eye on nature.[37] If anything I suspect the orators learned these aspects of their occupation from the players rather than the reverse. The relationship was certainly described on that assumption by an anonymous writer in 1616 (T. G., *The Rich Cabinet*), who claimed that

as an Orator was most forcible in his ellocution; so was an actor in his gesture and personated action. (Q4r)

For us the really important thing in the relationship between oratory and acting is its effect on the terminology used to describe acting, and some of the implications of the changes in terminology.

In the sixteenth century 'acting' was occasionally used as a verbal form of the noun generally used for the 'action' of the orator, his art of gesture. What the common stages offered was mere 'playing'.[38] From this distinction came Jonson's bitter jibe when he inscribed on the titlepage of *The New Inn* that his play was 'never acted, but most negligently play'd, by some, the Kings Servants'. That the academic term 'acting' should become so completely the prerogative of the common players as it did early in the seventeenth century is a quite striking testimony to the growth of their predominance over the orators, who were to a large degree their direct competitors in church pulpits. More significantly perhaps what the players were presenting on stage became distinctive enough to require a wholly new term to describe it. This term, the noun 'personation', suggests that a relatively new art of individual characterisation had begun to develop, an art distinct from the orator's display of passions or the academic actor's portrayal of the character-types described by Jonson in *Cynthia's Revels* and by earlier academic playwrights such as Richard Edwardes in the prologue to his *Damon and Pithias* (1565). The author of the comparison between oratory and acting quoted above spoke of the player's 'personated action'; Heywood's *Apology for Actors* specified that the good actor should 'qualifie everything according to the nature of the person personated' (C4r). Even the author of a puritanical reply to Heywood (I. G., *A Refutation of the Apology for Actors* (1615)) told a story in which a 'jesting-Plaier ... so truely counterfeited every thing, that it seemed to bee the very persons whom he acted' (E3v).

Gradually the term 'personation' became the word to praise actors with. For all the pulpit fulminations against illusionism, the essential virtue of the character of 'An Excellent Actor' was held to be that 'what we see him personate, we thinke truely done before us'. *The Oxford English Dictionary* records the first use of the term 'personation' in the Induction to Marston's *Antonio and Mellida*, a play crammed with neologisms, written probably in 1599–1600, at the end of the great decade in which Alleyn and Burbage made their reputations.[39] It is not stretching plausibility too far to suggest that the term was called into being by the same developments – in the kinds of part given the actors to play and their own skill in their parts – that made two great tragedians succeed the extemporising clowns on the pinnacle of theatrical fame. By 1600 Burbage's Hamlet exemplified the chief requisite of a successful player, his ability to characterize.

To know that natural acting, 'counterfeiting' nature and playing a part 'to the life' or with 'lively action' became the Elizabethan player's aim[40] is not necessarily to know just how anyone cautious of illusionism would have performed his part on stage. Such descriptions as we have of Elizabethan displays of feeling do not entirely correspond with the postures the same feelings evoke today. The paralinguistic language of gesture is almost as conventional and capable of change as ordinary language, and therefore almost as liable to change as are spoken forms. In Field's *Amends for Ladies* (1616) 1.1, a gentleman complains that his mistress does not take his love seriously because he uses the wrong actions:

> 'cause I doe not weepe,
> Lay mine arms ore my heart, and weare no garters,
> Walke with mine eyes in my hat, sigh, and make faces.

Field himself in his portrait is shown with his hand on his heart, perhaps acknowledging his success as a lover in life. Like the other gestures it looks strident to a modern eye. So too are the poses described by the 'country man' who composed *The Cyprian Conqueror* in about 1633 and wrote a preface instructing the potential actors of his play how to perform:

The other parts of action, is in ye gesture, wch must be various, as required; as in a sorrowfull parte, ye head must hang downe; in a proud, ye head must bee lofty; in an amorous, closed eies, hanging downe lookes, & crossed armes, in a hastie, fuming, & scratching ye head &c …[41]

Still, the difference between then and now was probably on the whole not too great. In 1644 a teacher of the deaf, John Bulwer, produced a manual of what he called with unconscious irony the 'Natural language of the hand', with illustrations to show the paralinguistic gesture appropriate to each emotion (*Chirologia* and *Chironomia*, 1644).[42] The thoughtful man is shown scratching his head, threats are made with a shaking of the clenched fist, a finger on the lips asks for silence, and oaths are sworn with raised palm, much as one might expect today if one were to seek out gestures with which to mime such processes. Of Bulwer's various illustrations, one hundred and twenty in all, perhaps twenty would not still be readily recognisable to a modern English audience.

Illustration 19. Gestures for miming, from John Bulwer's treatise for the deaf, *Chirologia, or the Naturall Language of the Hand* (1644), p. 255.

Such gestures might also be recognised today as rather more appropriate to mime than to acting. Bulwer was writing not for the stage but for the orator. He wrote from the standpoint of the inventor of a sign-language for the deaf, his illustrations belonging more properly with dumb-show than acting with words. When the Player Queen in *Hamlet* '*makes passionate Action*' of grief during the dumb-show (3.2.134) she in all probability raised her joined hands to heaven just in the way Bulwer's sorrowful orator does. That Queen Gertrude in the play proper was expected to do the same seems unlikely.

By the time *Hamlet* was written, in fact, 'Pantomimick action' was openly being condemned as old-fashioned. Thomas Campion in his *Book of Airs* (1601) spoke contemptuously of old-fashioned academic acting, the

old exploided action in Comedies, when if they did pronounce *Memeni*, they would point to the hinder parts of their heads, if *Video*, put their finger in their eye. But such childish observing of words is altogether ridiculous. (B2v)

And in 1602 Thomas Tomkis showed that it looked dated even in Cambridge, where plays in Latin were still performed, when in his student play *Lingua* he produced an affected young man called Phantastes who tries to show his peers how to 'pronounce'.

PHA[NTASTES]. Pish, pish this is a speech with no action, lets here Terence: *quid igitur faciam, &c*

COM[EDUS]. *Quid igitur faciam? non eam ne nunc quidam cum accusor ultro?*

PHA. Phy, phy, phy, no more action, lend me your baies, doe it thus. *Quid igitur, &c.*

He acts it after the old kinde of Pantomimick action

COM[MUNIS]SEN[SUS]. I shold judge this action *Phantastes* most absurd: unles we should come to a Commedy, as gentlewomen to the commencement, only to see men speake. (4.2)

Men's body language is more attractive than what they say. Tomkis at least, one presumes, used his ears as well as his eyes, and would have listened to his Shakespeare as well as watching him. Bulwer's concern was primarily with the academic schooling of orators and teachers of the deaf so that their audiences could literally 'see men speake'.

Certain conventions of gesture on the Elizabethan stage clearly did differ from what would be familiar today. They were the shorthand of stage presentation, and in a packed repertory with plays performed at high speed there can have been little chance for deeply studied portrayals of emotions at work. There were many ways of utilising such a shorthand.[43] Conventions like love at first sight had an established way to convey them on stage. Marston evidently knew of one, since in *The Insatiate Countess* (1607–8) he sets down at one point the bald stage direction '*Isabella fals in love.*' Some method of presentation involving mimed gestures was necessary in such cases, especially with love at first sight, since it usually struck the lover dumb.[44] Another convention that seems less than natural today though it was basic to metatheatrical practice is the tradition of direct address to the audience. Falstaff's catechism on honour is a relic of the clown's tradition of 'interloquutions with the Audients'.[45] Like explanatory prologues, the self-revelatory soliloquy or aside to the audience was a relic of the less sophisticated days that developed into a useful and more naturalistic convention of thinking aloud, but it never entirely ceased to be a theatre convention.[46]

Shorthand in the conventions of body language that mimed the internal passion must have been essential to the Elizabethan actor. The repertory was hardly ever the same two days running, and opportunities for rehearsal can have been few in comparison with modern standards. With a part in every play, the leading players had little time for doing more while studying their parts than the essential learning of the lines. As Bernard Beckerman puts it of the Globe actor:

There was no opportunity for him to fix a role in his memory by repetition. Rarely would he play the same role two days in succession. Even in the most popular role he would not appear more than twice in one week, and then only in the first month or two of the play's stage life. The consequences of such a strenuous repertory were twofold. First, the actor had to cultivate a fabulous memory and devote much of his time to memorization; various plays testify to the scorn of the playwright for the actor who is out of his part. Secondly, the actor had to systematize his methods of portrayal and of working with his colleagues.[47]

The Chamberlain's Servants had barely more than a day to revive the defunct *Richard II* for performance when the Essex conspirators paid them to do so in 1601. In 1633, when the Master of the Revels stopped them from performing Fletcher's *The Tamer Tamed* on the morning of the day the performance was advertised for, the King's Men replaced it with *The Scornful Lady* that same morning.[48] In such rushed conditions when changes had to be made at extremely short notice a player's mindset guaranteed the use of stock poses. These conditions of performance would also have reinforced the practice of allocating parts according to acting types. Such procedures would have reduced the strain on the actor's ability to 'personate' and left him to concentrate as he had to on remembering his lines.

One question given too little consideration is what sort of accent the London-based players used in their speech. As travellers they were used to hearing the different dialects of the whole country, but as a company playing regularly in London they must have developed a common language that would be recognisable to all and yet more and more must have come to reflect whatever was the received pronunciation of perhaps the Court and certainly of fairly well-educated men. Most of them were Londoners (the only two immigrants in Shakespeare's company were John Heminges, born in Droitwich in Worcestershire, and Shakespeare, born in nearby Warwickshire), but London had and still has its own variety of accents.

What little evidence can be garnered from distinctive spellings suggests that, apart from Llewellyn's comic Welsh and versions of the modern 'Mummerset', a broad west-country dialect used by rustics such as the mechanicals in *A Midsummer Night's Dream*, most parts, whether spoken by courtiers or commoners, were to be delivered in a standardised and educated London form. Mummerset relished its rhoticisms, rolling its 'r's more than modern English in a relatively Americanised form of speech. Some regional accents were used for particular plays. One in particular, Day's *Isle of Gulls*, was staged by the Blackfriars boys using English and Scottish accents. There does seem to have been not just regionality in speech and vocabulary but a degree of class distinction that must have been recognised and adopted by the players. George Puttenham, in his *Arte of English Poesie* (1589), specified it as the language of the country's centre, the 'mother speech', and recommended it for poets to use. A poet must ensure that his or her language

be naturall, pure, and the most usuall of all his countrey: and for the same purpose rather that which is spoken in the kings Court, or in the good townes and Cities within the land, then in the marches and frontiers, or in port townes, where straungers haunt for traffike sake, or yet in Universities where Schollers use much peevish affectation of words out of the primative languages, or finally, in any uplandish village or corner of a Realme, where is no resort but of poore rusticall or uncivill people: neither shall he follow the speach of a craftes man or carter, or other of the inferiour sort, though he be inhabitant or bred in the best towne and Citie in this Realme, for such persons do abuse good speaches by strange accents or ill shapen soundes, and false ortographie … Neither shall he take the termes of Northern-men, such as they use in dayly talke, whether they be noble men or gentlemen, or of their best clarkes all is a matter: nor in effect any speach used beyond the river of Trent, though no man can deny but that theirs is the purer English Saxon at this day, yet it is not so Courtly nor so currant as our Southerne English is, no more is the far Westerne mans speach: ye shall therfore take the usuall speach of the Court, and that of London and the shires lying about London within lx. myles, and not much above. I say not this but that in every shyre of England there be gentlemen and others that speake but specially write as good Southerne as we of Middlesex or Surrey do, but not the common people of every shire, to whom the gentlemen, and also their learned clarkes do for the most part condescend. (fol. 120–1).

Puttenham's ring of sixty miles around London included Oxford and Cambridge, though he did suggest that the accents and vocabulary used there were undesirable in a poet. We must conclude that the plays were normally delivered in his 'good Southerne', however that sounded.[49]

5. THE REPERTORY SYSTEM

The single most characteristic feature of all the companies was their repertory system. Nothing can have shaped the nature of playing so much as having to perform a different play every day and to produce new plays at frequent intervals. In their 1594–5 season the Admiral's, performing six days a week, offered their audiences a total of thirty-eight plays of which twenty-one were new to the repertory, added at more or less fortnightly intervals. Two of the new plays were performed only once, and only eight survived through to the following year. Even the company's most popular plays by Marlowe would be put on stage not more often than once every month or so. The first part of *Tamburlaine* appears in Henslowe's records for the new company's first year fourteen times, its second part six, *Faustus* twelve, *The Massacre at Paris* ten and *The Jew of Malta* nine. The repertory in the next year, 1595–6, was again large – thirty-seven plays, of which nineteen were new – and in 1596–7 thirty-four plays were performed of which fourteen were new. The most popular play over the whole three seasons, *The Wise Men of Westchester* (*John a Kent and John a Cumber*), was performed altogether in the three years thirty-two times, less than once per month even allowing for the closures of Lent.

The Admiral's Men's appetite for new plays was at its height at this time, of course, with their new security backed by Privy Councillors, a half-monopoly of London playing, and Marlowe's plays as the most famous of the day performed by the leading player of the day, Alleyn. Their appetite slackened off markedly later on. None the less, the stringent organisation and the feats of memory required from the company would have involved a number of consistent practices that must have persisted through the whole period and that we can recognise as equally characteristic in later years. The most important of these must have been the custom of type-casting parts. It is a ready presumption that each player would have been allocated the part in each new play that most closely suited his talents. Also no player would wish to change his part in a play once he had learned it – there were enough new parts in new plays without that – so if one player left the company his successor would have to take over all his abandoned parts, and would therefore be admitted to the company on the understanding that his type sufficiently matched that of the departed player. Such a system probably explains the insistence of the company agreements on a player being reimbursed for his share in the company only if he left with his fellows' consent. Once the repertory became as intense as it was in 1594–5 sharers had duties too specific to allow easy coming and going. That helps to explain the extraordinary longevity of some players in the same companies, like Hemminges and John Lowin with the King's and Sam Rowley and Charles Massey with the Admiral's.

The most tangible testimony for such a custom is to be found in the plays written by a company's resident poet, most notably the sequence of plays written first by Shakespeare and later by the multiple authors of the Beaumont and Fletcher canon for the King's Men. Such plays written by members of the playing company could quite reasonably be presumed to have been tailored to the company's personnel and particular talents at the time of writing. A number of cast-lists that survive from the later years of the company (1623–32) confirm that presumption for at least those years. From the lists it appears that all members of the company were employed in every play, that there were consistently seven or eight major speaking parts, two or three of them for women, who were played by the boys, and that hired men never took major speaking parts.

The question of type-casting the players' roles in specific acting 'lines' has been much debated since it was first proposed and set out by T. W. Baldwin in 1927.[50] Baldwin characterised what he saw as the major kinds of role, and tried to fit the later King's players to them. Heroes would be played by Burbage and later Joseph Taylor, tyrants or burly soldiers by John Lowin, smooth villains by Eyllaerdt Swanston, dignitaries or aged kings by Robert Benfield, young lovers by Richard Sharpe and comic figures by Thomas Pollard. By this casting John Shanks, the chief clown, did not figure prominently in the cast-lists, leading Baldwin to the assumption that he was generally left to his own devices.[51] This bland interpretation of the repertory system and consistent type-casting of parts has been rightly challenged on the ground that Baldwin used the evidence too sloppily, and that he tried to press a pattern of nineteenth-century repertory practices onto seventeenth-century conditions. It is certainly true that Baldwin's ascription of 'lines' to particular players is overconfident and inaccurate. In the few cases where the parts that players took are known precisely there is certainly not the consistency of type-casting that he tried to make the evidence show. The repertory system in its first stable years of the 1590s had the sort of intensity that would have preferred specific type-casting, but it is likely that in later years the speed and the intensity eased off, inviting a rather more relaxed approach to the allocation of roles.

Nonetheless by modern standards the repertory system was always intense. So long as each day needed a different play some systematisation would have been unavoidable. The same players had to take one or more parts in a different play each afternoon with very little time for rehearsal.[52] They had to provide every speaking part in the different plays, and the most regular way of allocating the parts would have been by type-casting. Hamlet's account of the players who come to Elsinore anticipates some such distribution of typical roles:

> He that plays the king shall be welcome; his majesty shall have tribute of me; the adventurous knight shall use his foil and target, the lover shall not sigh gratis, the humorous man shall end his part in peace, the clown shall make those laugh whose lungs are tickle o'th' sere, and the lady shall say her mind freely – or the blank verse shall halt for't. (2.2.298–302).

On the other hand we might note Webster's praise of 'an excellent actor' for his versatility. 'All men have been of his occupation,' says Webster, 'and indeed, what hee doth fainedly that doe others essentially: this day one plaies a Monarch, the next a private person. Heere one Acts a Tyrant, on the morrow an Exile.'[53] But Webster is playing games with the world as a stage here, and his comment is focused more on the changes in life than on the stage. It is more to the point to consider the likely effects of doubling, and the limits that such a practice would necessarily impose on type-casting. We know that John Sincler played five parts in the Strange's Men's *2 The Seven Deadly Sins*, while Richard Cowley, later to play Verges in *Much Ado*, took seven. Players taking so many parts could not readily be type-cast. Consistent type-casting of the major roles is the easiest way to cope with the demands of any repertory system, but it could not have been an invariable practice. The illness or absence from the company of a single player or perhaps someone's fit of pique in rehearsal might easily cause a square player to be cast in a round part.

All that can be said positively about the likelihood of type-casting is that one of the values of the sharer system was to provide insurance against the casual absence of any of the leading players from the company and consequent shifts in casting. Henslowe no doubt had that sort of motive in mind as well as some milk of human kindness when he advanced William

Bird's wife £3 to get her husband out of prison, where he had been put 'for hurting of a felowe which brought his wiffe a leatter' (*Diary*, p. 83). Marital concord free from prison and availability for playing set roles went together.

What we know of the sharer system and the careers of individual sharers does seem to indicate that they recognised fairly distinct playing types, although the clowns were always a distinct entity. New sharers joining a company took on the parts of the players they replaced. Joseph Taylor joined the King's Men shortly before May 1619 to replace Richard Burbage who died in March of that year, and certainly took over several of Burbage's parts.[54] Benfield joined the company in 1615 most likely to replace William Ostler, who died at the end of the previous year, and took over his part as Antonio in *The Duchess of Malfi*. There was certainly consistency in casting and consequently in the tying of particular parts to particular players. On the other hand early in the seventeenth century the King's company was enlarged from eight sharers to ten and then to twelve, and with the larger numbers to draw on the allocation of roles must have become easier. Some sharers seem never to have taken major parts. Shakespeare was not celebrated for his playing apart from a joke by Davies of Hereford in *The Scourge of Folly* (1610) about his kingly roles. It is also true that the many non-resident poets who did not know the company well or who did not know in advance which company would buy their work could not have written parts with specific players in mind as Shakespeare was able to do. Some plays, possibly Shakespeare's, possibly Jonson's for the Blackfriars boys and possibly the later plays by Fletcher and Massinger for the King's Men might have been written in the expectation that certain players would take certain parts. But casting was never in the hands of the poets, and especially in the early years the repertory system and regular doubling must have made it more a matter of administrative convenience than aesthetic choice.

Several of the Admiral's Men's 'plots' show how tricky it could be to allocate parts in a play full of doubling. One in particular, Peele's *The Battle of Alcazar*, staged in 1594 and revived in 1601 when Alleyn returned to the Fortune stage, shows how tricky the allocation of parts could be, especially when several of the major parts were for 'blackamoors' who needed not only special costumes but blacked-up faces. You could not readily double a white man if you were blacked up for another role. *Alcazar* is the only play for which a copy of the text survives in print from 1594 along with the book-keeper's record in his 'plot' of how it was to be staged. David Bradley has produced a whole book analysing the difficulties the man he calls the 'plotter' had to match Alleyn, blacked up as the leading villain, with a family and escorts also in blackface without losing too many of the other players taking the white-faced parts, Portuguese, Spanish, Italian and English. At least for the revival in 1601 quite a few of the Moors had to appear in their normal white complexion.[55]

A certain amount of evidence does seem to show how well the companies worked in their repertory system. These are the few cases where a play-text has survived in *two* versions where one might be the author's original text and the other a version based on a text copied down by a pair of players, one dictating to another who wrote it down (perhaps sometimes using their memory of playing their own parts to supplement the manuscript). The variant texts of *Faustus* and the so-called 'bad' quartos of several of Shakespeare's plays seem to have been transcribed to some extent with the help of memory. A particularly revealing text of this kind is the 1594 quarto of Greene's *Orlando Furioso*. W. W. Greg in his edition[56] maintains that the play was written after August 1591 and played possibly at Court for Christmas 1591 and certainly in February 1592 by Alleyn and Strange's Men at the Rose. The Christmas performance may have been by the Queen's Men, who would have relinquished the play to Alleyn when they left for the provinces at the beginning of 1592 – unless, as the anonymous *Defence of Conny-Catching* maintained, Greene resold the play to the other company after its owners had left London. Alleyn must have bought the play as his own, since it stayed with him in the Admiral's repertory when he started the new company in 1594.

The most engaging piece of text to set against the 1594 quarto is the 'Part' of Orlando, a fragment comprising two-thirds of a scribal transcript of the leading role. It has corrections made in Alleyn's hand, so was presumably made at the beginning of 1592, since it is unlikely that Alleyn would ever have needed the part copied for him a second time. The only text of the full play is the quarto printed in 1594. Greg writes:

The text of *Orlando* printed in 1594 proves on examination to be a version severely abridged by the excision of scenes, speeches, and passages of dialogue, as well as by compression and the omission of characters, for performance by a reduced cast in a strictly limited time. Further than this the version has been adapted, by the insertion of episodes of rough clownage and horseplay, to the tastes of a lower class of audience … Thus the quarto contains what would appear to be essentially a stage version: the text is dependent on, not antecedent to, actual performance … based almost throughout on reconstruction from memory, while there seems likewise to be an oral link in the transmission. Modifying this, however, to some extent is the fact that a couple of short passages appear to reproduce written copies that happened to be preserved in the stock of the company, while a few incidental points reveal a knowledge of the original version, though this knowledge was clearly not obtained directly from any written source. Certain features, lastly, prove that the copy used for the printed quarto was in the first instance prepared for playhouse use.[57]

Modern bibliography calls much of this view into question. Greg suggests, implausibly, that the cause of the compilation was the reduced circumstances of the Queen's Men, who made it while on tour, possessing the original properties such as the roundelay scrolls that Orlando reads from; these were certainly written out to be read on stage, since Alleyn's Part does not transcribe them, and (even less plausibly) prepared for a company reduced to seven men and two boys. They lacked the promptbook, the 'allowed book' authorised by the Master of the Revels, which had been sold to Alleyn before they left London. He assumes their limited resources made them cut progressively more and more, for fewer players, made them build up the action sequences in place of words, and elaborate the comic scenes. The verse, he notes, where it was preserved was kept with remarkable accuracy, at least in its metre. That is the closest to the truth of the matter that Greg could achieve. We now know that companies routinely shortened and altered their plays for staging, that clown scenes were routinely invented by the clowns and that the 'memory' factor in the text's transmission was as likely to come from dictation by one player to another working as scribe as it was by players writing down what they could recall of their lines in performance. The quarto and the 'Part' were pieces of the standard material players used for memorizing their parts in any play.

Greene's printed text as a whole stands firmly on the 'drumming decasillabon', with a few alexandrines or half-lines to interrupt the flow. Altogether it may not be greatly different from the author's original manuscript, though rather less adroit. It is, however, revealing to see the way the printed version irons over the patches it puts on badly mangled verses in order to make them as smooth as their neighbours. It even makes up rhymes. One such case is Q1019–20, which adjusts the 'Part' with extra words to make up for the possibly forgotten polysyllable of Angelica's name.

Part 171–2:

> and yet forsooth Medor durst enterprise
> to reave Orlando of Angelica

Quarto 1019–20:

> And yet forsooth, Medor, base Medor durst
> Attempt to reve Orlando of his love.

Greg conjectures that this corruption started with the change of verb, necessitating the repetition in the first line and the shortening of the second. But the repetition is a characteristic acting exclamation, and the alteration of the second line creates a rhyme with the one following, line 1021, which is

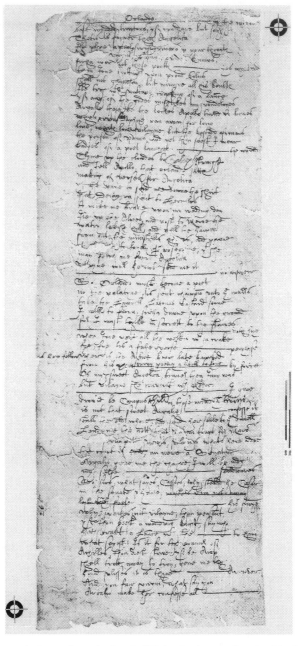

Illustration 20. A section from the 'part' of Orlando, preserved in the *Henslowe Papers*.

identical in both texts. Greg may be right, but the creation of a new rhyme suggests something more positive operating than simply improvising to cover forgotten metre. It implies a strong concept of the need for high poetry. The result in Q is metrically no less correct than Greene's original as given in the transcript of the Part.

A second instance of patching is even more positive. In the quarto line 604 the player substituted for Greene's abstruse 'Clor' the more familiar 'Flora' from two lines earlier, then added a phrase to make the reference seem more apt, and still kept his metre:

P10–11:

> kinde Clora make her couch, fair cristall springes
> washe you her Roses, yf she long to drinck

Q604–6:

> Fair Flora make her couch amidst thy flowres,
> Sweet Christall springs, wash ye with roses,
> When she longs to drinke.

The addition leaves Q with a three-foot line at 606, the first half of a rhymed couplet, but the extra phrase itself is fitted into the metrical pattern and leaves it little more nonsensical than Greene's original.

Textual evidence suggests that players consistently cut long-drawn similes and passages of classical name-dropping, such as P410–13 which is appallingly full of classical name-dropping.

> Extinguish proud tesyphone those brandes
> fetch dark Alecto, from black phlegeton
> or Lethe waters, to appease those flames
> that wrathfull Nemesis hath sett on fire.

Another seven lines, equally crowded, are cut after Q1550. It is possible, of course, that whoever it was from the Queen's Men who put the quarto text together simply felt they could not match Alleyn's trenchant delivery of such lines.

The exclamations that seem to occur regularly in the quarto as player's additions are sometimes absorbed into their line, sometimes not.

P18:   venus hath graven hir triumphes here beside
Q614:   What? Venus writes her triumphs here beside
P22:   this gordyon knott together counties
Q620:   But soft this Gordion knot together co-unites

This last exclamation does not fit its context as aptly as it should, because there is no reason for the speaker to be surprised over who is co-united by the Gordian knot. A still more inapt exclamation is one that the quarto adds to line 1385 – Orlando's 'Sacrepant', a surprised recognition of the villain of the piece, when Orlando already knows perfectly well who it is. Greg calls this 'just the sort of touch that a blustering actor would introduce'. By Greg's criterion there was a good deal of such bluster in the company and the performances that generated the quarto text.

Following a line of thought similar to Greg's, when editing his great edition of *Hamlet* Harold Jenkins noted a tendency of the actors to inflate their lines that he thought must have got recorded in the Folio version. The classic instance of this he found in Hamlet's 'O vengeance!' in his second soliloquy, a cry that appears in the Folio text but not in the Second Quarto, which Jenkins thought was printed from Shakespeare's own manuscript untouched by any of the players' hands.[58] It does seem likely that players chose to augment their scripts in such ways on occasion, and that some of their elaborations were noted in the playhouse copies. Identification of such instances is usually difficult because normally only the one version of a play ever got into print.

The key distinguishing factor in the hundreds of surviving play-texts from the time is their provenance. Some came directly from the author's manuscript, others from a text roughly assembled from various papers and memories of what previous productions had used to get the words right. Almost no copies of what we in a rather facile way call the 'playbook', the authoritative text that might have served later generations as a promptbook, have come down to us. In effect the companies had only one manuscript with the authority to make a performance from, the text with the licensing signature of the Master of the Revels on it. This was what has been called the 'maximal' text, because it contained all that the company was allowed to speak on stage. Lesser or more 'minimal' versions might be taken from it for use when for whatever reason a shorter text was required. Such a text would have many cuts, especially to the longer and more ponderous speeches. Individual scenes might be shifted round in the sequence of playing or cut entirely. Problems with doubling found in rehearsal might call for cuts or for elaborations from other scenes to give the doubling players time to change costume. Some version of the playbook in between the maximal and the minimal versions would be used on any one occasion. As has been said above, playbooks were a far less fixed entity than printed texts.

Almost none of these key versions, the maximal texts, would ever have gone to the press. Every playing company held them as their most prized asset, the only document that authorised their use for performance. The 'allowed books', will hardly ever have been given to the press, because they could never be retrieved from the printer in good enough condition to return to their original use afterwards. Of the six hundred or more plays that have survived from the Shakespearean time only three 'allowed books' have come to us. Two are play manuscripts: the King's Men's *Second Maiden's Tragedy*, so-called by the Master when he authorised it, and probably written by Middleton in 1612 or so, and Massinger's heavily revised *Believe As You List*, a play he wrote for the King's Men in 1628 about the alleged survival of the Portuguese king from the battle of Alcazar. Since Spain had used his death to annex Portugal, the survival of a pretender to the Portuguese throne was a major political issue, and even fifty years later it was too hot for the censor to allow it. Massinger had to rewrite the story, basing it instead on Rome's annexation of Carthage. The third is a copy printed in 1657 of a Red Bull play, *The Walks of Islington and Hogsdon*, when 'allowed books' were no longer important. In this case the printer not only set the whole play but included the Master's licence at the end. Only three such authoritative playbooks out of the possible six hundred is a dreadful statistic for those of us who would like to know the texts that actually were put on stage.

One pair of texts that shows much more substantially than any others just what the company did to the manuscript the writer gave them when they were preparing it for staging is the two versions of Shakespeare's *Henry V*. The First Quarto, printed in 1600, less than a year after the first performances, is a remarkably compressed and speeded-up version of the play most of us know only in its form as Shakespeare's original, the First Folio text, generally thought to be printed directly from the author's manuscript. That makes sense because the company would always have made a transcript out of the manuscript the author sold or gave them for their 'allowed book', and so the only copy of the play free to be given to a printer (who would always destroy a manuscript in the process of setting from it), would have been the author's own. The licence the Master of the Revels had inscribed on the 'allowed book' made it far too valuable to be handed over to a printer. So uniquely in this instance we seem to have both a text printed from the author's untouched original manuscript and a specimen of what the company did to it for production.

While the Folio text of *Henry V* runs to 3,253 lines, the Quarto has only 1629. The Folio is what has been called the 'maximal' text, the fullest possible version that would be sent to the Master of the Revels for his approval to become the 'allowed book'.[59] What the company then seems to have done with the playbook was to compress it massively so that it could easily fit into the two or so hours usually allocated for a performance. To do that with *Henry V* they cut out all six choruses, shortened all the longer speeches, and eliminated several complete scenes, including the discussion between the Archbishop and the Bishop of Ely that starts Shakespeare's original version. The adjustments made on each side of a cut are often clumsy, though they retain the verse metre well. Internal evidence suggests that the Quarto text was compiled not long after the play was first staged by two sharers who probably took the parts of Exeter and Gower in the first performances.[60] On the whole they got their own speeches right, but they had hopeless memories for numbers and for proper names, and, like many more recent actors, sometimes failed to grasp the meaning of what they had been given to speak. One dictated a line and the other copied down what was given him, with the effect that the entire play was set by the compositor as lines of verse. Even the Eastcheap prose and Henry's long anonymous debate with his soldiers were set as verse, which is one reason the text has been scorned by most subsequent readers, and has created a major difficulty for editors of the Folio text when they face Ancient Pistol's extravagantly poetic prose, since the quarto makes it all into verse.

As a whole, the sharers' version suggests that the play was performed with an urgency that prevented any dalliance at specific moments. The slow awakening of King Henry from the depths of prayer when summoned by Gloucester for instance, which is delicately presented in the Folio version as a slow arousal, was made through the copyists' memories into a vigorous leap straight back into the action:

Folio 4.1.323–6:

> GLOUC. My Liege.
> KING My Brother *Gloucesters* voyce? I:
> I know thy errand, I will goe with thee:
> The day, my friend, and all things stay for me.

Quarto:

> GLOST. My Lord.
> KING. My brother *Glosters* voice
> GLOST. My Lord, The Army stayes upon your presence.
> KING. Stay *Gloster* stay, and I will goe with thee,
> The day my friends, and all things stayes for me.

Like Burbage playing Hamlet in Jenkins's reading the clowns seem to have intensified the exclamations in what was set down for them, particularly repeating their comic catchphrases. Nym's 'and theres the humor of it' turns up on three extra occasions in Q, and Fluellen's catchphrases get even harder wearing. His favourite oath, 'Godes plud', crops up three extra times, and once Q elaborates it to 'Gode plut, and his' when he has just been struck a blow that he has every intention of repaying. 'Looke you' is sprinkled almost at random throughout his speeches, and four times he addresses Henry with a phrase not found anywhere in F – 'and it shall please your Majesty'. One late entry appears twice in Q to once in F – 'in the worell', an oddity of pronunciation that crops up again with the Welsh-speaker of the quarto text in *The Merry Wives of Windsor*. And there is also the peculiar frequency with which Ancient Pistol is faced in Q with his own name, perhaps because it was ambiguously though then correctly pronounced 'Pizzle'.

Perhaps the most revealing feature of the 1600 Quarto of *Henry V* is how the company altered the presentation of Henry from the ambivalent figure open to criticism for his brutality that Shakespeare so delicately set out in the Folio, killing the French prisoners at Agincourt but first failing with his spectacular attempt to charge into the breach at Harfleur. The Quarto text for Act 3, where the siege of Harfleur takes place, was the most radically altered section of the whole play, and with good reason if the company was not to make too much of Henry's failures. They evidently decided to trim the staging, especially of one wordless but highly revealing feature of the siege. In the Folio the opening stage direction calls for '*scaling ladders at Harfleur*' (3.1.1). The intention in calling for such devices would have been that as soon as Henry concluded his 'Once more unto the breach, dear friends' exhortation the onstage soldiers with their ladders would have put them up against the *frons scenae*, or tiring-house façade, so that they could climb them onto the stage balcony and exit inside the tiring-house, which then represented the besieged city. The conclusion to that display of valour three scenes later would have been the appearance of the governor of Harfleur on the same balcony, still representing the walls of the city, its gates the central opening below him, while Henry stands on the stage platform in front of the gates and demands that Harfleur surrender. Although modern directors ignore this signification of Henry's initial defeat, this confrontation was meant to be a tacit admission that the attack on the breach had failed and that the governor was still in command of the town. So the soldiers who scaled the ladders to the balcony must have been killed in the failed attack. In the Folio Harfleur does not fall until this later scene, when the governor admits that his hope of relief from the Dauphin has failed and he must surrender the town to Henry. The company did not want such a delay. They cut entirely all of Henry's now-famous speech about assaulting the breach along with the ladders and the consequent quiet indication that Henry's attack on the breach had failed. The whole revision set out in the Quarto text makes Henry into an unquestionable hero, swift and brutal, with no failures. It leaves no evidence at all besides the simple order to kill the prisoners of Shakespeare's qualms about Henry's conduct. At least by keeping that it retained the reason why Pistol appears at the end still penniless, lacking his egregious ransom for having captured Monsieur Le Fer.

The quarto text of *Henry V* is remarkable because it is unique as a record of what the company was ready to do in revising, shortening and simplifying its author's texts. In form and printing the quarto is not unlike several of the Admiral's company plays from the same period, many of which seem to have been printed from minimal theatre versions rather than from the author's manuscript. Speed and economy of production with no great concern for precision in the verse language was always a company's major need when staging its plays. In *Henry V* historical precision in detail and versification came a poor second to the vigorously simple characterisation and speed of production. Modern productions oversimplify the Folio version of the play too, though for different reasons. None allow the 'Once more unto the breach' speech to be a flop, and few cut the choruses, for all the fact that they disagree with what the acts they precede go on to demonstrate.

All this implies a great deal about the players' approach to their repertory, and how they treated their playbooks. Above all it reaffirms the likelihood that what we read in modern editions is likely to come closer to the 'maximal' allowed book than to the cut versions actually staged. We will return to the difference between the fixity of print and the fluidity of performance in Chapter 5.

6. ACTING QUALITY

Finally here we must make an attempt to assess the quality of the acting, in so far as it can be differentiated at separate points in time and amongst the various companies or individual players. We have already seen evidence suggesting that by 1600 discerning critics were inclined to reject the scholastic 'Pantomimick action', that they recognised a concept of 'personation' and had begun to deplore exaggerated or affected acting. After 1600 there appears to have been little in the way of substantial change to these criticisms. Richard Brome in 1638 looked right back to the 'dayes of *Tarlton* and *Kempe*' to find the 'barbarisme' that had been successfully purged from his own stage (*The Antipodes*, 2.2). Through the seventeenth century exaggeration was the only charge commonly flung at the players.

The players of the northern outdoor playhouses, the Fortune and Red Bull, were targets for attacks on 'over-doing' more commonly than any others. Tomkis jibed at them in *Albumazar* (1615), Wither in *Abuses Stript and Whipt* in the same year, and Thomas Carew in verses prefixed to Davenant's *The Just Italian* in 1630. In 1654 Edmund Gayton ironically claimed to have heard that 'the Poets of the Fortune and red Bull, had alwayes a mouth-measure for their

Actors (who were terrible teare-throats) and made their lines proportionable to their compasse, which were *sesquipedales*, a foot and a halfe' (*Pleasant Notes upon Don Quixot*, p. 24). Soon after Gayton Richard Flecknoe showed what a standard comparison for affectation Red Bull acting used to be, writing (in his 'Character' *Of a Proud [Wo]man)* 'She looks high and speaks in a majestique Tone, like one playing the *Queens* part at the *Bull*' (*Aenigmaticall Characters*, B1v). That, together with the indoor plays of the 1630s that derided outdoor audiences because they still liked jigs and tales of bawdry along with noisy swordfights, is the clearest mark of how audience tastes changed.

Grand gestures seem to have matched the *sesquipedales*, to judge by such incidents as one in 1622 when Richard Baxter, while acting on the Red Bull stage, accidentally wounded a feltmaker's apprentice, who was watching the play from the edge of the stage.[61] With some reservations we might even trace the acting tradition to which Baxter's swashbuckling belonged back as far as Alleyn himself. It was Alleyn after all who was owner of the Fortune and first creator of the 'majestick' roles that the Red Bull and Fortune players inherited from him. Most of his repertoire, including *Tamburlaine* and *Faustus*, went to his Fortune company, and it was at the Fortune in Caroline times that Richard Fowler built himself a reputation for valiant acting and strenuous swordfighting along the lines that Alleyn started with his Tamburlaine. His early parts such as the Marlowe roles were what got him most remarked on for his characteristic 'stalking and roaring' as Orlando and Tamburlaine.[62] His peer, Burbage, on the other hand, who spoke Hamlet's words to the Players about unnatural actors strutting and bellowing, was only ever spoken of as a master of 'lively' or life-like acting. His elegist wrote of his most famous 'personation',

> oft have I seene him, leap into the Grave
> suiting the person, wch he seem'd to have
> of A sadd Lover, with soe true an Eye
> that theer I would have sworne, he meant to dye,
> oft have I seene him, play this part in jeast,
> soe livly, that Spectators, and the rest
> of his sad Crew, whilst he but seem'd to bleed,
> amazed, thought even then hee dyed in deed.[63]

And Thomas May in *The Heir* (1620), also written shortly after Burbage's real death, speaks of him 'painting' another famous role:

> ROSCIO .... has not your Lordship seene
> A Player personate Hieronimo?
> POL[YMETES]. By th'masse tis true, I have seen the knave paint grief

> In such a lively colour, that for false
> And acted passion he has drawne true teares
> From the spectators. Ladies in the boxes
> Kept time with sighs, and teares to his sad accents
> As had he truely been the man he seem'd. (1.1)

Burbage's technique of subtler and less vigorous 'personation' is suggested by such things as his apparent elaboration in *Hamlet* of the hero's habit of repeating words, as a trait peculiar to a very singular mind,[64] and in other roles by references like Samuel Rowland's to gentlemen who copied his body language from his playing of Richard III (*The Letting of Humours Blood in the Head-Vaine* (1600), A2r):

> *Gallants*, like *Richard* the usurper, swagger,
> That had his hand continuall on his dagger.

In playing as in so many other ways, Shakespeare's own company, more restrained than their fellows on the public stages, and more life-size, as well as more life-like, than the boy companies, appear to have been the outstanding group of their time in their stage characterisations.

And one final point about how the difference of then from now affects our thinking about how the actors treated their plays. Nowadays we expect to take them very slowly and usually fairly respectfully. The impact of physical and mental changes on us through the last four centuries of playgoing has affected the shape and the comfort levels of the playhouses, our distancing from the language of Shakespeare, and more than anything else a slowing down of the pace. The inherent passivity expected of modern audiences, all seated in silence, imposes this long-pausing Shakespeare on modern staging. The summary 'two hours traffic of the stage' that the Chorus of *Romeo and Juliet* expected has extended to a minimum of three. Respect, even worship, of Shakespeare makes the imposition not just of high-speed staging but of radical cuts to the text quite difficult to contemplate. We reject the Quarto text of *Henry V* because it cuts as well as simplifies the Shakespearean complexity, even though modern productions impose their own gross simplifications. We could not bear to lose 'Once more unto the breach, dear friends' yet we prefer to ignore the visible failure of the attack it leads to. It was not only the repertory that had a much more rapid turnover in the early modern time than we are accustomed to now, but the players' performances.

CHAPTER 4

The Playhouses

I. MOBILE PLAYERS

The structure of the playhouses is the most well-trodden subject of all the background aspects of the drama. Consequently precision in identifying playhouse design involves trudging through a morass of mud, with all the lack of confidence and clarity that entails. Playhouse design, being more tangible than other matters, has attracted the most material disputes. It is simpler to argue over fixities like the shape of a stage than such intangible matters as an Elizabethan audience's awareness of itself as a visible presence during a performance in daylight. The discovery in 1989 of some real playhouse remains has added some fixity to what is known, and burrowing into the warren of legal papers has yielded up still more evidence. But the weight of the many footprints planted in this part of the terrain has not altered the muddy nature of most of the evidence.

Evidence about the playhouse structures, however slippery, needs to be kept in some kind of perspective. The playhouses themselves were no more than convenient accessories to the business of playing. Both plays and players operated in London long before any permanent structures were built for the performance of plays. Throughout the Shakespearean era companies retained the capacity at the end of an afternoon's playing to take their plays off to a nobleman's house or to Court and play again there with no more aids to performance than the arena itself and what they could carry to it. The Revels Office did supply costumes and scaffolding for performances at Court, but even there most of the work went into erecting stages and seating in halls normally used for other purposes.

The adaptability of the early players in their use of playing venues is an element in the long story of the innovation of commercial playing in London and its gradual climb up the ladder of social respectability.[1] There were radical differences in the design of each playhouse. The first commercial theatres, built in 1567 and 1576, were probably simpler structures than

139

Illustration 21. Travelling players performing at a market-place outside an inn in Holland. From 'Kermesse', by David Vinckboons (1576–1629). It seems to offer a fairly standard version of a market-place performance. Note the gentleman and lady standing off to the right, where her pocket is being picked.

those built later in the shapes of both stage and auditorium. Like most of the subsequent designs, they were certainly built as cheaply as possible, however brightly they were painted. Each seems to have been quite distinct from the others, whether in size, in the provision of stage features such as trapdoors or 'heavens' for descents, or in the forms of access provided for the audience. The Swan was very different from its near neighbour the Rose, built eight years earlier. Their neighbour the Globe, built four years later than the Swan, was different from either of them, although on an older frame, that of the 1576 Theatre. Hall playhouses, the first of which were created along with the first open-air stages, were different again.

The earliest amphitheatres, like the Red Lion in the suburb of Stepney, built by John Brayne probably for his brother-in-law James Burbage and his Leicester's company, were conceived in terms revealing most of the traditional practices they catered for. The Red Lion was an extraordinary precursor. Built in 1567, it was put up in the yard of a local house in Stepney, east of the City. Brayne and Burbage gave the open space they rented a circuit of scaffolding that provided seating for three levels of spectators, with inside it a stage built against a turret standing thirty feet high from ground level, made of 'Tymber and boords', a peculiar structure with a single floor 7 feet from the top. It is not clear why it stood so high, unless its roof was meant to cover the stage from rain and snow. Nor is it clear just where inside the stage space it was to stand. Presumably if only to give it support it was at the rear next to the surrounding gallery scaffolding, although the lawsuit where these specifications are listed does not specify any linkages between the turret and the stage. Besides the high turret the extensive stage included a hole for a trapdoor. It was raised 5 feet (1.5 metres) above ground level and its area was specified as 40 feet by 30 (12.2 by 9.1 metres), a little bigger than the Fortune's stage was to be in 1600.[2] There can be no doubt that, given the cost, it was a wildly ambitious piece of construction, and it is surprising that no comment about it besides the lawsuit from which this information comes has survived.

Silence about the Red Lion suggests that it did not survive long, or get any major publicity. Nonetheless the rush of playhouses that began eight years later must have taken lessons from the early experience, above all for James Burbage's Theatre of 1576. The Theatre and its neighbour the Curtain each had a large protruding stage, presumably not unlike the platforms set up in market-places for travelling players, which were normally backed by a narrow curtained booth for the players. Each had a tiring-house in the bays behind the stage. The Theatre's auditorium was a scaffolding of galleries like those provided for the Red Lion and the bear-baiting arenas and innyards. This scaffolding served a double function, increasing the quantity of spectators by banking them upwards and providing a wall to keep out anyone who could or would not pay for admission. Burbage was likely to have been motivated to build his scaffolds chiefly by the control they gave him over his audience's purses. He could now collect money at the door instead of going through the crowd with a hat when setting up his stages in country market-places. This was no more than an adjustment of long-familiar travelling company practices. The cheapest patrons stood in the yard closest to the action just as they stood around the stage in market-places, whereas the wealthier had seats more removed in the roofed galleries which now surrounded the stage and the standing patrons. The highest in social status sat in a special section of the galleries above the stage called 'lords' rooms'.

This disposition of amphitheatre audiences, set by the early traditions of the travelling players, was in total contrast with the hall playhouses. Their auditoria had the more modern form adopted later by opera houses and nineteenth-century theatres. The audience members who paid least sat at the furthest remove from the stage. The more you could pay the nearer you could be to the action, a principle followed after 1594 in the locations of the favoured playhouses too. The indoor halls were inside the City while the amphitheatres stood outside in the mud and distance of the suburbs. All of the halls were located much closer to the haunts of the wealthy playgoers than were the suburban amphitheatres. Paul's playhouse, starting business in 1575, nestled under the walls of the cathedral itself in the centre and most promenaded area of the City. The first Blackfriars playhouse, which started up within a year of Paul's, was not far away, down Ludgate Hill towards the Inns of Court and the residences of the rich who lived in the Blackfriars precinct and along the Strand in Westminster.

Throughout the period for reasons that must have started with social snobbery the halls were called 'private' playhouses to distinguish them from the licensed 'public' open-air theatres. After the turn of the century, as we have seen, their 'private' identity may have survived for a time chiefly as an excuse to keep them free from the supervisory functions of the Master of the Revels, who had no official concern with the more genuinely private entertainments in great houses and in the London houses of the nobility. In later years the halls' 'private' label merely renewed the feeling of social difference between the clientele of the expensive and therefore more exclusive halls and those who attended the much cheaper 'public' amphitheatres.

The two kinds of playhouse differed radically in the numbers they could hold, too. Johannes de Witt estimated in 1596 that the Swan could hold three thousand people, and the Spanish ambassador gave the same figure as the minimum capacity at the Globe in 1624.[3] The Rose and its successor the Fortune were rather smaller, but all the amphitheatres could take in far more customers than the halls could. Paul's playhouse may not have squeezed in more than a couple of hundred, and both Blackfriars playhouses can hardly have seated many more than six hundred. These smaller capacities, however, were more than compensated for by the higher prices the halls charged. When Shakespeare's company started to run playhouses of both sorts, as they did after 1608, they seem to have made distinctly more money from the smaller indoor Blackfriars than from the Globe.

Hall playhouses were designed for the wealthy in their auditorium layout and in their central locations. By contrast the amphitheatres were built closer to the working-citizen parts of the City, and aimed chiefly at them. The first amphitheatres were built on London's perimeters in fields alongside the poorest residential areas, the suburbs of the east and the north. This was probably not so much because of any particular allegiance to the poor but more because the suburban location put them under the more lenient care of the justices of Middlesex and Surrey, beyond the hostility of the City's magistrates. The first Middlesex amphitheatre, the Red Lion, built before the players had any government protection and probably as temporary in its playing life as in its design, was set up to the east, in Stepney. The next innovation was a small outdoor playhouse built a mile south of the Thames at Newington Butts in 1575, probably for the company patronized by the Earl of Warwick, Leicester's brother. It proved too remote from the City ever to be popular, although it was used through one week by the 'duopoly' companies for their first performances at their beginning in June 1594.

The first durable playhouse, the Theatre, was built on land leased for twenty-one years in Shoreditch, near Finsbury Fields, nearly a mile north of the City's eastern perimeter. By then, in 1576, its builder, James Burbage, held the patent for Leicester's Company which for the first time secured their status. His name for the new structure was pretentious, referring to classical Roman precedents, although at the time the term was chiefly used for world atlases produced by Mercator and others. Its later name, the Globe, reflected the same concept as well as the famous saying that all the world's a stage. The Theatre went up while the first two halls were opening in the City. Its neighbour the Curtain appeared a year later, two hundred yards nearer the City on the same highway to the north. Ten years later, in 1587, Henslowe opened the Rose south of the river in Southwark, not far from the baiting-houses and with the consent of the magistrates of Surrey.

Access across the river into Surrey was by London Bridge for the poor and by ferry for the wealthier playgoers. All the Southwark playhouses apart from the one a mile south of the river at Newington Butts were conveniently accessible by ferry, since the busiest City wharves were directly opposite, below St Paul's. The Swan became the Rose's first playhouse neighbour in 1595. When Shakespeare's company crossed the river and

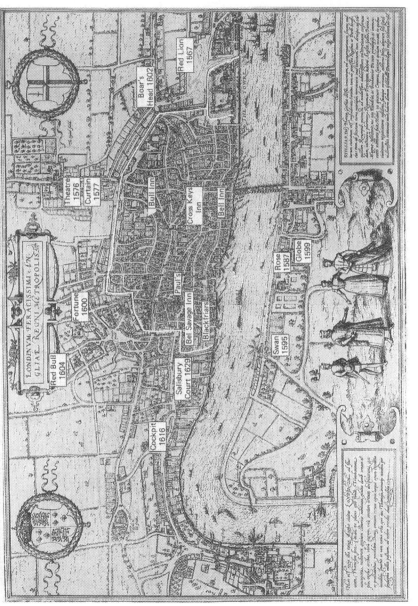

Illustration 22. A panorama of London in 1572. It was engraved by Braun and Hogenberg, and printed as the second image in *Civitates Orbis Terrarum* (1572). The approximate location of each playhouse built between 1567 and 1629 has been added. The City walls are clearly marked with a thick white line ending at the Tower of London to the east. To the west of the walls sprawls the City of Westminster. The main road north through Middlesex where the Theatre and Curtain were built can be seen flanked by open fields, as are the baiting houses on the Bankside in Surrey to the south of the Thames. For further information see Ida Darlington and James Howgego, *Printed Maps of London*, London, 1964, and *Tudor London: A Map and a View*, ed. Ann Saunders and John Schofield, London, 2001.

opened within 40 yards (36.6 metres) of the Rose at the Globe, a little closer to London Bridge, in 1599, Alleyn moved to the northern space they had vacated, building the Fortune in Middlesex, still close to the City but some way to the west of where the Theatre had been. The Red Bull opened soon after, still more to the west and a little further north, in Clerkenwell. Meanwhile the Boar's Head playhouse had been converted in 1599 out of an innyard on the eastern edge of the City in Whitechapel. Henslowe and Alleyn built the last of the traditional amphitheatres, the Hope, near the site of the old Beargarden in Southwark in 1614, planning to use it as a dual-function playhouse and baiting house. In the event the players soon gave it up to the bears, for reasons Ben Jonson cited explicitly in *Bartholomew Fair*, the first and only play he wrote for the new venue. He got his stage-keeper to announce that it was the right setting because the bears and dogs made it 'as durty as *Smithfield*, and as stinking every whit'. Smithfield was London's meat market, where the annual fair that is the play's setting was run on St Bartholomew's Day.

After the Hope, the only new playhouses built before the closure in 1642 were halls. Once Shakespeare's company retrieved the Blackfriars playhouse for themselves in 1608, others soon set out to imitate them. The Whitefriars was south of Fleet Street, close to the Inns of Court, a little west of Blackfriars. The abortive Porter's Hall was to have been built between Paul's and Blackfriars. The Cockpit was built to the north-west of it in 1616, in Westminster's Drury Lane, and the last hall playhouse, Salisbury Court, built in 1629, was again positioned in Whitefriars. The hall play-houses stretched in a line from St Paul's westwards, with the amphitheatres to the north and south, and rather more to the east. All of them except for Paul's and the Blackfriars were positioned outside the jurisdiction of the City Fathers. The Blackfriars precinct was officially made part of the City of London in 1608, when James had to gratify the City because he needed its wealth, but by then the playhouse, originally built in what had been a 'liberty' free from City control, was secure from Guildhall's interference, and its new occupants had a royal patron.

2. THE HISTORY OF PLAYHOUSE BUILDING

The story of where and when the players accommodated their plays in London would also make a short history of their lives up to 1642. In the early years, while they struggled to gain a secure footing, they used such scaffolds as they could find or construct, whether custom-built like the Red Lion, the Theatre and the Rose or buildings adapted for playing, like the Bel Savage or the Boar's Head, inns which had open-air yards surrounded by a balcony. As often as they could in winter they used City inns like the Bell and the Cross Keys in Gracechurch Street, where they must have had an indoor space to perform in.[4] They kept this up despite Guildhall's opposition until, in 1594, all the City's inns were finally barred to them. In the meantime, when the first amphitheatres were opening, Richard Farrant rented a hall to use for plays in Blackfriars, and another chorister company had opened in the City at Paul's by 1576. These boy groups ran first as two companies and then as a merged company until the Marprelate troubles closed them down in 1590.

Through the next decade only the adult companies performed, and only the amphitheatres were available for playing. Then in 1596, largely because access to the City inns had now been lost and perhaps because his lease of the land on which he had built the Theatre was due to expire in 1597, James Burbage thought that he could combine the adult company practice of occasionally using rooms at inns in winter with the boy company practice of performing in 'private' halls. In that year he built a second hall playhouse in the Blackfriars.

This radical and costly commitment was either intended to make it an accessory to his existing outdoor playhouse, making it possible to play outdoors in summer and indoors in winter as had been done while the city inns could provide acting space, or it was designed to replace it. There is nothing to say whether he intended to keep the Theatre for use in summer and supplement it with the Blackfriars for winter. He does not seem to have expected to lose the Theatre when its lease expired in April 1597. Possibly he hoped to replace his ageing outdoor playhouse with the new indoor one, which his company would thenceforward use in summer as well as in winter, but renewal of the old outdoor-indoor seasonal switch had certainly been the implication behind the company patron the Lord Chamberlain's request to the Lord Mayor in October 1594 to let them reopen at the Cross Keys Inn.[5]

It does seem most likely that old Burbage thought the use of both venues for summer and winter playing was going to be possible. The company certainly renewed this policy when they rebuilt the Globe after its 1613 fire, though it is not easy to say whether they did so because they remembered it had been Burbage's ambition so many years previously or that they had found they enjoyed the seasonal switch between the two sorts of venue. That is an intriguing question, especially since the decision to renew the Globe in 1613 put the sharers to the cost of rebuilding the most expensive of all the playhouses, and may indeed have been the reason why Shakespeare chose that time to opt out of the otherwise highly profitable business of playhouse owning.

The arguments used by the residents in their petition to prevent playing at the new Blackfriars boiled down essentially to their objection to the noise of public playing, the crowds they attracted and their drum and trumpet accompaniments. The advent of a boy company, more socially respectable and performing only once a week, seems to have raised no such problems. Three years after Burbage's scheme failed the two boy companies reopened, one at Paul's and the other at the unused Blackfriars, while the adult companies reshuffled themselves between the northern and southern suburbs, building a new generation of amphitheatres for the purpose. Not until the boy companies had finally faded from the scene in 1608 did the adult company gain belated access to a hall playhouse. From then on with the sole exception of the Hope all development went into the building of hall playhouses for adult companies.

This brief history needs amplifying not just with some detail about the structure of the various playhouses but with an account of the constraints on building. From 1594 in order to control the number of playhouses the Privy Council insisted that each one be licensed. The Council's attempts to appease the Lord Mayor by restricting the number of playing companies and the available playhouses was accompanied by their 1594 accord to the Mayor's ban on any City inn being used for playing. The formal conversion of the Boar's Head and the Red Bull from inns into playhouses was a predictable consequence of this restriction. The most popular of the inns, the Bel Savage, had been used for plays, prize-fights and other sorts of show since the 1570s. It was easily recognisable as a form of playhouse, with its three ranges of galleries like Burbage's Theatre and a similar system of admission and pricing. All the playhouses had arrangements for selling ale on their sites, so that whether they counted as taverns or playhouses was a matter of name rather than function. The Boar's Head conversion when it was formally made into a playhouse kept not only its taproom but also four parlours and eleven bedrooms. The Globe and the Fortune both built taprooms alongside for selling ale to playgoing customers. Converting the Boar's Head and the Red Bull was in part a matter of altering Elizabethan nomenclature to suit Jacobean regulations.

The Privy Council's licensing of playhouses from 1594 is in some degree a mark of a rapid rise in the status of playing. By as early as 1599 playing had completely outgrown its association with London's inns, although when the London companies went on tour they seem most often to have used the large yards of country inns to stage their plays. The request in October 1594 by Henry Carey on behalf of his company asking the Lord Mayor for them to use the Cross Keys in Gracechurch Street through the winter, which no doubt the Mayor refused, is the last record of City of London inns being considered for playing. In many ways the policy of making seasonal changes of venue that the Chamberlain's was able to impose once they were secure under James was a throwback to earlier practices. In 1583, as the City's main contribution to their establishment as a royal company, the Queen's Men had been assigned to use the Bell in Gracious (Gracechurch) Street near Bishopsgate, and the Bull in Bishopsgate. The Bull was an open amphitheatre like the Theatre and the Curtain, and it is most likely that the Bell and Cross Keys offered roofed venues.[6] So it seems that the Queen's Men were allocated the two inns because one could accommodate large numbers outdoors and the other was useful in bad weather. If so, James Burbage's construction of the Blackfriars in 1596 was no more than a premature attempt to reproduce the playing conditions originally laid down for that greatly favoured first royal company. It makes the King's Men's eventual preference once they had two playhouses not quite the novelty it has been thought. To alternate in summer and winter between the Globe and Blackfriars would have merely renewed the privileged routine that Elizabeth seems to have got the Lord Mayor to concede for her royal players in 1583.

Converting the Boar's Head and the Red Bull from inns into playhouses is evidence not just of the ban on staging plays at inns but of the higher status that playing had acquired by the turn of the century. Robert Browne, who leased and converted the Boar's Head, was the leader of a company of players trying to establish themselves as the third of the adult companies resident in London. He evidently made a good job of his conversion.[7] When James authorised three adult companies in 1604, Queen Anne's Men chose to nominate the Boar's Head as their base even though the Curtain, Swan and Rose, the last of which they had been using, were still available to them. They soon abandoned the Boar's Head with its single level of gallery and consequent limited seating for the new Red Bull, however, and that playhouse remained their regular home for the next twelve years until 1616, when their co-sharer and financial manager Christopher Beeston used his and probably their profits to build himself a hall playhouse, the Cockpit.

The three amphitheatres that won the authority of licensing under King James were the Globe, Fortune and Red Bull. The Curtain and Swan were kept open for prize fights or other types of spectacle and sometimes plays, but were rarely occupied by resident companies. The Boar's Head got itself entangled in litigation (Langley had a thick thumb in that pie too). The

Rose was demolished in 1605, though in a sense it grew up again in 1614 when the adjacent Globe burned down and Henslowe and Alleyn decided to replace their other main business venue, its near neighbour the Beargarden, with a new multipurpose playhouse, the Hope. As a playhouse the Hope was something less than the last of its kind, for it was designed from the start as a dual-purpose arena for playing and for bull- and bear-baiting, with a stage that could be removed when the bears needed the yard. Playing was more frequent there at first than baiting, three afternoons out of four so far as we can tell. The two forms of entertainment did not work well in partnership, however, and there were quarrels over priority which led to the players more or less giving it up altogether by about 1620.

Two more playhouses were opened along with the second generation of amphitheatres after the Swan in 1595, and another three up to 1629. These were all halls. Paul's started up in the business again in about 1599, playing at their small roofed playhouse in a location abutting the cathedral, and the Chapel Children reopened in 1600 at the second Blackfriars theatre. In 1608 another private playhouse opened in the Whitefriars. In 1615 a fourth, Porter's Hall, opened in the Blackfriars precinct but was immediately stopped from use. In 1616 the more durable Cockpit or Phoenix was opened in Drury Lane near the Inns of Court. It seems to have been based like some of the amphitheatres on a gaming house, though this time on the much smaller roofed hall used for displays of cockfighting. The royal Cockpit in Whitehall – probably a larger building than the commercial ones – had occasionally been used as a venue for plays since Henry VIII first built it. Whether a set of plans by Inigo Jones, thought by some commentators to be originally made for the Drury Lane structure, was for Beeston's Cockpit is a question still in dispute.[8] Lastly, in 1629, while Henry VIII's royal Cockpit was being redesigned by Inigo Jones as a regular playhouse, another and rather smaller commercial venue, Salisbury Court, was opened by Richard Gunnell, a former Fortune player, near to the old Whitefriars. The earlier Whitefriars had closed after only a few years when its lease fell in, and its impresario then foundered on the abortive Porter's Hall project. The life of the three hall playhouses that existed from 1629, the Blackfriars, the Cockpit and the Salisbury Court, was every bit as healthy as the three public play-houses still flourishing, the Globe, Fortune and Red Bull. It is an accurate sign of the times that, after 1608, the first year an adult company was able to get possession of an indoor playhouse, the only new ones built or projected were halls.

This brief history of playhouse-building can be summarised in the words of the reviser of Stowe's *Annales*:

In the yeere one thousand six hundred twenty nine, there was builded a new faire Play-house, neere the white Fryers. And this is the seaventeenth Stage, or common Play-house, which hath beene new made within the space of threescore yeeres within London and the Suburbs, viz.

Five Innes, or common Osteryes turned to Play-houses, one Cockpit, S. Paules singing Schoole, one in the Black-fryers, and one in the White-fryers, which was built last of all, in the yeare one thousand six hundred twenty nine, all the rest not named, were erected only for common Playhouses, besides the new built Beare garden, which was built as well for playes, and Fencers prizes, as Bull Bayting; besides, one in former time at Newington Buts; Before the space of threescore years above-sayd, I neither knew, heard, nor read, of any such Theaters, set Stages, or Play-houses, as have beene purposely built within mans memory.[9]

3. EARLY AMPHITHEATRE DESIGN

For the first generation of playhouses information about their shape is sparse and not entirely consistent. Samuel Kiechel, a German merchant visiting London in 1584, noted of its entertainments that

there are some peculiar houses, which are so made as to have about three galleries over one another, inasmuch as a great number of people always enters to see such an entertainment. It may well be that they take as much as from 50 to 60 dollars [£10 to £12] at once, especially when they act anything new, which has not been given before, and double prices are charged. This goes on nearly every day in the week; even though performances are forbidden on Friday and Saturday, it is not observed.[10]

Another traveller, William Lambarde, within a decade or so of Kiechel recorded that

such as goe to Parisgardein, the Bell Savage, or Theatre, to beholde Beare baiting, Enterludes, or Fence play, can account of any pleasant spectacle, [if] they first pay one pennie at the gate, another at the entrie of the Scaffolde, and the third for a quiet standing.[11]

The amphitheatres were usually round or polygonal buildings,[12] built on a timber frame with lath and plaster infills, on brick and pile foundations, with thatch or tile to roof the galleries. The yard and three ranges of galleries were reached, to judge by Lambarde's account, through one or more gates into the yard, and by stairs into the galleries. To enter the yard cost a penny, to enter the galleries cost another, and to sit in comfort in the gentlemen's rooms cost another ('to get a standing' meant to find a viewing-place, whether standing or sitting). More central than the gentlemen's rooms were lords' rooms costing sixpence. They were partitioned off from the galleries closest to the stage and given access directly from a penthouse-roofed back door through the tiring house at the Theatre, Rose and Globe, and presumably at the others too.

The stage was a platform measuring as much as 40 feet (12.2 metres) across and extending out to the middle of the yard. At the rear of the stage was the 'tiring-house' or players' changing-room, occupying several bays of the surrounding galleries. Its front face, what De Witt at the Swan labelled the '*mimorum aedes*', the players' room, otherwise known as the *frons scenae* or front of the stage, had two or more openings for the players to enter and leave the stage by. At the first gallery level in the tiring-house façade was a balcony or gallery (sometimes in the seventeenth century called the 'tarras' or terrace), occasionally used as a supplementary playing area in conjunction with the stage itself, but more often used to accommodate the lords who paid most and whose rooms gave them the closest view of the stage along with the privilege of being most in view themselves.[13] Near the front of the stage in most playhouses was a large trapdoor. Over the stage, extending out from the tiring-house above the balcony or tarras, was a cover, 'shadow' or 'heavens' usually supported by two pillars rising from the stage. The Hope's stage was built in 1614 with a 'heavens' but no pillars so that the entire stage could be easily removed to make space for the baitings. Set on top of the heavens or cover was a 'hut' or huts, within which stage hands operated the machinery for the 'flights', windlass-driven descents on to the stage. Stage hands would also produce thunder and lightning effects from the heavens. If we can credit the Swan drawing, alongside the hut was a small platform level with the gallery roof, from which a trumpeter announced the imminent start of a performance, to hurry any latecomers. Beside the platform or on the hut a tall mast flew a flag to mark that a play was being performed. These last features, taken from De Witt's drawing of the Swan (illustration 26), were probably not dissimilar in the other playhouses.

According to the Puritan preachers of the 1570s and 1580s the decor of these playhouses was 'sumptuous' and 'gorgeous', although unless they put themselves at risk by visiting plays we must assume their testimony to have been second-hand. We do know from contemporary documents such as the building contract for the Fortune that the woodwork of the playhouse interior was painted, at least in one case so as to imitate the appearance of marble, like the Italian theatres.[14] Some of the woodwork was carved, and monkey-like 'satyrs' or grotesque faces decorated the interior posts. The underside of the 'heavens' was painted with sun, moon and stars, and probably the signs of the zodiac. Curtains or 'hangings' covered part of the tiring-house façade, and sometimes green rushes were strewn on the stage itself.[15]

Illustration 23. The foundations of 60 per cent of the Rose as excavated in 1989, seen from above in Park Street (once Maiden Lane). The photograph was taken by Andrew Fulgoni from the top of a ten-storey office block on the south side of Park Street, facing north. The four hexagonal blocks and sets of piles inside the foundations were used to support Southbridge House, built on the site in 1957. Photographer: Andrew Fulgoni.
Copyright: Fulgoni Copyrights Ltd © 1989–2009.

These generalisations probably do not apply to all the early amphi-theatres. There is precise and tangible evidence about elements in just three of them: most of the foundations of the Rose, a fragment of the Globe, and a Dutch tourist's sketch of the interior of the Swan. The two different types of evidence tell variable stories, and seem to indicate that all three Southwark playhouses differed from each other in numerous ways. Balancing the different kinds of evidence and assessing the value of each kind is a difficult exercise made trickier by the uniqueness of each item and probably of each playhouse. Even the amount of corroborative evidence about the playhouses diverges widely. The Rose was the venue where more than thirty extant plays of the 1590s were staged, and many papers con-cerned with running the Rose have survived too. But no more than one play definitely staged at the Swan still exists, and little else about its operations besides a flysheet of 1602 for an event to be staged there which turned out to be a con trick. As for the Globe, even after thirty years of debate and calculations over its shape and size there is still not much agreement that the Wanamaker project on Bankside got its reconstruction right.[16] Trying to measure the reliability of evidence about these three playhouses and using it to find something about the history of playhouse design at large is delicate, complex and largely unrewarding.

Much of the ground plan of the Rose was identified early in 1989 when a team of archaeologists, given access to about 60 per cent of the area, found most of the foundation walls and the yard surface under a pile of debris dating from when the playhouse was demolished in 1605 or so, largely lath and plaster from the walls and thatch from the gallery roofing. An office block had been built on the site in 1957 and its ferro-concrete piles had penetrated some sections of the site, but a remarkable amount of the playhouse footprint was still there for study and record. Forty per cent of the eastern flank was not available for digging, but enough of the rest was exposed to make the basic shape and structure of the design clear. First built in 1587 as a thatched polygon with fourteen symmetrical sides, it was roughly 72 feet (21.9 metres) in outside diameter, with an interior yard slightly under 50 feet across. The yard was surfaced in mortar, which seems to have originally been slanted downwards from the encircling galleries towards the stage. The stage was markedly smaller than the measurements given in surviving papers for other amphitheatres, and its sides were not square like the Swan's but tapered. The tiring-house wall or *frons scenae* had three angles in conformity with the inner walls of the surrounding galleries. The foundations show evidence of a major reconstruction done at some time in its life, presumably in 1592 when Alleyn's company arrived and

Henslowe recorded the expenditure of £130 to rebuild part of it. This alteration turned the originally symmetrical polygon into a bulging cup-shape.[17]

Just how the fourteen sides of the polygon were first laid out to mark the ditches to be dug for the foundations has now been worked out. A surveyor's rod (sixteen feet six inches) and a length of cord were the only tools, starting with a triangle of a rod's length on each side and elaborating it into a seven-sided shape measuring 72 feet (21.9 metres) in diameter, then simply doubling the number of the sides.[18] One of the peculiar effects of this design was that, with the playhouse entrance to the south, where Maiden Lane was, the stage had to be positioned facing it across the northern side. But a fourteen-sided polygon meant that, if the main doorway occupied a single bay, one of the angles with its vertical framing post stood directly opposite to the north. So the stage, which was constructed after the timber frame had been set up, had to be positioned a little to the east of centre on the northern flank. The reason for this can easily be explained by what we know of the staging practices of the 1580s. Plays such as *Tamburlaine* show that the players had a very good use for a large central opening. To have a *frons scenae* angled across three bays of a fourteen-sided amphitheatre meant that the central opening would be flanked by a single door in each of the neighbouring bays, slightly confrontational, so that players entering from either flanking door could meet directly. The central opening was vital for large-scale entrances such as Tamburlaine's grand and often-cited arrival on stage in his chariot pulled by four of the kings he had defeated, and whom he hails in the words later declaimed by Ancient Pistol, about the 'hollow pampered jades of Asia, / Which cannot go but thirty mile a day' (*2 Henry IV* 2.4.131–2). The problem was that, if the stage had been positioned directly opposite the entrance to the yard, no such opening would have been possible because a vertical gallery post would have been in the middle. So the stage was shifted a little to one side to give a whole bay's width for the central opening.

Henslowe's *Diary* preserves a mass of information about the operations of the Rose, much of it wonderfully incomprehensible. It lists his daily takings from the galleries, naming all the plays performed there up to 1597 and their takings; it details loans he made to the players for stage materials and includes inventories of their properties. It notes the sequence of payments he made to his teams of writers for their plays. It records Henslowe's regular payments of fees to the Master of the Revels,[19] and includes his copy of the original agreement with John Cholmley, his fellow financier, to build the Rose in 1587, along with detailed accounts of the moneys paid and the items paid for when the Rose was altered in 1592. These records help to make sense of the ground plan with its remnants of thatch, bricks, chalk and rubble found on the site in 1989.

The *Diary* starts with the arrival of Strange's Men led by Alleyn at the Rose in February 1592. It was shortly before this event, and evidently because of it, that Henslowe undertook major alterations, the evidence for which only became apparent during the final days of the Rose excavation in May 1989. Henslowe enlarged his auditorium, levelling the original gallery walls and stage foundations on the northern side down to the pile caps and rebuilding them to make the originally symmetrical polygon bulge some way further out. The fourteen sides of 1587 thus became a misshapen ovoid, elongated so as to extend the yard and the side galleries, pushing the stage area back so that a new stage and tiring-house frame covered the pile caps of the original foundations and repositioned themselves 6 feet 6 inches (2 metres) further north.

This peculiar enlargement was made at what was probably a crucial time in the history of the evolution of Shakespearean playhouse design. Burbage was refurbishing his Theatre at the same time. In part Henslowe's motivation must have been the need to accommodate the large Alleyn with his large gestures and even larger plays in a playhouse that already seemed markedly smaller than the Theatre or the nearby Swan. Besides *Tamburlaine, The Spanish Tragedy* and *Dr Faustus*, the Rose staged the heroic Talbots of Shakespeare's first *Henry VI* play and *Titus Andronicus*, all noted by Henslowe as first appearing in those years and setting a fashion that was still able to draw London playgoers to similar amphitheatres for the same plays fifty years later. We do not know what use was made of the Rose from 1587 to 1592, when it was altered. But five years can hardly have been long enough to wear it out and justify such expensive refurbishing. Presumably its original design, only the fourth of the ten amphitheatre playhouses ever built in London, was found unsatisfactory in some way, most likely its small size. There is no other obvious reason why Henslowe should lay out so much money, a quarter of the whole playhouse's original cost, after only five years.

Henslowe's famous *Diary* includes an itemised list of the costs of the 1592 alterations, headed 'A note of suche carges as I have lady owt a bowte my playe howsse in the yeare of or lord 1592 as ffoloweth' (p. 9). The list includes a number of items of the design in the remade playhouse that confirm features found in 1989. Lime and sand were used along with loads of chalk and brick to cement in new foundation walls and probably some of the brick partition walls too. Cheap deal for boards and laths supplied the

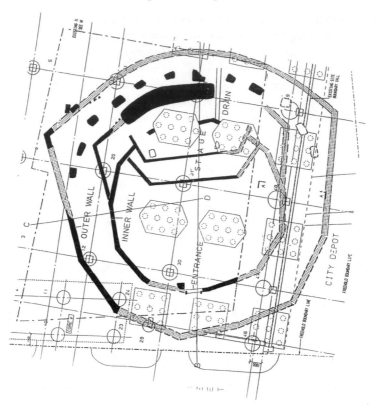

Illustration 24. An archaeological plan of the Rose site, aligned north–south, showing
the remains uncovered in 1989 in black with the conjectured remains still to be dug in grey.
The intermittent black blocks near the top show the original outer-wall foundations of
1587, while the greater black block and the long lines to the left show the extensions made in
1592. The two stages appear near the centre, the lower lines marking the original hexagon
while the upper lines show the later stage foundation moved to the north. Maiden Lane, now
Park Street, is at the bottom of the diagram.

basic materials for the walls and floors. The gallery walls were made from
timber frames, each section infilled with lath and plaster. Some ceilings were
covered with plaster too – the 'Rome over the tyer-howsse' and 'my lords
Rome' are specified for plastering. A series of payments to a thatcher
confirm the type of roofing used for the galleries, and probably the stage
roofing too. There are no payments for a tiler and no remains of any tiles
were found on this site, though the archaeologists found masses of Norfolk
reed, the usual materials used for thatch in the south, on the site. Another
note about buying dozens of turned balusters tells us what the gallery fronts
facing the yard were fenced with. The archaeologists turned up one broken

baluster, which shows its essentially normal shape. Henslowe also paid to have the stage painted, though we are not told in what colours.

The list shows how much care Henslowe himself took in supervising the work. John Grigg, the builder, who was on good terms with the Henslowes, as we know from family letters which have survived, supplied some of the building materials himself but most of them were bought by Henslowe directly from his regular suppliers, whether it was nails from the ironmonger at the sign of the Frying Pan, or from 'braders', or loads of timber brought in by boat. He paid the workmen, including the bricklayer, the thatcher and the plasterer, himself. Evidently by this time his original partner John Cholmley, a grocer who had the right to sell his food and drink to playgoers, had retired or had been bought out, since Henslowe bore all the costs from his own purse. The whole job, ending with payments to the plasterers and the painter, took about two months to complete.

This evidence confirms the large scale of the 1592 extensions, but it does nothing to explain why the enlargement was made. From the position of the foundations it seems that the galleries were stretched by 6 or 7 feet (2 metres) on either side of the stage, increasing the likely space there for audience by two hundred or more seats. If we ignore the possibility that the wooden stage platform was made to jut out into the yard well forward of its chalk foundations the enlargement increased the yard space for the audience from roughly 1,400 square feet to nearly 1,800 square feet. This would have admitted rather fewer than another two hundred understanders. Calculations based on the groundplan as it is now exposed, assuming three levels of galleries, give a total audience capacity of less than two thousand originally plus another four hundred at the enlarged Rose. A rough estimate of the audience at a very popular play in the enlarged Rose (the lost play *Hercules*, on 6 January 1596), based on the half-gallery takings plus a guess at the yard figures, indicates a possible audience of about two thousand two hundred fee-payers. The more usual attendance figure seems to have been about six hundred,[20] so calculations of the total capacity may not be greatly significant. On the other hand, a normally low attendance only makes the increase in the playhouse's maximum capacity more puzzling. Like all theatre impresarios, Henslowe as a businessman must have been inherently an optimist.

Increasing the audience capacity is the most likely explanation of the changes. Its original capacity left the Rose markedly smaller than the other playhouses, so far as we can tell. It was only two-thirds the size of its 1576 predecessor the Theatre, for instance, which must have had an outside diameter of almost 100 feet (30 metres) if we accept the Globe measurements as corresponding to the Theatre's framework. The Globe, like its neighbour the Swan, was said to have an audience capacity of over three thousand, so the Theatre, like the Globe and the Swan, would have made an obvious contrast in size with Henslowe's playhouse. No new playhouses were built between the Rose's first erection in 1587 and its reconstruction five years later, so Henslowe was not forced into a change of mind about the size of his playhouse by any fresh competition on the London scene. The desire to increase his auditorium capacity to something closer to that of the Shoreditch playhouses must have been one consideration behind his financial outlay in 1592. But it is unlikely to have been the sole reason.

The Rose's enlargement presents many puzzles, the greatest of which relates to the stage area. The enlargement had to be to the north, because the southern flank adjoined Maiden Lane. That meant altering the tiring-house and stage, where the experience of players like Alleyn might have made itself felt. But the actual changes seem to have been minimal. The original stage was small, noticeably smaller and less square in shape than the stages of any of the other known playhouses. As early as 1567 the Red Lion's stage had been set out at 30 feet (9.1 metres) deep and 40 feet (12.2 metres) across. The Rose's replacement, the Fortune, had a stage 27 feet 6 inches (8.4 metres) feet deep and 43 feet (13.1 metres) across. But the original stage of the Rose, while it ran 37 feet 6 inches (11.4 metres) across at the rear, tapered to only 27 feet 6 inches (8.4 metres) wide at the front, and most significantly was as little as 15 feet 6 inches (4.7 metres) deep. The replacement in 1592 seems to have been about seventeen feet deep, but with the same width as its predecessor if the angled rear wall of the *frons scenae* was retained. If it was fronted with a flat-plane *frons scenae* of the sort shown at the Swan in Johannes de Witt's sketch of it in 1596, then the depth of the Rose's stage either in 1587 or 1592 would have been reduced to about twelve feet at most. A *frons scenae* of this kind, built in timber with no foundations (and therefore with no remains surviving on the site, since all the original timbers have gone), is, of course, possible. But it seems unlikely if only because it would have reduced the area of the stage to far less than the 500 square feet (46.5 square metres) provided by a stage with angled rear walls. Even that compares poorly with the nearly twelve hundred square feet at the Red Lion and the Fortune. So the Rose's stage can be seen as an elongated hexagon, not square, stretched across the yard in front of the northern gallery bays, with angles on each side made by the bays themselves and the tapering stage edges running into them.

The question of the depth of the stage belongs with the related question of the stage pillars. The archaeologists found a pillar base just inside the foundation wall of the later stage front, built after the wall itself and abutting closely to it. If the clunch (chalk aggregate) footings of the stage front mark its exact limit then the pillar supported by this column base would have to have risen from the very edge of the stage. There is no sign of any pillar base for the first stage. This may mean that part of the intention of the reconstruction in 1592 was to add supports for the stage heavens. That might of course mean that the 1587 Rose had no cover over the stage, and one was added in 1592. Such a conclusion would involve making a large deduction from the inadequate evidence so far available, however, and does not match other hints of evidence. The two plays that might have been performed at the Rose before 1592, *Orlando Furioso* and *Alphonsus of Aragon*, both seem to require stage posts.

The question whether the heavens and stage roof were not constructed until 1592 is complicated by the fact of a large square-shaped drain found in 1989 which ran from the tiring-house northwards to a large ditch crossing the site. This wooden drain was positioned too high in the ground to drain the yard, and most likely functioned to take the run-off of water from the stage roof. Conceivably it was put there in 1587 and repositioned in the reconstruction of 1592 to where it is now. However, thatch cannot be provided with guttering, and there is no mention of lead for gutters in Henslowe's records of the 1592 alterations. The roofing of the reconstruction, like many other questions about the shape of the Rose's design above ground level, is still a mystery.

Erosion trenches were found in the mortar surface of the yard, and the evidence they supply about the driplines from the eaves of the thatched gallery and stage roofs create another enigma. A circular erosion trench, about eighteen inches in from the inner gallery walls, is easily explained as the dripline from the gallery thatch, but it seems to be too near the inner gallery walls if the Rose had the three levels of gallery usually ascribed to it. If each of the two upper gallery levels had a 'jutty' of a foot or so like those specified in the Fortune's contract for its upper galleries the two jutties should have left the erosion trench resulting from the raindrops some way further forward of where the archaeologists found it. The footprint showing the playhouse's foundations does not say much about how many levels were built on them.

A straight erosion trench across the front of the stage is equally puzzling because its depth, which is comparable to that around the galleries, suggests that the water that made it also dropped from a high roofline. Water dripping off the wooden surface of the stage platform itself if it projected forward of the stage foundation could not have made such a deep trench because the platform would have been only five feet or so above the yard surface, the height specified for the Red Lion's stage, compared with the

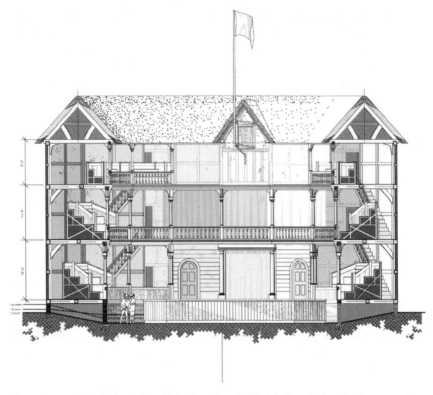

Illustration 25. A hypothetical profile by Jon Greenfield of the Rose's three levels as seen from Maiden Lane. The gallery levels correspond in size to those specified for the Rose's replacement, the Fortune, as specified in its contract.

thirty or so feet of the gallery roof thatch. This erosion trench's position, a foot in front of the stage foundation wall, suggests that the wall marked the forward limit of the stage platform, and perhaps that high above it at the level of the gallery roof there was a hipped stage roof, also of thatch, positioned to drip water onto the members of the audience who pressed closest to the platform. Part of the problem in that enigma is that the trench at the front of the stage is more scuffed by audience feet than the trenches round the gallery walls. This scuffing has its own intriguing implications, because we might expect rainfall to make the yard's standers take shelter under the gallery jutties and so scuff that trench with their feet too. The trench round the gallery edge is far less trodden than the stage edge, however, whatever that implies for spectators taking refuge from the rain.

Other evidence about the auditorium is also far from complete. The galleries were constructed in segments, with partition walls at each angle. The fourteen outer angles of the polygon must have been supported by huge oak timbers each weighing two tons and standing thirty feet high. The main or only entrance to the yard was opposite the stage on the south side, by Maiden Lane. No signs of stair turrets were found in the 60 per cent of the site that was uncovered, and it therefore seems most likely that access to the galleries was by steps up from the yard, as Lambarde and other tourists described them. This may or may not mean that the stairs to the upper levels would have been constructed inside the galleries themselves, as seems on De Witt's evidence to have been the case at the Swan. In fact, though, the Swan must have had two exterior stair turrets, because the contract for the Hope specifies that it was to have external access through stair turrets, essential for the baitings if customers were to be kept out of the yard, and that they were to be built like those of the Swan. If the Rose had internal stairways the space they required would have reduced the audience capacity in the galleries still further.

A lesser puzzle is the mortar-surfaced yard, with its irregular but quite steep ten-degree rake. The inward slope supplied an obvious means of coping with the rainwater dropping into the yard and funnelled in from the surrounding gallery eaves. The rake would also have helped with sight-lines for the standing spectators. The first mortared surface was itself subsequently covered with new layers of a deposit of cement, ash and clinker. This deposit, 18 inches (40 centimetres) thick, had an equal mix of ash and hazel nutshells throughout, probably indicating that the ash was laid at intervals to provide a secure footing on the mud which would have been tramped in daily onto the original mortar surface. The audience then scattered its own debris into the ash underfoot, stirring it in as they shifted their feet through the performance. The whole deposit must have built up gradually through the fifteen years (1587–1600 and 1602–3) that the play-house was in regular use.

Between them the yard and the area under the gallery benches were found by the archaeologists to hold over twenty thousand fragmentary items left by playgoers. Many were pieces of clothing, including beads and laces from ladies' dresses and men's gowns, broken and worn-out footwear, along with pieces of pottery, mostly for food but some money-boxes, a ring, half a scabbard and a broken spur, and some money tokens. Remnants of the food evidently consumed during performances include hazelnut shells, walnut shells, plumstones, figs, cherrystones, grape pips, remnants of apples and pears, elderberry seeds, plus seeds of blackberry, raspberry and sloeberry, along with remnants of rye, oat and wheat bread and marine and freshwater oyster shells.[21] Food must have been a ready feature of playgoing.

One clear deduction can be made about the Rose: its design was in most respects distinctly different from that of its later neighbours the Swan and the Globe, as well as its successor the Fortune on the northern side of the city, for which there is a builder's contract, and also from the Boar's Head to the east, about which there is some evidence from legal documents. The Rose therefore has limited value when we try to deduce the features of other playhouses from it. But as an early playhouse, rebuilt at a crucial time in theatre development, accompanied by Henslowe's unique record of its use for performances, it forms a striking testimony to the diversity of Elizabethan thinking about playhouse design. The foundations make it look more like a practical man's piece of carpentry than carefully designed architecture. They give it the look of a patched-up, jerry-built contrivance. It is perhaps inevitable that the work of the Roman Vitruvius and his resurrection in the sixteenth century by Serlio as a handbook for architects have elevated Roman architecture into an assumed model for Elizabethan design. But the Rose seems to have been built like its neighbours, so we must be cautious about using Vitruvius or Serlio as any sort of precedent for the design of these thoroughly home-made constructions using vernacular materials and domestic traditions for their building. The chief input from Roman sources must have been in the painted decorations.

The second major piece of evidence about early playhouse design needs to be approached with a rather different kind of caution. In 1596 the Dutch scholar Arend van Buchell made a copy of a sketch sent to him by his friend Johannes De Witt, showing the interior of the Swan. De Witt made the sketch shortly after the playhouse was built, though Buchell's copy was discovered in Amsterdam only in 1888.[22] De Witt was a visitor to London and like most foreign tourists took particular note of the playhouses then in use, the Theatre, Curtain, Rose and Swan. As he noted in his diary,

There are four amphitheatres in London of notable beauty, which from their diverse signs bear diverse names. In each of them a different play is daily exhibited to the populace. The two more magnificent of these are situated to the southward beyond the Thames, and from the signs suspended before them are called the Rose and the Swan ... Of all the theatres, however, the largest and the most magnificent is that one of which the sign is a swan, called in the vernacular the 'Swan Theatre'; for it accommodates in its seats three thousand persons, and is built of a mass of flint stones (of which there is a prodigious supply in Britain), and supported by wooden columns painted in such excellent imitation of marble that it is able to deceive even the most cunning. Since its form resembles that of a Roman work, I have made a sketch of it.

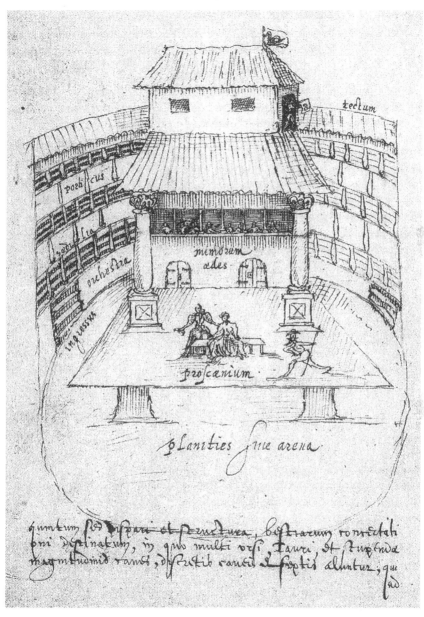

Illustration 26. The copy of the drawing of the Swan made by
Johannes De Witt in 1596 and found in 1888.

De Witt's drawing shows the three galleries (the '*orchestra*') noted by other tourists, with two internal entry-points from the yard (the '*planites sive arena*', or flat arena) to the lowest level of galleries. It shows a square stage with three players performing on it. The tiring-house façade ('*mimorum aedes*') has two pairs of closed double doors, and above it a partitioned balcony or tarras containing several spectators (or players or musicians). Two shapely and massive stage-posts support the small cover or heavens, which is tiled.[23] The hut, trumpeter and flag appear above the cover. To show this superstructure more clearly the perspective has been shifted sideways from that of the rest of the picture. De Witt labelled the various sections of the shape with the equivalent names from the Roman theatre that the Swan reminded him of.

To say that a number of the features illustrated by De Witt are debatable is to put it mildly. Many other items of evidence about the public play-houses seem to conflict with what is shown in the sketch, and have accordingly created doubts about De Witt's accuracy, or that of Van Buchell as his copyist, or both. For one thing what is supposed to be happening in the picture is not clear – the trumpeter would seem to be announcing the commencement of the performance but the players are in mid-show on stage. The audience is there (if it is audience, as it seems to be) in the tiring-house gallery, but nobody is portrayed in the circular galleries or the yard (it has even been conjectured that De Witt was bearing witness to a rehearsal). If the gallery figures are audience, where is the 'above' or playing area above the stage, where Juliet stands when she calls out Romeo's name? The two double entry doors onto the stage are at odds with the multitude of evidence that Elizabethan, Jacobean and Caroline plays all call for three stage entrances, one of them a wide central opening. There is certainly no 'inner stage', nor even a 'discovery-space' such as many plays require, and no hangings anywhere. Furthermore the two curious 'bulks' or 'trestles', as they have been called, underneath the stage seem to be uphold-ing it in a very awkwardly impractical position. Even the roof over the stage seems much smaller than the heavy posts would seem to demand, and its extent seems grossly inadequate as a shelter for the stage itself (it has been called a 'car-port' roof). As the only drawing from the time that claims to show the interior of an outdoor playhouse, it is, to say the least, frustrating.

It is pointless to go into the many attempts to explain these anomalies here. But one specific question does need raising, about the stairs that De Witt calls '*ingressi*', giving access to the lowest galleries. Their positioning accords with the two contemporary statements that the audience first entered the playhouse, presumably the yard, before going up into the galleries, but they are at odds with the two external staircases which are noted as existing at the Swan in the contract for the Hope, where the builder was asked to imitate those at the Swan. Where would external staircases be going if not up into the galleries? The internal stairs which De Witt illustrated would hardly have been used just as exits, though they would have had the useful function of allowing the yard's standers to get under cover for an extra penny when it rained. The '*ingressus*' label that De Witt gave them seems to mean that they were ways into the galleries from the yard, not just exits from the galleries down to the yard for people who originally got there from the stairs outside the playhouse. Some resolution of these uncertainties is necessary before we can accept that De Witt's sketch is an accurate depiction of the Swan or not.

The varying perspective positions the viewer above the roof level and at a middle gallery level simultaneously. There are six partitions in the stage gallery when in a polygonal structure there should be five. Such indications of a less than exact method of recording by the observer, together with the fact that the surviving drawing is a copy, besides enigmas like the hatched markings under the stage (which I conjectured long ago might show openings in the hangings around the stage rim) and the conflict of several features with other evidence have led some critics to dismiss what the drawing seems to offer altogether. It has too many peculiarities for comfort. So some consideration of at least one of the anomalies is appropriate here, a particular anomaly which has been heightened by the archaeological work done on the Rose and the Globe.

The drawing's '*ingressus*', or stairway from the yard up into the lowest gallery, conforms with the evidence for the admission system described by other visitors to London at the time, who said that spectators first paid one penny for admission to the yard, then a second for admission to the galleries. De Witt shows the form of access into the lowest galleries that this early process indicates would have made necessary. But it was a clumsy system, and not very economical. At the Rose, if it lacked any stair turret, and apparently at De Witt's Swan, latecomers wanting a gallery place paid a first gatherer to enter at the back of the yard, and then to get into the galleries they had to press through the yard's crowd before, after paying a second gatherer, forcing their way up the internal stairs of the '*ingressus*' through the spectators sitting on the stairs or at the front of the gallery degrees, to eventually find a seat at the back of the crowd. By contrast at the Globe, if the archaeological testimony is right, entrants to the yard and the galleries would have divided themselves off as soon as they entered one of the two outer lobbies. These lobbies, at the base of the two stair turrets, gave initial access to both standers and sitters. We know the Globe had only the two means of access in all, since when it burned down in 1613 the witnesses said that everyone had to escape by just 'two small dores'. So the Globe's standers would have entered the yard from the lobby at the back through a passage under the galleries as they did at the Rose, but unlike at the Rose the seekers after seats in the Globe's galleries when in the lobby immediately turned up a stairway. Patrons making for the galleries paid only once, in the entrance lobby, and then spiralled up the stair turret going directly from the lobby to enter at the back of the galleries. The firstcomers thus got the best seats without the fear that they must have had at the Rose of being subsequently elbowed by latecomers who had to push their way through them to the back. The puzzle about De Witt's drawing is that the Hope contract's reference to the Swan indicates that it had stair turrets like the Globe's, which would have made the '*ingressus*' from the yard unnecessary except when customers wanted to pay extra to get out of the rain into the lowest level of gallery. It is most unlikely that the Swan ever had a major overhaul to install stair turrets some time between De Witt's visit in 1596 and the Hope contract of 1614.

Conceivably De Witt's drawing shows features from more than the one playhouse. Its square stage and planar *frons scenae* with its two stage doors may have belonged to the Swan, but the redundant '*ingressus*' may have come from the Rose. De Witt was certainly not thinking of the Rose's narrow and tapered stage when he made his drawing, but he may have conflated his memories of other features. The drawing may be accurate in some respects for the Swan itself, but it would be unwise to use it for more general observations about playhouse details. Van Buchell's copy of whatever De Witt drew for him shows that the Swan was as different from the Rose as it was from the Globe and the Fortune. Even the Rose's rake in its yard does not seem to have been copied at the Swan, since the word '*planities*' which Van Buchell applied to the Swan's yard indicates that it was flat. The Swan drawing's evidence cannot be wholly discounted, but it can only be used hesitantly, even for the Swan itself.

At the least what the Swan drawing does confirm is how very variable the design of each outdoor playhouse was. Given the huge amount of tangible evidence provided by the work of archaeologists on the sites of the Rose and the Globe it is an agonizing pity that English Heritage, controller of all such early sites, has in its wisdom decreed that, while the whole of the Rose site may be excavated when enough money can be found to do it, the site of the Globe and every other early playhouse must remain secure from further intrusion. This seems to follow the old tourist principle that when you've seen one you've seen them all, and is quite mistaken. All the evidence we have says that the Rose and the Globe were utterly different from each other, and that the Swan, Fortune and Hope were different again. The fragment of the Globe dug up in 1989 is particularly tantalizing and inconclusive, as we shall see shortly.

Apart from doubt over the Swan's '*ingressus*' and the stair turrets, what little other evidence there is about that playhouse does not seriously contradict De Witt. The two stage doors are quite sufficient for the staging of the only play we know to have been performed at the Swan, *A Chaste Maid in Cheapside*, which does actually specify in a stage direction entries '*at one Dore ... At the other Doore*'. It has also been pointed out that one pair of double doors opened out would have been sufficient for any normal 'discovery' or display scene, or for the pushing out of a bed onto the stage, or the carrying out of large properties. Conceivably any stage hangings might have been omitted by De Witt because they would have obscured the location of the stage doors. Alternatively they might have hung inside the doorways behind the doors, so that when the doors were open the hangings would become visible to conceal a 'discovery', and when they were closed the hangings would be hidden and so would not impede the normal use of the doors. It has even been suggested that perhaps De Witt wished only to show the physical structure and that, because the players used only two gaps in the hangings for their entrances, that left him assuming there were only two doors instead of three, one a 'discovery-space' in the centre that was not used the day he was there. The drawing leaves a lot of room for such guesswork.

The figures watching the players from above the stage have caused as much controversy as the non-existent discovery-space. About one-sixth (45 out of 276)[24] of the extant plays written in the period when the Swan was in use require a playing space '*above*' or '*aloft*', but De Witt's sketch leaves little room for it. The partitions of the gallery suggest that they are the Swan's equivalent to the 'gentlemen's roomes' specified in the Fortune contract, or the 'lords roome' that Jonson describes as 'over the stage' at the Globe in *Every Man Out of his Humour*. It has been suggested that the players simply moved into one of the gentlemen's rooms when they required an area aloft and shared it temporarily with the gentlemen.[25] There would then be no loss of revenue from the rooms and perhaps a gratifying proximity to the action for the gentlemen, much as they enjoyed at the Blackfriars sitting on their stools on the stage. Or one of the rooms might be the musicians' room, in which case there would be no problem in asking them to move over to give the players access.

The 'bulks' or 'trestles' underneath the stage are curious chiefly because they seem to be drawn so crudely and so out of proportion in comparison with the rest of the sketch, so that their presence actually discredits much of the rest. As noted above, I suspect they are in fact quite accurately if incompletely drawn, and that they represent not under-stage supports but gaps in the hangings draped round the stage to conceal the under-stage area. Some form of concealment there must have been – at the Fortune it was wooden palings – or the operation of the stage trap could hardly be secret. There must have been apertures, though, because it was from under the stage that devils were expected to run amongst the audience in *England's Joy*, a non-existent play for which an ingenious trickster attracted large crowds to the Swan in 1602.[26] When the audience realised they had been caught by fraud they are said to have revenged themselves on the playhouse, including the 'hangings', of which the most accessible would have surrounded the stage. Such a theory would explain the curiously soft outlines of the two shapes and the splay of their feet, as a depiction of soft material dragging on the ground, in contrast with the sharp outlines of all the wooden features in the sketch. All that is missing if De Witt was trying to depict such a feature are vertical lines at the outer edges of the stage to mark where the hangings turned. De Witt would have sketched the apertures in order to show where the devils emerged. Such a theory on the other hand contradicts the idea that he showed no hangings because he was only concerned with the physical features, not the furnishings. The drawing is rich in such anomalies.

4. LATER AMPHITHEATRE DESIGN

Besides the often tenuous Globe evidence the best information we have about the second generation of public playhouses is the builder's contract for the Fortune. Built in about six months, from 17 January 1600, it was created in competition with the Globe and constructed by the same builder, Peter Streete. He had supervised the demolition of the old Theatre and its reconstruction on the Bankside in the previous year. Unfortunately much of his Fortune contract simply instructs him to copy what he had done in constructing the Globe, and to follow a plan that has not survived. Nonetheless it is well worth quoting in detail:

Phillip Henslowe & Edward Allen, the daie of the date here of, have bargayned, compounded & agreed with the said Peter Streete For the erecting, building & setting up of a new howsse and Stadge for a Plaiehouse in and upon a certeine plott or parcell of ground appointed out for that purpose, scytuate and beinge nere Goldinge lane in the parishe of Ste Giles withoute Cripplegate of London, to be by him the saide Peeter Streete or somme other sufficyent woorkmen of his provideinge and appoyntemente and att his propper costes & chardges, for the consideration hereafter in theis presentes expressed, made, erected, builded and sett upp in manner & forme followinge (that is to saie); The frame of the saide howse to be sett square and to conteine Fowerscore foote of lawfull assize everye waie square withoutt and fiftie five foote of like assize square everye waie within, with a good suer and stronge foundacion of pyles, brick, lyme and sand bothe without & within, to be wroughte one foote of assize att the leiste above the grounde; And the saide Frame to conteine three Stories in heighth, the first or lower Storie to conteine Twelve foote of lawfull assize in heighth, the second Storie Eleaven foote of lawfull assize in heigth, and the third or upper Storie to conteine Nyne foote of lawfull assize in height; All which Stories shall conteine Twelve foote and a halfe of lawfull assize in breadth throughoute, besides a juttey forwardes in either of the saide twoe upper Stories of Tenne ynches of lawfull assize, with Fower convenient divisions for gentlemens roomes, and other sufficient and convenient divisions for Twoe pennie roomes, with necessarie seates to be placed and sett, aswell in those roomes as throughoute all the rest of the galleries of the saide howse, and with suchelike steares, conveyances & divisions withoute & within, as are made & contryved in and to the late erected Plaiehowse on the Banck in the saide parishe of Ste Saviours called the Globe; With a Stadge and Tyreinge howse to be made, erected & settupp within the saide Frame, with a shadowe or cover over the saide Stadge, which Stadge shalbe placed & sett, as alsoe the stearecases of the saide Frame, in suche sorte as is prefigured in a plott thereof drawen, and which Stadge shall conteine in length Fortie and Three foote of lawfull assize and in breadth to extende to the middle of the yarde of the saide howse; The same Stadge to be paled in belowe with good, strong and sufficyent newe oken bourdes, and likewise the lower Storie of the saide Frame within-side, and the same lower storie to be alsoe laide over and fenced with stronge yron pykes; And the saide Stadge to be in all other proporcions contryved and fashioned like unto the Stadge of the saide Plaie howse called the Globe; With convenient windowes and lightes glazed to the saide Tyreinge howse; And the saide Frame, Stadge and Stearecases to be covered with Tyle, and to have a sufficient gutter of lead to carrie & convey the water frome the coveringe of the saide Stadge to fall backwardes; And also all the saide Frame and the Stairecases thereof to be sufficyently enclosed withoute with lathe, lyme & haire, and the gentlemens roomes and Twoe pennie roomes to be seeled with lathe, lyme & haire, and all the Flowers of the saide Galleries, Stories and Stadge to be bourded with good & sufficyent newe deale bourdes of the whole thicknes, wheare need shalbe; And the saide howse and other thinges beforemencioned to be made & doen to be in all other contrivitions, conveyances, fashions, thinge and thinges affected, finished and doen accordinge to the manner and fashion of the saide howse called the Globe, saveinge only that all the princypall and maine postes of the saide Frame and Stadge forwarde shalbe square and wroughte palasterwise, with carved proporcions called Satiers to be placed & sett on the topp of every of the same postes, and saveinge also that the said Peeter Streete shall not be chardged with anie manner of Pay[ntin]ge in or aboute the saide Frame howse or Stadge or anie parte thereof, nor rendringe the walls within, nor seeling anie more or other roomes then the gentlemens roomes, Twoe pennie roomes and Stadge before remembred. Nowe theiruppon the saide Peeter Streete dothe covenant, promise and graunte For himself, his executours and administratours, to and with the saide Phillipp Henslowe and Edward Allen and either of them, and thexecutours and administratours of them and either of them, by theis presentes in manner & forme followeinge (that is to saie); That he the saide Peeter Streete, his executours or assignes, shall & will att his or their owne propper costes & chardges well, woorkmanlike & substancyallie make, erect, sett upp and fully finishe in and by all thinges, accordinge to the true meaninge of theis presentes, with good, stronge and substancyall newe tymber and other necessarie stuff, all the saide Frame and other woorkes whatsoever in and uppon the saide plott or parcell of grounde (beinge not by anie aucthoretie restrayned, and havinge ingres, egres & regres to doe the same) before the Fyve & twentith daie of Julie next commeinge after the date hereof; And shall alsoe at his or theire like costes and chardges provide and finde all manner of woorkmen, tymber, joystes, rafters, boordes, dores, boltes, hinges, brick, tyle, lathe, lyme, haire, sande, nailes, lade, iron, glasse, woorkmanshipp and other thinges whatsoever, which shalbe needefull, convenyent & necessarie for the saide Frame & woorkes & everie parte thereof; And shall alsoe make all the saide Frame in every poynte for Scantlinges lardger and bigger in assize then the Scantlinges of the timber of the saide newe erected howse called the Globe; And alsoe that he the saide Peeter Streete shall furthwith, aswell by himself as by suche other and soemanie woorkmen as shalbe convenient & necessarie, enter into and uppon the saide buildings and woorkes, and shall in reasonable manner proceede therein withoute anie wilfull detraccion untill the same shalbe fully effected and finished.[27]

    In summary the most significant points in the contract are that the shape was to be square inside and out, unlike the 'round' or polygonal Globe, probably imitating square innyards instead of polygonal baiting-houses. The square measured 80 feet (24 metres) on the outside and 55 feet (16.8 metres) inside. It was built in timber infilled with oak laths and clad with lime plaster ('lathe lyme & haire') on a brick and pile foundation, and roofed with tiles over the 'Frame, Stadge and Stearecases'. The first gallery was to be 12 feet (3.7 metres) high, the second 11 feet (3.3 metres) and the third 9 feet (2.7 metres), a total height of 32 feet (9.7 metres), each of the upper galleries having a 10 inch (25 centimetre) overhang or 'jutty' into the yard. The stage, tiring-house and cover were set up inside the main framework, the stage measuring 43 feet (13 metres) across and extending halfway, i.e. 27 feet 6 inches (8.4 metres), into the yard. The stage itself and the lowest gallery were 'paled in' with oak boards, and the gallery paling was reinforced with iron 'pykes' to stop the yard standers from trying to haul themselves over into the seating. The tiring-house was to have glass windows, presumably at the rear on the outer face of the framework. Richard Hosley's analysis of the Fortune[28] adds the likelihood that the two entrances from the street were on the south flank, probably from a lobby like the

Globe's including the beginning of the spiral staircases that led up into the galleries. The stage would most likely have been on the northern side of the yard, as at the Rose, where it would have most light from the afternoon sun.

The cost of building the Fortune playhouse was £520, the total cost to Henslowe and Alleyn £1,320. Although its decorative scantlings were made larger than those at the Globe, its cost was cheap in comparison with the second Globe, which had to be rebuilt from foundation level after the fire of 1613. It took £120 a year in upkeep between 1602 and 1608. Its sign was a picture of Dame Fortune, who smiled on the building until 9 December 1621, when it was burned to the ground. Alleyn promptly rebuilt it in brick at a cost of £1,000, possibly this time with a circular design. Much later James Wright described it as 'a large, round Brick building'.[29] Despite vigorous opposition from Dulwich College, by then the owners, it was finally dismantled in 1649.

The Boar's Head has some information about its shape in its legal documents. Wrangles which brought it to the notice of the courts started in 1599, soon after Francis Langley took a share in its finances. Since they concerned the various outlays of cash, and what the cash was spent on, some fairly detailed descriptions of the building works are given in the records that survive.[30] Its first conversion from a galleried innyard to a playhouse started in 1598. The Privy Council order of July 1597 to pull all the amphitheatres down had wafted away, so with the Theatre standing now unused in its 'vast silence, and dark solitude'[31] and Langley in trouble at the Swan, only the Rose and the Curtain were then available as regular venues for use by the two licensed companies. The Boar's Head thus became the third candidate for use by whatever ambitious company could occupy it. The locality and perhaps the inn itself were not unused to plays. Many years before, in September 1557, the Privy Council had intervened to stop the performance of *A Sackful of News* at 'the Bores hed without Aldgate'.[32] Its position at the eastern gateway to the City made it an obvious candidate for such a function. Oliver Woodliffe, owner of the site in 1598 along with a yeoman called Richard Samwell, joined finances to put up a stage and convert the surrounding structures into galleries for audience and a tiring-house. Woodliffe provided the tiring-house and the gallery over the stage, Samwell two levels of galleries opposite the stage and a single gallery down each side of the rectangular enclosure. Samwell was to be the manager, handling the running costs, the players and the takings, Woodliffe the sleeping partner.

The playhouse they constructed was not very large, and seems to have had a stage standing free of the tiring-house, truly a 'theatre in the round', except that it was square. It evidently did not prove adequate, because in 1599 its financiers launched a major improvement, setting the stage 6 feet (1.8 metres) further back to butt against the tiring-house, putting a roof over it, and increasing the gallery seating capacity till the whole theatre could accommodate about one thousand spectators. The total cost was near £500. By this time Samwell had Robert Browne and Derby's Men as his clients, and Browne had come in as a part-financier. In August 1599 Browne bought Samwell out. Trouble started soon after, because the venturesome Langley had bought Woodliffe out in November of the previous year.

Langley's subsequent flow of lawsuits was aimed mostly at Samwell, and ran until 1601. The flood might have been one reason why Browne and his company moved elsewhere. In late 1601 the aggressive new Worcester's Men pushed themselves in with a three-month tenure of the playhouse, and on 31 March 1602 the Privy Council allocated Worcester's to the Boar's Head when it confirmed them as the third London company. But that arrangement did not last long. By 17 August Worcester's were at the old Rose while Browne and Derby's Men had returned to their former house. Whether because of its small capacity or for other reasons they did not stay there for many months, since by late 1604 Worcester's, now Queen Anne's Men, were settled at the Red Bull. After that the Boar's Head died as a playhouse.

The stage at the Boar's Head was rectangular, almost 40 feet (12.2 metres) across at the front and about 25 feet (7.6 metres) deep, only a little less than the Fortune and the Globe, with two rooms of about 12 feet 6 inches (3.8 metres) deep behind the stage, deeper than the gallery bays at the Rose and the Globe, to make the tiring house.[33] Plays written for the Boar's Head stage needed two entry doors, and made no demand for any machinery in the heavens. Only one surviving play needed a trap, and one an 'above'. The yard was similar in size to the Fortune's, measuring 54 feet 6 inches by 55 feet 7 inches (16.6 by 16.9 metres). The galleries were originally only 3 feet (90 centimetres) deep, making a shallow seating and passageway space that was broadened in 1599 to about 6 feet (1.8 metres). It was this limited gallery depth and only the one or two levels instead of the three at the Swan and the Fortune which made it so much smaller in audience capacity than the others. At Samwell's end of the building there was a privy, the only interior privy on record at any of the playhouses. Apart from that feature it seems to have been not unlike a square and shorter version of the Swan as De Witt shows it, with a rectangular stage, two stage doors, and a gallery for audience above the stage.

A small word or two might be appropriate here about privies, since even the one on record at the Boar's Head cannot have done much to supply an outlet for a thousand spectators, let alone the large proportion of them who were female. Given the evidence for such an ample supply of foodstuffs and drink at the Rose, suggesting that playgoing commonly included all the ingredients for a picnic, even the two hours traffic of the Elizabethan stages must have given many spectators problems, at least with their urine. It has been suggested that for those seated in the galleries the topmost gallery's back wall would have been useful for men, since the steep angle of vision there allowed only about three steep ranks of seating, which left several feet of empty space behind for other uses. Tests done at Wanamaker's Globe on Elizabethan lime plaster as wall-filling indicate that it could easily withstand erosion from flows of urine. Women might have had special pots under their skirts to receive their outflows, subsequently decanted into available buckets. Women did that at the Spanish theatres, though one does have to give some credit to a report by Gail Kern Paster that a maker of gunpowder, the saltpetre element for which was taken from urine, got the right at Ely Cathedral to scrape the sections of floor where women stood at church services. The masses of lime plaster from the wall in-fills found in the yard of the Rose received no testing for possible urine content.

Knowledge about the other Elizabethan and Jacobean public playhouses is more fragmentary, deriving mainly from casual mentions in contemporary writing such as the inevitable lawsuits and from the analysis of stage directions in the plays, filled in with deductions based on the Swan sketch and Fortune contract. Of the original Theatre in Shoreditch we know from lawsuits that it was built in timber with some ironwork, and had a tiring-house and galleries, one of which had rooms for gentlemen to sit in.[34] The leading companies used it regularly in the 1580s, but by 1597 it was empty because the lease of the land on which it stood had expired. After Christmas 1598 the players employed twelve workmen under the supervision of Peter Streete to pull it down, and on 20 January 1599 they transported its oak framing timbers across the river to a new site near the Rose and Swan. Exit Theatre.

Techniques of building in timber were on the decline in Tudor times, partly under the influence of Renaissance brick and plaster construction, partly because timber became more costly as the oak forests were cut back. In Jacobean times new fire regulations added their pressure towards building in brick and tile instead of timber and thatch. We can see some changes at work in theatre building, in the Swan's painted marbling, and perhaps in the switch from a timber frame structure to brick at the second Fortune and the later private playhouses. The first playhouses like the Theatre and the Globe, however, belong in the vernacular wood-based tradition. Building in timber involved highly standardised construction techniques, and a very precise module or dimensional code for interlocking beams. The beams were mortised and tenoned, and held at the joints only by dowel pegs (iron nails were expensive, as Henslowe's payments in 1592 show). The component timbers were prefabricated, since construction by means of interlocking pieces required a whole section or bay of a framework to be fitted together before the components could stand in their places – beams could not be fitted with the interlocking mortices once they were erected. If they were prefabricated in large quantities or if they were to be transported from one site to another the main component beams were numbered with standard markings. This is what Streete would have done when he dismantled the Theatre's framework and took them south of the river to Bankside.[35]

The playhouse built out of the timbers transported across the Thames early in 1599 is the most misinterpreted piece of hardware the Elizabethan players had. Constructed on a second-hand frame as a second-best option by the company which had hoped to use the Blackfriars hall built for it to use three years before, the Globe's beginning was unpromising. The fact that subsequently most of Shakespeare's greatest plays were written for it has obscured these scrambled origins and has fertilised elaborate fantasies about its design for hundreds of years. This account will try to prune or lop the more extravagant fantasies about the Globe's original shape by examining the only two reliable pieces of evidence about it that we have, a drawing of the second Globe made in the 1630s and the fragments of its foundations uncovered in 1989.[36]

The story of the Shakespeare company's loss of the Theatre and its abortive partner the Blackfriars followed by the dubiously legal acquisition of the Theatre's frame timbers to build the Globe has been told above in Chapter 2. One feature of that story is the cut-price circumstances in which the first Globe was built, and the contrasting opulence of its rebuilding in 1614. That creates difficulties for the evidence about the original Globe, because the two best pieces of evidence both relate principally to the reconstruction of 1614. To identify the original Globe we have to weigh the likelihood of improvements to the design that were made in the rebuilding against the probability that the nostalgia which persuaded the company to rebuild it would have required any changes to be fairly minimal. A testimony in the 1630s asserted that the new Globe was built on the foundations of the old. This indicates that the groundplan should have been the same, so that the outline in Hollar's illustration of the second Globe and the fragment of the foundations dug up in 1989 should reflect the dimensions of the first Globe. Whatever alterations may have been introduced above the foundations is a matter for conjecture.

Illustration 27. Wenceslas Hollar's drawing of the second Globe made in the 1630s from Southwark Cathedral's tower for his 'Long View' of London.

Only those two kinds of good evidence about the Globe survive. One, like the Rose dig, is archaeological, the other a contemporary's graphic picture, like De Witt's Swan drawing. Both are principally of the second Globe. The archaeological evidence has uncovered a section of the gallery walls with a stair turret lobby attached round an angle of the outer wall. Wenceslas Hollar's 1630s drawing for his famous 'Long View' of London from the south shows what he could see of the second Globe from the tower of the church that is now Southwark Cathedral. The archaeological evidence provides information chiefly about the foundations, while Hollar's view shows only the exterior shape of the lavishly built replacement for the original Globe. Such imperfect evidence has to be eked out with thoughts from the plays we know were written for the first Globe if we are to locate any secure indications of what Shakespeare expected from his workplace.

The archaeological evidence comes from a small section of the total foundations, most of which lie under another building.[37] It shows a broad foundation of 'clunch', or chalk stones in an aggregate which evidently filled the trench, forming a basis for the outer gallery wall foundation. Two sections or bays of the outer walls of a polygon were uncovered, angled at about 158° or 160°. This angle indicates that there might have been twenty or perhaps eighteen sides to the full polygon. Another angle was discovered in a very small fragment of the inner gallery wall, in brick and mortar. It measures the same as the outer wall. Since it stands one bay round from the outer gallery angle, the likely radius of the outer walls can be measured by bisecting the two angles, subtending a line through them and noting where they intersect at the centre of the polygon. So far as it is possible to measure the angles exactly they seem to cross at about 50 feet (15 metres) from the outer gallery wall. It thus appears that the Globe was roughly 100 feet (30 metres) in its outside diameter, markedly larger than the approximately 72 feet (22 metres) of the Rose. The outer and inner gallery walls enclose a space a little over 11 feet (3.4 metres) deep, much the same as the Rose's gallery bays. The Globe's yard must therefore have been nearly 78 feet (24 metres) in diameter.

The fraction of the Globe's remains so far excavated have other foundations attached to the gallery walls. They appear to form the base of one of the two entrances to the playhouse on the north-eastern flank. Two crosswalls stretch between the inner and outer gallery foundations, to the right (looking from the yard) of the outer wall angle. Hazelnut shell debris was found at the yard end between the two crosswalls, indicating that they formed a passageway into and from the yard. Outside the outer gallery wall two sets of foundations jut out from the centre of each side, turning at right angles to run parallel to the faces of the outer gallery until they meet and make an enclosure or lobby framing the angle of the outer gallery wall. These lobby walls stop short of the angle itself, thus making an open doorway into the lobby. Outside this doorway a deposit of gravel was found, evidently laid in order to provide footing for pedestrians arriving at the playhouse from Maiden Lane to the north. The positioning of the lobby walls around the angle of the outer gallery wall perhaps suggests that the huge 30-foot-high (9.1-metre) timber beam upright in the angle, part of the main structural frame for the gallery scaffolding, was used as a newel post. If so, the stairway into the galleries would have spiralled round it with the stair treads mortised into it.

Such a lobby design indicates that audiences, when they entered through the outer opening, would have either gone to the left of the angle and walked through the passageway into the yard, or have gone to the right and climbed the stairs into one of the galleries. This entranceway would have

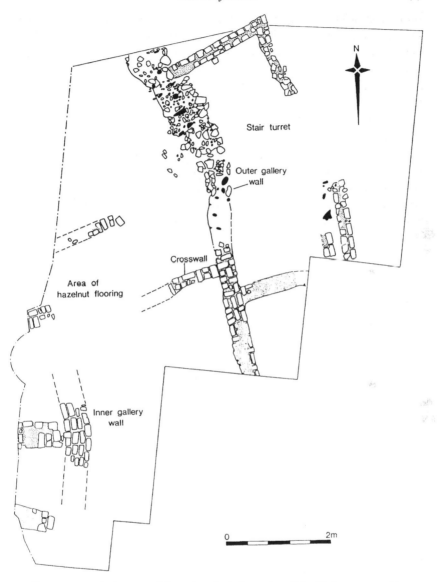

Illustration 28. A diagram of the archaeological remains of the Globe uncovered in 1989. They appear to show an angle of the outer gallery wall and a tiny section of the inner wall, with a lobby or entranceway to the right, fixed on one of the timber uprights making an angle of the twenty-sided polygon. A walled corridor runs south of the post marking the lobby to the yard on the left, to the west.

given access to the yard and the galleries on the eastern side facing the stage. The other entranceway, shown as another stair turret in Wenceslas Hollar's picture of the second Globe, was positioned symmetrically on the other flank of the yard and would have given access to the western side of the auditorium. If this is reliable evidence for the admission system at the Globe it clearly indicates an improvement in the design of the later generation of amphitheatres compared with the Rose generation, if indeed the Rose had no stair turret.

It is regrettable that English Heritage has barred any further excavation, even in the basement of Anchor Terrace, which was built in the 1840s on a foundation not consisting of piles like Southbridge House at the Rose site but a concrete raft, the base of which seems to be at least a foot higher than the Globe foundations. The remains are thus preserved for what English Heritage hopes will be the superior technology of future archaeology. The one supplementary dig that was undertaken in 1992 and that established the existence of the raft of concrete on which Anchor Terrace was built was ordered to stop as soon as it found anything that might belong to the Globe. Three pits were dug, finding only one fragment that might have been the Globe. From the top surface it seemed to be a pile cap, the basis for a vertical post of some kind. Since it was within the area where the stage is thought to have been, it could be the foundation for one of the two stage posts that we know both Globes had.

One thing the main particles of archaeological evidence do confirm about the first Globe is also a distinctive feature of Hollar's depiction of the second Globe. In this kind of exercise, when one piece of evidence supports the testimony of another the coincidence is devoutly to be celebrated. Hollar positioned the second Globe's stage cover precisely adjoining what John Orrell calculated was the point where the sun rose in Southwark at midsummer.[38] In other words the stage had its back to the summer sun, the 'shadow' or cover or 'heavens' over the stage providing shelter from direct sunshine as well as rain. This was opposite to where the Rose and the Fortune had their stages. Such a calculation was confirmed by the location of the auditorium lobby uncovered in 1989. Having its back to the sun may in part reflect the Globe designers' knowledge that their playhouse was bigger than the Admiral's company venues, where the smaller diameter of their galleries with the same heights might have given better protection against incoming sunlight. Elizabethans had constant trouble with the sun, which not only turned faces an unseemly brown and forced many women to walk abroad wearing headscarves or face-masks but made its ultra-violet light fade the bright colours of their velvets and satins all too quickly. So the Globe was

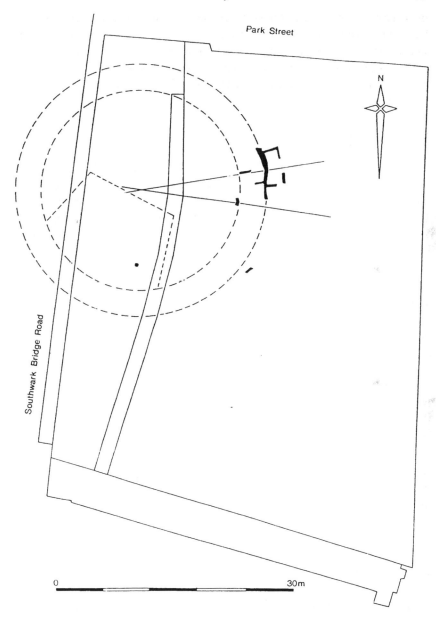

Illustration 29. A diagram of the Globe foundations in relation to the rest of the (conjectured) building. Much of it lies under a listed nineteenth-century structure, Anchor Terrace, facing Southwark Bridge Road and now a block of flats. The one fragment in its basement that was uncovered in 1992 (marked in the stage area) could have been the support for a stage post.

designed to protect the players from direct sunlight as well as rain, and to leave only those customers who chose to sit in the upper galleries opposite the stage (a much-favoured modern cinema-goer's position) suffering from its rays.

We know that the Globe had its stage facing north, where direct sunlight did not intrude. On the other hand the Rose and probably the Fortune had their stages facing the southerly sun. Apart from this being a further testimony to the variability of playhouse design, it suggests that sunlight was not enough of a problem to prevent the Rose from being constructed so that it faced Maiden Lane on its southern side, and therefore required the stage to be on the northern flank. We should not forget that Elizabethans routinely wore hats, and that ladies wore black face masks, both of which helped to shelter faces against the sun. Richard Knolles in his history of the Turks (1603) reported that Tamburlaine preferred to remain bare-headed. Marlowe, however, made some play with crowns in his text. Whether Alleyn would have chosen to represent Tamburlaine's appearance on stage bare-headed or at first hooded and later crowned is open to serious question.

Both the Rose and the Globe's archaeological evidence tells us more about their auditoria than it does about their stages. Foundations give little firm information about the details of timberwork constructed on them, and there is little evidence of the stage and all its furnishings apart from the outline of the stage's shape at the Rose and a base for one of its stage posts. The Swan drawing is some help, but the best evidence about the stages is still what can be deduced from the plays that were written for specific playhouses. Of these there is happily more evidence about the Rose and the Globe than any of the others.

It does seem that the Globe's yard was markedly larger than the Rose's, and its stage may in consequence have had a distinctly different configuration. Probably square or rectangular, it could afford to have a flat-faced *frons scenae*, instead of the three angled faces at the Rose. Its size must have compared with the Fortune's 43 feet wide by 27 deep, probably more if like the Fortune it extended to the middle of the yard. It had a large trap, big enough for two men (Hamlet and Laertes, for instance) to descend at once, and two stage pillars supporting the heavens, which Hamlet says were fretted with golden fire. It had two stage doors (the Quarto of *Pericles* has a stage direction speaking of '*one door*' and '*the other*'), flanking a set of hangings across what was probably a central discovery-space recessed into the *frons*. This central space was necessary for bringing on large properties such as the chair of state or throne required for all court scenes, and the curtained bed for Juliet and for Desdemona in *Othello*. Its cover of hangings was the cloth of arras that Hamlet stabs through to kill Polonius. It was used for regal entries and for the clowns, who usually made their presence known first by sticking their heads through the hangings, as we have seen.

At the upper level of the *frons* on the stage balcony were the lords' rooms, which Guilpin said were 'o're the stage'.[39] One such room, probably the central one, would have been used for balcony scenes. It was required for rather more than half of the plays written for the Globe between 1599 and 1609.[40] For some of the scenes, a '*window*' above the stage is mentioned in the stage directions or the text, in others players appear '*on the walls*' or above the gates of a besieged town, as at Harfleur in *Henry V*. Other scenes require a non-specific locality above as a place for observation. In Shakespeare fourteen references indicate the place simply as '*aloft*' or '*above*'. Ten references, not all of them in plays originally written for the Globe, call it '*on the walls*', four '*the windows*', one '*the Tarras*', and others are simply implied in the dialogue.[41] Two references to a place '*on the top*' occur in plays not written specifically for the Globe (*1 Henry VI* and *The Tempest*) though most likely staged there. They seem to refer to places above the upper playing area. Such an elevated place may have been adjacent to the heavens or the huts – possibly even the trumpeter's place, if the Globe had one like De Witt's sketch. Thirteen scenes in Shakespeare need descents from the upper area to the stage, and five require ascents, three by way of the tiring-house interior, a climb which occupies the time of two or three lines of verse.

Action above was usually brief, twenty-eight of Shakespeare's instances averaging only thirty-seven lines there, and a maximum of three players.[42] They use speech rather than movement. From these observations it is easy to deduce that the space available above the stage was limited. Scholars have accordingly been quick to point out that an above-stage gallery area given over to spectators like the partitioned gallery of the Swan sketch could easily have accommodated all the above-stage requirements of the Globe plays. The one likely exception to this is the raising of Antony's body to the monument in *Antony and Cleopatra*, of which there is something to be said below. Therefore it seems likely that the upper levels of the Globe tiring-house façade were constructed in a manner not essentially different from those shown at the Swan. Jonson's reference to 'the lords roome over the stage' at the Globe seems to confirm this. The players could have simply used one of the lords' rooms when a play demanding such an area was to be put on. Later the company's musicians from the Blackfriars consort occupied one.

There is a strong likelihood that one of the rooms in the gallery after 1608 became reserved as a 'music-room', and – a further conjecture – that it was this room that doubled as the above-stage playing area. It has even been suggested that the figures in the third and fourth sections of the gallery (the middle two) in De Witt's sketch were meant to represent musicians.[43] There certainly was a music-room at the Swan when *A Chaste Maid in Cheapside* was performed because it calls at one point for '*a sad Song in the Musicke-roome*'. Use of the '*above*' is complicated and possibly explained by a change in the function of music in the amphitheatres towards the end of the first decade of the seventeenth century under the influence of the King's Men's acquisitions of 1608. The induction to the version of the Shakespeare company's *The Malcontent* stolen from a boy company and played at the Globe speaks bluntly of the 'not received custome of musicke in our Theater'. This presumably means that they lacked the concert musicians performing with strings and woodwinds that the boy company at Blackfriars employed. Drums, trumpets, fiddles and flutes were standard accessories to performances from early in the history of playing, but these instruments were most employed on stage or '*within*'. The fashion for string and woodwind chamber-music began in the hall theatres, where it was played as a kind of overture and between the acts. The Blackfriars musicians had a considerable reputation even in 1602, the year the visiting Duke of Stettin-Pomerania heard an hour-long concert before the play by a consort of lutes, mandolins, bandores, violins and flutes.[44] The Blackfriars music-room was probably a curtained alcove above the stage like the musicians' gallery 'above' in a hall screen.

In the open-air playhouses at least up to the end of the sixteenth century music seems always to have sounded from '*within*', i.e. from the tiring-house, not a room above the stage, or else by the players on the stage itself. Soldiers often marched on stage to a drum, while drum and trumpet-calls in battles that sounded orders to advance or retreat were usually played off-stage. This not only makes it unlikely that the middle rooms of De Witt's balcony in 1596 were for musicians but also makes it doubtful whether the Globe's balcony originally had any use for music either. The Boar's Head was not given a room in the gallery for musicians when it was designed in 1599. Not until some time later than 1604 at the Globe, when the players of *The Malcontent* acknowledged they were still not accustomed to providing music, could it have had a music-room set up. It is a fairly safe bet that the company made the change in 1608 when the boys at Blackfriars relinquished their playhouse to the King's Men and the company took on their consort of musicians. We do know that after 1608 the public playhouse poets began to follow the private playhouse practice of dividing their plays into acts. This may also signal the adoption of the related practice of inter-act music. *The Chaste Maid* was performed at the Swan in 1613, by which time one of the lords' rooms could easily have been taken over for musicians. The Red Bull had a music room 'above' by about 1608 and the second Globe's music room certainly had fiddlers in a curtained alcove '*above*' as we learn from a passage in *Late Lancashire Witches*, performed at the Globe in 1634:

ARTH [UR]. Play fidlers any thing.
DOUGH [TY]. I, and lets see your faces, that you play fairely with us.
Musitians shew themselves above.

There is a strong likelihood that in the hall playhouses it was always the alcove for the musicians amongst the spectators sitting over the stage that the players used for action '*above*'.[45] The players at the Globe could have done the same, but there is no evidence that they did so before 1608. In 1638 Jasper Mayne praised Jonson for his care in staging, his metatheatrical realism, in that 'Thou laid'st no sieges to the music room'.[46] Sieges of the tiring-house like the Harfleur scenes of *Henry V* were less fashionable in the seventeenth than in the sixteenth century at the Globe, and in any case Mayne's memory could not have stretched back as far as 1608.

The second and more vexed question, what the central opening below the tiring-house balcony might have been, and what it was used for, is less easy to resolve if only because the evidence provided by the plays is difficult to reconcile with any single kind of structure. Twenty-one of the thirty plays known to have been performed at the Globe between 1599 and 1609 need no discovery-space at all.[47] Of the remaining nine, seven use the feature only once. So it was for special effects, not standard use. I suspect its main function was as the '*locus*', or authority place, for formal entrances onto the stage, as will be described below.

There must in fact have been two kinds of stage feature in or near the centre of the *frons*. One was permanent, the curtained alcove or discovery-space in the tiring-house wall which served as a shop, tomb, cell, study or closet, and as the entry-point and exit-point for major processions. The other must have been a special property, possibly a raised platform or sometimes even a curtained 'booth' of the kind used in the early years by the travelling players as their tiring-house. If there was such a structure it seems to have had a variety of shapes. It might be a tent, or a canopied 'state' (a regal throne on a dais), both carried on stage whenever they were needed. Perhaps the biggest puzzle is what was used for *Antony and Cleopatra's* 'monument'. It had to be a structure big enough to hold Antony's body and three boys playing women on top, and yet allow the three boys to haul Antony's living body up on to it with an overt and explicit struggle. The stage balcony might have been used, though that sets up difficulties in explaining the various stage directions and verbal orders. When it was staged at the new Globe in 1999 Cleopatra and her two maids, all played by adult men, needed a rope from the windlass above the stage to help them haul Antony, bound on a chair, up to the balcony. On the other hand any special construction taken out onto the stage seems unlikely since it would need to hold five people at once and would have to be a sturdy piece of carpentry that was nonetheless easily portable. It would have had to be moved offstage during or immediately after the performance, since no two afternoons ran the same play. Since Cleopatra has to state how heavy her lord is and they all puff and heave to get him up to the monument, it is difficult to deny that the balcony would have been the most likely location for the monument at least for that one scene.

Several plays need a raised platform like the dais of the 'state' for such actions as the mountebank speeches in *Volpone*. A platform with three or four steps up to it, which could be used as an executioner's scaffold, is needed in *The Fair Maid of Bristow*. These constructions could not have been the 'discovery-space' unless they were curtained and the discovery-space was the area inside, a kind of discovery-booth. If it were such a structure, it would have had to be adjacent to the tiring house in front of a door so that the objects and players to be discovered could be changed without the audience seeing. *The Devil's Charter* uses the discovery-space six times for different tableaux, as well as two '*tents*', all requiring changes to be made inside the discovery-space. And as there seem to have been two doors at the Globe which could be used even when the discovery-space was in service, a discovery booth can hardly have been set in front of either door. Moreover in *The Devil's Charter* apparitions enter by one door and leave by the other while the discovery space is in use, and one of the same play's stage directions speaks of a discovered player coming '*upon the Stage out of his study*'. This is not the kind of terminology likely to be used if the discovery-space or study were really a booth already set up on the stage.[48] If a platform or booth construction were put up only for plays needing it and the discovery-space was simply a curtained central alcove in the tiring-house wall neither feature would have been obtrusive when any of the plays not using them were performed.

On the other hand the central opening had a positive function as the '*locus*', the site of authority, in contrast to the '*platea*', the street area round the margins of the stage closest to the groundlings standing in the yard. The '*platea*' encompassed the loop from one flanking door to the other, and was walked by the parties opposed to each other in the play. More will be said about this symbolic role for the different parts of the stage in the next chapter. Here we can only note the focal role of the central opening, and the likelihood that it formed the centre from which the chief stage actions emerged and into which they exited at the end of the play. The likelihood that the most expensive spectators sitting in the lords' rooms over the stage would not be able to see into the discovery-space is one of the oddest features of the public theatre stages and staging. It invites the sort of speculation about staging practices that does not belong in this most materialist chapter.

With a repertory demanding a different play every afternoon it is unlikely that the players made much use of booths or demountable structures that took a long time to set up. Such constructions would have to be simple enough to be erected on the morning of the performance and removed the same evening or early the next morning before the players came to start rehearsals for that day's play. Large structures demanding extra storage space would also get the players into difficulties when they had to transfer their play for an evening show at a private house or at venues like the Middle Temple Hall, as the Shakespeare company did with *Twelfth Night* in February 1602. Even their largest properties, the chair of state on its dais and the curtained bed, had to be readily transportable. Desdemona did not die on the stage floor when *Othello* was performed at Oxford in 1610.[49]

There was certainly some sort of enclosed space at the back of the stage which could be pressed into use for the Globe plays. Its use seems to have been chiefly for static tableaux, in accordance with long-established theatrical tradition. The '*brazen Head*' that was revealed '*in the middle of the place behind the Stage*' in *Alphonsus of Aragon* (c. 1587) is echoed in *Volpone*'s unveiling of his gold and Nerissa's 'discovery' of the caskets in *The Merchant of Venice*. The players who are 'discovered' in the Globe plays are almost all single figures who do not usually move, unless to step out onto the stage. They are usually studying, sleeping or dead. In Shakespeare's plays seven are studiers, six are sleepers and five are corpses.[50] This kind of static display is the most distinctive feature of the discovery scenes. Recognition that they are designed as tableaux can save us from thinking of all scenes that are said in the dialogue to be in bedchambers or other interiors as being tucked away at the back of the stage.

The discovery-space seems to have had a number of lesser uses, some of which can explain other details about the staging. Most importantly it made a third entry-point. In *The Devil's Charter* 4.5 the leading character enters '*out of his studie*', and later exits '*into his studie*', which we might suppose to be through one of the normal entry doors if it were not that in two other scenes he is discovered in his study and speaks six or eight lines there before moving out onto the stage. Secondly, the curtain or hangings covering the

Illustration 30. The Hall at Middle Temple, dating from 1574, was used to stage the Shakespeare company's *Twelfth Night* for John Manningham and other students there on Candlemas Night, 2 February, 1602. For the 400th anniversary of the event the Shakespeare's Globe company restaged it there in February 2002. This scene shows Mark Rylance playing Olivia.

discovery space could also be used for concealment, for Polonius's arras in *Hamlet*, or Galatea in *Philaster*, who eavesdrops from '*behind the Hangings*'. Volpone peers over a curtain to watch his gulls ('Ile get up / Behind the Curtain, on a stool, and hearken; / Some time peep over'). And of course noises off or music '*within*' could most easily be heard from behind a curtain. All three extant illustrations of stages in use between De Witt's Swan and 1642, *Roxana* (1632, see illustration 2), *Messallina* (1640) and perhaps Kirkman's *The Wits*)[51] show the whole tiring-house façade curtained off. This practice must have derived from the curtained booth of the street theatres and was probably fairly general. It is always easier to make an entrance through a curtain than through a closed door. Hangings would always have been the most easily modifiable feature of any stage.

A raised platform, canopied 'state' or curtained booth was a more variable feature. It might usually have been employed for animated action, as we might expect with any construction set up on the stage proper. It or they might have been portable enough to be brought in for a particular scene – certainly substantial properties such as canopied beds as well as tables were pushed or carried on and off the stage, and Volpone's rostrum for his mountebank scene where he sees Celia on her balcony is explicitly said to be carried out on stage. The same rostrum might have been used for the speeches to the crowd in *Julius Caesar*. They were less common than discoveries, but they certainly were used. They took the form of tents (*The Devil's Charter, Richard III* and *Troilus and Cressida*), a dais with a 'state' or scaffold (*The Fair Maid of Bristow*, and the rostrums in *Volpone* and *Julius Caesar*), or a raised monument as perhaps in *Antony and Cleopatra*. All in all, the various possible features that the tiring-house may have presented to the stage could be said to be like a handsome nose in a face, flexible but not obtrusive.

Only one other public playhouse, the Red Bull, has been granted the kind of detailed analysis of the staging of its repertory that Shakespeare's Globe has received. The main conclusion to be drawn from this analysis is that the Red Bull plays 'could be given on a stage structurally like that of the Swan, with the single important addition of a third stage door'.[52] The Red Bull was square in shape, like its near neighbour the Fortune. As we learn from a petition by Martin Slater, a player involved in the enterprise, the builder

altered some stables and other rooms, being before a square court in an inn, to turn them into galleries, with the consent of the parish.[53]

Like the Fortune it was probably similar to the round Globe and Swan in its stage fittings. It had stage posts, a heaven and a large trap. It offered only a small upper playing area, normally reached by stairs in the tiring-house. It had a fair number of discovery scenes, and possibly a removable curtained booth, as well as a dais for the 'state' or throne which was also removable. The Red Bull was more inclined to favour spectacle than Shakespeare was, so the Red Bull plays contain a greater use of properties of all kinds amongst their stage effects. But there is nothing that indicates any significant structural differences in the design of the stage area from the Globe, nor of the other amphitheatres.

Evidence for the playhouses as a whole, both amphitheatre and hall, supports this analysis of the Globe and Red Bull plays. T. J. King has examined carefully all the evidence, mainly in stage directions, of 276 plays performed between 1599 and 1642, and found no significant variations in the requirements for staging them.[54] As many as 87 of the plays need only the minimal two doors and floor space, with large properties 'thrust out' as they are required. Of these plays 30 were in the King's Men's repertoire. Only 45 of the 276 need a playing space '*above*'; 42 need a trap, and 102 need a discovery-space, half of them King's Men's plays. Everything else that was needed was portable.

One other fairly substantial piece of evidence about the amphitheatres remains to be considered: Henslowe's contract for building the Hope, similar to his contract with Peter Streete for the Fortune. Henslowe and Alleyn constructed the Hope in 1614, primarily out of their interest in bull- and bear-baiting, though they did sign the contract barely a month after the nearby Globe burned down. It replaced the old Beargarden, though that place of entertainment had provided only baitings with occasional jigs as interludes.[55] For their new venue Alleyn and Henslowe planned a regular alternation of baiting and playing. The contract stipulates the usual timber construction on a brick foundation, with three galleries of the same height as the Fortune's, tile roofing, and two external staircases for access to the galleries. Its other fittings were to be like those of its neighbour half a mile upriver, the Swan, except that it was to have boxes in the lowest gallery level, and the stage had to be removable and therefore without pillars to support the heavens. The contractor was to

not onlie take downe or pull downe all that same place or house wherein Beares and Bulls have been heretofore usuallie bayted, and also one other house or staple wherin Bulls and horsses did usuallie stande, sett, lyinge, and beinge uppon or neere the Banksyde in the saide parish of St Saviour in Sowthworke, commonlie called or knowne by the name of the Beare garden, but shall also at his or theire owne proper costes and charges uppon or before the saide laste daie of November newly erect, builde, and sett upp one other same place or Plaiehouse fitt &

convenient in all thinges, bothe for players to playe in, and for the game of Beares and Bulls to be bayted in the same, and also a fitt and convenient Tyre house and a stage to be carryed or taken awaie, and to stande uppon tressells good, substanciall, and sufficient for the carryinge and bearinge of suche a stage; And shall new builde, erect, and sett up againe the saide plaie house or game place neere or uppon the saide place, where the saide game place did heretofore stande; And to builde the same of suche large compasse, Forme, widenes, and height as the Plaie house called the Swan in the libertie of Parris garden in the saide parishe of St Saviour now is; And shall also builde two stearecasses without and adjoyninge to the saide Playe house in suche convenient places, as shalbe moste fitt and convenient for the same to stande uppon, and of such largnes and height as the stearecasses of the saide playehouse called the Swan nowe are or bee; And shall also builde the Heavens all over the saide stage, to be borne or carryed without any postes or supporters to be fixed or sett uppon the saide stage, and all gutters of leade needfull for the carryage of all suche raine water as shall fall uppon the same; And shall also make two Boxes in the lowermost storie fitt and decent for gentlemen to sitt in; And shall make the particions betwne the Rommes as the are at the saide Plaie House called the Swan; And to make turned cullumes uppon and over the stage; And shall make the principalis and fore fronte of the saide Plaie house of good and sufficient oken tymber, and no furr tymber to be putt or used in the lower most, or midell stories, except the upright postes on the backparte of the saide stories (all the byndinge joystes to be of oken tymber); the inner principall postes of the first storie to be twelve footes in height and tenn ynches square, the inner principall postes in the midell storie to be eight ynches square, the inner most postes in the upper storie to be seaven ynches square; The prick postes in the first storie to be eight ynches square, in the seconde storie seaven ynches square, and in the upper most storie six ynches square; Also the brest sommers in the lower moste storie to be nyne ynches depe, and seaven ynches in thicknes, and in the midell storie to be eight ynches depe and six ynches in thicknes; The byndinge jostes of the firste storie to be nyne and eight ynches in depthe and thicknes, and in the midell storie to be viii and vii ynches in depthe and thicknes. Item to make a good, sure, and sufficient foundacion of brickes for the saide Play house or game place, and to make it xiii^{teene} ynches at the leaste above the grounde.[56]

Like its predecessor it was a polygonal structure.[57]

Jonson's *Bartholomew Fair* was one of the first plays written for the new Hope, and was played there and at Court by the reconstituted Lady Elizabeth's Men in 1614. Not surprisingly Jonson put in his Hope script a number of pointed references to the dual-purpose nature of the playhouse. The Hope version begins with a stage-keeper coming out to beg the audience's patience for a delay while one of the players' costumes is sewn up, and is later accused of collecting the apples thrown by the impatient audience to feed 'the bears within'. Jonson claimed to have kept a 'special decorum' in the depiction of his fairground, since the playhouse is as quite as full of the stench of animals as Smithfield, the real venue of the fair. He also speaks of a spectator paying sixpence at the door, which, unless it refers to the grandees who would have entered through the tiring-house for a seat in a room above the stage, might indicate that the old system of paying for places out penny by penny to a series of gatherers may have been dropped at the later playhouses.

It is usually thought to be an indication of the reduced status of the public playhouses that the last of them was built as a dual-purpose place of entertainment. It should be noted, though, that the building it replaced was designed solely as a baiting-house, and to add playing to its bill of fare actually gave the players an extra venue they had not had before. With more than four companies in competition for space in London and one company holding onto two of them there was just then a distinct shortage of play-houses. Moreover Henslowe drew up his contract for the Hope within a month of the Globe's fire, which took it out of use for most of the next year. In theory it was a sound commercial device for Alleyn and Henslowe to combine their two interests at the one house, since for the sake of the animals baiting could not be provided every day. Nonetheless it was not a happy notion. The players and the playhouse owners quarrelled frequently over the priorities the owners gave to baiting over playing, and after 1620 the Hope was hardly used by players at all. By the 1630s it had reverted to its old name of Beargarden. By then there were enough open-air playhouses – the Globe and Fortune were both rebuilt more lavishly after their fires, and substantial improvements seem also to have been made to the Red Bull in the 1620s, if we can trust William Prynne's claim that it was 'reedified' and 'enlarged' at around the time the Fortune was rebuilt.

5. THE HALL PLAYHOUSES

With possibly one striking exception the other main venues, the hall play-houses, are less well documented. Two fairly general presumptions are all that we can make initially about them with any confidence. First, the auditorium areas differed markedly from those of the public playhouses because of the different origins for the two kinds of structure. Secondly, their playing areas are likely to have differed rather less, if only because the first builder of the most important of both kinds was the same man, James Burbage, and also because the King's Men had so little apparent trouble after 1608 in switching themselves and their repertory between the Globe and Blackfriars. Queen Anne's Men also passed from the Red Bull to the Cockpit and back again in 1616 and after. The two most potent physical differences were the much smaller stages at the indoor venues and the absence from them of any stage posts. What difference it made to have the richest members of the audience not only crowded all round the stage but even sitting on the stage itself is more a matter of staging, considered in the next chapter, than of structure.

About the first commercial indoor playhouse, Richard Farrant's first Blackfriars, we know very little. It had the advantage enjoyed only by its later namesake of being located inside the City walls and yet free from the City's jurisdiction. As a former monastic precinct the five acres of Blackfriars were until 1608 technically a 'liberty', with a vague form of local self-government like that of a rural parish. The independence of the Blackfriars precinct was a continued irritation to the Lord Mayor, and a new City Charter of 1608 finally abolished all the liberties and brought them under City government. Fortunately for the players by that time the play-houses were not only long established but under royal protection.[58] Farrant leased property there late in 1576 in order to obtain a room in central London where his Chapel Children could perform to the public. The room he used was the Frater of the original monastery. When Farrant rented it, it was partitioned into smaller rooms by partitions, which Farrant promptly pulled down, as later did Burbage for his playhouse. William More, the owner of the building, liked neither Farrant's pulling down of the partitions nor his use of the room as a playhouse. After Farrant died in 1580 his successor as company manager kept the lease from More by various dodges, but More none the less repossessed the building and turned the players out in 1584, after only eight years of playing.

A similar attitude to playing in the precinct showed up amongst the residents when James Burbage tried to set up his playhouse there in 1596. He bought a considerable property from the same William More who had closed the first playhouse, and converted it into the famous Blackfriars for the sum of £600.[59] It did in the end prove to be a splendid investment, but Burbage himself did not live to see it. He had bought the freehold of the property, so it could not be taken from him as Farrant's was and as the Theatre was about to be. None the less, he could be stopped from using it as a playhouse, and thirty-one prestigious Blackfriars residents, including the company's new patron George Carey and Shakespeare's printer, the other Stratford exile Richard Field, promptly made sure he was stopped, though not until after Burbage had made all the alterations to turn the building into a playhouse. The petition told the Privy Council that

one Burbage hath lately bought certaine roomes in the ... precinct neere adjoyning unto the dwelling houses of the right honorable the Lord Chamberlaine and the Lord

of Hunsdon, which romes the said Burbage is now altering and meaneth very shortly
to convert and turne the same into a comon playhouse, which will grow to be a very
great annoyance and trouble, not only to all the noblemen and gentlemen thereabout
inhabiting but allso a generall inconvenience to all the inhabitants of the same
precinct, both by reason of the great resort and gathering togeather of all manner of
vagrant and lewde persons that, under cullor of resorting to the playes, will come
thither and worke all manner of mischeefe, and allso to the great pestring and filling
up of the same precinct, yf it should please God to send any visitation of sicknesse as
heretofore hath been, for that the same precinct is allready growne very populous; and
besides, that the same playhouse is so neere the Church that the noyse of the drummes
and trumpetts will greatly disturbe and hinder both the ministers and parishioners in
tyme of devine service and sermons; – In tender consideracion whereof, as allso for
that there hath not at any tyme heretofore been used any comon playhouse within the
same precinct, but that now all players being banished by the Lord Mayor from
playing within the Cittie by reason of the great inconveniences and ill rule that
followeth them, they now thincke to plant them selves in liberties.[60]

The writers of the petition had noted the Mayor's success in 1594 with his
ban on playing at inns inside the City. They clearly saw Burbage's inten-
tions for the Blackfriars as an attempt to circumvent the ban. No hall
playhouses were operating in 1596, and the petitioners' objection to the
'noyse of the drummes and trumpetts' makes it evident that part of their
complaint was to the loud instruments common at the amphitheatres being
sounded in an enclosed space. The boy company which opened there three
years later used neither drums, trumpets or fireworks, and played woodwinds instead of brass horns and trumpets for their music. Eventually
Shakespeare's company was to do the same. Where the Globe might have
used a trumpet fanfare to herald the visit of foreign dignitaries such as
Aragon and Morocco in *The Merchant of Venice* the Folio text of the play,
prepared for the Blackfriars, specifies a cornet. The dumb-show in *Hamlet* is
heralded in the 1604 Quarto by trumpet-calls but in the Folio text of 1623 by
hautboys, another indoor equivalent.

The second Blackfriars property included the paved hall of the old Priory
and a great chamber above it, sometimes called the Upper Frater. Like
Farrant's property it was subdivided, and consisted of:

All those Seaven greate upper Romes as they are nowe devided being all upon one
flower and sometyme beinge one greate and entire room W^{th} the route over the
same covered W^{th} Leade ... And also all that greate paire of wyndinge staires W^{th}
the staire case thereunto belonginge W^{ch} leadeth upp unto the same seaven greate
upper Romes oute of the greate yarde.[61]

It was this high-roofed hall of seven rooms rather than the low-ceilinged one
in the old Priory that Burbage made into his theatre. The 'greate paire of

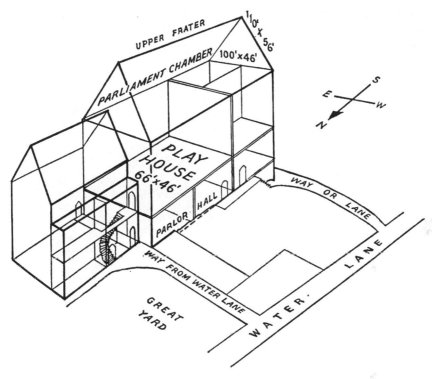

Illustration 31. The location of the second Blackfriars in the medieval stone-built complex of the Dominican monastery. A conjectural drawing by Richard Hosley based on the known location and dimensions.

wyndinge staires' is implied in various references to access being from 'below' and to the theatre being up a set of stairs. The total dimensions of the Upper Frater were 110 feet (33.5 metres) by 46 feet (14 metres), although the actual dimensions of the theatre are stated to have been 66 feet (20.1 metres) north to south and 46 feet (14 metres) east to west.[62] The stairway and as we know from other evidence the playhouse entrance were to the north.[63] The full space was grand enough to have once been used for meetings of Parliament under Richard II. Clearly it was beautifully convenient in its geographical and social location and in its inward dimensions and appearance for use as a 'private' playhouse.

The interior dimensions of 66 feet (20.1 metres) by 46 feet (14 metres) compare with the external dimensions of 72 feet (22 metres) for the round Rose and 80 feet (24.4 metres) square for the Fortune. The Blackfriars

Illustration 32. A section of Hollar's 'Long View' of London from the east showing the tower of St Bride's Church on the left (later rebuilt by Christopher Wren), with below and to the right a long, steep-pitched roof with two tall lanterns or chimneys protruding from its centre. This is thought to be the roof under which Burbage constructed his Blackfriars playhouse.

auditorium was paved, with wooden benches supplied in the pit and degrees for sitting on built in the galleries. The galleries, probably with three levels above the pit, were curved or polygonal timber structures arranged around three sides in front of the stage.[64] The line of the Blackfriars roof shown in Hollar's 'Long View' indicates that the rectangle was aligned with the longer sides roughly north–south. A reference to the eastern side of the stage indicates that it was aligned east–west, which would put it across one of the shorter sides, probably the southern one, since the great staircase was at the northern end. For afternoon performances what sun there was would have shone in from the high windows at the southern end and along the western flank above the galleries.

Behind the stage end stood the tiring-house, under the music room flanked by several rows of seating for audience. The tiring-house provided separate and privileged access for up to fifteen gallants, who paid an extra sixpence for a stool so that they could view the play from the stage itself, reaching the stage through the hangings in the *frons* like the players. The stage itself was small, the width of the hall being reduced by boxes which flanked the stage on either side.[65] These would have taken at least 20 of the available 46 feet. In 1640 Shirley claimed in the prologue to *The Doubtful Heir* that the Globe's stage was 'vast' in comparison with the Blackfriars.[66] The contrast in the known measurements of 25 feet (7.6 metres) or so of width against the 43 (13 metres) of the Fortune and a nearly similar width at the Globe makes that a reasonable statement. Add to the smaller size all the well-dressed feathered and sword-wearing gallants occupying stools on the stage itself and we must conclude that the acting space was certainly cramped, the effect an intimacy that the open-air stages never enjoyed, if that is the word for the experience at Blackfriars and the Cockpit. It is hardly surprising that after the adults started using the Blackfriars stage in 1609 swordplay began to be confined to the occasional fencing bout and that the old-fashioned history plays with their battles and what Shirley called 'target fighting' seem not to have been tried there.

The Blackfriars easily had the height for three ranges of galleries in the auditorium, but it is not certain how many there actually were. They are referred to in a lawsuit in the plural, which implies at least two levels. Occasional references to 'the middle region' possibly apply to the middle gallery of a range of three, but at the indoor venues that term might also apply to the pit. I suspect the allusions were to the former. One reference specifies an ex-soldier positioned there, the kind of man with little money but too high a social status to join the 'sixpenny mechanicks' in the topmost gallery. The galleries were curved round inside the rectilinear auditorium, giving them some kinship to the polygonal amphitheatres,[67] following the principle of an audience wrapped around the stage.

Admission prices at Blackfriars began at a basic sixpence for entry to the topmost gallery. A further shilling provided a bench in the pit and to any of the seating closest to the stage other than the boxes. Some of those had keys to their doors, for exclusivity and privileged access. A place in a box on either side of the stage cost half-a-crown, two shillings and sixpence. As many as fifteen gallants who wished to display themselves at the same time as they got their intimate view of the play could enter through the tiring-house, hiring a stool to sit on the stage itself at a minimum cost of two shillings.[68]

The audience literally surrounded the players as they did at the outdoor venues. The grandest sat in the flanking boxes, probably on two levels, while lesser bodies on the stage balcony were on 'degrees' or benches on either side of the music room. A reference to a tiff between two spectators at the Blackfriars in 1632 proves that the boxes were close enough to the stage for a spectator without a stool who was on his feet on the stage to obscure a box-holder's view. In the event the standing spectator, Lord Thurles, shortly to become the Earl of Ormond, lunged with his sword at the box-holder when told to move out of the way. The box that Thurles obscured must have been at the side, not the back, because that was occupied by the tiring house. Such a position roughly accords with the location of the 'two Boxes in the lowermost storie' of the galleries in the Hope contract. It certainly would have allowed the 'discovery-space' more room at the back of the stage. The Blackfriars boxes were the prime resort for the great of the country. In 1636 King Charles's uncle the Duke of Lennox had a spat with the Lord Chamberlain over possession of a box for which the Lord Chamberlain, the fourth Earl of Pembroke, held the key.

Boxes flanking the stage must have seemed better to the grand than the lords' rooms at the amphitheatres because, unlike the balcony rooms, they gave their inhabitants a view of the discovery space in the tiring house wall. Less advantageous were the 'degrees' for spectators in the gallery flanking the central upper-stage music-room, shown in the theatre that Inigo Jones designed some time in the Jacobean period to copy the Blackfriars (see illustration 33). Like the Globe's rooms for lords on the stage balcony they gave their occupants no view of the discovery-space. It may well be that the Blackfriars boxes were set up at the sides of the stage to satisfy that lack.

It is our two-dimensional thinking derived from viewing cinema screens that makes it difficult for us to think of the lords' rooms as privileged locations for watching a play. Under the early Stuarts the key difference in stage playing from modern theatre was that it was conceived in three dimensions, not two. Mostly we think of the early indoor playhouses as differing from the open-air venues partly in their smallness and consequent intimacy but chiefly as the precursors of modern theatres. In fact, while they certainly must have made the playgoing experience feel like intimate theatre compared to the spaciousness of modern structures, the indoor venues like the Blackfriars and the Cockpit had their own distinctive features that separate the experience of witnessing a play there from modern playgoing quite as widely as the amphitheatres, if not in some ways even more intensely.

Even at the modern Globe in Southwark audiences expect to stand in front of the stage while the actors perform in front of them across the stage, using only two dimensions. Actors and audience are equally complicit in this difference from early staging. Modern audiences are conditioned to be passive and to be mute, and to use their eyes more than their ears. Cinemas, lectures and talks, like modern theatres with footlights and proscenium arches, all expect actors to stand and walk in front of their audiences in two dimensions. One side confronts the other. But Elizabethan and early Stuart playgoers were raised to listen rather than to watch, which meant that being within hearing distance was far more important than seeing something in front of you. So they expected to gather in a circle all round the speaker. A circle has no front, and the early playhouses relished using their three dimensions rather than the scenic two which is what the primacy of the eye requires. Looking at the stage was secondary to hearing what was said. Shakespearean plays were far more dependent on their words than on whatever visual spectacles the players might augment them with. Both outdoor and indoor playhouses were built on that principle. Christopher Wren called the huge dome he designed for St Paul's after the fire of 1666 a 'vast auditory', a circle of listeners, not watchers. The Protestant revolution gave priority to the word of the Bible from the pulpit in the church's centre, not the visual ceremonials conducted by the remote priests at the high altar at one end. Playhouses were designed to a broadly similar principle.

The most misleading feature of De Witt's drawing of the Swan is also its most insidious. He drew his image of the amphitheatre from a perspective point roughly where the camera and projection booth in a cinema would be. He made us confront the Swan's stage from a modern perspective, not from where the great and the wealthy would have been. Such a position would have seemed even more incongruous at any of the indoor playhouses because there such a position would have been occupied by the cheapest payers. The poorest seats at Blackfriars were at the back of the topmost gallery facing the stage from in 'front'. The richer playgoers sat on stools on the stage itself in front of the tiring-house and of the flanking boxes. Otherwise they occupied the boxes on either side of the stage, probably at two levels, and they sat on 'degrees' or benches across the back of the music-room on the stage balcony. Nearly a third of all the playgoers, certainly the wealthiest, were at what we think of as the 'back' of the stage, behind the non-existent footlights. Players certainly had to act in three dimensions to cater for the self-important dignitaries surrounding them.

The best graphic evidence from the time is an odd case which just might present at one remove the most remarkably precise image of a Jacobean indoor playhouse that we have. It is a set of drawings now at Worcester College Oxford, and once thought to be drawn by Inigo Jones in 1616 as the builder's plan for Christopher Beeston's Cockpit. The latest scholarly view is that the drawings are copies by Jones's assistant John Webb, who drew them in 1660.[69]

What is most remarkable about this drawing is how firmly it echoes what we know about the Blackfriars auditorium. Boxes on each flank of the stage

Illustration 33. A copy by John Webb of a design by Inigo Jones perhaps originally
made in the Jacobean period for an indoor playhouse, probably the Cockpit. This element,
showing the stage end, exhibits two levels of boxes on each side of the stage, three stage
doorways in the *frons scenae* and a music-room over the stage flanked by four ranks of
'degrees' or benches for audience seating.

are there along with the music-room over, and benches for more audience at
what we usually think of as the back of the stage. Even more remarkable is the
groundplan shown below, which puts the stage in the centre and ranks the
audience in almost equal numbers all around the stage. It suggests that even
the benches in the pit were curved to face the 'front' edge of the stage centre.

Evidence from plays performed at the Blackfriars suggests that the stage
fittings there and presumably at the other indoor playhouses were basically

similar to those of the outdoor playhouses. The indoor plays make no references to stage posts, which of course were unnecessary at the indoor venues. There must have been a 'heavens', though, because flights were not unusual. A mid-stage trap existed according to *Poetaster*, which begins with '*Envie. Arising in the midst of the stage.*' There was certainly a playing area above, probably doubling as the music-room. Chapman in *May-Day* several times calls it a '*tarras*' and uses it as a window or balcony. In *Poetaster*, 4.9 Jonson shaped his stage directions ambiguously, as in '*Shee appeareth above, as at her chamber window*', but in *The Devil is an Ass*, 2.6 he noted in the margin of the text '*'This Scene is acted at two windo's, as out of two contiguous buildings*'. Elizabethan windows were not always glazed, of course, nor necessarily even papered, and it need not be assumed that he was calling for more than two adjacent apertures, possibly curtained like the music room.

What may have been below the music room, tarras or windows is as much a matter of conjecture for the hall theatres as it is in the

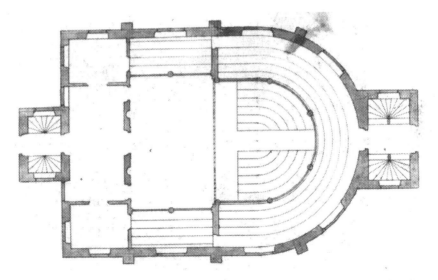

Illustration 34. John Webb's copy of the plan drawn by Inigo Jones for a Jacobean playhouse, probably the Cockpit of 1616. The circular shape of a cock-fightinig arena has been broken into and enlarged, the square extension accommodating the stage near the centre and the tiring-house behind it. Audience surrounded the stage on all sides. Perhaps its most striking feature is the disposition of the benches in the pit for audience, which retains more than half of the circular structure of the original cockpit. The sitters in the pit confronted each other more easily than they faced the stage, a striking testimony to the concept of an encircling audience.

amphitheatres. Their plays have much less evidence for the use of large constructions than the amphitheatre plays, and not much more for a curtained discovery space. The opening stage direction of *Eastward Ho!* is about as explicit as one could hope for:

Enter Maister Touchstone, and Quicksilver at several dores ... At the middle dore, Enter Golding discovering a Goldsmiths shoppe, and walking short turnes before it.

This implies three doors, the central one large enough to conceal a shop. It suggests the possibility that the arrangement was for a broad doorway or set of double doors in the centre flanked by two single doorways. Some authors certainly expected one of the doors, presumably the middle one if it was used for discoveries, to be curtained. Davenant's prologue to *The Unfortunate Lovers* speaks of a half-dressed player peeping through the hangings before the play starts to see how the playhouse is filling up. The 'silke cortaine, come to hang the stage here' mentioned in the induction to *Cynthia's Revels* would have hung in such a doorway. It did not hang around the outer edge of the stage to conceal the understage area, because the Citizen and Wife in *The Knight of the Burning Pestle* comment on the hangings within their view as they sit amongst the gallants on the stage. Understage hangings would have been out of sight for them. Either the double doors or the hangings could have opened for discoveries like the one in *A Staple of News*, when *'The study is open'd where she sit in state'*.

Evidence from the plays at the other two hall playhouses is more fragmentary, but presents a picture largely consistent with that of the Blackfriars. The playhouse used by Paul's Boys, particularly the stage area, seems to have been markedly smaller, since the stage was not large enough to allow gallants to sit on stools on it. Admission charges there may have been lower too at one time, perhaps no more than twopence when they first reopened in 1599. Their space above had a balcony or window, which included a place for musicians. Two entry doors probably flanked a discovery-space. A structure called a 'canopy' in two of the plays was big enough to seat five boys holding books.[70]

The shapes of the Whitefriars theatre that came into being in 1608 after Paul's had closed down and its abortive successor, Porter's Hall, are almost totally obscure. Whitefriars was built in the former monks' refectory and measured approximately 85 feet (26 metres) by 35 feet (10.7 metres), longer and narrower than Blackfriars, which almost certainly means that its stage would have been set across one of the shorter sides of the hall. Of Porter's Hall we cannot even be sure that it was private, though the fact that it was intended for use by boys and that all the urban playhouses were indoors makes it more than likely.

As noted above we know more, conceivably a great deal more, about the Cockpit or Phoenix that Beeston built in 1616. Whether or not the plan copied by Webb was one intended for use in building the Cockpit it has features which suggest that it could have been designed originally as an enlargement of the former cockpit in Drury Lane into a playhouse. The extension with a squared shape on one side would have satisfied the restriction of the time that no new buildings should be built and that extensions should not be bigger than the original structure by more than one-third. King James tended to use Drury Lane when he drove north for his hunting, and was insistent that any new building he saw was a curse. The plan's curious shape, round at the auditorium end and squared at the other, might well have been an adaptation of an existing circular cockpit. Jones was the King's Surveyor by 1615, and would have known what could and could not be done with the structure Beeston had leased for his playhouse.[71]

Some features of Jones's elegant and eloquent plans are less than perfect, either in detail or in their provenance. Confusion between levels in the drawings and the absence of any staircase has led at least one scholar to conclude that it could never have been built.[72] Gordon Higgott, whose work on the Jones drawings and those of his student and heir John Webb puts him at the forefront of Jones scholarship, considers that they may be copies made by Webb in 1660 or so, after Jones's death, of something that Jones had drawn much earlier, though not necessarily for Beeston in 1616. For us its chief peculiarity and its main attraction is that it shares all the features we know the Blackfriars had in the Jacobean years, making it certainly relevant to a period much earlier than the Restoration years when Webb copied it. It would not be the first architect's design to require modification in practice, and the circumstantial evidence linking it to Beeston's Cockpit is plausible enough to warrant taking the plan seriously as at least a possible model for that playhouse. For the necessarily speculative purposes of this study the name 'Cockpit' seems still to be the most appropriate name for the design that appears on the plans.

Judging from their measurements its interior dimensions were 52 feet (15.8 metres) by 37 feet (11.3 metres), a little smaller than the Blackfriars. James Wright, who reported from near the end of the seventeenth century that the Blackfriars, the Cockpit and Salisbury Court built in 1629 were almost exactly the same size,[73] might have been misled by the similarity of the Blackfriars interior curve of its galleries inside its rectangle with the Cockpit's elongated circle. In Jones's designs (see illustration 34) the stage area is 23 feet 6 inches (7.2 metres) by 15 feet (4.6 metres), which cannot have been very different from the Blackfriars dimensions. It is 4 feet

(1.2 metres) high, and the tiring-house behind it is 10 feet (3 metres) in depth running the whole breadth of the playhouse at the squared end. The galleries on each side of the stage are a little under 7 feet (2.1 metres) wide. There are only two levels of galleries, the first 11 feet (3.3 metres) above stage level and the second 7 feet (2.1 metres) above that. Each of the boxes has four degrees or steps for sitting on with a passageway for access at the back. Above the stage are three sets of seats except in the centre, where an ornamental window 4 feet (1.2 metres) wide dominates the tiring-house façade. A central arched door of the same width as the window above it stands at stage level in the façade, 8 feet (2.4 metres) high at the apogee of the arch. On each side of it is a rectangular door 2 feet 6 inches (0.7 metres) wide and 6 feet (1.8 metres) high. There is no sign of any trapdoor. The replica built in 1997 alongside the new Globe in Southwark, which looks exactly right from the outside, has actually been made 10 per cent larger than the original plans in order to provide better access for modern audiences round the outer edges of the auditorium.

Evidence from plays staged at the Cockpit and for that matter at the Blackfriars does not contradict this layout. It simply indicates that the Cockpit's tiring-house must have had at least two doors, a gallery or 'Balcone' capable of holding a maximum of three players, and that a curtained booth was available for some plays.[74] None of this is out of step with the evidence for the other venues. Jones's drawings are of an extremely handsome Palladian design, which the customary painting, marbling and gilding would have made quite splendid. For all the strength of its decorative features it is a practical design, too, far less ruled by the classical requirements of Vitruvian theatre that Jones followed when he designed the Cockpit-at-Court in 1629. Beeston ought to have been pleased with it.

Almost the one feature that we might have expected to see at the Cockpit but which is missing from Jones's drawing is a set of low rails surrounding the stage. These are shown in both of the early illustrations of indoor stages (not only *Roxana*, illustration 2, but on the titlepage of *Messallina*, 1640). There are none in the Swan drawing, and it would be tempting to see them as a feature only of the indoor playhouses, a sensible protective consequence of having a more crowded auditorium and a lower stage height, built also perhaps for the safety of the peacocks on their stools, if Jones's drawing had included them. Perhaps, as with traps and other such devices, some playhouses had them and some did not.

A third indoor playhouse was successfully completed and put to use under Charles before the closure in 1642. This was the Salisbury Court in Whitefriars not far downhill and across the Fleet river from the Blackfriars just outside the City. Built by Richard Gunnell of the Fortune and William Blagrave of the Revels Office in 1629, it was based on a barn with walls largely of brick, by then an obvious precaution against loss by fire, of which Gunnell had first-hand experience at the Fortune. It was most likely rectangular like the Blackfriars, at least on the outside. Converting it to a playhouse cost roughly £600.[75] A specification that has survived, for the construction of a dancing-school room 40 feet (12.2 metres) square over the stage, suggests that the width of the hall was 40 feet, only slightly less than the Blackfriars. It probably also means that the stage was built like the others across one of the narrower sides of the rectangle.

6. COURT THEATRES

We should not pass from considering the playhouses without a look at the third major venue for the plays, the halls at Court. One company or another performed at Court in the festivities almost every Christmas throughout the period. Used in the murk of winter, indoors, with stages and 'degrees' or tiers of seating set up on temporary scaffolding for the occasion, the Court venues obviously resembled the hall playhouses rather than the amphitheatres. Because performances were seasonal the first Court venues for plays had to be temporary structures built inside one of the great halls at Court, of which the one at Hampton Court is the most spectacular survivor. Under Elizabeth most performances were held in the old Banqueting House in Whitehall, a substantial building in the shape of a 'long square', measuring 332 feet (101.2 metres) in circumference, 40 feet (12.2 metres) high, and fitted with 292 glass windows. In 1607 under James it was pulled down and rebuilt on a rather larger scale, 120 by 53 feet (36.6 by 16.2 metres). Pillars supported galleries along the east, north and west sides, under which the scaffolding for the 'degrees' of seating was installed by the Revels Office whenever a play was to be put on. Most of the seating was partitioned into boxes, and the stage was set at one end, with the royal chair on its dais positioned directly facing the stage.

At first the Whitehall theatre was used only for masques, matters of spectacle rather than story, which were no doubt felt to be more suitable for the lavishly equipped new building. It opened with Jonson's *Masque of Beauty* in 1608. Plays were put on there from 1610, though more often they were assigned to the Hall or Great Chamber, or the royal Cockpit, an enclosed wooden amphitheatre built under Henry VIII for cockfighting, which James's son Prince Henry paid to have altered to show plays in 1611. Often a different venue might be prepared for each play. The Revels men were paid in January 1618 for six days' work at Whitehall preparing 'the Banquetting-house the Cockpitt and the Hall … for three severall plaies'.[76] Of course masques and plays were by no means the only form of entertainment for royalty. Baiting, which normally took place in the adjacent tiltyard, and cockfighting in the royal Cockpit even after its conversion for playing still appeared regularly on the festive programme. Occasional baitings were held in the Banqueting House itself (certainly in 1611–12, 1612–13 and 1628–9).[77] Players summoned to perform before royalty in the seventeenth century faced the same kind of competition from animals that they faced through the sixteenth century in the amphitheatres.

There is not much surviving evidence about the design of any of these buildings, let alone the temporary structures put up inside them by the Revels Office for the festivities.[78] Only one out of all the buildings used to stage plays before royalty is well documented. What it can tell us is a revelation of how the Court organized its hardware for the royal pleasures.

In the middle of the 1618–19 Christmas season, on 12 January 1619, the Banqueting House followed the model of several public theatres and burned to the ground. It was replaced by a building that has rightly been called the most substantial architectural project of the whole early Stuart period. This was Inigo Jones's Banqueting House in Whitehall, a building so valued by Wren that when the rest of the royal palace in Whitehall went up in flames in 1698 he directed the fire-fighters to save Jones's building at all costs, even the loss of his own designs. It is true that its survival into this century is rather like George Washington's axe, but it stands as a greatly impressive monument to its time. Charles I had his head cut off on a scaffold outside it, in front of a gigantic crowd of both delighted and of appalled spectators. It was finished in 1622 at a cost of £9,850. The basic shape is a double cube measuring 110 by 55 feet (33.6 by 16.8 metres), and 55 feet in height. Magnificently decorated, it attracted masques more than plays, beginning with Jonson's *Masque of Augurs* on Twelfth Night of 1622. The stage was set at the north or lower end in front of the entrance screen, across the whole width of the hall, a matter of 40 feet (12.2 metres) once allowance is made for the flanking galleries. The depth of the stages built for different occasions varied between 27 and 40 feet (9.2 and 12.2 metres). They were usually set up at about 6 feet (1.8 metres) high.[79]

Some of the stages set up at Court in the last years were weirdly complex affairs. One, designed by Jones for Queen Henrietta Maria's pastoral *Florimène* in 1635 and staged in Whitehall's Great Hall, for which the groundplan has survived, had a rear stage closed off by shutters, a French innovation, with in front of it a stage proper, flanked on each side by wings

Illustration 35. The interior of Jones's Banqueting House, showing the Rubens ceiling installed in the 1630s and the furniture for a twentieth-century musical entertainment.

in perspective and finally a shallow forestage framed by a proscenium arch, with steps at each side for the final descent of the masquers on to the floor for dancing. It must be remembered that this was a royal spectacle, put on by the Queen herself and her French ladies-in-waiting, not a professional theatrical performance.

For the presentation of masques in the Banqueting House an empty space was kept clear in front of the stage for the dancing that concluded each show. This space ended at the King's 'state', his dais with its throne, to which all the sight-lines of Jones's perspective scenery were drawn. For this the Revels Office was responsible. Perspective staging was far too costly a business for the professional players, and would have sharply reduced the numbers paying to attend, since it left the only perfect view with the king.

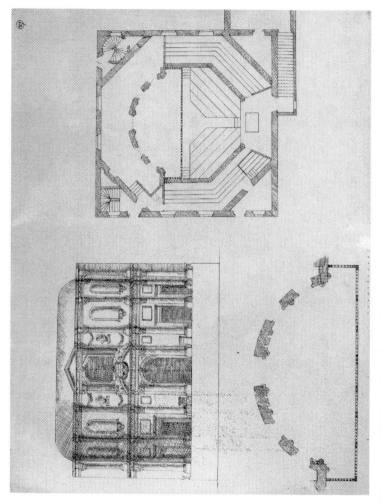

Illustration 36. The Inigo Jones designs for the conversion of the royal Cockpit into a permanent playhouse.

In 1635 the famous Rubens ceiling-paintings arrived at the Banqueting House, and King Charles put a ban on performing there for fear of damage to the paintings from the candle-smoke. Instead a new masquing-house was built in its place, of wood. As Davenant, whose *Britannia Triumphans* was the first masque to open the new house in January 1638, recorded,

There being now past three yeers of Intermission, that the King and Queenes Majesties have not made Masques with shewes and Intermedii, by reason the roome where formerly they were presented, having the seeling since richly adorn'd with peeces of painting of great value, figuring the acts of King *James* of happy memory, and other inrichments: lest this might suffer by the smoake of many lights, his Majestie commanded the Surveyor of his workes, that a new temporary roome of Timber, both for strength and capacitie of spectators, should bee suddenly built for that use; which being performed in two moneths, the Scenes for this Masque were prepared.[80]

It cost £2,500, the walls being of fir weather-board cladding, and it was set on the Whitehall 'tarras' next to the Banqueting House, which it resembled in size.[81]

Plays had already been found a venue of their own in 1630 at the new Cockpit-at-Court. This was another of Inigo Jones's handsome buildings. It replaced Henry VIII's old gamehouse on the same foundation, octagonal internally like the old building but square externally. It was built during 1629–30. Not only have detailed accounts of the interior decoration for this building survived, but drawings of the groundplan probably again copied in 1660 by Jones's assistant John Webb.[82] They show a building about 57 feet (17.7 metres) square, with an octagonal auditorium, each side about 28 feet (8.5 metres) across the gallery rear. One side of the octagon provided the entrance, and four sides, two to the left and two to the right of the entrance, made up the galleries. The stage occupied the space of the sixth, seventh and eighth sides, extending almost to the middle of the building. It was shaped like a shallow apron of about 35 by 5 feet (10.7 by 1.5 metres), with the tiring-house front backing it in the form of a concave bay, giving a maximum stage depth at the centre of the tiring-house front of about 16 feet (4.9 metres). The tiring-house was lavishly pilastered, and pierced by five stage entrances, a large central doorway and four smaller doorways arranged symmetrically on each side. Above the central opening was an equally wide 'window' or balcony. Even though the king had exclusive access complete with his own private stairway to the dais and chair of state at one end facing the stage, as he had for the masques staged at other halls, the Cockpit-at-Court's small, shallow stage would prohibit anything at all elaborate in the way of spectacle. Charles, who paid for it, clearly intended it purely for playing.

Not that the theatre was bare. Its interior was lit by iron candelabra, two large and ten small ones around the stage, and three others in the auditorium. The stage was covered in green cloth, the rest in matting. The whole stage area was painted and its pilasters were gilded. The cover over the stage was made of calico painted sky-blue with silver stars and fitted on a roller to allow it to be drawn back when the folding and suspended throne had to be lowered to the stage. It was royally finished. As the Office of the Works accounts show,

for pryminge stoppinge and payntinge stone Cullor in oyle divers Cornishes pendaunt[es] and mouldings in the viii' Cant[es] of the Cockepitt wth the postes both belowe and in the gallery above in the insyde all Cont: in measure ccclvi ya^{ds} did at xvi^d the yarde £xxiii xv^s iiii^d, for new Couleringe over wth fayre blewe the viii' upper squares on the wall three of them beinge wholy shaddowed and the rest mended xl^s, for pryminge and payntinge like glasse xx^{ty} panes wth had bin Lightes xxx^s and for Clenzinge and washinge the gold of the pendaunt[es] and Cornishes and mendinge the same in divers places wth gold Cullor in oyle and mendinge the blew of the same in sondry places 1st ...

Carvers for moulding and clensinge of twoe great Statuaes of Plaster of Parris for the Cockpitt mouldinge and castinge three Ballastleavo^{rs} and cuttinge and flutinge the Bodies of twoe Corinthian Columnes ciiii^s ...

Candlestickes of Iron beautified wth branches Leaves and garnished wth other ornament[es] to beare Lights in the Cockpitt x^{en} at xxx^s the peece £xv ...

John Walker Property maker viz:' for hanging the Throne and Chaire in the Cockpit wth cloth bound about wth whalebone packthred and wyer for the better foulding of the same to come downe from the Cloud[es] to the Stage cutting fitting and soweing of Callicoe to cover all the roome over head wth in the Cockpitt cutting a great number of Starres of Assidue and setting them one the Blew Callicoe to garnish the cloath there setting one a great number of Coppring[es] to drawe the cloth to and fro ... for divers times Cullouring in Gould cullo^r the Braunches of xv^e Candlesticks in the Cockpitt whereof tenn smaller and twoe greater then thother about and before the Stage and for Hatching and Guilding them wth fine gould cullouring the great Braunches in the front of the stage and Hatching and Guilding all the ptes to be seene forwards allowed by agrem' £x in all.[83]

At least some of the playhouses went out in a blaze of glory.

CHAPTER 5

The Staging

I. MOBILE STAGING

Print has a fixity that performance never presumes to. We suffer from reading Shakespeare and his contemporaries in editions that give an illusion of permanence to their words and their stage directions that the originals never had. The original staging of Shakespeare's plays lacked consistency even for the playhouses they were staged in, and the idea that each play on stage became perfectly fixed in the minds of the company playing it is a hopeful delusion. Plays were subject to constant change, not just in memory but in such transient features of the performance event as the mood of the audience and the condition of the day, whether the playhouse was outdoors or in. A playgoer struggling through inner London's crowds to get by coach to the Blackfriars, would, once seated in the playhouse, at the least have first to recover from the state of the narrow streets and greet his or her acquaintances in the crowd and slowly start to breathe more easily before he or she could focus their mind on the anticipated play, which perhaps or perhaps not they knew about from playbills or previous visits. Even the size of the playgoer in front with or her his tall hat and feather could become a nuisance, getting in the way of the gradual process of preparing oneself for the coming event. Backstage the state of mind and health of even a single player let alone the costumes and properties being made ready for the occasion could throw the planned performance off track. Any attempt to examine the conditions and the traditions of Shakespearean staging is inhibited by the distance between the event as fixed in print and the flexible actualities of the local conditions of performance.

With that in mind we must move on from the quality of the players and the material structure of the stages to look at the product of the two put together, the staging. If there were a suitable plural for the singular word 'staging' I would use it, because syncretism is misleading in this section more than any other. The classification into public and private or amphitheatre and hall which serves as at least a basic division for the playhouse structures is not very helpful when categorising the different forms of staging. In some respects it may be actively misleading. At first sight there is some justification for adopting such a well-publicised division, because it is easy to see staging as done on a bare platform with portable properties in the outdoor playhouses on the one hand, and according to more modern practices with pictorial scenery and set-pieces at the indoor venues on the other, as in the Restoration theatres, which seem to resemble the halls more than they do the amphi-theatres. The boy companies that first occupied the hall playhouses had stability of tenure as well as a roof over their heads, some of them had access to the resources of the Revels Office, and their early repertory, especially under John Lyly, shows the kind of sophistication that could well have found the Italian influence of Vitruvian perspective scene-presentation agreeable. But, as we noted above, it is not so simple.

Assumptions about 'scenic' staging that so dominated thinking about theatre in the last century have been fixed, not to say fixated, by the predominance of the camera. The camera eye creates for us many of the features that dominate our thinking about what we see on a screen, not least the great privilege it gives us to intrude far more intimately and yet impersonally on faces and expressions than we would in normal life, or be taken to see remote natural beauties that once would never have been visible except after long and arduous journeying. This is not just a matter of stage realism, as we registered in Chapter 2. The experience of viewing at second hand through a camera's eye keeps us safe from direct involvement in what we are seeing, passive and secure, far more than a playgoer at Blackfriars could be watching whatever fiction the players provided. Whether you sat there on the stage itself or at the far back of the topmost gallery the experience was shared. Today we have almost totally lost the feeling of experiencing a play as a member of a crowd. Crowds packed together develop a strength of collective emotion that energises everyone and con-ditions their reception of the theatre event. The old aphorism that you laugh and the world laughs with you is true, but its corollary that cry and you weep alone is not. Shakespearean audiences were far more active than we are in their collective responses to the plays they viewed, consciously sharing the joint experience as members of a crowd, whereas we sit in the dark in private and almost secret comfort, falling asleep as easily as we might weep at the fiction of tragedy we are silently witnessing.

Perspective staging, with the expectation that is built into its design that the stage will do things to a wholly passive audience viewing a two-dimensional scene, certainly did become predominant on the Restoration stages. The separation of audience from actors by footlights helped the actors to feel in control of their show. Every technical advance in theatre since then has worked to intensify audience passivity and remoteness, distancing the individual from the collective experience of the stage event that Shakespeare expected his audiences to generate. Staging then had an essential economy, and at least half the vigour of the event came from the audience sharing it. Adult companies might be seen to reflect their mobile origins and their susceptibility to the travelling sickness in their preference for representing bedchambers simply by the presence of a bed and battle-fields by the flourishing of swords whereas indoor performances might be seen as more sophisticated in the sense that they relate more closely to modern experience. But the evidence for the staging of plays at the hall playhouses shows if anything that even plays using the most elaborate of Inigo Jones's Vitruvian scenery at Court in Caroline times were put on without it when they returned to the hall playhouses.[1] T. J. King's examination of the Cockpit repertory led him to the conclusion that 'in usual practice the playwrights for the [Cockpit] were following the conventions of the earlier Elizabethan "open stage" rather than anticipating the modes of presentation usually associated with the Restoration period'.[2]

Differences in staging at the different playhouses were dictated by a variety of factors. Each company and each playhouse had its own reputation that broadly reflected or anticipated the preferences of the audiences who went to them. On the whole the companies and their different repertories were a much stronger identifying factor than were the different venues, indoors or out. Through the early years the amphitheatres and the shifting adult companies developed a fashion for vigorously noisy plays and extravagant verse. In the last thirty years the Blackfriars became the predominant resort for the new and the fashionable. Its repertoire of Shakespeare and Beaumont and Fletcher plays was supplemented in the 1630s by the courtier poets Davenant, Carew and Suckling, who helped to make it the favoured venue for the rich and fashionable. Its small enclosed shape and half-sized stage helped to make it more a place for witplay than swordplay. The northern amphitheatres, the Fortune and the Red Bull, maintained their repertoire of the older plays that first established the Rose's reputation in the 1590s, including the battle plays of that militant decade. But these were changes of fashion, not of staging. In the 1620s and 1630s Beeston regularly took Red Bull plays and players from the amphitheatre play-house to his Cockpit hall, and their traditions of staging must have gone with them. The King's Men's regular transfer of their Globe plays to the Blackfriars each season indicates the durability of the same staging traditions at both venues. The Blackfriars consort added music to the King's Men's resources from 1609 onwards but there are few other signs that they made substantial changes in staging when transferring their repertory from one to the other.

Contrast between the attractions of witplay and swordplay is part of the larger story of the conflict between stage verse and stage spectacle, and the priority that the poets fought the players for, writing for audiences rather than spectators, for listening to their verse against watching the spectacles. The poets wanted audiences, hearers, to use their ears for the words, while the players found it easier to cater for spectators and the pleasures of the eye.[3] Spectacle became a notable excitement for playgoers from the earliest days. Jonson, to whom the phrase 'judicious spectator' was a contradiction in terms, fought unavailingly for the priority of his words even though in the masques that he wrote for the Court he made full use of Inigo Jones's potent visual symbols. When he first wrote for the amphitheatres at the end of the 1590s new tastes in staging were beginning to assert themselves. The revived boy companies with their trained but non-realistic eloquence offered words more than spectacle, and there were enough Hamlets in the audiences to offset Polonius's preference for 'a jig or a tale of bawdry, or he sleeps'. The clown's jig provided the standard end-piece for adult company plays throughout the early years. As we suggested in Chapter 3, keeping or abandoning jigs provides a clear if possibly oversimplified means of distinguishing the trends of the different companies in the years before and after 1600.[4]

The dance that we now think of as the jig is a good place to start about early staging. Irish jigs are related to the stage jig of Elizabethan times, but the stage versions seem to have involved song as much as dance, and relate most closely to the story-telling popular ballads of the kind that Autolycus sells the country folk in *The Winter's Tale*. In their fullest form as we have seen they were offered as end-pieces after the plays were finished, an incidental item of entertainment quite separate from the play. Short songs or dances might be used as interludes in the course of a play, as they are in Peele's *James IV*, but the full-scale jigs led an independent existence. So far as the limited evidence tells us the most popular were bawdy knockabout song-and-dance farces, though extempore rhyming on given themes and various forms of dance were equally common at least with the most famous clowns. John Harington in *Metamorphosis of Ajax* (1596) even mentions 'Machachinas' or sword dances as a stage treat.

Perhaps most pointedly the songs in jigs resembled the popular ballads in their function as commentaries on topical matters, political, religious or personal. Will Kemp has a hostile word at the end of his *Nine Days' Wonder* for the 'Jig-monger' who manufactured ballads about his celebrated morris-dancing all the way from London to Norwich in 1599, and ten years before that Tarlton just before his death certainly involved himself in the Marprelate controversy with his jigs and extemporising. The author of the tract *Mar-Martine* claimed that the violent abuse that was a feature of the anti-bishop Marprelate controversy began with the clown:

> These tinkers termes, and barbers jestes first *Tarleton* on the stage,
> Then *Martin* in his bookes of lies, hath put in every page.[5]

Tarlton was the first and probably best of the famous jigging clowns. He had parts to perform in the plays his company presented, but he was renowned above all for his comedy as a country clown in jigs and as an extemporising ballad-maker. One of the *Jests* describes how, when travelling with a company of players, 'Tarlton's use was, the play being done, everyone so pleased to throw up his theame.'[6] He seems to have worn a standard country garb for his end-piece, 'his sute of russet, his buttond cap' (illustration 15), and to have entered beating a tabor or light drum (pronounced 'tabber', which may be an onomatopoeic description of its rapid tapping), which he carried slung around his neck.

After Tarlton's death in 1588 the most famous clowns were the Chamberlain's Will Kemp and the Admiral's George Attewell. One jig performed by each of them found its way into print, and the two, the rhyming ballad known as 'Attewell's Jig' and the ballad of 'Singing Simkin', are the best examples we have of the kind.[7] The second is not specifically named as Kemp's, though if it is not it must have borne a very close resemblance to 'Kemps newe jygge betwixt, a souldiour and a Miser and Sym the clown', entered for printing as a ballad in 1595. 'Singing Simkin' is a rhyming farce for four players, a housewife, the clown who appears as the housewife's first lover, a soldier who is her second lover and whose arrival causes the clown to hide in a chest whence he adds lines to the sung dialogue, and finally the old husband, who is told when he enters that the soldier is there hunting for a thief. The wife and husband persuade the soldier to leave and let Simkin out of the chest. The husband leaves, Simkin makes up to the wife, the husband catches him at it and wife and husband together beat the clown off the stage.

The jig reached the height of its fame with Tarlton and then Kemp. In the seventeenth century the word became conspicuous chiefly as a term of contempt used by one type of gentlemanly playgoer against another, the artisan and the old-fashioned gentry from the country. In the eyes of satirists it epitomised all that was disgusting in popular entertainment. Jonson in his

Epistle to *The Alchemist* and induction to *Bartholomew Fair* disowned 'the concupiscence of jigs and dances'. Hamlet dismisses Polonius's taste in light entertainment for jigs or tales of bawdry. Massinger's dedication to *The Roman Actor* (1626) for the King's Men specifically rejects the censure of those who prefer 'jigs and ribaldry'. Mostly it was the obscenity that drew attacks from the satirists but jigs did get associated with uproar generally. In 1612 the jigs at the Fortune even drew the official displeasure of the Middlesex magistrates for the disturbances they caused and the kind of audience they attracted:

Complaynte have beene made at this last Generall Sessions that by reason of certayne lewde Jigges songes and daunces used and accustomed at the playhouse called the Fortune in Goulding-lane divers cutt-purses and other lewde and ill disposed persons in great multitudes doe resorte thither at th' end of everye playe many tymes causinge tumultes and outrages wherebye His Majesties peace is often broke and much mischiefe like to ensue thereby.[8]

Dekker painted a similar picture in his *Strange Horse-Race* (1613), where he testified:

I have often seene, after the finishing of some worthy Tragedy, or Catastrophe in the open Theaters, that the Sceane after the Epilogue hath beene more blacke (about a nasty bawdy Jigge) then the most horrid Sceane in the Play was.

The audience at such a time are in commotion, he says, 'the stinkards speaking all things, yet no man understanding any thing' (C4v). Very likely the jig was the one feature of a play not evaluated in advance by the Master of the Revels. Like the clown's extempore rhyming and joking it was the only medium allowing free comment on contemporary events.

   It is probably significant about the divergence in taste and fashion that after 1600, or to be precise after Kemp left the Chamberlain's Men in 1599, the only playhouses that were named as presenting jigs were the three to the north of the city, the Fortune, Curtain and Red Bull.[9] These were the playhouses covered by the Middlesex County Order of 1612 that tried to suppress jigs. Shortly after, William Turner's *Dish of Lenten Stuffe* (1613) seems to uphold the northern playhouses in comparison with the two Bankside playhouses so far as the performing of jigs went:

> That's the fat foole of the Curtin,
> and the leane foole of the Bull:
> Since *Shanke* did leave to sing his rimes,
> he is counted but a gull.
> The players of the Banke side,
> the round Globe and the Swan,

> Will teach you idle trickes of love,
> but the Bull will play the man.[10]

If we discount the contrived word-play in the last line we can read this as meaning that Shanks has left the Fortune and jig-making to join the Globe company (which he in fact did in 1613), a change for the worse so far as Turner is concerned. The contrast is between the romantic love stories offered by the Bankside playhouses and the virile and bawdy jigs at the northern playhouses.

Jigs certainly did persist in spite of the voice of official displeasure through to the closure, though their history is obscure. Some jigs including 'Singing Simkin' were printed with the prose farces and drolls that the playhouses continued furtively and fugitively to offer during the Commonwealth. Their persistence must be a sign of how the fashion in plays that they accompanied survived in the northern suburbs after it had been supplanted on the Bankside.

2. HALL AND AMPHITHEATRE STAGING

Differences in staging fashions that went with the different repertories are complicated by a number of further variations that do seem to have grown out of the differences between the outdoor and indoor playhouses. The fact that the indoor playhouses were smaller and roofed, for instance, created variations in what each kind of playhouse did with music. The indoor consort of musicians with their curtained-off room on the balcony of their playhouses has been mentioned already. The amphitheatres did not use nearly as much song and music as the halls.[11] The chief difference lay in the tradition of beginning an afternoon's performance with a concert overture, particularly at the Blackfriars, and the use in the open air of instruments the decibel capacity of which might have been painful indoors. When the Grocer in *The Knight of the Burning Pestle* demands to hear music, his familiarity with the open-air playhouses leads him to ask for shawms, a form of hautboy sometimes used as a kind of bagpipe. The hall playhouse boy diplomatically tells him that the boy company only has recorders. War trumpets and military drums, designed to be audible in the uproar of a battlefield, were instruments more fit for the open-air theatres than inside a 60-foot hall.

Only one boy company play, Marston's *Sophonisba*, has battles with trumpet-calls. Its stage directions are notable in specifying not the brass instruments used to convey orders to cavalry on the battlefield and to summon latecomers to the amphitheatres but cornets, a woodwind which gave out a similar but quieter sound compared with a trumpet. Only one boy company play calls for a brass instrument, and that is Jonson's *Epicene, or The Silent Woman*, where a hunting horn's volume is used to torment the comically noise-sensitive (hyperacusic) gull Morose.

Other noisy devices must also have had to be scaled down indoors. The firing of cannon and the use of fireworks were neither of them pleasant devices for use inside. The cannon that fired at the Globe for the death of Hamlet and burned it down at *Henry VIII* obviously had to be reproduced for similar performances at the Blackfriars, but it was reduced in scale. In *Love's Pilgrimage*, played at the Blackfriars in 1635, an order is given to shoot off a cannon (4.1). The Folio text of the play accordingly has a book-holder's direction to an aide '*Joh. Bacon ready to shoot off a Pistol*'.[12] Besides the volume of noise from gunpowder there was the smell, an objection that also applied in an enclosed space to the fireworks essential to *Faustus* and other plays with devils in them. Marston's *The Fawn* (1605) has the following passage (1.2):

PAGE. IThere be squibs sir, which squibs running upon lines like some of our gawdie Gallants sir, keepe a smother sir, with flishing and flashing, and in the end sir, they do sir,-
NYMPHADORO. What sir?
PAGE. Stink sir.

Comments on the stench from fireworks sometimes accompanied references to the increasingly popular habit of smoking tobacco in the playhouses. That was not confined to the indoor venues, though the more confined indoor space was no help to the many who did not indulge in the costly fashion of smoking tobacco.

Lighting was another feature that differed between the open-air and indoor venues. In London plays were always staged in the afternoons, presumably to get the brightest daylight whether outdoors or in. Indoors the high windows in stone-walled playhouses like the Blackfriars provided some illumination, but the chief light came from candles and perhaps cressets, a smoky light given out from coils of tarred rope in an iron frame. They were an expensive item in the Shakespeare company's recurrent wintertime bills. In his admirable *Lighting the Shakespearean Stage, 1567–1642* R. B. Graves notes Dekker's comment in *The Seven Deadlie Sinns of London* (1606) that indoor playhouses might be made darker by closing the windows in his simile saying that 'all the Citty lookt like a private Playhouse, when the windows are clapt downe, as if some *Nocturnall*, or dismall *Tragedy* were presently to be acted' (D2). This may indicate by its opposite how much the light from the windows could add to the brightness inside, but Graves also notes that even the large windows in the Middle Temple Hall where Shakespeare's company staged *Twelfth Night* on Candlemas in 1602 only bring in 2 per cent of the external daylight today.[13] I suspect that candlelight was always preferable to daylight for the ladies at the Blackfriars, whose clothing was commonly adorned with spangles that glittered in candlelight whereas in the open air they lost their shine. The multitude of beads from male and female clothes found at the outdoor Rose in 1989 included no spangles, but in the hall at Berkeley Castle, where ladies and gentry watched plays indoors through dark evenings, archaeologists found even more spangles than beads. In daytime the high price of candles, for all the substantial addition they made to running costs at the indoor venues, was a feature designed to suit wealthy audiences. Plays at Court were always staged in dark winter evenings by candlelight.

One important change in staging generally which does seem to have become universal may have been brought about by the influence of the indoor playhouses. This was the practice of breaking off the performance between each act. It seems to have been a practice that began to spread from the indoor to the outdoor repertories after the usual crossover date of 1608. In the hall playhouses pauses in the action were essential if only to give time for attendants to trim the candles that lit the stage or to replace them. Jonson's Induction to *A Staple of News* has a stage direction '*The Tiremen enter to mend the lights*', and the Book-keeper instructs them 'Mend your lights, Gentlemen' in preparation for the Prologue's entry to start the play. Regularly trimming or replacing of the candles in the chandeliers and wall sconces, which supplied far more light than came in from the high windows, was essential if the customers below were not to have their clothes suffer from the wax that would always drip from them. Wax candles were far more costly than tapers, but they still shed their wax with all too familiar regularity.

All the early public-theatre plays ran continuously, without intervals, the incidental entertainment being confined to before and after the performance. Beer and bread were sold during the play so unless the action actually needed a pause there was no point in an interval. Continuous staging helped to fit the stage traffic into its two hours. Some plays do contain a few hints of pauses, but they are slight, and very brief. The lovers in *A Midsummer Night's Dream* '*sleep all the Act*', that is, between the end of Act 3 and the beginning of 4; but that stage direction is to only be found in the Folio text printed in 1623 and might have found its way there at any time up to 1622. *James IV* (1590) has songs or dances including a hornpipe and a jig after Acts

1, 2 and 4 to mark pauses in the story, and the plot of Strange's *Dead Man's Fortune* which dates from about 1590 has a line of crosses drawn at each act break, with a note '*musique*' alongside. The manuscript also has lines drawn at each scene-end, however, and scene-changes were certainly not marked by pauses in staging even in the private playhouses. They may be simply scribal markings, or relics of the authorial manuscript. I would be inclined to believe that some authors in the 1590s acknowledged act breaks by inserting song interludes or by placing their mid-play choruses at them, but not that they expected the players to mark them with the kind of pause that was adopted with later staging.

The chief significance of act breaks, which were usually occupied with music and dancing,[14] is that they altered the practice of continuous staging traditional on the amphitheatre stages. What that might say about an early audience's expected concentration span is not a relevant subject here. In the earlier plays scene divisions are identifiable only by the departure of one group of players as another group enters. Act divisions were probably treated similarly, except when the chorus or perhaps in the early academic plays like *Gorboduc* a plot-foreshadowing dumb-show came to herald the next act. Speech was almost non-stop. The only silences were for heavy breathing in the formal pauses during hand-to-hand sword-fights (in *Orlando Furioso*, '*they fight a good while and then breath*'), or in the voiceless uproar of battles. Real silences are truly noteworthy, as in Tamburlaine's exit after he has caught Agydas denigrating him to Zenocrate (*1 Tamburlaine*, 3.2):

Tamburlaine goes to her, & takes her away lovingly by the hand, looking wrathfully on Agidas, and sayes nothing.

There are only three such eloquent silences in all Shakespeare.[15]

With the players accustomed to holding the attention of audiences, many of them on their feet closest to the stage, the flow of words must have been not only constant but rattled off at speeds markedly higher than modern armchair audiences are now used to. The absence of formal intervals on the amphitheatre stages would certainly have helped to speed the performances and keep audience attention. Even in the indoor theatres act-breaks were designed to last the length of no more than thirty lines of verse, little more than a minute.[16] That is an element in the much-debated question of how long performances were normally expected to last. Through the 1590s contemporary accounts claimed that performances of plays of average length, 2,500 lines, took no more than two hours. That was for plays that with an interval take three hours now, even with cuts. Plays grew longer in the seventeenth century, to an average nearer 2,900 lines, and yet the evidence about performance times does not vary. The prologue to Shirley's *The Duke's Mistress*, a play of roughly 3,000 lines, refers in 1636 to its length as 'but two howers'. Even *Bartholomew Fair*, an exceptionally long play for its time at over 4,000 lines, was said by its author to take only 'the space of two houres and a half, and somewhat more'.[17] Possibly here of course Jonson was mocking the official line about the permitted length for the performance of plays. The Lord Chamberlain had laid that down in his letter to the Lord Mayor in October 1594, when he declared that his new company, Shakespeare's, had given an undertaking

that where heretofore they began not their Plaies til towardes Fower a clock, they will now begin at two and have done betwene fower and five.[18]

This is quite specific. Considering the jigs took extra time at the end of the play, this undertaking allowed precious little time for the 3,700 lines of *Richard III*, still less the 4,000 or so of *Hamlet* or *Bartholomew Fair*. It is likely that most performances would be cut, sometimes very drastically, to fit the time available, especially in winter when the nights were drawing in early. Shakespeare's company trimmed his *Henry V* from his manuscript's 3,400 lines to the First Quarto's 1,700. The two hours' traffic of the stage proclaimed in *Romeo and Juliet* was a conventional claim, and two hours became a strikingly pervasive statement about the timing, although most people would judge it by the church clocks, most of which struck only once each hour. Henry Carey's statement that his company would perform for between two and three hours, prescriptive as it was, seems a fair estimate of the standard period performances lasted for. Whatever the regular time, few folk had watches, so it must have been a stock assumption based on the hourly chimes of the City's clocks. It seems unlikely that breaking the two or three hours of continuous playing at the amphitheatres with act breaks at the indoor halls had anything to do with the concern of modern TV producers about the limited concentration span of modern audiences.

Continuous and high-speed staging went hand-in-hand with unlocalised settings. The 'scene' was changed when one person departed and another entered, only occasionally specifying where they now were. *Catiline* offers as similes for rapid movement 'a veil put off, a visor changed, / Or the scene shifted'. The word 'scene' provides some problems, because it could mean the tiring-house (John Florio's dictionary defines it as 'a skaffold, a pavillion, or fore part of a theater where players make them readie, being trimmed with hangings, out of which they enter upon the stage'), or it could mean the fictional localities where the action of a play was supposed to happen. Only much later did it come to mean the canvas flats or 'scenery'

that provided backgrounds for such localities. The use of the word in these
three senses misled some scholars into thinking that scenery was used in the
hall theatres. Thomas Nabbes, for instance, has been cited as using the word
to mean scenery in the following passage in the prologue to *Hannibal and
Scipio* (1637):

> The places sometimes chang'd too for the Scene
> Which is translated as the musick playes
> Betwixt the acts ...

but the rest of the passage shows he meant fictional localities:

> ... wherein [the author] likewise prayes
> You will conceive his battailes done.[19]

The same play specifies all the entries for its characters as 'by the right
Scoene', '*by the middle* Scoene', and '*by the left* Scoene' (using the 'tiring-
house' sense of the term), and '*in the* Balcone'.

Almost all the action took place on the main stage or platform, the only
area known at the time as the 'stage' (which is why I avoid using the term
'upper stage'). Analyses of staging in the repertories of the Globe on the one
hand and the Cockpit on the other indicate that the stage was almost never
left empty of characters.[20] Since the only means of separating players from
audience was the height of the stage,[21] the crowd of 'understanders' jostling
alongside the amphitheatre platforms would have had little patience with
players who left them to their own devices for any period. References to
audiences showing their impatience by such actions as hurling apples at the
hangings in order to get the players to start their play are not unknown. The
chief feature of the staging and its interaction with the audience was their
intimate interconnection. The spectators were as visible as the players, and
more potently they completely surrounded the players on their platform, at
the hall playhouses sharing the stage space itself with the action. So the
clown's tricks and Hamlet's soliloquies both had to be aimed at the visible
presences around the stage.

With unlocalised staging and freely variable 'scenes' all that the poet
had to do was slip in a reference early on in each scene to the locality to be
imagined if he wanted anywhere specific. Jonson in *Every Man Out of His
Humour* went to the length of providing two Presenters, constantly on
stage, who inform the audience of each change of locality. At the beginning
of Act 3, for instance, one says 'we must desire you to presuppose the stage,
the middle isle in *Paules;* and that, [pointing to the tiring-house?] the west
end of it'. Occasionally the stage doors might be called on to serve as

specifically separate locations, as in the Globe's *Merry Devil of Edmonton* (1602?), where a group of characters are tricked about the names of two inns by a switch of signboards – presumably one over each flanking stage door. Occasionally the boy companies seem to have hung up title boards in the private playhouses. *Wily Beguiled* at Paul's and *The Knight of the Burning Pestle* at Blackfriars in 1607 both begin with some by-play about changing their play's title boards, and *Cynthia's Revels* at Blackfriars in 1601 mentions them. Some sixteenth-century Court plays appear to have used both title and locality boards, but on the whole they appear to have been an early phenomenon, a cumbersome and literal-minded way of telling an audience where the scene was supposed to be located. Inn signs such as those used in *The Merry Devil of Edmonton* were a rather different matter. Some plays such as the Admiral's Men's *Look About You* in 1595 give the names in the dialogue of each inn which is to be visited, suggesting that the players did hang up inn signs marking their destinations. The Boar's Head in Eastcheap might have been signalled in such a way, though all its scenes take place only after the participants are already inside the inn.

3. STAGE REALISM

The main features of amphitheatre and hall staging can conveniently be divided into a number of the most conspicuous categories: stage realism, stage business and effects, properties, costumes (known as apparel) and scenery. By far the most awkward of these to assess is realism. As has been noted above, lacking any proscenium arch to separate players from audience the presentation of illusion as reality for Shakespeareans was inevitably more complicated than in modern theatres or in cinema, quite apart from the pulpit insistence that deceptions were the work of Satan. The players stood in the midst of the audience and had no facilities for presenting the pictorial aspects of illusion because they were appearing in three dimensions, not the two that proscenium-arch staging or the camera's picture frame establish. Awareness of the illusion as trickery was therefore close to the surface all the time. It was because of this that so many of the plays began with prologues and inductions openly acknowledging that the play which follows is a fiction.

Both poets and players admitted quite often that their business was a cheat, whether illusion or delusion. In numerous plays a masque or a play within the play (*The Spanish Tragedy, Hamlet, The Revenger's Tragedy, The Maid's Tragedy*) serves as an explicit emblem of deceit. Playing is counterfeiting, a continual pretence, so the illusion had to be acknowledged openly as an illusion. From there it was only a slight further twist to develop inductions in which the players come on stage to talk about their play and in so doing actually play themselves, performing what the playwright has written for them to speak in their own personality as if reality and illusion were the same. *Cynthia's Revels*, the 1604 King's Men's *Malcontent, Bartholomew Fair* and other Jonson plays all use such metarealistic fictions. Playwrights such as Beaumont in *The Knight of the Burning Pestle* bring players disguised as audience on stage to comment on the play they are seeing, confusing the illusion/reality borderline with a sophistication rarely matched in any drama at any time. *Twelfth Night* is crammed with jokes about stage illusion. At 3.4. 131–2 Fabian watches Malvolio making a gull of himself and offers the obvious comment that 'If this were played upon a stage now, I could condemn it as an improbable fiction.' In *The Malcontent*'s induction Will Sly comes on stage pretending to be a gallant looking for a stool and accuses the stage attendant: 'lle hold my life thou took'st me for one of the plaiers.' Later he asks if 'Harry Cundele, D: Burbidge and W: Sly' might be brought on stage, and begins to flourish his hat like Osric in *Hamlet*, perhaps in imitation of his own playing of the part. The fictional reality was a running paradox, a matter of what Shakespeare once called 'Tragedy / Played in jest, by counterfeiting actors' (*3 Henry VI*, 2.3.27).

Such interplay between illusion and reality went easily with the conventions of continuous staging and non-localised settings. Sidney's mockery of the playwrights and players who failed to remember that their reality was illusion stayed in the minds of at least some of the dramatists. In his *Defence of Poesy* (*c.* 1583) Sidney wrote:

you shal have *Asia* of the one side, and *Affrick* of the other, and so many other under-kingdoms, that the Player, when he commeth in, must ever begin with telling where he is, or els the tale will not be conceived. Now ye shal have three ladies walke to gather flowers, and then we must beleeve the stage to be a Garden. By and by, we heare newes of shipwracke in the same place, and then wee are to blame if we accept it not for a Rock. Upon the backe of that, comes out a hidious Monster, with fire and smoke, and then the miserable beholders are bounde to take it for a Cave. While in the meantime two Armies flye in, represented with foure swords and bucklers, and then what harde heart will not receive it for a pitched fielde?[22]

Shakespeare used a choric presenter to introduce the improbable fictions of war on stage in the last of his plays about English history in 1599, and acknowledged the inadequacy of his illusion by asking the audience to 'piece out our imperfections with your thoughts', though that modest induction was axed from the first performances by a company impatient to tell the more obvious aspects of the story. Jonson echoed Sidney in a prologue to *Every Man in his Humour* published in the Folio version of the play in 1616, when he claimed that:

>   he himselfe must justly hate,
> To make a child, now swadled, to proceede
> Man, and then shoote up, in one beard, and weede,
> Past threescore yeeres: or, with three rustie swords,
> And helpe of some few foot-and-a-halfe-foote words,
> Fight over *Yorke*, and *Lancasters* long jarres:
> And in the tyring-house bring wounds, to scarres.
> He rather prayes, you will be pleas'd to see
> One such, to day, as other playes should be.
> Where neither *Chorus* wafts you ore the seas;
> Nor creaking throne comes downe, the boyes to please;
> Nor nimble squibbe is seene, to make afear'd
> The Gentlewomen; nor roul'd bullet heard
> To say, it thunders; nor tempestuous drumme
> Rumbles, to tell you when the storme doth come.

Jonson was echoing Sidney in his contempt not for realism in itself but for a too literal-minded use of mechanical devices and for the simple-minded belief that illusion can successfully become delusion. It was a matter on which for his own reasons he tended to face both ways, especially while composing his masques.[23]

Not that the whole theatre and its stage lacked decorations, colourful and symbolic, in forms often reflected by the staging. The design by Inigo Jones for a hall theatre stage considered in Chapter 4 was a Jacobean flourish with neoclassical features, but was not at a far remove from many surviving examples of Tudor decorative arts. The painting and sculptural features of the stage and auditorium embodied a symbolism that gave the different elements their own character. The stage itself was represented as earth, and earthly. The painted heavens above covering the stage in the amphitheatres provided automatic visual signals of their place, with gods and the sun, moon and stars and perhaps other heavenly figures. The middle level and the stage balcony may have shown interactions between divine and human forms, like the goddess Venus and human Adonis, or Apollo and the Muses. The trap provided another level, its position under the stage surface offering a hell for Marlowe's Barabbas and Faustus to sink into, for devils to spring from, and for the ghost of Hamlet's father to descend into before he speaks from his purgatorial grave under the ostensible earth of the stage floor.

Painted skies on ceilings had a standard form. The Oxford antiquary Brian Twyne described the stage set up for James's visit at Christ Church in 1605 as having 'over all, delicate paynttinge resembling ye Cloudes & Sky cullur &c'.[24] Tiring-house fronts were painted, serving equally as the inside or outside of a house or royal court. The tiring-house wall was used when towns were to be besieged, when the central doorway became the town gate as in *Henry V*'s Harfleur scenes. It served as the exterior of the Capulet house when Romeo climbed to its balcony. Specific sets of stage hangings might similarly be used to give signals to the audience. Dekker wrote an induction in which an observer comments that 'the stage is hung with black, and I perceive / The auditors prepared for a tragedy'. Not much effort was given to catering for Sidney's literal-minded realism of localities, but the structural iconography of heaven and hell above and below the stage and the attendant architectural features were fully exploited, and carefully depicted in paint and sculptural features.

Besides these symbolic signals permanently on the scene, stage realism did have its simpler levels too, especially when the effect had to be gruesome or sensational. Bladders and sponges of vinegar concealed in the armpit and squeezed to produce the semblance of blood were not unknown, and many other realistic details testify to the esteem the players retained for touches of colourful realism on this level. In the plot of the Admiral's *Battle of Alcazar*, when three characters are executed and disembowelled in a dumb-show on stage, the appropriate book-holder's instruction is '*3 violls of blood & a sheeps gather*', that is, a bladder holding liver, heart and lungs and one small flask of blood for each victim to burst open. A little earlier in the same plot the annotator calls blandly for '*raw flesh*'. The flasks may even have contained real blood, since calf's or sheep's blood does not usually congeal. White shirts would, however, need some heavy laundering afterwards. In *The Spanish Tragedy* a letter said to be written in blood is accompanied by a marginal note '*red ink*'. Some plays had execution scenes involving decapitation. A late anonymous play printed in 1649, *The Rebellion of Naples*, has a stage direction for such an execution, '*He thrusts out his head, and they cut off a false head made of a bladder fill'd with bloud. Exeunt with his body*'. Since the play was written during the closure of the theatres the odds are that this was fanciful, but it might explain how the decapitations in plays like *Faustus, The Insatiate Countess* and *Sir John Van Olden Barnavelt* were done.[25] In the 1616 text of *Faustus* the decapitation is preceded by a direction, '*Enter Faustus with the false head*'. A list of simpler but equally useful pseudo-realistic devices might include the appearance of the mariners '*wet*' after the shipwreck in *The Tempest*, a device used also in the horse-courser scene of *Faustus* and

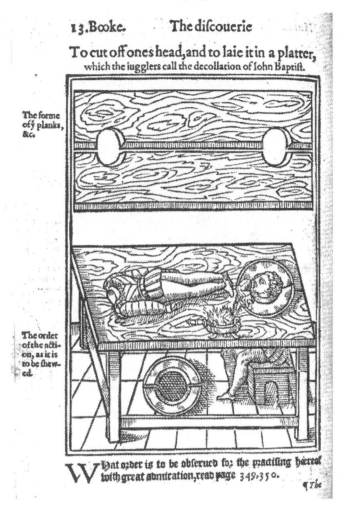

13.Booke. The difcouerie

To cut off ones head, and to laie it in a platter, which the iugglers call the decollation of Iohn Baptift.

The forme of ÿ planks, &c.

The order of the acti-on, as it is to be fhew-ed.

WHat order is to be obferued fo; the practiling herrof with great aduniration, read page 349,350.

¶The

Illustration 37. A device for displaying decapitated bodies. The orginal woodcut is in Reginald Scot's *Discoverie of Witchcraft* (1504). Described as a 'juggler's' trick for deceiving the ignorant, it may resemble the kind of device used to display decapitated bodies onstage, though usually just detached heads were flourished, as with Macbeth.

other plays. Smoke was provided to make mists and fog, as in the masque in Act I of *The Maid's Tragedy*, which starts with Night coming up through the trap '*in mists*'.

Other tricks of realism akin to the references to the required locality for a specific scene could easily be supplied by means of noises off, and was. Marston in *The Insatiate Countess* 2.6 ordered '*a trampling of Horses heard*', and Fletcher in *The Chances* 3.4 similarly asked for '*A noise within like horses*'. Massinger's *The Guardian* has '*a noyse within, as the fall of a Horse*' (4.1), after which a character enters and shouts 'Hell take the stumbling Jade.' The firing of cannon and peals of bells were other means of producing noises off, especially in the outdoor playhouses, and the indoor playhouses may have been able to produce bird-song when required. Dekker's *Blurt Master Constable*, a Paul's play of 1601, has the stage direction '*Musicke sodainly plaies and Birds sing*', and Marston's *Dutch Courtesan* at the Blackfriars in 1603 has '*the Nittingalls sing*'. *The Pilgrim*, performed by the King's Men in 1621, has two stage directions, one simply '*Musicke and birds*', the other '*Musick afar off. Pot birds*'. The last reference is probably not to fat capons but the Elizabethan device of producing a warbling note by blowing through a pipe into a pot of water.[26] Players could easily become adroit at imitating bird-calls themselves.

Realism of this kind was by no means uniform, of course. It appears usually as a special effect designed to intensify the inherent comedy or tragedy of its occasion. 'When the bad bleedes,' as Vindice says in *The Revenger's Tragedy*, 'then is the Tragedie good.' We must be careful to measure such effects against the many totally non-realistic conventions of the kind suggested by Henslowe's note of a 'robe for to goo invisibell' (*Diary*, p. 325). It is healthy to note what the book-keeper appended in the manuscript of the anonymous *Two Noble Ladies*, a Red Bull play of 1619–23, when two soldiers are drowned on stage in the following passage:

1ST [SOLDIER], what strange noise is this?
2ND [SOLDIER], dispatch, the tide swells high, what feind is this?
1ST. what furie ceazes me?
2ND. Alas, I'm hurried headlong to the streame.
1ST. And so am I, wee both must drowne and die.

The book-keeper's accompanying stage directions show how the players managed to drown themselves. Opposite 'what strange noise is this?' is written '*Thunder. Enter 2 Tritons with silver trumpets*', and after 'what feind is this?' '*This tritons ceaz the souldiers.*' They drown as '*The Tritons dragge them in sounding their trumpets.*'[27] If the play had gone to the press it is unlikely that the book-keeper's informative notes would have been printed.

The occasional attempts at stage realism are closely linked with spectacle and other stage business and effects, which themselves were likely to vary according to the nature of each playing company's repertory. Here the distinction drawn earlier between on the one hand the plays dating before about 1600 and the plays at the northern playhouses after that and on the other the indoor theatre plays and Globe plays crops up once again. Some general impression of the older style might be found in the English Wagner Book of 1594, a fantasy on the life and death of Faustus that seems to be strongly coloured by memories of the play in performance:

there might you see the ground-worke at the one end of the Stage whereout the personated divels should enter in their fiery ornaments, made like the broad wide mouth of an huge Dragon ... the teeth of this Hels-mouth far out stretching.[28]

The hell-mouth that is 'discovered' in the 1616 text of *Faustus* has usually been identified with the curt entry 'i Hell mought' in Henslowe's inventory of the Admiral's Men's properties at the Rose. The Fortune players offered up *Faustus* in much the same way in 1620, when, as a contemporary witnessed,

a man may behold shagg-hayr'd Devills runne roaring over the Stage with Squibs in their mouthes, while Drummers make Thunder in the Tyring-house, and the twelve-penny Hirelings make artificiall Lightning in their Heavens.[29]

The public-theatre players had considerable resources and resourcefulness for this kind of staging. A foreign visitor wrote this account of what he saw at the first Beargarden as early as 1584:

There is a round building three storeys high, in which are kept about a hundred large English dogs, with separate wooden kennels for each of them. These dogs were made to fight singly with three bears, the second bear being larger than the first and the third larger than the second. After this a horse was brought in and chased by the dogs, and at last a bull, who defended himself bravely. The next was that a number of men and women came forward from a separate compartment, dancing, conversing and fighting with each other: also a man who threw some white bread among the crowd, that scrambled for it. Right over the middle of the place a rose was fixed, this rose being set on fire by a rocket: suddenly lots of apples and pears fell out of it down upon the people standing below. Whilst the people were scrambling for the apples, some rockets were made to fall down upon them out of the rose, which caused a great fright but amused the spectators. After this, rockets and other fireworks came flying out of all corners, and that was the end of the play.[30]

A suggestion of the traveller's tale hangs round this, though the baiting and the jig that followed it are easily enough authenticated, and fireworks were freely used. It seems, however, to merge a bear-baiting occasion into a play performance since the audience were standing in the yard when they scrambled after the apples and pears, so it may be mere fantasy. The pyrotechnics in Heywood's *Ages* plays at the Red Bull in 1610–12 on the other hand involved some extraordinary feats that the company author clearly expected to be put into practice on stage. In *The Silver Age*, for instance, '*Enter* Pluto *with a club of fire, a burning crowne ... and a guard of Divels, all with burning weapons*'; '*Jupiter appeares in his glory under a Raine-bow*'; '*Thunder, lightnings*, Jupiter *descends in his majesty, his Thunderbolt burning ... As he toucheth the bed it fires, and all flyes up*'. One of Heywood's stage directions in *The Silver Age* concludes with '*fire-workes all over the house*'. So far as their extant plays indicate, the hall playhouses and the Globe made less use of such spectacular scenic resources.

The fact that the amphitheatres used daylight while the halls relied on candles seems to have made surprisingly little difference to the means of presenting night scenes at the two sorts of venue. In plays written for both night scenes are signified in words and by the players or stage hands bringing on candlesticks or flaming torches. Other atmospheric effects, thunder, lightning and mists, noises off and mood music of various kinds, occur routinely in plays put on at all the playhouses. Thunder came from what Jonson called the 'roul'd bullet' trundled down a sheet of metal, or a 'tempestuous drum'. Lightning was produced from squibs set alight in the heavens, and mists were made with smoke. There are even some hints that the heavens were not beyond dropping a gentle rain upon the earth beneath in *The Brazen Age* and in Dekker's *If It Be Not Good, the Devil is in It*, both at the Red Bull.

Atmospherics in a metaphorical sense appeared in the colouring of the stage hangings, which, as we have noted, might be black for a tragedy,[31] and in offstage music. The Blackfriars with its famous consort of musicians made this readily available in plays like *The Duchess of Malfi*, where the Madmen sing '*to a dismall kind of Musique*', and *The Tempest's* mood music from offstage was clearly presented by the Blackfriars consort. Marston's *Sophonisba* has a stage direction '*Infernall Musicke plaies softly whilst Erictho enters and when she speakes ceaseth.*' Martin Peerson, who had a financial interest in the second Blackfriars Boys, was a professional musician. He left the Blackfriars to become singing master at Paul's School. Phillip Rosseter, who started the abortive Porter's Hall playhouse in 1615, was another professional composer. Music in the amphitheatres was more limited, commonly introduced as song with or without accompaniment, and the musical atmospherics were supplied in forms such as a sennet or flourish of trumpets of the kind and possibly from the place where the commencement of a play was heralded. Drums provided martial music as well as thunder, and accompanied battle scenes in consort with the trumpets. The equipment of the

Admiral's Men in 1598 included three trumpets, one drum, a treble and bass viol, a bandore, a sackbut, 'iii tymbrells' and 'i chyme of bells'.

4. STAGE PROPERTIES

Besides their function in the dramatic action, displays and discoveries were matters of stage business as spectacle, a moment for the audience to stop listening and admire. The early playhouses offered displays of special properties such as the brazen head in *Friar Bacon and Friar Bungay* and *Alphonsus of Aragon*, the hell-mouth of *Faustus* or the cauldron for the finale of *The Jew of Malta*. The Globe 'discovered' Volpone's gold and Portia's caskets while the revelations of the Red Bull included a Trojan Horse. Shops, studies and cells in all the playhouses appeared furnished to show what they were, as in the Red Bull's *If It Be Not Good*, where a cell has '*A table … set out with a candle burning, a deaths head* [i.e. a skull] *a cloke and a cross*'. *The Devil's Law-case* at the same playhouse discovered a table with '*two Tapers, a Deaths head, a Booke*'. The study in the Globe's *Devil's Charter* is equipped for one discovery with '*books, coffers, [a] triple Crowne upon a cushion …*' and in another a player is revealed '*beholding a Magicall glasse with other observations*'.

Properties were tangible assets to a playing company, and the list of properties that Henslowe and Alleyn compiled in March 1598 is a business-man's inventory of his stock. It is also the most precise indication we have of a company's normal resources in time of prosperity. The full list, in Henslowe's characteristic spelling, is as follows:

> *Item*, i rocke, i cage, i tombe, i Hell mought.
> *Item*, i tome of Guido, i tome of Dido, i bedsteade.
> *Item*, viii lances, i payer of stayers for Fayeton.
> *Item*, ii stepells, & i chyme of belles, & i beacon.
> *Item*, i hecfor for the playe of Faeton, the limes dead [a heifer for a sacrifice?]
> *Item*, i globe, & i golden scepter, iii clobes.
> *Item*, ii marchepanes, & the sittie of Rome.
> *Item*, i gowlden flece; ii rackets; i baye tree.
> *Item*, i wooden hatchett; i lether hatchete.
> *Item*, i wooden canepie; owld Mahemetes head.
> *Item*, i lyone skin; i beares skyne; & Faetones lymes, & Faeton charete; & Argosse heade.
> *Item*, Nepun forcke & garland.
> *Item*, i erasers stafe; Kentes woden leage.
> *Item*, Jerosses head & raynbowe; i littel alter.

Item, viii viserdes; Tamberlyne brydell; i wooden matook.
Item, Cupedes bowe, & quiver; the clothe of the Sone & Mone.
Item, i bores heade & Serberosse iii heads.
Item, i Cadeseus; ii mose banckes, & i snake.
Item, ii fanes of feathers; Belendon stable; i tree of gowlden apelles;
    Tantelouse tre; ix eyorn targates.
Item, i copper targate, & xvii foyles.
Item, iii wooden targates; i greve armer.
Item, i syne for Mother Readcap; i buckler.
Item, Mercures wings; Tasso picter; i helmet with a dragon, i shelde, with
    iii lyones; i elme bowle.
Item, i chayne of dragons; i gylte speare.
Item, ii coffenes; i bulles head; and i vylter.
Item, iii tymbrells; i dragon in fostes.
Item, i lyone; ii lyone heades; i great horse with his leages; i sack-bute.
Item, i whell and frame in the Sege of London.
Item, i paire of rowghte gloves.
Item, i poopes miter.
Item, iii Imperial crownes; i playne crowne.
Item, i gostes crown; i crowne with a sone.
Item, i frame for the heading in Black Jone.
Item, i black dogge.
Item, i cauderm for the Jewe.

The lists of Revels Office properties for Court performances of about the
same time as this inventory are broadly similar.

   A few of these properties were evidently designed for display, specially set
out on the stage or set in the central opening behind a curtain until needed.
The great majority however were portable, equipment rather than set-
pieces.[32] That fitted the general expectation that plays and their properties
had to be easily moved from one venue to another, whether to Court or to a
grandee's private hall. For staging purposes the portable nature of most
properties means that somebody or some bodies had to be employed to
bring on those properties that were not actually worn or carried on and off
the stage by players. *King Lear*'s direction at II.ii, '*Stocks brought out*', means
that a pair of anonymous hirelings carried the required object on and set it
down at a suitably conspicuous place. There is an elaborate stage direction
in the Blackfriars play *Bussy D'Ambois*, 5.1,

*Montsurry bare, unbrac't, pulling Tamyra in, … one bearing light, a standish, and
paper, which sets a Table.*

This requires an entry by a hatless Montsurry (we have to remember that
hats were normally worn indoors and therefore on stage), with his doublet

unlaced, dragging the boy playing Tamyra with him, followed by an invisible boy (a which not a who), with a candle, an inkstand and a sheet of paper, which he sets out on a table already in position on stage. One feature of what we probably rightly know as the bare stage that was far more conspicuous then than our reading of the texts tells us now was the presence of servants and attendants, standing silently, ready to carry properties on or off, and if messengers standing by a stage door ready to take a letter and depart with it. Usually, like all house servants, dressed in a blue tunic, they would stand there in silent attendance when nobility was on stage unless the noble explicitly dismissed them. Messengers would similarly stand waiting by the flanking stage doors until summoned to deliver a letter.

All too often the surviving stage directions understandably fail to state the obvious such as the presence or entry of servants, because such uses of the stage were far more recognisable then than they are to us as readers of the texts. The original texts frequently fail to bother to supply an '*Exit*' when a player is to leave the stage, because so far as the writer was concerned it was the player's job to know when he had to leave. Neither poet nor player had much reason to bother with later generations of readers. Something similar applies to the many far from explicit stage directions. So far as we can judge, for instance, even the most substantial properties were likely to be carried onto the stage more often than they were discovered, and they would never be in position from the outset of the play they were to be used in. Some of the directing terminology is ambiguous, though, and a stage direction like '*Enter X upon a bed*' may mean either that the bed was pushed out onto the stage or that it was discovered, and the term '*set out*' seems sometimes to mean 'carried on to the stage' and sometimes 'discovered'.[33] That is one of the many unclarities befogging subsequent generations of readers. They ought to keep our mind on the absence of much fixity in performance compared with the apparent authority of print.

It seems logical to assume that a four-poster bed 'put out' for a bedroom scene would be put back again afterwards. But would the same thing have happened to trees, mossy banks and similar less obtrusive objects? Some scholars think they could have been on stage throughout the play.[34] Personally I should think the blue-coated stage-keepers were kept busier than that. An essentially metatheatrical approach to stage realism could easily cope with invisible stage hands carrying trees and mossy banks on stage at the beginning of a scene, as readily as banquet tables or benches and stools for players to sit on when at a tavern. The three trees listed in Henslowe's inventory are all designed for specific purposes. One is of Atlanta's golden apples, one is for Tantalus and one is a bay tree. There is no hint that Henslowe bothered at all about undifferentiated trees for forest scenes, and he might not even have supplied rose bushes for the Temple garden scene (2.4) in *1 Henry VI*, where one of the rival families plucks a red and the other a white rose It seems highly unlikely that any special tree like the one for Tantalus would have been left on stage throughout the play. *A Warning for Fair Women* performed by Shakespeare's company has a dumb-show in which the trap-door is used to spectacular effect: '*suddenly riseth up a great tree*'. It is subsequently felled and, I would expect, dragged off. How 'great' it was if it could rise suddenly out of the trap we can only guess. There is little to justify the view that all such devices when needed for a play were left on stage throughout the performance.[35] If tables, chairs, benches, beds and thrones could be shifted by the stage hands so could every other portable object.

One very spectacular form of display utilising only readily portable properties was of course the procession. Like a mannequin parade it showed off costumes and accessories to advantage, and as in mannequin parades its members 'passed over the stage' in solemn march, probably arriving on the stage by one door, walking all the way round the stage edge and back into the tiring-house again by the other. A long time ago Allardyce Nicoll conjectured that 'passing over the stage' meant exactly that, climbing onto the stage from the yard on one side and descending into the yard again on the other.[36] This is extremely unlikely, if only because the stage doors leading straight from the tiring-house onto the stage were already in existence and because there is no evidence that steps ever existed from the yard up the five feet or so to the stage. Such stairs would have made it all too easy for the groundlings to ascend where the players would not want them to go. There would otherwise have been no point in building a stage five feet higher than the yard level. Certainly even at the Blackfriars, which had a deterrent rail surmounting the low stage rim, there was no easy way up onto the stage for the Citizen's wife in *The Knight of the Burning Pestle*.

An archetype for stage processions can be found in the several stately pomps of the two plays about *Tamburlaine*, most notably the one for the death of Zenocrate:

Tamburlaine, with Usumcasane, and his three sons, foure bearing the hearse of Zenocrate; and the drums sounding a dolefull martch; the Towne burning.

So far as this may have been the company's direction rather than Marlowe's own, which is unclear, it seems to order a funeral procession issuing from one flanking stage door to the other, possibly with fire and smoke belching out at balcony level, all figures marching in time to a doleful drum with the usual four carrying the coffin.

Every company liked processions, though the earlier companies and those playing at the Fortune and Red Bull made more of the martial and pompous aspects and the hall playhouses more of the sumptuous and elegant. Both kinds of venue not infrequently used processions for dumb-shows, or at the hall playhouses for masques. Nathanael Richards in his tragedy *Messallina*, written for the King's Revels at Salisbury Court in 1635, appended this hopeful direction:

Cornets sound a Flourish, Enter Senate who placed by Sulpilius, cornets cease, and the Antique maske consisting of eight Bachinalians, enter guirt with vine leaves, and shap'd in the middle with Tunne Vessells, each bearing a Cup in their hands, who during the first straine of Musick playd foure times over, enter two at a time, at the tune's end, make stand; draw wine and carouse, then dance all: the antimasque gone off, and solemne musicke playing; Messallina and Silius gloriously crown'd in an Arch-glittering Cloud aloft, court each other.

Richards was offering his attempt at a version of the Court masques, chiefly their anti-masque phase of the full masque performed by Bacchanalian grotesques pretending to get drunk, the sort of fake onstage carousal seen all too often today.

Descents and ascents of deities from the stage heavens like the gradual delivery of Juno over (or through) thirty lines of *The Tempest* at Blackfriars were similarly matters of spectacle. In the earlier plays the gods tended to walk on from the stage doors like any mortal. After *As You Like It*'s Hymen enters on foot the first of Shakespeare's gods to fly in was Jupiter on his eagle in *Cymbeline*, throwing thunderbolts as he flew (in 5.3 one witness says 'his celestial breath / Was sulphurous to smell'). Flights were more favoured by the boy companies than the adults, since the smaller size of the boys gave them a weight advantage on the heavens' windlass. The ingenuities of Inigo Jones in the Court spectacles of later years, which allowed boys to fly in not only vertically but at a slant, may have encouraged more limited imitations at the commercial venues.

Dumb-shows were affairs of pure spectacle, the only silent moments in any play, and employed relatively far more properties than the rest of the plays in which they were incorporated. At their simplest they were parades of spectacle, formal processions using all the company's most glorious apparel, with crowns, sceptres and other fake regalia, swords and often blazing torches. State occasions like the coronation in *The Devil's Charter* or the funeral at the beginning of Act 2 in *Antonio's Revenge* were characteristic of this kind. The stage direction for the latter gives a hint of what they were like.

The Cornets sound a cynet [sennet]

    Enter two mourners with torches, two with streamers; Castilio & Forobosco, with torches: a Heralde bearing Andrugio's helme & sword: the coffin: Maria supported by Lucio and Alberto, Antonio by himselfe: Piero, and Strozzo talking: Galeatzo and Matzagente, Balurdo & Pandulfo: the coffin set downe: helme, sworde and streamers hung up, placed by the Herald: whil'st Antonio and Maria wet their handkerchers with their teares, kisse them, and lay them on the hearse, kneeling: all goe out but Piero. Cornets cease, and he speakes.

Marston specified cornets rather than trumpets because the Paul's play-house was so small, but it did not stop him creating a fire hazard with the torches.

    Earlier classical plays such as *Gorboduc* and *Jocasta* used dumb-shows at the end of each act to summarise the plot of the act to follow. Some later plays of the boy companies also used their interacts for dumb-shows, as in *Histriomastix* 3, *Antonio and Mellida* 3 at Paul's and *The Malcontent* 2 at Blackfriars. By the turn of the century, though, dumb-shows that mimed a plot-story were seen by some of the more acid playwrights as laughably archaic, to judge by their contempt for 'pantomimick action'. Dumb-shows were deliberately used as old-fashioned devices in *Hamlet* and Middleton's *Your Five Gallants*. For a while after *Pericles* in 1607 they became fashionable again, regularly appearing in the King's Men's reper-tory, usually inset as tableaux or spectacles like the show of madmen and the waxworks in *The Duchess of Malfi*. Heywood, in a prologue to a Red Bull play printed in 1615, *The Four Prentices of London*, still insisted on their value for abridging a story

        in dumbe shewes, which were they writ at large,
    Would aske a long and tedious circumstance.

and as late as 1634 a Cockpit play by the same author, *A Maidenhead Well Lost*, had a dumb-show as plot-thickened as this:

Musicke. A Dumbe Shew. Enter Millaine, to him Storza, and brings in Lauretta masked. The Duke takes her and puts her into Bed, and Exit. Enter both the Dukes and Julia, they make signes to her and Exit; Storza hides Julia in a corner, and stands before her. Enter againe with the Prince to bring him to bed: They cheere him on, and others snatch his points, and so Exit. The Dukes Imbrace and Exeunt.[37]

Stage business and spectacle of this kind should not be allowed to obscure the fact that the stages themselves were colourful but essentially bare apart from their normal fixed painting and carvings. We might add that as a general rule the better the playwright the less spectacle was likely to be used in his plays. Of all Shakespeare's scenes written for the Globe it has been estimated that 80 per cent could have been performed on a completely bare stage platform.[38] The one play of Shakespeare's that makes great use of stage spectacle and business is *The Tempest*, a play in which Shakespeare seems almost to have been mocking his own art by the closeness with which he observed the neoclassical unities of time and place. The contrast that made with *The Tempest*'s immediate predecessor, *The Winter's Tale*, which swings in time through a whole generation and in place between Sicily and the sea-coast of Bohemia, is as complete as it well could be. Most of the stage business in *The Tempest* can be seen as setting up a metaphor for Prospero's and perhaps for Shakespeare's arts, of course, including the broken-off spectacle of the Act 4 masque, and is closed to our questions for that reason.[39] But it does raise a suspicion about how deeply Shakespeare's tongue was embedded in his cheek while he wrote his last plays.

The relative frequency with which properties were discovered for display rather than carried on stage is hard to tell because the stage directions are ambiguous. The Globe, Red Bull and Cockpit, the three venues whose plays have been most closely scrutinised for the evidence of their stage directions, all seem to have favoured either method without much consistency. In any case, the occupants of canopied beds, the most substantial properties of all, usually emerged from them onto the stage fairly promptly. The Swan's double doors may not have provided a large enough discovery-space for such properties, since *The Chaste Maid* 3.2 opens with a bed being '*thrust out*', but this is no evidence to draw general conclusions from. Tables and chairs, more easily portable than beds, were revealed in the discovery-space when they represented a study or a cell but were carried on for banquet or tavern scenes. Benches and stools, the 'state' or royal throne, a 'bar' for judgement scenes, trees and arbours and a mossy or flowery bank could all be carried on. Servants always brought banquets on, sometimes already set out on a table. The '*quaint device*' by which Ariel makes the banquet vanish in *The Tempest* was, I would think, a kind of reversible table-top with dishes fastened to one surface and the other bare – in which case the banquet would certainly have been brought out already fastened to the table.

Even a property as heavy as a regal throne with its canopy of painted cloth and its pedestal or dais, the 'state', would have been carried or trundled on. The 'creaking throne' scorned by Jonson that descends from the heavens in *Faustus* and *A Looking-Glass for London and England*, which Henslowe notes as being stored in the heavens, was a chair for flights and nothing else, quite distinct from the 'state'.[40] Hirelings would have brought out the chair of state from which Claudius conducts the business of Denmark in 1.2

Illustration 38. A detail from the engraving by Wenceslas Hollar (p. 551), showing Parliament debating the trial of the king's strong man, the Earl of Strafford, in 1641. He was subsequently found guilty and executed. At the scene the royal chair of state stands empty at the top of the picture, on its dais. Charles chose to sit behind his son, Prince Charles, seated alongside the throne, refusing to occupy his seat of authority as *rex in parliamento*. He is shown to the left of the canopy of what Hollar called 'the seate of state', while Henrietta Maria sits in the bay second right. A portable version of such a great but vacated apparatus, with its dais to raise the king above common eye level and the royal coat of arms on the tapestry hanging behind the chair, would have been brought on stage for court scenes. Hollar's depiction notably reproduces the Parliament scene of *Richard II* (4.1), where the throne was left empty on stage while Richard and Bullingbrook debated who should occupy it.

of *Hamlet* and over which he makes his little joke about how Fortinbras wrongly assumes 'our state to be disjoint and out of frame' as a result of its previous occupant's sudden death. It was a solid piece of furniture. The dais on which the chair of state usually rested was as much as four steps high, to judge by the counting of Mariana in 2.1 of *The Dumb Knight*. She ascends it to be executed, saying,

> this first step lower,
> Mounts to this next; this, thus and thus hath brought
> My bodies frame unto its highest throne.

This dais or scaffold was certainly carried on for the relevant scene by stage hands, to judge by the stage direction in the same play, '*Enter Chyp, Shaveing and others with a Scaffold.*'[41]

Given the storage space that they got from their fixed London venues after 1594 the wealthier and longer-lived companies could accumulate a good many such standard properties. Some of course had to be custom-built for particular plays in the repertory. Lord William Percy's curious plays, which seem to have been written for Paul's in the years after 1599, contain lists of the properties needed for performing them. *Cuckqueans and Cuckolds Errant* needed two inn-signs specially painted, besides a title board, a rope-ladder and a bench:

The Properties
  Harwich, In Middle of the Stage Colchester with Image of Tarlton, Signe and Ghirlond under him also. The Raungers Lodge, Maldon, A Ladder of Roapes trussed up neare Harwich and Aloft the Title The CuckQueanes and Cuckolds Errants. A Long Fourme.

Percy's *The Faery Pastorall* was more demanding:

The Properties
  Highest, aloft, and on the Top of the Musick Tree the Title The Faery Pastorall, Beneath him pind on Post of the Tree The Scene Elvida Forrest. Lowest of all over the Canopie *ΝΑΠΑΙΤΒΟΔΑΙΟΝ* or Faery Chappell. A kiln of Brick. A Fowen Cott. A Hollowe Oake with vice of wood to shutt to. A Lowe well with Roape and Pullye. A Fourme of Turves. A greene Bank being Pillowe to the Hed but. Lastly A Hole to creepe in and out.

Pretty well all of these properties, with the exception of the 'greene Bank' and possibly the enigmatic 'Fowen Cott' would have had to be constructed for the performance. They might well merely be the poet's wishful thinking, and may never have been staged. The modesty of Shakespeare's demands for his plays probably reflects his financial interests as well as his dramatic sophistication.

5. STAGE COSTUMES

Colour was a major source of stage symbolism. The decorums of social status were rigidly marked by dress and its colours in accordance with the Tudor sumptuary laws. Hamlet's 'nighted colour' and Malvolio's yellow garters stood out as conspicuously discordant elements in a tradition of dress that everyone knew in detail. Such colours were an advertisement, a flaunted message. Colourful costume was an instrument of paralinguistic meaning as well as spectacle and the eye-catching shades of colour that Elizabethans could contrive. Henslowe's 'tyer man' at the Rose, Steven Magett, was as vital a member of the playhouse operation as the book-keeper.[42] Apparel and playbooks were the company's two most vital resources. They needed constant care, both for repairs and for remaking into new costumes and play manuscripts. Considering that most of the players owned and used on stage their own gentrified or regal clothing, Henslowe still had to invest almost as much money in apparel for the players as in playbooks, much more than he did on stage properties. When the Globe and the Fortune were burned and when Beeston forsook Queen Anne's Men for his own enterprises it was the loss of playbooks and apparel that the players bewailed, not the properties. Alleyn's accounts list some quite startling totals for clothing by present-day priorities: £20 10s. 6d. for a 'black velvet cloak with sleeves embrodered all with silver and gold' was more than a third the cost of Shakespeare's official payment for his great house in Stratford. No wonder Henslowe had a rule against players leaving the playhouse wearing his apparel.

It was the flaunted magnificence of playing apparel that made the players common symbols of the distance between appearance and reality in Elizabethan society. Greene in *A Quip for an Upstart Courtier* (1592) wrote enviously of a player wearing a

murrey cloth gowne … faced down before with gray conny, and laide thick on the sleeves with lace, which he quaintly bare up to shew his white Taffata hose, and black silk stockings. A huge ruffe about his necke wrapt in his great head like a wicker cage, a little Hat with brims like the wings of a doublet, wherein he wore a Jewel of Glasse, as broad as a chancery sale.

The image of the player jetting it in borrowed apparel is given point by the custom that Thomas Platter noted in 1599:

it is the English usage for eminent lords or knights at their decease to bequeath and leave almost the best of their clothes to their serving men, which it is unseemly for the latter to wear, so that they offer them then for sale for a small sum to the actors.[43]

Whether they did sell directly to the companies or whether a noble's attire when it became second-hand went via their servants to be sold and remade at the frippery shops is guesswork.[44] Certainly house servants would not be able to wear such hand-outs themselves because they were made for a social rank the servant class could never aspire to. Moreover rich clothes with lace, ribbons and embellishments of all kinds were always likely to be in need of repair, and London was full of tailors. Clothing was portable property, and there to be displayed. The bright colours of the costumes matched the spectacular painting of the playhouse interiors. Henslowe's and Alleyn's papers list cloaks in scarlet with gold laces and buttons, and in purple satin adorned with silver; a doublet in copper lace (for Tamburlaine), carnation velvet, flame, ginger, red and green; and women's gowns of white satin and cloth of gold. There is one complete inventory of apparel in Alleyn's hand, undated but probably of the same time as Henslowe's list of properties made in March 1598 (*Diary*, pp. 291–4). It speaks for itself.

Clokes
1 A scarlett cloke wth ii brode gould Laces: w^t gould buttens of the sam downe the sids
2 A black velvett cloke
3 A scarlett cloke Layd downe wth silver Lace and silver buttens
4 A short velvett cap clok embroydered w^t gould and gould spangles
5 A watshod sattin clok w^t v gould laces
6 A purpell sattin welted w^t velvett and silver twist
7 A black tufted cloke
8 A damask cloke garded w^t velvett
9 A longe blak tafata cloke
10 A colored bugell for a boye
11 A scarlett w^t buttens of gould fact w^t blew velvett
12 A scarlett fact w^t blak velvett
13 A stamell cloke w^t gould lace
14 blak bugell cloke
Gownes
1 hary ye viii gowne
2 the blak velvett gowne w^t wight fure
3 A crimosin Robe strypt w^t gould fact w' ermin
4 on of wrought cloth of gould
5 on of red silk w^t gould buttens
6 a cardinalls gowne
7 wemens gowns
8, 9 i blak velvett embroyde^d w^t gould
10 i cloth of gould candish his stuf
11 i blak velvett lact and drawne out w^t wight sarsnett

12 A black silk w^t red flush
13 A cloth of silver for pan
14 A yelow silk gowne
15 a red silk gowne
16 angels silk
17 ii blew calico gowns
Antik sutes
  1 a cote of crimosen velvett cutt in payns and embrydered in gould
  2 i cloth of gould cote w^t grene bases
  3 i cloth of gould cote w^t oraing tawny bases
  4 i cloth of silver cott w^t blewe silk & tinsell bases
  5 i blew damask cote the more
  6 a red velvett horsmans cote
  7 A yelow tafata pd
  8 cloth of gould horsmans cote
  9 cloth of bodkin horsmans cote
10 orayng tany horsmans cot of cloth lact
11 daniels gowne
12 blew embroyderde bases
13 will somers cote
14 wight embroyd^r bases
15 gilt lether cot
16 ii hedtirs sett w^t stons
Jerkings and dublets
  1 A crymosin velvett pe^s w^t gould buttens & lace
  2 a crymasin sattin case lact w^t gould lace all over
  3 A velvett dublett cut dimond lact w^t gould lace and spang^s
  4 A dublett of blak velvett cut on sillver tinsell
  5 A ginger colored dublett
  6 i wight sattin cute on wight
  7 blak velvett w^t goul^d lace
  8 green velvett
  9 blak tafata cut on blak velvett lacte w^t bugell
10 blak velvett playne
11 ould wight sattin
12 red velvett for a boye
13 A carnation velvett lact w^t silver
14 A yelow spangled case
15 red velvett w^t blew sattin sieves & case
16 cloth of silver Jerkin
17 faustus Jerkin his clok
frenchose
  1 blew velvett embr^d w^t gould paynes blew sattin scalin
  2 silver paynes lact w^t carnation satins lact over w^t silver
  3 the guises

 4 Rich payns w^t long stokins
 5 gould payns w^t blak stript scalings of canish
 6 gould payns w^t velvett scalings
 7 gould payns w^t red strypt scaling
 8 blak bugell
 9 red payns for a boy w^t yelo scalins
10 pryams hoes
11 spangled hoes
Venetians
 1 A purpell velvett cut in dimonds lact & spangels
 2 red velved lact w^t gould Spanish
 3 A purpell vellvett emproydored w^t silver cut on tinsell
 4 green velvett lact w^t gould Spanish
 5 blake velvett
 6 cloth of silver
 7 gren strypt sattin
 8 cloth of gould for a boye

These appear to be as much eulogies as descriptions of the particular items of clothing.

The age was not only colourful but intensely fashion-conscious. The range of available fabrics was enormous, and the turnover of fashionable fabrics and cuts was enormous too, which probably helped the players a little in acquiring their lordly cast-offs. It was an age of glorious variety in which, as always in the world of fashion, new names had constantly to be chosen for the newest shades of colour. Pepper, tobacco, sea-water and puke (a dark brown) were a few of the many new Elizabethan colours.[45]

Colour symbolism was inevitable and universal throughout the Renaissance, though the range of possible interpretations of the significances of colours was almost as wide as the range of colours. Red for blood, yellow for the sun and for lovers, white for purity, black for gloom, evil and death were all traditional. Tamburlaine's famous degrees of mercy, signified by his white, red and black tents and on stage by the changing colours of his robes, reflect a set of values for colours that can still be recognised. Other significances were more local. When Malvolio in *Twelfth Night* is gulled into appearing cross-gartered like a lover his yellow hose as well as his crossed garters signify his new role, in contrast to the customary black of his steward's office. When he says he is 'not black in my mind, though yellow in my legs' he means that his yellow stockings show him to be a lover, but that he is not a melancholy (black-minded) one. The black of a Hamlet and a Bosola, the yellow of a Malvolio, Parolles or Iachimo were all standard signals.

Illustration 39. An Elizabethan gallant, a miniature by Nicholas Hilliard painted in about 1590 of an unknown young man. The original is in the Victoria and Albert Museum in London. It is inscribed *Dat poenas laudata fides* (my praised faith causes my sufferings), a quotation from Lucan's *De Bello Civili*. It has rather too confidently been identified as the Earl of Essex registering his love for Queen Elizabeth. It shows a lover and the lover's standard gesture, hand on heart. The crossed legs show idleness if nothing more.

A particularly intriguing question is what version of women's dress did the boys wear when they took a woman's part. For the most part Henslowe's *Diary* suggests that women's gowns were specially made by the company tailor, Steven Magett, presumably because the boys themselves could not afford to supply any themselves as the adult players did. They do seem to have been complete imitations of normal women's wear. But other questions arise for which easy assumptions or answers are misleading. David Mann, in *Shakespeare's Women: Performance and Conception* (Cambridge, 2008) has an excellent chapter about the likely display of such specifically female features as bare breasts in costume. Bare breasts sometimes appear in Inigo Jones's illustrations for wear in masques. It seems likely that boys tried to imitate such nudity, and they certainly used female make-up. Mann's account of Rosalind's epilogue in *As You Like It* (p. 120) suggests that the staging might have entailed a metatheatrical game, with the boy appearing half-changed from the wedding outfit he wore to accompany Hymen's entry, and so, as Mann puts it, stripped of any illusion.

There were costumes to match vocations, of course: doctors' gowns of scarlet, lawyers' gowns in black, blue coats for serving-men, a 'friars gown of gray', a 'cardinalls gowne' of scarlet, shepherds' brown or grey coats, motley fools' coats with cap and bauble, and of course soldiers' leather coats or jerkins. These were worn with little concern for historical accuracy if Henry Peacham's drawing of a scene from *Titus Andronicus* made in about 1595

Illustration 40. A drawing attributed to Henry Peacham and dated 1594 of a performance of *Titus Andronicus*. Accompanied by thirty lines of text, it seems to have been taken from the stage, and shows different incidents from the play.

is any indication. In his drawing the leading character wears a form of Roman dress reasonably like a toga, but the men flanking him are clearly Elizabethan soldiers. Aaron the Moor is in blackface with black gloves. 'Turkish bonnets', perhaps turbans, get a mention in *Soliman and Perseda*, and Henslowe's lists include 'ii Danes sutes', 'i mores cote', four 'Turkes heds' and 'the suit of motley for the Scotchman', which sounds suspiciously like a tartan plaid.

Some costumes gave information about locality or setting. Nightcaps and candles signified night scenes and bedrooms, riding boots signified travel. Different kinds of hat were used to signal status and for gestures of respect such as doffing. The higher the hat the higher the social status. A workman or servant wore a flat cap or bonnet, a citizen a taller hat with a small feather, a gallant or courtier a high hat with a long plume. All hats were doffed as a mark of respect in the presence of a lord or ruler. Anyone addressing the King knelt hat in hand while speaking. The story of King James in 1600 when he was threatened by the assassins of the Gowrie conspiracy says that the assassin holding a dagger to James's heart had some trouble with his own headgear:

having such crueltie in his lookes, and standing so irreverently covered with his Hat on, which forme of rygorous behaviour, could prognosticat nothing to his majestie, but present extremitie. But at his majesties perswasive language, he appeared to be somewhat amazed, and discovering his head againe, swore and protested that his majesties life should be safe.[46]

Taking his hat off required the use of his right hand to do it, where the dagger would have been before. The games played in *Richard II* over Bullingbrook kneeling to York and Northumberland kneeling to the king are other indications of how potent were the decorums of costume and behaviour.

Mad women such as Cassandra in *Troilus and Cressida* or Queen Elizabeth in *Richard III* wore long-haired wigs unbound, a fairly realistic symbol of their condition. Costumes for 'Negro Moors' as Peele called them, like Aaron in Peacham's drawing of *Titus Andronicus*, were spectacular rather than realistic.[47] None the less considerable efforts were made on occasions to simulate dark skin and curly hair. Face masks with elbow gloves of velvet and black leather leggings were topped with 'Corled hed Sculles of blacke Laune' in early Court performances. In the seventeenth century paint superseded black velvet masks, commonly worn by women to protect themselves from the sun, on the initiative of Queen Anne herself, who appeared with eleven of her ladies in blackface for the *Masque of Blackness* in 1605. Sir Dudley Carleton acidly reported that

Illustration 41. A Barbary Moor from Cesari Vecellio's *Degli Habiti* (1590). Such a large cloak would make it easy to do a quick change from barbarian to European if the role was to be doubled with other parts. The hood might then conceal an unblackened face.

instead of Vizzards [i.e. masks], their Faces and Arms up to the Elbows, were painted black, which was Disguise sufficient, for they were hard to be known; but it became them nothing so well as their red and white, and you cannot imagine a more ugly Sight, then a Troop of lean-cheek'd Moors.[48]

Exotic costumes existed for various gods. Henslowe's lists include specific costumes for Juno, Phaeton, Neptune and Iris, together with an intriguing 'Eves bodice', which may have shown the breasts that David Mann takes note of. Henslowe also had a 'fairys gown of buckram', 'a pair of gyants hose' and 'coats for giants', and a ghost's suit and bodice. From his function as bear-ward he could no doubt have imitated the game in *The Winter's Tale* by introducing a real bear on stage, but his players, perhaps understandably, seem to have preferred doing it themselves, and his lists accordingly show 'i bears head' and 'i bears skin' as well as a bull's head, the three heads of a Cerberus, 'i lions skin' and 'ii lions heads'. In *The Battle of Alcazar* Alleyn as the black-faced Moor enters with lion's flesh on his sword to nourish his 'fair' Calipolis.

In the later years under the lavish Stuarts some players seem to have collected cast-offs not just from dead nobles but from Court shows of plays and masques, for which costumes were made specially. Suckling paid out several hundred pounds to stage his play *Aglaura* at Court over Christmas 1637, and afterwards passed the costumes on with the play to the King's Men, who restaged it at Blackfriars. In the words of a contemporary:

Two of the King's Servants, Privy-Chamber Men both, have writ each of them a play, Sir *John Sutlin* and *Will. Barclay*, which have been acted in Court, and at the *Black Friars*, with much Applause. *Sutlin's* Play cost three or four hundred Pounds setting out, eight or ten Suits of new Cloaths he gave the Players; an unheard of Prodigality.[49]

Several other plays, similarly produced by rich gallants, benefitted the professional players who took them back to their own playhouses.

6. COURT STAGING

It has been argued that in Caroline times the players took with them from Court some of the elaborate perspective 'scenes' and costumes that Inigo Jones designed for such plays.[50] I think it has been fairly conclusively proved that they did not, unless they acquired some of the costumes. Scenic apparatus was less costly, less portable and far less readily reusable in the three-dimensional staging of the indoor stages than was apparel. Furthermore the Court stages, which used perspectives regularly for masques and plays, always took several days to prepare. The public playhouses could not have afforded the loss of playing-time involved in setting up such non-traditional devices. Much more to the point their staging was three-dimensional while Jones's scenery was designed for use in perspective as a tightly two-dimensional mode directed chiefly at the royal presence. One wonders how much of the optimum spectacle all the other courtiers could ever have seen. Palladio's wonderful Teatro Olympico in Vicenza, which Jones studied, was built for the Doge of Venice, who was the only audience member given a perfect view of its perspective scenery. The specificity of the perspective lines prevented most of the other audience members from getting such a view. After its first use in 1584 the Teatro was left unused for over a hundred years.

Certainly the professional companies spent little time and money making their own pictorial shows. There are occasional references to pieces of scenery being employed in the private playhouses from the earliest days, but they cannot ever have been a prominent feature of the staging or they would have drawn more comment. *Periaktoi*, great prisms with a different scene painted on each of the three faces, set on a pivot to revolve when required, are mentioned in connection with the first Blackfriars,[51] and Jonson speaks of a 'piece of *perspective*' in the induction to *Cynthia's Revels*, but there are few other references except when writing about Court staging. Henslowe's inventories include 'the sittie of Rome', but that was probably a painted cloth suspended somewhere on the *frons scenae*, or a specially painted set of hangings. The bare stage backed with a curtain on which Tudor moralities and farces were played was the traditional basis for Elizabethan staging and seems to have remained firmly entrenched at all the Stuart playhouses up to the closure. The Stuart Court, largely through the person of Jones, the English Bernini, was converted to Italian perspective staging early on, but tradition and commerce combined to keep it off the common stages.

Court masques were intricate affairs combining music and dance with verse-speaking in visually gorgeous settings designed as banquets for all the senses. Once the shows and speeches were done they also became a participation sport for courtiers to dance and flourish their costumes. The plot or allegory and the words of the masques belonged in a form quite distinct from the drama. Professional players could never match what were in effect the most lavish family charades England has ever seen. As Bentley has said, their scenery was conceived of as 'a special display exhibition'.[52] It seems to have been a feature designed for special occasions rather than for particular plays, and was used as an extra adornment, a garnish to the event.

The players did participate in the masque performances at Court that used scenery, however, and it may be worth looking at a contemporary description of one such Court spectacle if only to see what the players became familiar with there. The best description by far is of a show at Court in 1618 reported by Orazio Busino, chaplain to the Venetian Embassy, with all the frankness of a homesick expatriate writing in the privacy and confidence of his personal diary about his outlandish hosts. I make no apology for quoting it at length.

In London, as the capital of a most flourishing kingdom, there are theatrical performances throughout the entire year in various parts of the city, and these are always frequented by many people devoted to pleasure, who, for the most part, dress grandly and colourfully, so that they appear, if possible, more than princes, or rather they appear actors. Similarly in the King's court after Christmas day begins a series of sumptuous banquets, well performed plays, and very graceful masques of knights and ladies. The most distinguished of the masques is performed on the day after the feast of the three wise men, in accordance with an ancient custom of this royal palace, where in a large hall arranged like a theatre, with well-secured boxes all around, the stage is placed at one end, and facing it at the other end, his majesty's chair under a large canopy, and near him stools for the foreign ambassadors. On the 16th of this month of January [i.e. 6th January English style] his excellency [the Venetian ambassador] was invited to see this performance and masque, prepared with extraordinary care and elegance, in which the chief performer was the only son and honoured heir of his majesty, the Prince of Wales, seventeen years of age, a lively youth, handsome and very graceful. At the fourth hour of the night we went to court privately, through the park, and entered the royal apartments. His excellency was entertained awhile by a principal courtier until everything was prepared, and we others of his retinue, all perfumed, escorted by the master of ceremonies, entered the usual box of the Venetian embassy, where, unfortunately, we were so crowded and uncomfortable that had it not been for our curiosity we would have given up or expired. Moreover we had the additional curse of a Spaniard who came into our box by courtesy of the master of ceremonies, asking for only two fingers of room, though we had no space to run around in, and by God, he placed himself more comfortably than all of us. In short, I have no patience with these crows; it was observed that they had settled in all the best locations. The ambassador was near the King; others with gold chains round their necks sat with the lords of the Council; others were in their own box attending the ambassadress; and this fellow comes into our place! While waiting for the King we took pleasure in admiring the decorations, in observing the beauty of the hall, with two orders of columns one on top of the other, their distance from the wall the full width of the passage, the upper gallery supported by Doric columns, and above these the Ionic, which hold up the roof of the hall. It is all of wood, including even the pillars, carved and gilded with great skill. From the roof hang garlands and angels in relief. There were two rows of lights, which were to be lit at the proper time.

Then there was such a crowd; for though they claim to admit only those favoured with invitations, nevertheless every box was full, especially with most noble and richly dressed ladies, 600 and more in number, according to the general opinion; their clothes of such various styles and colours as to be indescribable; the most delicate plumes on their hats, and in their hands as fans; and on their foreheads strings of jewels, and on their necks and bosoms and in their girdles, and on their garments in such quantity that they appeared so many queens; so that at first, when there was little light, as if it were the twilight of dusk or dawn, the splendour of the diamonds and other jewels was so brilliant that they appeared so many stars. During the two hours' wait we had time to admire them again and again; because of my poor vision, I could not form an accurate judgement from afar, and I referred myself in everything to my colleagues, who reported to me that they discerned beautiful and delightful faces, and at every moment they would say, 'Oh look at this one, oh see that one; whose wife is that one in the third row, and whose daughter is that pretty one nearby?' However, they concluded that among much grain there were also husks and straw mixed in, that is to say, some withered ladies, and some votaries of San Carlo; but that the beauties were of superlative quality. Even though I am old and half blind, I can testify to the accuracy of this account. The dress worn by these ladies is very beautiful, for those who like it, and for some of them it serves to hide the defects of nature, because in the back it hangs almost from the neck to the ground, with long, tight sleeves, and no waist, and without folds; so that any deformity, however monstrous, remains hidden. The farthingale also plays its part. The plump and buxom show their bosoms very openly, and the lean go muffled up to the throat, all of them with men's shoes, or at least with very low slippers. Face masks are as important to them as bread at table, but for these public spectacles they put them aside willingly.

At about the 6th hour of the night his majesty appeared with his court, having passed through the apartments where the ambassadors were waiting, and he graciously brought them along with him, that is to say, the Spanish and Venetian ambassadors, it not being the turn of the French ambassador, because of his and the Spaniard's disputes over precedence. As he entered the hall fifteen or twenty cornets and trumpets began to play, antiphonally and very well. After his majesty had been seated under the canopy alone, the Queen not being present because of some indisposition, he had the ambassadors sit on two stools, and the great officers and magistrates sat on benches. The Lord Chamberlain then had the way cleared, and in the middle of the room there appeared a fine and spacious area all covered with green cloth. A large curtain – painted to represent a tent of gold with a broad fringe, the background of blue canvas flecked all over with golden stars – was made to fall in an instant. This concealed the stage at the beginning; on its being removed there appeared first of all Mount Atlas, and one saw only his huge head at the peak, right under the very roof of the hall; it rolled its eyes and moved itself with wonderful cunning. To make the main ballet and masque seem more light and elegant, they had some mummers in the first scene, for example a very fat Bacchus in a car drawn by four men in long robes, who sang *sotto voce* before his majesty. There was another fat man on foot, dressed in a short red costume, who spoke, and during the speech went reeling about like a drunkard, cup in hand, so that he seemed to be Bacchus's cupbearer; this first scene was very light and funny. Then followed twelve extravagant masquers, one with a barrel round his middle, the others in great wicker flasks very well made; and they danced for a while to the sound of the cornets and trumpets with various and most extravagant movements. Then came a huge man in the shape of Hercules with his club, who wrestled with Antaeus, etc.; and then appeared twelve masked boys, like so many frogs, who danced together with various grotesque gestures. All at once they fell to earth, and were quickly driven

Illustration 42. A design by Inigo Jones for a Daughter of Niger in
The Masque of Blackness (1605). The original is in the collection of the
Duke of Devonshire, the Chatsworth Settlement.

off by Hercules. The mountain then opened by the turning of two doors, and from behind the low hills of a distant landscape one saw day break, some gilded columns being placed along the sides to make the distance seem greater. Next Mercury appeared before the King and made a speech, and then came a musician with a guitar, dressed in a long robe, who played and sang some trills, implying that he was some deity; and then came a number of musicians dressed in the long red robes of high priests, with golden mitres, and in their midst was a goddess in a long white costume. They sang some short pieces that we did not understand; it is true that this performance was not much to our taste, accustomed as we are to the elegant and harmonious music of Italy.

Finally six [i.e. twelve] masked knights appeared, dressed as if in livery, six having full hose and breeches with slashes or folds of white silk trimmed with gold and silver, and the other six with their breeches below the knee, their half hose also crimson, and white shoes. Their doublets went well with this, cut in the manner of ancient Roman corslets; and on their heads they had long hair, crowns, and very large white feathers, and on their faces black masks. These all descended from the scene together in the figure of a pyramid, with the Prince alone always at the apex. When they reached the ground one suddenly heard the music of violins, to the number of more than twenty-five or thirty, all in a box. When the knights had made their bows to his majesty they began to dance in tempo and with a variety of steps, keeping the same figure for awhile, and then changing places with each other in divers ways, always ending their leaps together. When this was finished, each one took his lady, the Prince accompanying the principal lady among those who were standing ready to dance, and the others doing the same in succession, making bows first to his majesty and then to each other. They did all sorts of ballets and dances of every country, such as passemeasures, corantos, canaries, Spanish dances, and a hundred other beautiful turns to delight the fancy. Finally they danced the Spanish dance once more with their ladies, and because they were tired began to lag; and the King, who is by nature choleric, grew impatient and shouted loudly, 'Why don't they dance? What did you make me come here for? Devil take all of you, dance!' At once the Marquis of Buckingham, his majesty's favourite minion, sprang forward, and danced a number of high and very tiny capers with such grace and lightness that he made everyone admire and love him, and also managed to calm the rage of his angry lord. Inspired by this, the other masquers continued to display their powers one after another, with different ladies, concluding with capers, and lifting their goddesses from the ground. We counted 34 capers in succession cut by one knight, but none matched the splendid technique of the Marquis. The Prince, however, surpassed them all in his bows, being very formal in doing his obeisance both to his majesty and to the lady with whom he was dancing, nor was he seen to dance once out of step, which cannot perhaps be said for the others. Because of his youth, he does not yet have much breath; nevertheless he cut some capers with considerable grace. When the performance of these twelve accomplished knights was completed, after they had overcome the sloth and drunkenness of Bacchus with their prowess, the Prince went in triumph to kiss his royal father's hands, by whom he was embraced and warmly kissed. The King then honoured the

Marquis with extraordinary signs of affection, touching his face. His majesty rose from his chair, and taking the ambassadors along with him, passed through a number of rooms and galleries and came to a hall where the usual supper was prepared for the performers, a light being carried before him. He glanced round the table and departed, and at once like so many harpies the company fell on their prey. The table was almost entirely covered with sweetmeats, with all kinds of sugar confections. There were some large figures, but they were of painted cardboard, for decoration. The meal was served in bowls or plates of glass; the first assault threw the table to the ground, and the crash of glass platters reminded me exactly of the windows breaking in a great midsummer storm. The story ended at two hours after midnight, and half disgusted and exhausted we returned home.[53]

Nathanael Richards's dumbshow masque in *Messallina* quoted above could do nothing comparable to this. The masque Busino saw was Jonson's *Pleasure Reconciled to Virtue*, performed at the first Banqueting House. It is our loss that Busino gave no comparable account of any of the occasions when the King's Men or the Cockpit company performed plays at Court on stages designed by Jones, as they did during the Christmas festivities in some years.

In Caroline times, of twelve plays that we know were performed for the Court with scenery three were put on privately by Henrietta Maria's ladies, two privately by the Earl of Pembroke, Philip Herbert's household, three at Oxford by the university, three at Court by the King's Men and one at Court by the Cockpit company of 1634. All but two or three of them used Jones's designs.[54] The four plays performed at Court by the professional players were all transferred to the private playhouses, some with the costumes used in the Court performance but none with the scenery. One of the Oxford plays went to London for a second performance before the Court, this time by the King's Men at the instigation of the Chancellor, Archbishop Laud (who, incidentally, claimed that the professionals performed the play less well than the students). It cost £100 just to make the costumes ready again for the second performance. Laud showed an understandable anxiety about the university's property that he had committed to London, and the Queen had to reassure him:

you may be confident that no Part of these things y^t are come to our hands, shall be suffered to bee prostituted upon any Mercenary Stage, but shall bee carefully Reserv'd for our owne Occasions and particular Entertainments att Court.

The mercenary players on the whole probably expected little else, though they were said to be waiting for any scraps that might fall from the royal stage.

Illustration 43. A painting of Lucy Countess of Bedford in masque costume, by Marcus Gheerhaerts, from the collection of the Marquis of Tavistock at Woburn Abbey.

7. DIRECTING PERFORMANCES

A large part of the business of staging must have depended on the amount of time available for rehearsals, which raises the related question whether anyone served as coordinator or stage director of performances. Henslowe's records for the Rose mention nobody serving as director and do not even give a name to the company book-keeper. They indicate that on average mounting a new play took three weeks from delivery of the completed playbook to the first performance on stage. Since the company was playing every afternoon, and probably spent most of each morning running through that day's play, the company cannot have had much free time for full rehearsals of its new plays.[55] Moreover in that three weeks the scribe had to take time to copy out all the major speaking parts, and the players had to learn them. Besides those practical needs there was the risk that the new play might not succeed on stage. Quite a few of the seventeen or more plays taken on each year at the Rose appear in Henslowe's performance lists only once.[56] So the temptation must have been great not to put too much effort into a new play until its success on stage and its retention in the repertory were assured. Only then would work be applied to giving the production any polish. As we have said, performances were far less fixed than editions, either then or now. With such large and rapidly changing repertories no company could afford to spend much time on the niceties of their staging. Such book-keeper's records as we have suggest that once a player was on stage he was left to his own devices to handle his part. Given the proximity of audience everywhere around the stage, and on it at the Blackfriars, no prompter was there to murmur a player his next words if he corpsed. On the stage the players were left largely to their own devices. Their fellows if they were to hand might help to prompt them, but backstage the work all went into setting up the next player's entrance. Such a high-speed repertory system put a high premium on traditional practices.

The manipulation of the business, the stage-management side, fell naturally into the hands of the only member of the company who had to be reasonably familiar with the whole text of the play, the book-holder or book-keeper. Surviving playbooks show that he took the responsibility for seeing that players backstage were ready on their cues and for having the properties on hand that were to be carried on or 'discovered' as and when they might be needed.[57] The book-holder was also responsible, presumably in discussion with the sharers, for allocating all the parts he copied out. More pressingly as the surviving 'plots' show he had to allocate all the smaller speaking parts that had to be doubled and the walk-ons by mutes. He had several 'stage-keepers' to help him, who also served as mutes and supernumeraries. It was the stage hands who helped to tidy up the stage after the performance, and who did routine jobs like drawing open the hangings and strewing rushes on stage.[58] They might also take walk-on parts, since one of the Admiral's Men's plots (*1 Tamar Cam*) specifies that everyone had to march in the final procession, including one anonymous helper noted merely as 'the red fast [faced] fellow'. More routine was a marginal note in Heywood's *The Captives* ordering '*stage keepers as a guard*'.

During the performance the book-holder lurked in the tiring-house, as we learn from such references as the one in *The Maid in the Mill*, a King's Men's play of 1623, where a woman's screams are heard '*within*' and a character says 'they are out of their parts sure: it may be 'tis the Book-holder's fault: I'll go see'. In the surviving 'plots' the terms '*within*' and '*without*' are used in the reverse way to what the poets specified in their stage directions, since their standpoint was backstage, not looking at the performance from in front. Ben Jonson, probably with an excess of modesty, disclaimed any direct responsibility for the staging of *Cynthia's Revels* by getting one of the boys in the induction to say:

wee are not so officiously befriended by him, as to have his presence in the tiring-house, to prompt us aloud, stampe at the booke-holder, sweare for our properties, curse the poore tire-man, raile the musicke out of tune, and sweat for everie veniall trespasse we commit.

In view of the pains Jonson obviously took in preparing this play especially so that the boys could show their paces it is likely that this denial is another of his interweavings of appearance and reality. His direct interest in the production of his plays was to become a byword with playgoers, one that he himself exploited in the induction he wrote for *Bartholomew Fair*, where the stage-keeper complains aggrievedly that the author has taken no notice of his experienced advice.

It was easier to tell youths how to perform their play than adult sharers, of course, which may be why the only other known statement about a super-vising or directing hand is about the manager of a young company. In Brome's epilogue to *The Court Beggar* he commended William Beeston for training his young players in their trade.

But this small Poet vents [no wit] but his own, and his by whose care and directions this Stage is govern'd, who has for many yeares both in his fathers dayes, and since directed Poets to write & Players to speak till he traind up these youths here to what they are now. I some of 'em before they were able to say a grace of two lines long to have more parts in their pates then would fill so many Dry-fats.

This is training in playing, of course, not directing the performance.

Apart from Jonson's the only clear hints I know suggesting that a poet participated in the staging of his plays come from the first cause of all the attention paid to Shakespearean drama in the last four centuries. He was, of course, a player on the stage as well as the company poet, present at rehearsals throughout, so his interventions should be recognizable. Perhaps surprisingly, though, there are very few obvious indications, and we must not lose sight of the way *Henry V* was cut ruthlessly from Shakespeare's own original 3,400 lines to a mere 1,700. Part of the object behind that trimming of the play in performance was to take it from the manuscript's deeply ambivalent image of Henry as not just the winner at Agincourt but the ruthless killer of his Eastcheap subjects and the French prisoners, whose charge at Harfleur was a failure, and leave him solely as the warlike victor. If this comparison of the two versions of *Henry V* is correct, Shakespeare connived at his fellows' selection of Henry just as the resolute victor of Agincourt, forsaking for whatever reason the more malign of the two sides he originally created.

I can find only three instances where Shakespeare does seem to have intervened to elaborate the staging of his plays. The first is the couplet quoted on page 138 about Burbage's mannerism in playing Richard III with 'his hand continuall on his dagger'. That must reflect a gesture for which there is some historical justification. Holinshed's account of Richard reads in part:

When he stood musing, he would bite and chaw busilie his nether lip; as who said, that his fierce nature in his cruell bodie alwaies chafed, stirred, and was ever unquiet: beside that, the dagger which he ware, he would (when he studied) with his hand plucke up & downe in the sheath to the midst, never drawing it fullie out.[59]

There was at least one fellow of Burbage who knew his Holinshed well and could have told him about that mannerism. The same author would most likely have been the one to elaborate on the bare stage direction '*Enter Clifford wounded*' in the Folio text of *3 Henry VI*, and to inform the player and the tire-man just what was needed to show his wound. The equivalent stage direction in the earlier version of the text reads '*Enter Clifford wounded, with an arrow in his necke*', the precise wound according to the sources of the play. Thirdly the early version of *2 Henry VI* tells us that the stage direction '*Enter Richard, and Somerset to fight*' was also amplified in the original staging by reference to the play's source. In Holinshed Somerset was said to have died at St Albans under an inn-sign, and the play follows that report, as the stage direction in the reported text says: '... *enter* the Duke of Somerset, *and* Richard *fighting and Richard kils him under the signe of the Castle in saint* Albones'. That would have entailed hanging up a painted inn sign as in other plays.

These three instances all appear to be cases of authorial intervention in the staging. They confirm, if incidentally, that Shakespeare must have been a fellow with Burbage and the others in the 1592 Pembroke's company that staged the three plays. It is logical to acknowledge some members of this Pembroke's including Shakespeare as the fellows who made up the early versions of *2* and *3 Henry VI* printed in 1594 and 1595. They helped to stage both of the *Henry VI* plays and were probably familiar with *Richard III* as well.

CHAPTER 6

The Audiences

1. SOCIAL ATTITUDES TO PLAYGOING

Crowd psychology has gained an enormous amount of attention in the twentieth century. Political, religious and racial riots have had their own interest for psychologists in a century when, as Eric Hobsbawm declared, new technology in and out of wars through the years from 1914 to 1991 killed far more ordinary people than the old world had ever tried to. What generated crowd disturbances excited many besides the governments wishing to stop them. No psychologist, however, has yet thought to look at theatre audiences as crowds. Since the technology of theatre in the centuries since Shakespeare has aimed to turn audiences into passive watchers invisible to the actors, and silent except for occasional bursts of laughter, audiences have not been thought of as crowds. Reviewers now give voice to their individual reactions to plays in newspapers and other media, thinking of audiences only as assemblies of individuals with private interests, sharing little with other audience members. A few audiences have occasionally reacted as angry crowds to plays, as Yeats found at the Abbey Theatre in Dublin and as the governments of Nazi Germany and Soviet Russia found in the 1930s when for diametrically opposed political reasons productions of *Coriolanus* provoked riots in Berlin and Moscow. Psychologists do not consider theatre audiences to be crowds, so even the new focus by theatre teachers and theoreticians on what is usually called performativity has ignored this fascinating new territory for study. Not until Sam Wanamaker's facsimile of the Globe opened in London did its crowds raise this new question.

On occasions in the past when speaking about what the original play-goers at the Globe might have been like I suggested that they must have resembled modern football crowds more than modern theatre audiences. Watching the show in daylight, feeling your kinship with a vocal gathering of like-minded supporters, possibly even hurling missiles when annoyed by what you see staged on the field, such behaviour did appear to me to reflect moods more likely to resemble those of audiences at the Rose or the Globe than the hidden armchair audiences in the dark of a modern auditorium. That rather idle speculation received a peculiarly strong endorsement when the new Globe opened in 1997. Working to build the site, we had wondered what people condemned to stand in the yard for three hours on end would do when it rained, and even whether anyone would enjoy the experience enough to stay on their feet all through it, let alone return for another uncomfortable session as a groundling. Much to our surprise, when it first rained on the groundlings nobody moved, and throughout at least the first five years of packed houses 70 per cent of the audiences were London regulars, returning each year for more. Without realising what we were doing we had returned theatre audiences into the role of crowds, and the effect was hugely popular. A crowd is unique in the way it shares the excitement of the experience. Being in a crowd enhances the feeling and makes it a collective, not an individual, pleasure.

Whether or not the Wanamaker reconstruction ended up as an accurate version of the original Globe it certainly proved to be one that, using original materials throughout, had the benefit of the Globe's amazingly good acoustics, the sound reflecting and being absorbed by the timbers, plaster, people and the open roof. The shape and the materials attracted tourists but the real impact was on the audiences. Michael Holden, responsible for completing the construction in the last years after Sam Wanamaker died, said that even holding only half the numbers of the original Globe it was the biggest intimate theatre in London. All good theatre is intimate in the sense that it holds a group of people together and hopefully helps them to share their feelings as a crowd. That collective feeling must have been what all the playhouses of Shakespeare's time generated, whether outdoor or indoor. Its audiences were active whereas we have been drilled for centuries into being passive. On stage the early players drew energy and inspiration from the audience's visible and audible participation in the experience. That, unstudied though it is, seems to be the essence of truly Shakespearean theatre. We need to keep it in mind when looking at what the available evidence tells us about the original audiences and their behaviour.

In 1623 a Catholic archpriest named William Harison discovered that some of his priests were in the habit of going to plays at the amphitheatres. With pained understanding he pointed out to them that

such playes are made to sport, and delight the auditorie, which consisting most of young gallants, and Protestants (for no true Puritanes will endure to bee present at playes) how unlikely is it, but that there are, and must bee, at least some passages in the playes, which may relish, and tickle the humor of such persons, or else good night to the players.[1]

Similar presumptions and similar deductions about the relationship between Shakespearean plays and their audiences have been made for centuries. Working in the reverse direction to Harison and noting that events shown in the plays were bloody and bawdy, scholars have found it easy to assume that the audiences to whom such plays were fed were correspondingly riotous and self-willed. The trouble is that this kind of presumption has no particular validity. We might look at twenty-first-century television and by the same presumption conclude that audiences now are quite as lecherous and disorderly in their living rooms as those of Shakespeare's day are assumed to have been in their playhouses.

For all we know it may be true that the basic mentality of Elizabethan and early Stuart audiences is not essentially different from that of the majority audiences of today, and that in consequence we do not need to look very deeply into their composition. It is knowing even that much which is difficult. Of course the returns on the labour of summarising and generalising about such intangibles are likely to be small. On average over that seventy years or so of London commercial theatre there were as many as a million visits to the playhouse a year. Any generalisation covering that number of visits would have to be stretched thinly. Three of the theatre's four estates, the playhouses, the staging and even the acting can evoke generalisations with far more strength. None the less the early audiences dominated the show, and their sharing of the playgoing experience as a crowd was the ruling feature of the whole event. Our picture of the Shakespearean stage is incomplete without some impression of them as a major factor in the performances. Unless we make Harison's kind of presumption we cannot really draw firm conclusions about the original playgoers' mentality or their influence on playwriting. There is evidence for their constituent members, those sections of society that did help the players to stay prosperous, and for their behaviour, their favourite habits and their tastes in everything from poetry to tobacco. It is from these elements that we have to make a recognisable if impressionistic picture of the theatre's fourth estate.

To take the broad perspective first: between 1574 and 1642 the London playhouses found their audiences amongst a population growing from about 200,000 to nearly 400,000 people. In 1594 the estimates suggest that the two authorised acting companies were visited by about 15,000 people weekly. In 1620, when six playhouses were open, three of them the smaller private houses, the weekly total was probably nearer 25,000.[2]

Perhaps 15 or 20 per cent of all the people living within walking distance of Shoreditch and Southwark were regular playgoers. Modern estimates of the capacities of the amphitheatres converge on about 2,500 as a maximum figure (de Witt estimated 3,000 for the Swan, and John Chamberlain said the Globe held over 3,000 in 1624).[3] According to Henslowe, the only impresario whose accounts we have in any detail, the largest audiences attended for new plays and on public holidays, the average being more like half of the capacity. Seasonal variation was less than might be expected, Henslowe's daily receipts dropping from £44 19s. in May to £37 11s. in January.[4] The auditorium space in hall playhouses such as Blackfriars was much less than half that of the amphitheatres, to judge by Beaumont's rather hopeful description in 1609 of the Blackfriars as a place where 'a thousand men in judgement sit'. He meant both men and women, of course, as we shall see, but with five playhouses, indoor and outdoor, all performing daily when he wrote that figure the total of the crowds of playgoers each day must have been in the region of 5,000.

Figures such as these, rough estimates as they are, do not say much about more revealing but less tangible matters such as the place playgoing occupied in Shakespearean society, how largely it figured in the flood of contemporary social life, or what image it offered the public. Shakespearean London more than most conurbations had a many-headed public divided against itself, and the images its members painted of playhouses and playgoing were highly variable and of very doubtful reliability, particularly when laid down by the non-playgoing 80 per cent. The spokesmen for Puritan London described playhouse audiences as riotous and immoral; the poets described them as ignorant and wilful; the City Fathers regarded them as riotous and seditious. If any of these images had been largely true the playhouses would have been closed much earlier than 1642. As it was, on the one distressing occasion when officialdom did investigate the playhouses – in 1602 on the instructions of the Privy Council to empty the places of resort of idle and disorderly persons and press a lot of them into the army – it found the image had misled them quite thoroughly. According to a gleeful account by Philip Gawdy the City Fathers chose to clear the playhouses first, even before the taverns and brothels, and found they had caught 'not only ... Gentlemen, and servingmen, but Lawyers, Clarkes, country men that had lawe cawses, aye the Quens men, knightes, and as it was credibly reported one Earle'.[5]

Any general picture based on contemporary evidence has to be built up piecemeal. It should rather be a moving picture, changing in space and time as the audiences changed, varying from playhouse to playhouse, from the audiences for Marlowe to the audiences for Davenant. Even contemporary generalisations of acknowledged impartiality need qualifying when the 'contemporary' label covers seventy years of rapid social change and growth.

One of the many types of witness that we can hope might be more reliable or at least less prejudiced than the locals is the traveller from abroad. The Elizabethan playing companies were famous across Europe and many of the foreigners who passed through London took care to see them. As tourists they also not infrequently recorded what they saw for the benefit of their fellow countrymen with the kind of detail that the Londoner, to whom such things were automatic knowledge, usually omitted. Thomas Platter, a young German-speaking Swiss who travelled widely in England in 1599, told of seeing a play at the Curtain:

in conclusion they danced [a jig] very charmingly in English and Irish fashion. Thus daily at two in the afternoon, London has two, sometimes three plays running in different places, competing with each other, and those which play best obtain most spectators. The playhouses are so constructed that they play on a raised platform, so that everyone has a good view. There are different galleries and places, however, where the seating is better and more comfortable and therefore more expensive. For whoever cares to stand below only pays one English penny, but if he wishes to sit he enters by another door, and pays another penny, while if he desires to sit in the most comfortable seats which are cushioned, where he not only sees everything well, but can also be seen, then he pays yet another English penny at another door. And during the performance food and drink are carried round the audience, so that for what one cares to pay one may also have refreshment.[6]

This is a typical if minimal portrait of an amphitheatre scene on the eve of the rebirth of the indoor theatres. Platter's admission prices are those confirmed by Lambarde, reflecting at least the current statements about the system, variable though we know it was from one playhouse to another. In addition to the standing room in the yard and the penny and twopenny galleries all the amphitheatres had one or more lords' rooms, where the charge was sixpence, six times the cost of standing in the yard. There is no positive evidence that these prices altered at any time in the period. In the hall playhouses, as we have noted, basic admission to the rear of the topmost gallery was sixpence, and a stool on the stage itself cost sixpence for the stool in addition to the shilling or more for admission. The boxes at the side of the stage cost half-a-crown, five times the basic sixpence.[7]

Against Platter's tourist report from 1599 it is worth adding one from a fictional account of a would-be gallant's visit to the Blackfriars in the 1620s, when the hall playhouses were the socially dominant place of fashionable resort. *The Life of a Satyrical Puppy called Nim* was not published until 1657, but it belongs to the time when the Blackfriars was where high fashion spent their time and where ambitious young men tried to profit from them ('Nim' was the term for a petty thief, like Shakespeare's Eastcheap character). He spends fifty pounds on a fashionable suit and goes to the Blackfriars in search of any rich lady, in the hope that she will be so attracted to him she will give him her finest jewels.

I entered the *Theater*, and sat upon the Stage: making low Congies to divers Gentlemen; not that I knew them, but I was confident, they would requite me in the same kinde: which made the Spectators suppose us of very olde, and familiar acquaintance. Besides (that I might appear no *Novice*) I observ'd all fashionable Customes; As delivering my Sute to a more apparent view, by hanging the Cloak upon one shoulder: or letting it fall (as it were) by chance. I stood up also at the end of every *Act*, to salute those, whom I never saw before. Two *Acts* were finished before I could discover any thing, either for my Comfort then, or worth my relation now. Unless it were *punycall* absurdity in a Country-Gentleman: who was so caught with the naturall action of a Youth (that represented a ravish'd Lady), as he swore alowd, he would not sleep untill he had killed her ravisher: and how 'twas not fit such Rogues should live in a Common-wealth. This made me laugh, but not merry.

Anon after, I spied a Gentlewomans Eie, fix'd full upon me. Hope and Despaire threw me into such Distractions, that I was about to bid a Boy (who personated *Cupid* in the play) to shoot at her with his counterfeit Arrow. But she presently disclaimed me her Object: and with the like inconstancy gaz'd upon another. About the beginning of the Fourth *Act*, my Face withstood a fresh encounter, given me by a Ladies Eie, whose Seate opposed mine. She look'd stedfast on me, till the Play ended; seeming to survey my Limbs with amorous curiosity: whilst I advanced them all, to encounter her approbation. A great desire I had to see her Face: which she discovered, by unmasquing it to take her leave of a Gentleman. But if I ever beheld one so ill-favour'd? do thou abhorre my Book. She look'd like *December*, in the midst of *April*, old and crabbed in her Youth. Her Nose stood towards the *South-East* point: and *Snot* had fretted a preposterous *Channell* in the most remote corner of her Lip. Sure she was chast, *chast* because *deformed*: and her *deformitie* (repugnant to the common course of *Nature*) might beget that *Chastitie*: but in whom? in others, not in her selfe; unlesse *Necessitie* did force it. For no doubt she would be as leacherous as the Mountaine-*Goate*, had not Natures qualmishnesse proved a strong contradiction to her desire: who heaved the Gorge, at her *imperfect* perfecting: therefore had no Stomach to make a Man fitting her embracements. Yet she wore *Jewells*, for the which I could willingly have kiss'd her in the *dark*. And perhaps too (by guilded provocation) supplied the Office of a Husband.[8]

Nim's attempt to seduce the lady as they leave the play fails, of course, and he loses his investment when the lady's brother threatens him with his sword. But his account does tell us that gallants on their stools found it usual to flourish their costly attire and handsome limbs on stage, that one of his companions on a stage stool was quite unaware of metatheatrical illusion, that the lady who kept staring at him from the pit with her mask on sat with what turned out to be her brother as her escort, and that Nim's attempt to pick the lady up outside the playhouse was neither unusual nor unexpected, either by the lady or her brother.

Nim's can hardly have been a common experience at the Blackfriars, we might hope. Otherwise the author, known only by his initials (T. M.) would not have thought it a story worth putting into print. Nim was a frill when a plain garment would be more valuable for our purposes. Rather than search for more of such fictitious anecdotes it might be better to begin by hunting out some of the more sociological kinds of evidence.

2. SOCIAL DIVISIONS IN THE PLAYHOUSES

Prices understandably tended to shape the distribution of social classes in the playhouses. The basic penny at the Globe in 1600 was cheap by the standards of most forms of entertainment at the time, though the hall playhouses' basic sixpence, roughly a twelfth of the London artisan's weekly wage,[9] was by amphitheatre standards truly a lord's price for the two hours of stage traffic. The other major pastimes available, however, gambling, whoring and drinking, were all by that standard lordly sports. Tobacco cost three pence for a small pipeful, and even the nuts that spectators commonly chewed during performances cost up to sixpence a bag. Only bear-baiting was as cheap as the yard of the public playhouses. The working classes seem to have paid up to twopence for their plays according to the author of *Father Hubburd's Tales* (1603), who writes of 'a dull Audience of Stinkards sitting in the Penny Galleries of a Theater, and yawning upon the Players'. Theirs were the cheaper seats, probably in the lowest of the three gallery levels just above the yard. There are several references to army captains and other sitting in 'twopenny galleries', though they may have been the same as the 'middle region', the central gallery of the three. By Platter's testimony the stinkards' seats cost them one penny to get into the yard and a second for a seat under the roof on a gallery bench. Sir Humphrey Mildmay, a landed gentleman about town in the 1630s, used to pay for a twelve-penny room at the hall playhouse, and a similar price, presumably for a lord's room, when he went to the Globe in the summer months.[10] Mildmay's amphitheatre's shilling may have been made up to that total in his accounts by a boatman's fee of sixpence to row him and his friends there.

The different pricing does seem to have had a substantial effect on the composition of the audiences. The praeludium to Goffe's *Careless Shepherdess*, played at a hall playhouse in 1629, has a citizen say:

I will hasten to the money Box,
And to take my shilling out again, for now
I have considered that it is too much;
I'll go to th'Bull, or Fortune, and there see
A Play for two pense, with a Jig to boot.

If a merchant or craftsman found the shilling too much it is not likely that many apprentices would have been tempted. Their income was truly minimal. They received nothing but board and lodging from their employer until they were skilled enough to produce their own saleable commodities after several years of training.

We have noted the number of beads and other items of dress found at the Rose in 1989. What such items do not tell us is whether they were dropped from clothes worn by women or by men. The question of how substantial a proportion of the audience at the Rose or any other playhouse was female has been a topic of some debate. We cannot take too precisely the point, made implicitly in Nim's account, that the proportion of women must have been less than half on the grounds that respectable women never went out without a male escort, whether a family friend, a brother, a lady's page or a citizen's husband's apprentice. But if you add the occasional whore looking for custom, the occasional family with young sons and daughters, and the individuals from the thousands of working women, fishwives, apple wives, or figures like Ursula the pig-woman in *Bartholomew Fair*, the proportions seem unlikely to have been heavily biased on the male side.

Beads at the Rose tell us nothing about the sexes. On the whole it was the menfolk who were the peacocks of London society, wearing at least as much beadwork and lace as the women. Neither clothing fragments nor the evidence from food remains are very helpful. We know whole families went, but not how often or how many. Philip Gawdy wrote in 1587 of an accident with a firearm at a playhouse, probably the Theatre, that killed a child and a pregnant woman, which suggests that whole families might be present on some occasions. The water poet John Taylor wrote in 1628 of how a beggar might get his whole family into a playhouse, 'all in for one penny'.[11] But that still says nothing about the proportions of male and female.

By the time I issued the third edition of my *Playgoing in Shakespeare's London* I had collected the names of 250 individuals who were actually known to have attended playhouses. To that sadly limited total more recently I added another thirty-six, eighteen men and eighteen women. But even that addition is subject to the limitations imposed by the small number of places where we can find evidence. Two of the thirty-six were aristocrats, Lord Aubigny and Lady Anne Cecil, rather obviously note-worthy figures, but almost all the other names come from the records of Bridewell, a 'house of correction' for minor offences, run as a church court. It was Bridewell that tried to deal with the feats of Mary or Moll Frith, the cross-dressing 'roaring girl' of Dekker and Middleton's play staged at the Fortune in 1612. The Bridewell list of playgoers included seventeen women, almost all of them charged with marital and sexual misdemeanours.[12] Finding names of playgoers in the Bridewell records shows how much the chief catchment areas for finding the names of real people who went to playhouses are heavily biased sections of the social territory.

In total, of the 286 names now identified at plays fifty are female, eight of them nobles, one a queen (Henrietta Maria, who visited the Blackfriars four times in the 1630s). The 286 together, perhaps 0.0004 per cent of all playgoers through the period, hardly give us a reliable cross-section of typical playgoers. The names provide an alarmingly rough outline of those sections of the community most likely to attend plays. Since the range is from beggars to a queen, it is not much help in identifying which sections went most frequently. The best we can say is that the presence of women does appear to have been a regular features of all crowds, not least those who flocked to the playhouses, outdoor and in.

We cannot avoid the point that a fundamental difference between all the various audiences must have existed between the social classes, in simple financial terms of those who could not afford the hall playhouse charges and those who could. It is all too easy to exaggerate the difference and see the bulk of playgoers as privileged. But the social mix of audiences can never be ignored. Certainly the Globe after 1608 when it began to serve as the King's Men's summer resort continued to attract the playgoers used to seeing them through the cold weather at Blackfriars. Mildmay's diary records several plays seen at Court, eighteen visits to Blackfriars and four to the Cockpit, but also four to the Globe. Even in the decade before 1608 the Globe company was summoned to play at Court twice as often as any other company, in fact as often as all the other companies put together. It is unlikely that those who favoured them so much at Court would have ignored them at the Globe when they were in town. The privileged and underprivileged audiences were not mutually exclusive; rather the rich went to hall and amphitheatre playhouse alike, the poor more exclusively to the amphitheatres.

Looking back from 1699, the antiquary James Wright summed up the general impressions of the different Caroline playhouses as they evolved after 1609 as follows:

Before the Wars, there were in being all these Playhouses at the same time. The *Black-friars*, and *Globe* on the *Bankside*, a Winter and Summer House, belonging to the same Company called the King's Servants; the *Cockpit* or *Phoenix*, in *Drury-Lane*, called the Queen's Servants; the private House in *Salisbury-court*, called the Prince's Servants; the Fortune near *White-cross-street*, and the Red Bull at the upper end of St. *John's-street*: The two last were mostly frequented by Citizens, and the meaner sort of People. All these Companies got Money, and Liv'd in Reputation, especially those of the *Black-friers*, who were Men of grave and sober Behaviour.[13]

Most of the evidence for the composition of audiences at these various playhouses supports Wright's description, though by no means straightforwardly. The boy companies at the new hall theatres in 1600 seem not so much to have drawn wealthy audiences away from the amphitheatres as for a time and in ways that changed to have excluded the poorer patrons. Marston, writing about St Paul's Boys in 1600 in *Jack Drum's Entertainment* 5.1, told his listeners

> I like the Audience that frequenteth there
> With much applause: A man shall not be choakte
> With the stench of Garlicke, nor be pasted
> To the barmy Jacket of a Beer-brewer.

and called them 'a good gentle Audience'. It was of course a hopeful pronouncement, and probably meant rather that the stinkard was banished from the yard or the penny gallery to the back of the galleries indoors than that he was totally excluded. By 1609 Jonson was writing of 'six-penny mechanicks' and the 'shop's foreman ... that may judge for his sixpence' attending Blackfriars. It is also worth bearing in mind that the first performance of Beaumont's *Knight of the Burning Pestle* at the Blackfriars in 1607 was a total flop because, as the publisher of the First Quarto (1613) said, the audience missed 'the privie mark of irony about it'. That such an extravagant burlesque of citizen plays should be construed by the audience as a straight pro-citizen play rather implies that the city element in the audience was much stronger than Beaumont bargained for.[14]

The wealthy and especially the young had patronised the amphitheatres readily enough before the reopening of the halls in 1599. Throughout the 1580s city apprentices and the Inns-of-Court law students were equally notorious for their behaviour in such public places, usually because their gangs fought each other. In the 1590s, with only the amphitheatres open to all Londoners, people from the whole social gamut, male and female, attended plays. The brief period from 1594 to 1600 marked an almost unique concordance from all social levels. As the law student John Davies put it, citizens and artisans joined with gentlemen and prostitutes, porters and household servants in the playhouse crowds.

> For as we see at all the playhouse dores,
> When ended is the play, the daunce, and song,
> A thousand townsemen, gentlemen, and whores,
> Porters and serving-men together throng …[15]

Davies' number, incidentally, was matched by Middleton and Dekker in *The Roaring Girl* when they wrote of a thousand heads at the Fortune in 1611. That suggests the usual crowd was closer to this number than the 3,000 of the maximum figures quoted for the Swan and the second Globe. Even if the average attendance at the outdoor playhouses was a thousand it meant over half a million visits to a playhouse every year. With a total population of around two hundred thousand and less than 20 per cent of them regular playgoers, it also means most of them must have gone to a play at least twenty times a year.

Inside the range covered by Davies' comprehensive list of playgoers we can of course find much more comment on the higher social levels than on the lower. Nashe in 1592 listed the most notorious groups enjoying their conspicuous leisure who became 'afternoon's men' (a euphemism for drunkards): 'Gentlemen of the Court, the Innes of the Courte, and the number of Captaines and Souldiers about London': that is, gentlemanly and therefore unemployed gallants, lawyers and soldiers on leave. Foreign tourists also normally visited the theatres, since they were counted as one of the famous sights of London.

Foreign emissaries in particular made their presence known by visits to the amphitheatres. The French ambassador and his wife took a party to the Globe to see *Pericles* in 1608. At a time of considerable hostility to Spain in 1621 the Spanish ambassador Gondomar and his train saw a play at the Fortune, and afterwards treated the players to a banquet in the adjacent garden. The scandal over the performances of the anti-Spanish *A Game at Chess* at the Globe in 1624 three years later produced the following note from a contemporary observer:

I doubt not but you have heard of our famous play of Gondomar, which has ben followed with extraordinarie concourse, and frequented by all sorts of people old and younge, rich and poore, masters and servants, papists and puritans, wise men etc churchmen and statesmen as sir Henry wotton, Sir Albert morton, Sir Benjamin Ruddier, Sir Thomas Lake, and a world besides; the Lady Smith wold have gon yf she could have persuaded me to go with her, I am not so sore nor severe but I that I wold willingly have attended her, but I could not sit so long, for we must have ben there before one a'clocke at farthest to find any roome.[16]

Chamberlain was impressed by the fact that the concourse at such a scandalous play was less extraordinary for its social altitude than its wide social range. A more run-of-the-mill occasion was reported by Busino, the wide-eyed Venetian chaplain, who visited the Fortune in 1617, and was impressed

to see such a crowd of nobility, so very well arrayed that they looked like so many princes, listening as silently and soberly as possible. These theatres are frequented by a number of respectable and handsome ladies, who come freely and seat themselves among the men without the slightest hesitation.[17]

He goes on to describe being accosted by one such masked gentlewoman, in two languages. She was probably set on him as a joke by his ambassador.

John Earle, writing of a leading actor in 1628, coupled gentlewomen with law students as the most frequent playgoers, claiming with characteristic malice that both types went for the pleasure the leading player gave them:

The waiting-women Spectators are over-eares in love with him, and Ladies send for him to act in their Chambers. Your Innes of Court men were undone but for him, hee is their chiefe guest and imployment, and the sole businesse that makes them Afternoones men.[18]

A more detailed though not necessarily more typical catalogue of a Blackfriars audience under the Stuarts was given in 1617 by the Inns-of-Court student Henry Fitzgeoffrey, in a book of verses called *Satyres and Satyricall Epigrams: with Certaine Observations at Black-Fryers*. In a looser version of the Theophrastan 'Characters' manner he describes a '*Captain Martio*, he ith' *Renounce Me* Band, / That in the middle Region doth stand' (meaning he sat in the six or ninepenny galleries at the middle level), '*Sir Iland Hunt*, a Travailer that will tell / Of stranger Things then *Tatterd Tom* ere li't of', 'A *Cheapside* Dame' (a citizen's wife), a high-heeled 'world of fashions' (male), 'A *Woman* of the *masculine Gender*', a 'plumed *Dandebrat*, / Yon Ladyes *Shittle-cocke*', and a 'misshappen *Prodigall*' who struts on to the stage from the tiring-house as if he had not a debt in the world. Later and perhaps a little inconsistently the audience is described as 'this *Microcosme*, Man's societie'.

Both Earle's and Fitzgeoffrey's descriptions are of the Blackfriars, unquestionably the most reputable playhouse of the whole later period. In 1630 it was the focus of a literary quarrel that in a small way illustrates the differences between the playhouses at that time. Davenant's second commercial-theatre play, *The Just Italian*, failed when put on at Blackfriars by the King's Men in 1629. His friends promptly supplied him with sympathetic prefatory verses for the publication of the play early in

1630. One of them was Thomas Carew, who wrote contemptuously of its hostile audience:

> They'l still slight
> All that exceeds Red Bull, and Cockpit flight.
> These are the men in crowded heapes that throng
> To that adulterate stage, where not a tong
> Of th'untun'd Kennell, can a line repeat
> Of serious sence: but like lips, meet like meat;
> Whilst the true brood of Actors, that alone
> Keepe naturall unstrayn'd Action in her throne
> Behold their benches bare, though they rehearse
> The tearser *Beaumonts*, or great *Johnsons* verse.

This slur, linking Beeston's company at the Cockpit with the tear-throat citizen fare of the Red Bull, found a prompt reply in verses attached to Shirley's *Grateful Servant*, one of the only two plays by Shirley to be printed with prefatory verses. One defender of Shirley and the Cockpit repertory, for which Shirley was the leading poet, called Carew's poem a cock and bull story:

> I must
> Be to my conscience and thy Poem just,
> Which grac'd with comely action, did appeare
> The full delight of every eye and eare,
> And had that stage no other play, it might
> Have made the critticke blushe at cock-pit flight,
> Who not discovering what pitch it flies
> His wit came down in pitty to his eyes
> And lent him a discourse of cock and bull
> To make his other commendations full:
> But let such Momi passe, and give applause
> Among the brood of actors, in whose cause,
> As Champion he hath sweat, let their stale pride
> Finde some excuse in being magnified,
> Thy Muse will live, and no adulterate pen
> Shall wound her, through the sides of common men
> Let 'em unkennell malice, yet thy praise
> Shall mount secure, hell cannot blast thy bayes.[19]

Others of Shirley's sympathisers upheld his 'So smooth, so sweet' verse against the 'mighty rimes, / Audacious metaphors' of Davenant at the Blackfriars. *The Just Italian* was crammed with extreme images, especially sexual. Lovers for instance are 'wrapt in curlings intricate', in 'slippery closures'. Shirley ignored Davenant's language and merely defended his actors – 'the most of them deserving a name in the file of those that are eminent for gracefull and unaffected action'.

It has been suggested that what gave Shirley's supporters so much exercise was not only the 'untun'd Kennell' charge but more particularly the 'cock and bull' association of the 'Cocke-pit flight' with the Red Bull. I think it more likely that the writers made it a slur by associating the indoor Cockpit's repertoire of plays with the amphitheatre Red Bull's. It is true that the Cockpit was then running plays usually associated with the outdoor playhouses. Several Red Bull plays including Heywood's *Rape of Lucrece* and Marlowe's *Jew of Malta* had found their way into the Cockpit repertoire by the late 1620s.[20] Heywood in fact later answered the slur on behalf of both playhouses. In Book 4 of his religious poem *The Hierarchy of the Blessed Angels* (1635), he broke out against Carew and Davenant in self-righteous if postponed indignation:

> Whence growes this Innovation? How comes it
> Some dare to measure mouthes for every bit
> The Muse shall tast? And those Approv'd Tongues call
> Which have pleased Court and City, indeed All;
> An untuned Kennel: when the populous Throng
> Of Auditors have thought the Muses sung,
> When they but spake? How comes it (ere he know it)
> A puny shall assume the name of poet,
> And in a Tympa'nous and Thrasonicke stile
> (Words at which th'Ignorant laugh but the learn'd smile
> Because Adulterate and Undenizen'd) he
> Should taske such Artists, as have took Degre
> Before he was a Fresh-man?

Like its more celebrated predecessor this was rather a quarrel amongst individual poets than a war about dramatic standards, since Heywood for one took it personally. But the question of differing standards did exist. Carew's assumption of the superiority of the Blackfriars repertory was reasserted by Leonard Digges in commendatory verses attached to Shakespeare's *Poems* of 1640 though written earlier, probably for the First Folio of 1623. Digges exhorted contemporary scribblers not to pollute Shakespeare's stage:

> But if you needs must write, if poverty
> So pinch, that otherwise you starve and die,
> On Gods name may the Bull or Cockpit have
> Your lame blancke Verse, to keepe you from the grave:
> Or let new Fortunes younger brethren see,

What they can picke from your lean industry.
I do not wonder when you offer at
Black-friers, that you suffer.

This is a celebration of the superior standards offered at the Blackfriars rather than a mark of any essential difference in the repertory. The whole quarrel shows an awareness by the rival poets of the homogeneity of each playhouse's audiences and their tendency to differ in their tastes and styles.

The chief problem in differentiating the playhouse audiences is not in fact so much between the citizen and amphitheatre Red Bull and Fortune on the one hand and the courtier Blackfriars on the other as in locating the place held by the Globe after 1608–9, when the King's Men became hall theatre as well as open-air players, using the Globe for their summer season from May to September and Blackfriars through the rest of the year. By 1630 the Blackfriars was taking nearly twice as much money as the Globe on the average, and was used for twice as long through the year. The titlepages of play quartos published between 1616 and 1642 mention performances at the Blackfriars alone forty-nine times; while ten name both Blackfriars and Globe and only five give the Globe alone as the venue. It is unlikely that many or even any of these plays had really been acted at only one of the playhouses, because the repertoire of the King's Men seems to have been almost completely interchangeable, at least down to the last decade.

Several people known to have visited plays of the King's Men were travellers from the country such as Nathaniel Tomkyns, up from Somerset on his master's business. He went to the Globe on 14 August 1634 and wrote back to his master reporting on *The Late Lancashire Witches*.[21] He told him how surprised he was to find so many gentry there in high summer. The Inns of Court were in vacation and most of the aristocracy out of town but it still drew a good cross-section of London society. More likely London's general loss of its dignitaries in the heat of summer than its amphitheatre image caused Tomkyns' surprise and made it seem less distinguished than the Blackfriars. Henry Glapthorne's *Poems* (1639) contains a prologue 'To a Reviv'd Vacation Play' which puts forward the hope that its wit will evoke a good response even from an audience just of citizens. On the other hand Davenant's *News from Plymouth*, acted at the Globe in summer, has a prologue expressing joy at the appearance there of a worthy Blackfriars-type audience:

A Noble Company! for we can spy
Beside rich gawdy Sirs, some that rely
More on their Judgments, then their Cloathes, and may

> With wit as well as Pride, rescue our Play:
> And 'tis but just, though each Spectator knows
> This House, and season, does more promise shewes,
> Dancing, and Buckler Fights, then Art, or Witt.

If the prologue was written along with the play, of course, Davenant must have been just making a hopeful prophecy, or preparing a loaded compliment for an audience that he did *not* expect to be keen on wit. His last lines suggest that the Globe now provided jigs and spectacles in spite of the success of the musicians at the Blackfriars. The implication is that the company deliberately chose plays they themselves expected to be more popular with outdoor audiences when they played at the Globe. The same point prompted the prologue to Shirley's *Doubtful Heir* (1640), which supplies a detailed catalogue of the differences he expected to exist between the two playhouses in his backhanded apology for presenting a play written for the Blackfriars at the Globe. It was actually a revision of a play originally composed for a select indoor audience of Dubliners.

> Our Author did not calculate this Play
> For this Meridian; the Bankside, he knows,
> Are far more skilfull at the Ebbes and flows
> Of water, than of wit, he did not mean
> For the elevation of your poles, this scene.
> No shews, no dance and what you most delight in,
> Grave understanders, here's no target fighting.

His catalogue of different types of play goes on at some length. We might wonder how much this reflects Shirley's recent arrival from Dublin in his echo of local gossip about the lesser status of the Globe compared with the Blackfriars. The seasonal shift of audience types must have been more influential than any difference in the types of play chosen for staging at the two company venues.

These distinct trappings of hall and amphitheatre performance evidently remained a feature of each theatre, and the repertories must have been divided accordingly in the later years, though not as much as some poets wished. On Davenant's testimony and evidence such as Mildmay's diary and comments on what he and his family went to it appears that in summer the Blackfriars audiences did not altogether forsake the King's Men just because they had moved to the Globe and were producing their plays with outdoor theatre appurtenances. In these later years both audiences were socially mixed, to judge by Lovelace's epilogue to his lost play *The Scholars,* published in 1649. The difference at Blackfriars between the cheap gallery and the more expensive pit required, he wrote, two plays in one:

> His *Schollars* school'd, sayd if he had been wise
> He should have wove in one two comedies.
> The first for th'gallery, in which the throne
> To their amazement should descend alone,
> The rosin-lightning flash and monster spire
> Squibs, and words hotter than his fire.
> Th'other for the gentlemen o'th'pit
> Like to themselves all spirit, fancy, wit.

No doubt the price differential reduced the proportion of commoners in the gallery of the Blackfriars in the winter compared with the numbers who stood around the Globe stage. The disappearance of the landed gentry to their estates and of the afternoon men from the Inns of Court no doubt similarly reduced the proportion of gallants at the Globe in summer. But at neither playhouse could the King's Men expect a complete change of audience. The most conspicuous difference was probably the relative positioning of the audience in each auditorium. At the Globe those who surrounded the stage were in the cheapest places. At the Blackfriars the witty and the elegant were closest and the poorer folk furthest from the stage.

The fact that all these references to a difference between the audiences of halls and amphitheatres appeared in Caroline times from about 1630 onwards reflects what is probably one of the consequences of social and political polarization through these last years. The sides that were to join battle after 1640 were moving into their entrenched positions. When Prynne was so savagely punished for his attack on Henrietta Maria's amateur theatricals in 1633 the world of playgoing was for the first time unambiguously identified as the exclusive avenue where the world of fashion most loved to stroll. For the first time respectable ladies were forming a noticeable proportion of the audience. Poets paid attention to them, giving their plays titles like *The Lady's Privilege* or *The Lady's Trial*, writing flattering prologues and dedicating their published texts to them. Brome's epilogue to *The Court Beggar* (1640) at the Cockpit addresses an audience divided into 'Ladyes', 'Cavaliers', and 'generous spirits of the City', in that order. These were all sections of the audience at the plays written for the hall playhouses, of course, in a repertory that saw the presence of women chiefly as a firmly restraining influence. Shirley in his prologue to *The Imposture* (1640) called the 'gentlemen' of his audience the 'commissioners of wit' while the 'ladies' were the arbiters of decorum.

In all his poems you have been his care,
Nor shall you need to wrinkle now that fair
Smooth alabaster of your brow; no fright
Shall strike chaste ears, or dye the harmless white
Of any cheek with blushes: by this pen,
No innocence shall bleed in any scene.

No bawdy, pure poetic justice and no fireworks in a playhouse where ladies are present. The assumption that ladies needed cosseting was a male attitude deeply opposed to the derision that earlier poets expressed over the apple wives and fishwives of the amphitheatre audiences.

3. AUDIENCE BEHAVIOUR

Evidence for the behaviour of Shakespearean audiences is much more plentiful than for their social constitution; rather too plentiful in fact. As Alfred Harbage once put it, most of the testimony for audience behaviour 'expresses a social attitude or comes from disappointed poets, disgruntled preachers, wary politicians, or spokesmen for threatened commercial interests'.[22] Harbage's point was that the bulk of unfavourable testimony can be discounted by analogy with the similar body of testimony against the depraved and corrupted nature of plays. Since the one set of testimonies can be proved false by reference to the plays accused of corruption equivalent testimonies for riotous behaviour among the audiences can similarly be distrusted. The inclination to do so is strengthened on finding that Stephen Gosson, once a player and writer of plays and later one of the most eloquent writers of testimonies against the playhouses took his descriptions of Elizabethan audiences from Ovid's accounts of Roman audiences in the *Amores*.[23] Harison's cautious and not implausible deduction about the nature of plays quoted at the beginning of this chapter was a safer argument for a non-playgoer to use than the accusations levelled by the non-playgoing Puritans and City Fathers. One might expect the poets to carry more weight with their condemnations, and they were certainly more eloquent. Nashe attacked audiences in 1592, Heywood in 1595, Marston in 1597, 1603 and 1604, Chapman in 1599, Beaumont in 1607 and 1609, Fletcher in 1609 and 1613, Dekker in 1609 and 1610, Webster in 1611, Middleton in 1613, Carew in 1630, and Jonson at frequent intervals throughout his career. But all their attacks were against bad judgement rather than bad behaviour, and can therefore hardly be thought disinterested. A few poets sometimes went to the other extreme of flattery, but with no more sign of disinterest than when they condemned.

Some evidence does exist for violence and lawlessness in the playhouses between 1574 and 1642, but there is nothing to show that it was more than the occasional consequence of large crowds gathering together for a length of time. Chambers lists a few instances of lawlessness in playhouses including a case of stealing at the Red Bull in 1613, a stabbing (the Fortune in the same year), fighting (the Red Bull in 1610), and receiving a stolen diamond (the Curtain in 1594).[24] There were also such minor consequences of ill manners as the lawsuit brought in Star Chamber by Captain Essex against the Irish Lord Thurles, a few weeks later to be the Duke of Ormond, in 1632, resulting from a brawl with swords when Thurles took up a position on the stage at the Blackfriars standing upright because no stools were left, so that he obstructed the view of Captain Essex and the Earl of Essex's new wife, whom the Captain was escorting, in their box.[25]

As in any crowd pickpockets and prostitutes were likely to be found at work, but even for them the taverns were better employment. A pickpocket caught in 1600 at one of the Middlesex amphitheatres, most likely the Curtain, was the only one amongst 118 proven cases in that year to be taken at a playhouse.[26] In all, one pickpocket in seven of those convicted at the Middlesex sessions was at a playhouse,[27] which is not a bad record considering the small range of places where crowds might foregather in the suburbs and countryside of sixteenth-century Middlesex. In the case of the Fortune there was even a rather self-conscious pride in the association of cutpurses and similar rogues with the house. Dekker and Middleton's *The Roaring Girl* celebrated Mary Frith, a well-known female transvestite, who herself favoured the Fortune and paraded on the stage there at a performance. In 1611 or 1612 the Bridewell *Consistory of London Correction Book* recorded Roaring Moll's bad reputation, and especially that

being at a play about three quarters of a yeare since at ye Fortune in man's apparel and in her boots and wth a sword at her syde she told the company then present y' she thought many of them were of opinion that she was a man, but if any of them would come to her lodging they should finde she is a woman, and some other immodest and lascivious speaches she also used at y' time and also sat upon the stage in the public viewe of all the people there present in man's apparel and played upon her lute and sange a song.[28]

Moll may in fact have sat on stage through a performance of *The Roaring Girl* itself. Certainly in the printed text at 5.1 she is utilised to identify her cutpurse associates in the playhouse audience. In 1.2 a leading gentleman character presents a detailed description of the Fortune audience and also identifies a cutpurse amongst them:

The furniture that doth adorne this roome,
Cost many a faire gray groat ere it came here,
But good things are most cheape, when th'are most deere,
Nay when you looke into my galleries,
How bravely they are trim'd up, you all shall sweare
Y'are highly pleasd to see whats set downe there:
Stories of men and women (mixt together
Faire ones with foule, like sun-shine in wet wether)
Within one square a thousand heads are laid
So close, that all of heads, the roome seemes made,
As many faces there (fill'd with blith lookes)
Shew like the promising titles of new bookes,
(Writ merily) the Readers being their owne eyes,
Which seeme to move and to give plaudities,
And here and there (whilst with obsequious eares,
Throng'd heapes do listen) a cut purse thrusts and leeres
With haukes eyes for his prey: I need not shew him,
By a hanging villanous looke, your selves may know him,
The face is drawne so rarely. Then sir below,
The very flowre (as twere) waves to and fro,
And like a floating Hand, seemes to move,
Upon a sea bound in with shores above.

In a neat ambiguity the 'galleries' are described as full of both pictures and of playgoers. The yard is a sea of faces, with the occasional cutpurse swimming amongst them. This compares with the fact that it was the Fortune that was singled out in the Middlesex order of 1612 to suppress its jigs because of the cutpurses they attracted. Which came first, the play advertising the cut-purses or the Middlesex order about them?

The presence of cutpurses and other criminals was a common claim made against the playhouses, although since there were almost no other places besides churches where large numbers of people assembled we need not take the claims too seriously. There are not many records of criminals being charged with offences at the playhouses. More frequent are accounts of affrays or fights between apprentices and others. But the criminal records only show the tip of what was probably a large iceberg of minor disturban-ces. The apprentices on holiday attacked the Cockpit in 1616 as noted above, and a similar display of crowd spirits eager to create a disruption is described by Edmond Gayton in 1654 from his colourful memory:

the players have been appointed, notwithstanding their bills to the contrary, to act what the major part of the company had a mind to. Sometimes *Tamerlane*, sometimes *Jugurtha*, sometimes *The Jew of Malta*, and sometimes parts of all these; and at last, none of the three taking, they were forced to undress and put off their tragick habits, and conclude the day with *The Merry Milkmaides*. And unless this were done, and the popular humour satisfied (as sometimes it so fortun'd that the players were refractory), the benches, the tiles, the laths, the stones, oranges, apples, nuts, flew about most liberally; and as there were mechanicks of all professions, who fell every one to his trade, and dissolved a house in an instant, and made a ruin of a stately fabric.[29]

So it might have 'fortuned'. The plays Gayton mentions were in the Red Bull and Fortune repertoires, and if they truly were the 'citizen playhouses' that James Wright called them in 1699 it is understandable that the more riotous happenings, like the lawbreaking, occurred there more than else-where. Captain Essex's altercation with Lord Thurles and a later squabble between the Lord Chamberlain and the King's uncle over who had a right to a key to a box were the only kind of incident recorded at the Blackfriars.

Riots, brawls and lawbreaking were hardly everyday happenings, and it is impossible to gauge the behaviour of a typical audience by them. Habitual practices tell us more than such exceptions. The most obtrusive habits were to be seen in the hall playhouses by the conspicuous gallants who sat on stools on the stage and made comments on the play, and in all the play-houses by the nut-cracking which was a favourite exercise for everybody. A gallant talking and smoking on a stool on the periphery of the stage was, and meant himself to be, an obtrusive feature of the performance. It was a popular habit from the time the hall playhouses first opened and however objectionable to the mass of the audience and the players it survived. The preface to the first Shakespeare Folio in 1623 complained of wits sitting 'on the Stage at Black-friers, or the Cock-pit, to arraigne Playes dailie'. The players were similarly unhappy about the noise of nuts being cracked during their performances. In fact nut-cracking was the only regular complaint apart from the prologue's customary plea for silence.[30] Jasper Mayne's prologue to *The City Match* bravely declares that the author has no fear of 'them who sixpence pay and sixpence crack' but according to Thomas Palmer in the 1647 Beaumont and Fletcher Folio it took a Falstaff to keep the audience from their cracking. Bottle ale, which was sold during the performance, was also occasionally remarked on for the potentially mis-understood hiss it gave when opened.

Just as contemporary commentators wrote mostly about the great who attended the playhouses, so they wrote about exceptional audience behav-iour rather than about the more normal audiences. Stephen Gosson may well have continued to see plays after being paid for his pamphlets attacking the theatre that he wrote in the early 1580s. Even after becoming a cleric he could still use analogies drawn from playgoing. One in particular reflects what was probably a standard feature of audience behaviour at the amphitheatres. At a sermon he delivered at the great public venue for preachers, Paul's Cross, on 7 May 1598 called 'The Trumpet of Warre', he said that

in publique Theaters, when any notable shew passeth over the stage, the people arise up out of their seates, & stand upright with delight and eagernesse to view it well.

Such actions today are more often found at football matches than in theatres. They were a consequence of the growing delight in spectacle more than speech, the press of people in the auditorium, and the informal crowded seating on wooden benches.

Hisses or 'mewes' as well as applause were given freely, and not only at the end of the play. Drayton speaks of

> Showts and Claps at ev'ry little pawse,
> When the proud Round on ev'ry side hath rung.[31]

And audiences were highly responsive in sentiment too. An academic spectator seeing a performance of *Othello* by the King's Men at Oxford in 1610 wrote (in Latin) that

not only by their speech but also by their deeds they drew tears. – But indeed Desdemona, killed by her husband, although she always acted the matter very well, in her death moved us still more greatly; when lying in bed she implored the pity of those watching with her countenance alone.[32]

The famous anecdote of the audience at *Faustus* being frightened when the theatre fabric gave a loud crack speaks of the tension that crowded audiences could generate. Not of course that they were often easily satisfied. Middleton echoed several fellow poets in complaining of the variousness of audience tastes in the prologue to *No Wit, No Help like a Woman's*:

> How is't possible to suffice
> So many Ears, so many Eyes?
> Some in wit, some in shows
> Take delight, and some in Clothes;
> Some for mirth they chiefly come,
> Some for passion, for both some;
> Some for lascivious meetings, that's their arrant;
> Some to detract and ignorance their warrant.
> How is't possible to please
> Opinion tos'd in such wilde Seas?

As in *The Roaring Girl*, he wrote that the Fortune audience was a heaving 'sea' of moods as well as faces.

The poets' complaints about the intelligence of their audiences some-times took the form of accusations that they came for the spectacle and the bodies, not the words, 'only to see men speak'. As Jonson put it, plays should be

> offered, as a Rite,
> To Schollers, *that can judge, and faire report*
> The sense they heare, above the vulgar sort
> Of Nut-crackers, that onely come for sight.[33]

We can count as many as thirty-four complaints from almost all the dramatists of the time other than Shakespeare about the kind of reception their plays were given. And yet very few of the plays that failed then, with the sole exceptions of *The Knight of the Burning Pestle* and possibly *The White Devil*, would stand much chance of success now. Where audiences then and now would be more inclined to differ is over the plays that were the greatest successes of the early period. Judging by the number of editions printed, with *Faustus*, *Hamlet* and the *Henry IV* plays, the most popular pieces from the whole seventy years of playing were *The Spanish Tragedy*, *Mucedorus*, *Philaster*, Heywood's *If You Know Not Me* and *Pericles*. The relative failures among the better plays of the period might be put down to the fickleness of individual audiences, but the successes among the better plays were made by the consistent judgements of a long series of audiences. They could hardly be called bad judges.

Finally on audience behaviour it is instructive to put beside each other two pieces of evidence that come from the same time and more or less the same place, the Blackfriars near the end of the boy company's tenure in 1608. The first is Dekker's splendidly vivid set of burlesque advice to the ambitious gallant on how he should try to show himself off in a playhouse. Dekker's remarks are meant to apply to any playhouse, but fit best at the leading hall playhouse while it was still occupied by the boy company.

let our Gallant ... presently advance himselfe up to the Throne of the Stage. I meane not into the Lords roome (which is now but the Stages Suburbs): No, those boxes, by the iniquity of custome, conspiracy of waiting-women and Gentlemen-Ushers, that there sweat together, and the covetousness of Sharers, are contempt-ibly thrust into the reare, and much new Satten is there dambd, by being smothred to death in darknesse. But on the very Rushes where the Comedy is to daunce, yea, and under the state of *Cambises* himself, must our fethered *Estridge*, like a piece of Ordnance, be planted valiantly (because impudently) beating downe the mewes and hisses of the opposed rascality ...

Present not your selfe on the Stage (especially at a new play) untill the quaking prologue hath (by rubbing) got culor into his cheekes, and is ready to give the trumpets their Cue, that hees upon point to enter: for then it is time, as though you were one of the *properties*, or that you dropt out of the *Hangings*, to creepe from behind the Arras, with your *Tripos* or three-footed stoole in one hand, and a teston [sixpence] mounted betweene a forefinger and a thumbe in the other: for if you should bestow your person upon the vulgar, when the belly of the house is but halfe full, your apparell is quite eaten up, the fashion lost, and the proportion of your body in more danger to be devoured then if it were served up on the Counter amongst the Powltry: avoid that as you would the Bastome. It shall crowne you with rich commendation, to laugh alowd in the middest of the most serious and saddest scene of the terriblest Tragedy: and let that clapper (your tongue) be tost so high, that all the house may ring of it: your Lords use it; your Knights are Apes to the Lords, and do so too: your Inne-a-court-man is Zany to the Knights, and (mary very scurvily) comes likewise limping after it: bee thou a beagle to them all, and never lin snuffing [lie sniffing], till you have scented them: ...

Now sir, if the writer be a fellow that hath either epigrammed you, or hath had a flirt at your mistris, or hath brought either your feather, or your red beard, or your little legs &c. on the stage, you shall disgrace him worse then by tossing him in a blancket, or giving him the bastinado in a Taverne, if, in the middle of his play, (bee it Pastoral or Comedy, Morall or Tragedie) you rise with a screwd and discontented face from your stoole to be gone: no matter whether the Scenes be good or no; the better they are the worse do you distast them: and, beeing on your feet, sneake not away like a coward, but salute all your gentle acquaintance, that are spred either on the rushes, or on stooles about you, and draw what troupe you can from the stage after you: the *Mimicks* are beholden to you, for allowing them elbow roome: their Poet cries, perhaps, a pox go with you, but care not for that, theres no musick without frets.

Mary, if either the company, or indisposition of the weather binde you to sit it out, my counsell is then that you turne plain Ape, take up a rush, and tickle the earnest eares of your fellow gallants, to make other fooles fall a laughing: mewe at passionate speeches, blare at merrie, finde fault with the musicke, whew at the childrens Action, whistle at the songs: and above all, curse the sharers, that whereas the same day you had bestowed forty shillings on an embrodered Felt and Feather, (Scotch-fashion) for your mistres in the Court, or your punck in the city, within two houres after, you encounter with the very same block on the stage, when the haberdasher swore to you the impression was extant but that morning.[34]

The advantage to modern actors of keeping their audiences in the dark is obvious. Dekker's satire is of course an exaggeration, but as a burlesque of a gull's actions and motivations it is exactly parallel to other burlesques of gallant behaviour such as the induction to *Cynthia's Revels*, one of the earliest boy plays at the Blackfriars in 1601, and *The Isle of Gulls*, another Blackfriars play of 1606.

The other item of evidence, from the Blackfriars in 1608, that is worth setting against Dekker's mockery tells of one effect of the kind of wilfulness and inattentiveness towards the play that he described. In 1608 John Fletcher wrote a careful and ambitious work, *The Faithful Shepherdess*, essentially an Arcadian pastoral drama of a type played previously only before Court or university audiences. It did not take at all on its first commercial appearance. So Fletcher angrily reported when it was published that

> It is a pastorall Tragic-comedie, which the people seeing when it was plaid, having ever had a singuler guift in defining, concluded to be a play of country hired Shepheards in gray cloakes, with curtaild dogs in strings, sometimes laughing together, and sometimes killing one another: And missing whitsun ales, creame, wassel and morris-dances, began to be angry.

Like Dekker's gulls, the audience that received Fletcher's play with such lower-class expectation was at the Blackfriars watching a boy company. Shortly afterwards the King's Men took over the theatre and performed Beaumont and Fletcher's *Philaster*, a modified version of the same kind of play which had an enormous success and created a fashion for tragicomedy to outlast the Stuart reign. Such apparent fickleness and inconsistency on the part of the Blackfriars audiences is a clear warning about the danger to us of our making too absolute a distinction between the audiences at one kind of playhouse and another. Henslowe's records show how reluctant audiences could be to start enjoying innovatory types of play. The subsequent success of *Philaster* and the flow of Beaumont and Fletcher plays that followed shows that the poets indeed were on occasion capable of forcing a new dramatic fashion onto their wayward brethren around them. Catering to existing tastes was not the sole function of the Shakespearean dramatists.

4. CHANGES IN FASHION

The perspective that remains to be laid down in this portrait of playhouse audiences is in time, not space. Tastes for different kinds of play changed, though not at all the playhouses and not always in the same general forms. Plays such as *Faustus* and *The Spanish Tragedy* remained popular at the Fortune all the way until the theatres were closed, but the plays that were written for the Cockpit and Blackfriars in Caroline times were vastly different from the products of Shakespeare's Globe and the playhouses that preceded it. One group of playhouses, the Curtain, Rose and Swan before 1600 and the Red Bull and Fortune afterwards, retained a fairly consistent repertory from the 1590s to the end. The plays of Shakespeare's company on the whole kept in step with their fellows' amphitheatre plays until some time after 1608, when the hall playhouses started moving away to end up with the Caroline and courtly fashion. One cannot really speak of a hall playhouse style of repertory before the King's Men themselves became hall players. Before that it was rather a boy company repertory, one not taken up by the adults until much later. To see the separate repertories in Harbage's term as 'rival traditions' before 1608, one working-class and the other aristocratic, is misleading and even later would be an over-simplification, though differences there certainly were. From the start the hall playhouse plays had music and masquing while the amphitheatres had jigs and fireworks. The hall plays of the later Blackfriars did take over the tradition of wit and aristocratic pastoral rather than rant and huffing parts, and the boys' Blackfriars plays had a good deal of sexual licence which soon returned under the King's company with their Beaumont and Fletcher repertory. With Fletcher the tyranny of kings always manifested itself in sexual misbehaviour. Neither tradition, however, was exclusive of features or even plays belonging to the other, and just where the Globe fits into the picture before 1609 is a still unresolved question. Even after the King's company had moved into the Blackfriars they chose to play a revised version of *Mucedorus*, the most popular and durable of all the lower-class plays, and they performed it before King James. The 'Untuned Kennel' debate of 1630 suggests that so much of a great gulf as there was had opened itself between individual hall playhouses as well as between halls and amphitheatres.

Not unless we knew the complete repertory of all the major playhouses for much of the period, which we do not, should we be able to trace the chronology or even the degree of change in these repertories with confidence and precision. We have the texts for about 160 Chamberlain's–King's Men's plays from between 1594 and 1642 and over 200 titles (thanks to Henslowe) for the Admiral's company and its successors at the Fortune, and thirty or so of the play-texts. Barely thirty of those 200 Admiral's titles got into print, a proportion probably rather greater those of any other company of the time. So in all much less than a quarter of all the plays composed by a multitude of writers and staged by a multitude of companies have survived till today. We can only hope that what did get into print was the best of that great multiplicity of work.

It takes a perspective of at least forty or fifty years to recognise real changes in the repertories and audience fashions. Differences did undoubtedly grow in the course of time. It is hard to visualise *Faustus* being staged in the hall playhouse repertory in 1620 quite as John Melton described it at the Fortune with its fireworks and running devils. By 1632 Jonson was looking back on the fashion still current at the Fortune as one belonging wholly to

former days. In *The Magnetic Lady* he summarised the plot of an old play
that sounds suspiciously like Beaumont's burlesque of the same fashion for
knight errantry in *The Knight of the Burning Pestle* in 1607:

if a Child could be borne, in a Play, and grow up to a man, I' the first Scene, before
hee went off the Stage; and then after to come forth a Squire, and bee made a
Knight: and that Knight to travell betweene the Acts, and doe wonders I' the holy
land, or else where; kill Paynims, wild Boores, dun Cowes, and other Monsters;
beget him a reputation, and marry an Emperours Daughter for his Mistris; convert
her Fathers Countrey; and at last come home, lame .... These miracles would
please, I assure you.[35]

Sidney and Beaumont had fired first long before in this contest, but it was
still a living target in the open-air playhouses. One of Jonson's tribe of
followers, Richard Brome, copied him in *The Antipodes* (1638) with a scene
in which a lord reproves an actor for various old-fashioned tricks including
extempore clowning:

>   when you are
>   To speake to your coactors in the Scene,
>   You hold interloqutions with the Audients.
>   *Bi[play].* That is a way my Lord has bin allow'd
>   On elder stages to move mirth and laughter.
>   *Letoy.* Yes in the dayes of *Tarlton* and *Kempe*,
>   Before the stage was purg'd from barbarisme,
>   And brought to the perfection it now shines with. (2.2)

   What seems to have happened in the twilight of the Stuart gods is that the
amphitheatre playhouses soldiered on with their principal offerings, an old
repertory and their citizen allegiance,[36] while the hall playhouses recruited
the new plays. In such circumstances the gulf would inevitably widen. The
analogy with the world of fashion in dress, where some try to keep up to
date and others stick to the clothes of their youth, was recognised by
Middleton in the epistle to *The Roaring Girl*:

The fashion of play-making, I can properly compare to nothing, so naturally, as the
alteration in apparell. For in the time of the Great-crop-doublet, your huge
bombasted plaies, quilted with mighty words to leane purpose was onely then in
fashion. And as the doublet fell, neater inventions beganne to set up. Now in the
time of sprucenes, our plaies followe the nicenes of our Garments, single plots,
quaint conceits, letcherous jests, drest up in hanging sleeves, and those are fit for the
Times and the Tearmers.

Middleton's analogy was drawn up as early as 1611, and the fact that it was as
pertinent in 1642 as in 1611 shows the slowness of the changes being

mapped, and perhaps the thoroughness of the split between the two kinds of playhouse that lasted so many years. The one play that, according to an inns of court writer (known only by the initials An. Sc.), had managed to 'please all' was *Hamlet*; but that was at the Globe in 1600.[37] When the plays that occupied the stage through the great years that followed fell out of fashion then by 1642 it was indeed, as Harison put it, good night to the players.

Appendix: A Select List of Plays and their Playhouses

The following list is designed as a basis for reference from specific plays to their company and playhouse. It is arranged in alphabetical order of plays, by the first proper name in the titles, which are given as they have been regularised in E. K. Chambers, *The Elizabethan Stage* (4 vols., Oxford, 1923) and G. E. Bertley, *The Jacobean and Caroline Stage* (7 vols., Oxford, 1941–68). It includes only those extant plays which can be assigned with reasonable confidence to a particular company and playhouse. The information has been compiled largely from *The Elizabethan Stage* III–IV, *The Jacobean and Caroline Stage* III–V and Harbage, *Annals of English Drama 975–1700*, third edition, revised by Sylvia Stoler Wagonheim, 1989, with a few modifications. With some reservations it adopts the dating sequence of Shakespeare's plays in the *Complete Works*, the New Oxford edition. Middleton's plays are attributed to the dates given in the recent Oxford *Collected Works*. Other entries incorporate, for instance, suggestions about dating Ford's later plays (post-1628) in Andrew Gurr, 'Singing through the Chatter: Ford and Contemporary Theatrical Fashion', in *John Ford: Critical Re-Visions*, ed. Michael Neill (Cambridge 1988), pp. 81–96.

Similar names were sometimes used by different playing companies, chiefly the various Queen's and Prince's companies, and the King's Revels. Here Queen Elizabeth's is called Queen's, while Anne's and Henrietta's are indicated by the personal name. The first Jacobean Prince's company is called Prince's, later the Palsgrave's, and the post-1615 companies are called Prince Charles's. All the boy companies have the name 'Children' in their title. Thus the King's Revels Children of 1607–9 can be distinguished from the Salisbury Court King's Revels company. The company of boys who played at the first Blackfriars are called the Chapel Children, and the company which ran at the second Blackfriars from 1599 to 1608 under a variety of names (Revels Children, Queen's Revels Children, Children of the Chapel) are uniformly called Blackfriars Children, even after their move in 1608 to the Whitefriars playhouse. However, both of the Paul's boy companies are called Paul's Children. Beeston's Boys retain their title because they were not strictly a company of children.

Some of the details in the list, notably those relating to Shakespeare's plays, are subjects for continuing debate. In particular the evidence for the assignment of Chamberlain's Company plays dated between 1597 and 1599 to a particular playhouse and King's Company plays from after 1609 to the Globe or the Blackfriars is inadequate. Where a playhouse is positively assigned it means that the playhouse named has been specifically linked with the play in question, although the naming of one playhouse does not mean that a play was necessarily performed only there. Where a later performance by a different company or at a different playhouse is known, it is also noted. A play noted as performed by Beeston's Boys in 1639 indicates that it appears on Beeston's list of that year, naming the plays he wanted protected for his company. The dates given for many plays are conjectural. They usually relate to first performance rather than to the time of original composition.

Play	Author	Date	Company	Playhouse
Aglaura	Suckling	1637	King's	Blackfriars
Albertus Wallenstein	Glapthorne	1634–9	King's	Globe
The Alchemist	Jonson	1610	King's	Blackfriars
All Fools	Chapman	1601	Blackfriars Children	Blackfriars
All's Lost by Lust	Middleton and Rowley	1617–19 1639	Queen Anne's Beeston's Boys	Red Bull Cockpit
All's Well That Ends Well	Shakespeare	1602?	Chamberlain's	Globe
Amends for Ladies	Field	1610–11	Blackfriars Children	Whitefriars
Amyntas	Randolph	1630	King's Revels	Salisbury Court
The Antipodes	Brome	1636–8	Queen Henrietta's	Salisbury Court
The Antiquary	Marmion	1634–6	Queen Henrietta's	Cockpit
Antonio and Mellida	Marston	1599	Paul's Children	Paul's
Antonio's Revenge	Marston	1600	Paul's Children	Paul's
Antony and Cleopatra	Shakespeare	1608	King's	Globe
Anything for a Quiet Life	Middleton	1620–1	King's	Blackfriars
Argalus and Parthenia	Glapthorne	1637–8	Beeston's Boys	Cockpit
The Arraignment of Paris	Peele	1581–4	Chapel Children	first Blackfriars

As You Like It	Shakespeare	1599	Chamberlain's	Globe
Friar Bacon and	Greene	1589	Strange's	Theatre?
Friar Bungay		1592	Queen's &	Rose
			Sussex's	
		1594	Admiral's	Rose
		1602	Prince's	Fortune
The Ball	Shirley	1632	Queen Henrietta's	Cockpit
Sir John Van Olden	Fletcher	1619	King's	Globe?
Barnavelt				
Bartholomew Fair	Jonson	1614	Lady Elizabeth's	Hope
The Bashful Lover	Massinger	1636	King's	Blackfriars
The Battle of	Peele	*c.* 1589	Admiral's	Theatre? Rose
Alcazar		1601	Admiral's	Fortune
The Beggar's Bush	Fletcher (and	1615–22	King's	Blackfriars / Globe
	Massinger?)			
Believe As You List	Massinger	1631	King's	Blackfriars / Globe
The Bird in a Cage	Shirley	1633	Queen Henrietta's	Cockpit
The Blind Beggar of	Chapman	1596	Admiral's	Rose
Alexandria				
1 The Blind Beggar	Chettle and Day	1600	Admiral's	Rose
of Bednal Green		*c.* 1631	Prince Charles's	Salisbury Court
		c. 1634		Red Bull
The Bloody Banquet	Drue	1639	Beeston's Boys	Cockpit
The Bloody Brother	Fletcher	1617?	King's	Globe / Blackfriars
(Rollo)				
Blurt Master	Dekker	1601	Paul's Children	Paul's
Constable				
The Bondman	Massinger	1623	Lady Elizabeth's	Cockpit
		1639	Beeston's Boys	Cockpit
Bonduca	Fletcher	1611–14	King's	Globe / Blackfriars
The Brazen Age	Heywood	1610–13	Queen Anne's	Red Bull
Brennoralt	Suckling	1639–41	King's	Blackfriars
The Bride	Nabbes	1638	Beeston's Boys	Cockpit
The Broken Heart	Ford	1629?	King's	Blackfriars
The Brothers	Shirley	1641?	King's	Blackfriars
Bussy D'Ambois	Chapman	1604	Paul's Children	Paul's
		c. 1606	Blackfriars	Blackfriars
			Children	
		1634	King's	Blackfriars
The Conspiracy and	Chapman	1607–8	Blackfriars	Blackfriars
Tragedy of Byron			Children	
Charles Duke of Byron	Chapman	1608	Blackfriars	Blackfriars
			Children	
The Captain	Fletcher	1609–12	King's	Globe / Blackfriars
The Captives	Heywood	1624	Lady Elizabeth's	Cockpit
The Cardinal	Shirley	1641	King's	Blackfriars
Catiline	Jonson	1611	King's	Globe / Blackfriars
Chabot	Chapman	*c.* 1613?	Lady Elizabeth's	Hope?
		1635	Queen Henrietta's	Cockpit

A Challenge for Beauty	Heywood	1635	King's	Globe / Blackfriars
The Chances	Fletcher	1617	King's	Globe / Blackfriars
The Changeling	Middleton and	1622	Lady Elizabeth's	Cockpit
	Rowley	1639	Beeston's Boys	Cockpit
A Chaste Maid in Cheapside	Middleton	1613	Lady Elizabeth's	Swan
1 The Cid	Rutter	1637–8	Beeston's Boys	Cockpit
The City Madam	Massinger	1632	King's	Blackfriars
The City Match	Mayne	1637–8	King's	Blackfriars
The City Nightcap	Davenport	1624	Lady Elizabeth's	Cockpit
		c. 1639	Beeston's Boys	Cockpit
Claracilla	Killigrew	1635–6	Queen Henrietta's	Cockpit
Coriolanus	Shakespeare	1608	King's	Globe
The Coronation	Shirley	1635	Queen Henrietta's	Cockpit
		1639	Beeston's Boys	Cockpit
The Costly Whore	Anon	1619–32	Red Bull Company	Red Bull
The Country Captain	Cavendish and Shirley	1639–40	King's	Blackfriars
The Court Beggar	Brome	1639–40	Beeston's Boys	Cockpit
Covent Garden	Nabbes	1633	Queen Henrietta's	Cockpit
The Coxcomb	Beaumont and Fletcher	1608–9	Blackfriars Children	Blackfriars? Whitefriars?
		c. 1614	Lady Elizabeth's	
		1622	King's	Globe / Blackfriars
The Cruel Brother	Davenant	1627	King's	Blackfriars
The Cunning Lovers	Brome, Alexander(?)	1638	Beeston's Boys	Cockpit
Cupid's Revenge	Beaumont and Fletcher	1608	Blackfriars Children	Blackfriars? Whitefriars?
Cupid's Whirligig	Sharpham	1608	King's Revels Children	Whitefriars
The Custom of the Country	Fletcher and Massinger	1620	King's	Blackfriars
Cymbeline	Shakespeare	1609	King's	Globe
Cynthia's Revels	Jonson	1600	Blackfriars Children	Blackfriars
Death of Huntingdon	Munday and Chettle	1598	Admiral's	Rose
The Deserving Favourite	Carlell	1629	King's	Blackfriars
The Devil is an Ass	Jonson	1616	King's	Globe / Blackfriars
The Devil's Charter	Barnes	1606	King's	Globe
The Devil's Law-Case	Webster	1617	Queen Anne's	Red Bull
The Distresses	Davenant	1639	King's	Blackfriars
The Double Marriage	Fletcher and Massinger	1619–23	King's	Blackfriars

Downfall of Huntingdon	Munday and Chettle	1598	Admiral's	Rose
The Duchess of Malfi	Webster	1614	King's	Blackfriars / Globe
The Duchess of Suffolk	Drue	1624	Palsgrave's	Fortune
The Duke of Milan	Massinger	1621–2	King's	Blackfriars
The Duke's Mistress	Shirley	1636	Queen Henrietta's	Cockpit
The Dumb Knight	Markham and Machin	1607–8	King's Revels Children	Whitefriars
The Dutch Courtesan	Marston	1605	Blackfriars Children	Blackfriars
Eastward Ho!	Chapman, Jonson and Marston	1605	Blackfriars Children	Blackfriars
Edward II	Marlowe	1592	Pembroke's	Theatre?
		c. 1617	Queen Anne's	Red Bull
The Elder Brother	Fletcher	1625?	King's	Blackfriars
The Emperor of the East	Massinger	1631	King's	Blackfriars / Globe
Endymion	Lyly	1588	Paul's Children	Paul's
Englishmen for my Money	Haughton	1598	Admiral's	Rose
The English Moor	Brome	1637	Queen Henrietta's	Salisbury Court
The English Traveller	Heywood	*c.* 1627?	Queen Henrietta's	Cockpit
Epicene	Jonson	1609	Blackfriars Children	Whitefriars
Every Man in his Humour	Jonson	1598	Chamberlain's	Curtain?
		1605	King's	Globe
Every Man out of his Humour	Jonson	1599	Chamberlain's	Globe
The Example	Shirley	1634	Queen Henrietta's	Cockpit
		1639	Beeston's Boys	Cockpit
Fair Em	Anon	*c.* 1590	Strange's	Theatre?
The Fair Favourite	Davenant	1639	King's	Blackfriars?
The Fair Maid of Bristow	Anon	*c.* 1604	King's	Globe
The Fair Maid of the Inn	Fletcher	1625	King's	Blackfriars
2 The Fair Maid of the West	Heywood	1630–1	Queen Henrietta's	Cockpit
A Fair Quarrel	Middleton and Rowley	1615–17	Prince Charles's	Red Bull
		1639	Beeston's Boys	Cockpit
The Faithful Shepherdess	Fletcher	1608	Blackfriars Children	Blackfriars
		1633	King's	Blackfriars
The False One	Fletcher and Massinger	1619–23	King's	Blackfriars? Globe?
The Famous Victories of Henry V	Anon	*c.* 1588?	Queen's	Bull Inn
The Fatal Contract	Heminges	1638–9?	Queen Henrietta's	Salisbury Court
The Fatal Dowry	Field and Massinger	1617–19	King's	Blackfriars

Dr Faustus	Marlowe	1588?	Strange's?	Theatre?
		1594	Admiral's	Rose
		1619	Palsgrave's	Fortune
The Fawn	Marston	1605	Blackfriars Children	Blackfriars
A Fine Companion	Marmion	1632–3	Prince Charles's (II)	Salisbury Court
The Fleer	Sharpham	1606	Blackfriars Children	Blackfriars
Fortune by Land and Sea	Heywood and Rowley	1607–9	Queen Anne's	Red Bull
The Four Prentices of London	Heywood	*c.* 1592?	Strange's?	Rose?
		1615	Queen Anne's	Red Bull
Gallathea	Lyly	1584–8	Paul's Children	Paul's
A Game at Chess	Middleton	1624	King's	Globe
The Gamester	Shirley	1633	Queen Henrietta's	Cockpit
The Gentleman Usher	Chapman	1602(?)	Blackfriars Children	Blackfriars
Sir Giles Goosecap	Chapman	1602	Blackfriars Children	Blackfriars
The Goblins	Suckling	1637–41	King's	Blackfriars
The Golden Age	Heywood	1610?	Queen Anne's	Red Bull
The Grateful Servant	Shirley	1629	Queen Henrietta's	Cockpit
		1639	Beeston's Boys	Cockpit
The Great Duke of Florence	Massinger	1627	Queen Henrietta's	Cockpit
		1639	Beeston's Boys	Cockpit
Greene's Tu Quoque	Cooke	1611	Queen Anne's	Red Bull
The Guardian	Massinger	1633	King's	Blackfriars
Hamlet	Shakespeare	1600	Chamberlain's	Globe
Hannibal and Scipio	Nabbes	1635	Queen Henrietta's	Cockpit
The Heir	May	1620	Red Bull Company	Red Bull
Hengist (The Mayor of Quinborough)	Middleton	1616–20	King's	Blackfriars
1 and *2 Henry IV*	Shakespeare	1596–7	Chamberlain's	Theatre? Curtain
Henry V	Shakespeare	1599	Chamberlain's	Curtain? / Globe
1 Henry VI	Shakespeare	1590? 1594	Admiral's / Strange's?	Theatre? Rose
2 and *3 Henry VI*	Shakespeare	1592–3?	Pembroke's	Theatre?
Henry VIII	Fletcher and Shakespeare	1613	King's	Globe
Herod and Antipater	Markham and Sampson	1619–22	Red Bull Company	Red Bull
Hoffman	Chettle	1602	Admiral's	Fortune
		c. 1630	Queen Henrietta's	Cockpit
The Hollander (Love's Trial)	Glapthorne	1636	Queen Henrietta's	Cockpit
Holland's Leaguer	Marmion	1631	Prince Charles's (II)	Salisbury Court

The Honest Lawyer	S.S.	1614–15	Queen Anne's	Red Bull
1 and 2 The Honest	Dekker and	1604–5	Prince's	Fortune
Whore	Middleton	*c.* 1635	Queen Henrietta's	Cockpit
The Humorous Courtier	Shirley	1631	Queen Henrietta's	Cockpit
An Humorous Day's Mirth	Chapman	1597	Admiral's	Rose
The Humorous Lieutenant	Fletcher	1619 (?)	King's	Globe / Blackfriars
Humour out of Breath	Day	1608	King's Revels Children	Whitefriars?
Hyde Park	Shirley	1632	Queen Henrietta's	Cockpit
If It Be Not Good, the Devil Is In It	Dekker	1611–12	Queen Anne's	Red Bull
1 and 2 If You Know Not Me, You Know Nobody	Heywood	1604–5 *c.* 1630	Queen Anne's Queen Henrietta's	Red Bull Cockpit
The Imposture	Shirley	1640	King's	Blackfriars
The Insatiate Countess	Marston and Barksted	1607–8	Blackfriars Children	Whitefriars
The Iron Age	Heywood	1612–13	Queen Anne's	Red Bull
The Island Princess	Fletcher	1619–21	King's	Blackfriars
The Isle of Gulls	Day	1606	Blackfriars Children	Blackfriars
The Jew of Malta	Marlowe	1589	Strange's / Admiral's	Theatre?
		1594	Admiral's	Rose
		c. 1632	Queen Henrietta's	Cockpit
John a Kent and John a Cumber (The Wise Men of Westchester)	Munday	1595	Admiral's	Rose
A Jovial Crew	Brome	1641	Beeston's Boys	Cockpit
Julius Caesar	Shakespeare	1599	Chamberlain's	Globe
The Just Italian	Davenant	1629	King's	Blackfriars
A King and No King	Beaumont and Fletcher	1611	King's	Globe / Blackfriars
King John and Matilda	Davenport	1628–34 *c.* 1640	Queen Henrietta's Beeston's Boys	Cockpit Cockpit
King Lear	Shakespeare	1605	King's	Globe
A Knack to Know a Knave	Anon	1592	Strange's	Rose
A Knack to Know an Honest Man	Anon	1595	Admiral's	Rose
The Knight of Malta	Fletcher and Field (and Massinger)	1616–19	King's	Blackfriars
The Knight of the Burning Pestle	Beaumont	1607	Blackfriars Children	Blackfriars

The Lady Mother	Glapthorne	1635	King's Revels	Salisbury Court
The Lady of Pleasure	Shirley	1635	Queen Henrietta's	Cockpit
		1639	Beeston's Boys	Cockpit
The Lady's Privilege	Glapthorne	1637–40	Beeston's Boys	Cockpit
The Lady's Tragedy (*The Second Maiden's Tragedy*)	Middleton	1611	King's	Globe? Blackfriars?
The Lady's Trial	Ford	1638	Beeston's Boys	Cockpit
A Larum for London	Anon	1598	Chamberlain's	Globe
The Late Lancashire Witches	Brome and Heywood	1634	King's	Globe
The Laws of Candy	Fletcher? and Ford?	1619–23	King's	Blackfriars? Globe?
Law Tricks	Day	1604	Blackfriars Children	Blackfriars
The Little French Lawyer	Fletcher and Massinger	1619–23	King's	Blackfriars? Globe?
The London Prodigal	Anon	1604	King's	Globe
Look About You (*Disguises?*)	Anon (Wadeson?)	1595	Admiral's	Rose
The Lost Lady	Berkeley	1637–8	King's	Blackfriars? Globe?
Love and Honour	Davenant	1634	King's	Blackfriars
Love Tricks (*The School of Compliment*)	Shirley	1625	Lady Elizabeth's	Cockpit
		1631	Queen Henrietta's	Cockpit
		1639	Beeston's Boys	Cockpit
The Lover's Melancholy	Ford	1628	King's	Globe / Blackfriars
Love's Cruelty	Shirley	1631	Queen Henrietta's	Cockpit
		1639	Beeston's Boys	Cockpit
Love's Labours Lost	Shakespeare	1591?	Chamberlain's	Theatre? / Globe / Blackfriars
Love's Metamorphosis	Lyly	1589–90	Paul's Children	Paul's
Love's Mistress	Heywood	1634	Queen Henrietta's	Cockpit
Love's Sacrifice	Ford	1631 (?)	Queen Henrietta's	Cockpit
		1639	Beeston's Boys	Cockpit
The Loyal Subject	Fletcher	1618	King's	Blackfriars / Globe
Macbeth	Shakespeare	1606	King's	Globe
A Mad World, my Masters	Middleton	1606	Paul's Children	Paul's
		c. 1640	Queen Henrietta's	Salisbury Court
The Madcap	Heminges	1633	King's Revels	Fortune
The Magnetic Lady	Jonson	1632	King's	Blackfriars? Globe?
The Maid in the Mill	Fletcher and Rowley	1623	King's	Blackfriars / Globe
The Maid of Honour	Massinger	1621–2	Red Bull Company	Red Bull
		1632	Queen Henrietta's	Cockpit
		1639	Beeston's Boys	Cockpit
The Maid's Revenge	Shirley	1626	Queen Henrietta's	Cockpit
		1639	Beeston's Boys	Cockpit

The Maid's Tragedy	Beaumont and Fletcher	1610	King's	Blackfriars
A Maidenhead Well Lost	Heywood	1625–34	Queen Henrietta's	Cockpit
The Malcontent	Marston	1603	Blackfriars Children	Blackfriars
			King's	Globe
The Martyred Soldier	Shirley	1627–35	Queen Henrietta's	Cockpit
A Match at Midnight	Rowley	1621–3	Red Bull Company	Red Bull
Match Me in London	Dekker	1621?	Red Bull Company	Red Bull
		c. 1630	Queen Henrietta's	Cockpit
May-Day	Chapman	1601–2?	Blackfriars Children	Blackfriars
Measure for Measure	Shakespeare	1603	King's	Globe
The Merchant of Venice	Shakespeare	1596?	Chamberlain's	Theatre
The Merry Devil of Edmonton	Anon	*c.* 1602	Chamberlain's	Globe
The Merry Wives of Windsor	Shakespeare	1597?	Chamberlain's	Theatre? / Globe / Blackfriars
Messallina	Richards	1634–6	King's Revels	Salisbury Court
Michaelmas Term	Middleton	1605	Paul's Children	Paul's
Microcosmus	Nabbes	1637	Queen Henrietta's	Salisbury Court
Midas	Lyly	1589	Paul's Children	Paul's
A Midsummer Night's Dream	Shakespeare	1595	Chamberlain's	Theatre
The Miseries of Enforced Marriage	Wilkins	1606	King's	Globe
Monsieur D'Olive	Chapman	1605	Blackfriars Children	Blackfriars
Monsieur Thomas	Fletcher	1612–15	King's	Blackfriars
Mother Bombie	Lyly	*c.* 1589	Paul's Children	Paul's
Much Ado About Nothing	Shakespeare	1598	Chamberlain's	Curtain? / Globe / Blackfriars
The Muses' Looking Glass	Randolph	1630	King's Revels	Salisbury Court
The New Inn	Jonson	1629	King's	Blackfriars? Globe?
A New Way to Pay Old Debts	Massinger	1625	Prince Charles's	Cockpit
		c. 1633	Queen Henrietta's	Cockpit
		1639	Beeston's Boys	Cockpit
News from Plymouth	Davenant	1635	King's	Globe? Blackfriars?
No Wit, No Help like a Woman's	Middleton	1612	Prince's	Fortune
The Noble Stranger	Sharpe	1638–40	Queen Henrietta's	Salisbury Court
The Northern Lass	Brome	1629	King's	Globe / Blackfriars

Northward Ho!	Dekker and Webster	1605	Paul's Children	Paul's
The Novella	Brome	1632–3	King's	Blackfriars
1 Sir John Oldcastle	Drayton, Hathway, Munday and Wilson	1599 1602	Admiral's Worcester's	Rose Rose
Old Fortunatus	Dekker	1599	Admiral's	Rose
The Opportunity	Shirley	1634	Queen Henrietta's	Cockpit
Orlando Furioso	Greene	*c.* 1591	Queen's Admiral's	Rose? Rose
Osmond, the Great Turk	Carlell	1622	King's	Globe? Blackfriars?
Othello	Shakespeare	1603–4	King's	Globe / Blackfriars
1 and *2 The Passionate Lovers*	Carlell	1638	King's	Blackfriars
Patient Grissil	Chettle, Dekker and Haughton	1600	Admiral's	Fortune
Pericles	Shakespeare	1607	King's	Globe
Perkin Warbeck	Ford	1632	Queen Henrietta's	Cockpit
Philaster	Beaumont and Fletcher	1609	King's	Globe / Blackfriars
Philotas	Daniel	1604	Blackfriars Children	Blackfriars
The Phoenix	Middleton	1603	Paul's Children	Paul's
The Picture	Massinger	1629	King's	Globe / Blackfriars
The Pilgrim	Fletcher	1621?	King's	Blackfriars
The Platonic Lovers	Davenant	1635	King's	Blackfriars
Poetaster	Jonson	1601	Blackfriars Children	Blackfriars
The Poor Man's Comfort	Daborne	1610–17	Queen Anne's	Red Bull
The Prisoners	Killigrew	1632–5	Queen Henrietta's	Cockpit
The Prophetess	Fletcher (and Massinger?)	1622	King's	Blackfriars
The Puritan	Middleton	1607	Paul's Children	Paul's
The Queen and Concubine	Brome	1635–9	King's Revels	Salisbury Court
The Queen of Corinth	Fletcher (and Massinger and Field?)	1616–18	King's	Blackfriars? Globe?
Ram-Alley	Barry	1608	King's Revels Children	Whitefriars
The Rape of Lucrece	Heywood	*c.* 1608 1628 1639	Queen Anne's Queen Henrietta's Beeston's Boys	Red Bull Cockpit Cockpit
The Rebellion	Rawlins	1629–39	King's Revels	Salisbury Court

The Renegado	Massinger	1624	Lady Elizabeth's	Cockpit
		1630	Queen Henrietta's	Cockpit
		1639	Beeston's Boys	Cockpit
The Revenge of Bussy	Chapman	*c.* 1610	Blackfriars Children?	Whitefriars?
The Revenger's Tragedy	Middleton	1606–7	King's	Globe
Richard II	Shakespeare	1595	Chamberlain's	Theatre? / Globe
Richard III	Shakespeare	1593?	Pembroke's	Theatre?
		1594	Chamberlain's	Theatre? / Globe
The Roaring Girl	Dekker and Middleton	1611	Prince's	Fortune
The Roman Actor	Massinger	1626	King's	Blackfriars
Romeo and Juliet	Shakespeare	1594?	Chamberlain's	Theatre? / Curtain / Globe
The Royal King and The Loyal Subject	Heywood	1602	Worcester's	Curtain
Rule a Wife and Have a Wife	Fletcher	1624	King's	Blackfriars? Globe?
Sappho and Phao	Lyly	1583	Chapel / Paul's Children	first Blackfriars
Satiromastix	Dekker	1601	Paul's Children Chamberlain's	Paul's / Globe
The Sea Voyage	Fletcher (and Massinger?)	1622	King's	Globe? (Blackfriars?)
Sejanus	Jonson	1603	King's	Globe
The Shepherd's Holiday	Rutter	1633–5	Queen Henrietta's	Cockpit
The Shoemaker's Holiday	Dekker	1599	Admiral's	Rose
The Silver Age	Heywood	1610–12	Queen Anne's	Red Bull
The Sisters	Shirley	1642	King's	Blackfriars
Sophonisba (*Wonder of Women*)	Marston	1605	Blackfriars Children	Blackfriars
The Sophy	Denham	1641	King's	Blackfriars
The Spanish Curate	Fletcher (and Massinger?)	1622	King's	Blackfriars
The Spanish Gypsy	Dekker, Ford, Middleton and Rowley	1623	Lady Elizabeth's	Cockpit
		1639	Beeston's Boys	Cockpit
The Spanish Tragedy	Kyd	*c.* 1587		
		1592–3	Strange's	Rose
		1597–1601	Admiral's	Fortune
The Sparagus Garden	Brome	1635	King's Revels	Salisbury Court
The Staple of News	Jonson	1626	King's	Blackfriars
Captain Thomas Stukeley	Anon	1596	Admiral's	Rose
Swetnam the Woman Hater	Anon	1617–18	Queen Anne's	Red Bull

Play	Author	Date	Company	Playhouse
The Swisser	A. Wilson	1631	King's	Blackfriars
The Tale of a Tub	Jonson	1633	Queen Henrietta's	Cockpit
1 and 2 Tamburlaine	Marlowe	1587–8	Admiral's Prince's Palsgrave's	Theatre / Rose / Fortune
The Taming of the Shrew	Shakespeare	1593?	Chamberlain's	Theatre? / Globe / Blackfriars
The Tempest	Shakespeare	1610	King's	Blackfriars
Thierry and Theodoret	Fletcher	1613–21	King's	Blackfriars
Thomas Lord Cromwell	Anon	1601	Chamberlain's	Globe
The Three Ladies of London	R. Wilson	1581	Leicester's	Theatre?
The Three Lords and Three Ladies of London	R. Wilson	1588	Queen's?	
'Tis Pity She's a Whore	Ford	1630? 1639	Queen Henrietta's Beeston's Boys	Cockpit Cockpit
Titus Andronicus	Shakespeare	1591?	Strange's / Pembroke's / Sussex's / Chamberlain's	Rose / Theatre / Rose Globe
The Traitor	Shirley	1631	Queen Henrietta's	Cockpit
The Travels of the Three English Brothers	Day, Rowley and Wilkins	1607	Queen Anne's	Red Bull
A Trick to Catch the Old One	Middleton	1605–6	Paul's Children	Paul's
Troilus and Cressida	Shakespeare	1602	Chamberlain's	Globe
The Turk	Mason	1607	King's Revels Children	Whitefriars
Twelfth Night	Shakespeare	1600	Chamberlain's	Globe
1 Two Angry Women of Abingdon	Porter	c. 1597?	Admiral's	Rose
The Two Maids of Moreclacke	Armin	1606–8	King's Revels Children	Whitefriars
The Two Merry Milkmaids	J.C.	1619–20	Red Bull Company	Red Bull
The Two Noble Kinsmen	Fletcher and Shakespeare	1613?	King's	Blackfriars
The Two Noble Ladies	Anon	1619–23	Red Bull Company	Red Bull
The Unfortunate Lovers	Davenant	1638	King's	Blackfriars
The Unnatural Combat	Massinger	1624–5	King's	Globe
Valentinian	Fletcher	1610–14	King's	Globe? Blackfriars?
The Variety	Cavendish	1641–2(?)	King's	Blackfriars

The Virgin Martyr	Dekker and Massinger	1620	Red Bull Company	Red Bull
Volpone	Jonson	1605	King's	Globe
		1635	King's	Blackfriars
A Warning for Fair Women	Anon	1597	Chamberlain's	Theatre? Curtain?
The Wars of Cyrus	Anon	1576–80	Chapel Children	first Blackfriars
The Wedding	Shirley	1626–9	Queen Henrietta's	Cockpit
		1639	Beeston's Boys	Cockpit
Westward Ho!	Dekker and Webster	1604	Paul's Children	Paul's
What You Will	Marston	1601	Paul's Children	Paul's
When You See Me, You Know Me	Rowley, S.	1604.	Prince's	Fortune
The White Devil	Webster	1612	Queen Anne's	Red Bull
		c. 1630	Queen Henrietta's	Cockpit
The Whore of Babylon	Dekker	1606	Prince's	Fortune
The Widow	Middleton	1615?	King's	Blackfriars
The Widow's Tears	Chapman	*c.* 1605	Blackfriars Children	Blackfriars
A Wife for a Month	Fletcher	1624	King's	Blackfriars? Globe?
The Wild Goose Chase	Fletcher	1621?	King's	Blackfriars
The Winter's Tale	Shakespeare	*c.* 1610	King's	Globe / Blackfriars?
The Wisdom of Doctor Dodypoll	Anon	1599	Paul's Children	Paul's
Wit at Several Weapons	Middleton and Rowley	1613	Prince Charles's	Curtain?
Wit in a Constable	Glapthorne	1636–8 (revised 1639)	Beeston's Boys	Cockpit
The Witch	Middleton	1616	King's	Blackfriars
The Witch of Edmonton	Dekker, Ford and Rowley	1621	Prince Charles's	Cockpit
The Wits	Davenant	1634	King's	Blackfriars
The Witty Fair One	Shirley	1628	Queen Henrietta's	Cockpit
The Woman Hater	Beaumont	*c.* 1606	Paul's Children	Paul's
A Woman is a Weathercock	Field	1609?	Blackfriars Children	Whitefriars
A Woman Killed with Kindness	Heywood	1603	Worcester's	Rose
The Woman's Prize	Fletcher	1610	King's	Globe? Blackfriars?
The Wounds of Civil War	Lodge	*c.* 1588	Admiral's	Theatre / Rose?
The Yorkshire Tragedy	Middleton (?)	*c.* 1606	King's	Globe
The Young Admiral	Shirley	1633	Queen Henrietta's	Cockpit
		1639	Beeston's Boys	Cockpit
Your Five Gallants	Middleton	1607	Blackfriars Children	Blackfriars

Notes

The following abbreviations have been used in the Notes and the Bibliography.

Bawcutt	Bawcutt, N. W., *The Control and Censorship of Caroline Drama. The Records of Sir Henry Herbert, Master of the Revels 1623–73* (Oxford, 1996).
C. S. P.	*Calendar of State Papers.*
Dramatic Documents	W. W. Greg (ed.), *Dramatic Documents from the Elizabethan Playhouses* (2 vols., Oxford, 1931).
EES	Glynne Wickham, *Early English Stages 1300–1660* (3 vols.; Vol. I, London, 1959; Vol. II, part 1 1963; Vol. II, part 2 1972; Vol. III, 1981).
ELR	*English Literary Renaissance.*
ES	E. K. Chambers, *The Elizabethan Stage* (4 vols., Oxford, 1923).
ET	*The Elizabethan Theatre.*
Henslowe's Diary	R. A. Foakes and R. T. Rickert (eds.), *Henslowe's Diary* (Cambridge 1961).
Henslowe Papers	W. W. Greg (ed.) *The Henslowe Papers* (London 1907).
Herbert	J. Q. Adams (ed.), *The Dramatic Records of Sir Henry Herbert* (New Haven 1917).
HLQ	*Huntington Library Quarterly.*
JCS	G. E. Bentley, *The Jacobean and Caroline Stage* (7 vols., Oxford 1941–68).
JEGP	*Journal of English and Germanic Philology.*
MLN	*Modern Language Notes.*
MLR	*Modern Language Review.*
MP	*Modern Philology.*
MRDE	*Medieval and Renaissance Drama in England.*
NQ	*Notes and Queries.*
Nungezer	E. Nungezer, *A Dictionary of Actors and of Other Persons Associated with the Public Representation of Plays in England before 1642* (New Haven 1929).
PMLA	*Publications of the Modern Language Association of America.*

RD	*Renaissance Drama.*
RORD	*Research Opportunities in Renaissance Drama.*
RES	*Review of English Studies.*
Revels History	J. Leeds Barroll, Alexander Leggatt, Richard Hosley and Alvin Kernan, *The Revels History of Drama in English*, Vol. III: *1576–1613* (London, 1975); and Philip Edwards, Gerald Eades Bentley, Kathleen McLuskie & Lois Potter, Vol. IV: *1613–1660* (London, 1981).
SB	*Studies in Bibliography.*
SEL	*Studies in English Literature.*
ShAB	*Shakespeare Association Bulletin.*
ShS	*Shakespeare Survey.*
ShStud	*Shakespeare Studies.*
SP	*Studies in Philology.*
SQ	*Shakespeare Quarterly.*
ThS	*Theatre Survey.*
TN	*Theatre Notebook.*
TR	*Theatre Research.*
TRI	*Theatre Research International.*
WS	E. K. Chambers, *William Shakespeare* (2 vols., Oxford 1930).

Besides the editions abbreviated as *Henslowe's Diary* and *Henslowe Papers*, R. A. Foakes has edited a facsimile version of all the papers in two volumes (London, 1978). Vol. I reproduces the *Diary* and Vol. II the *Papers*. Texts quoted from either transcription have been checked against the facsimiles. References to plays of Shakespeare are to the New Cambridge editions. References to the *Works* of Jonson are to the edition of C. H. Herford and P. and E. Simpson (11 vols., Oxford, 1925–52). References to Massinger are to *The Plays and Poems of Philip Massinger*, eds. Philip Edwards and Colin Gibson (5 vols., Oxford, 1976). References to Middleton are to *The Collected Works*, gen. ed. Gary Taylor and John Lavagnino (Oxford, 2007). Other specific play editions are cited in the notes.

CHAPTER 1: INTRODUCTION (pp. 1–37)

Several general works have dealt in recent years with the background to the period, for instance Peter Thomson's *Shakespeare's Theatre* and the more specific *Shakespeare's Professional Career*, and Martin White's *Renaissance Drama in Action*. Various *Companions* have appeared, to Shakespeare in particular and to the drama at large, with assemblies of essays on aspects of the subject, and several collections of specialised papers, the best of which is *A New History of Early English Drama* edited by John D. Cox and David Scott Kastan. Historians of London have amplified in gritty detail the story of the city for which most of this drama was created. Studies of the economics of the playmaking business through the period by writers such as Douglas Bruster and Theodore Leinwand have stimulated study (and controversy). While more and more of the evidence accumulated by Chambers in *The Elizabethan*

Stage's four volumes and the seven of G. E. Bentley's *Jacobean and Caroline Stage* has been superseded by new information, their reliability as transcribers is still unmatched. Much of the most relevant archive material has been retranscribed (in modernised spelling) along with incisive essays on the various periods of study in a large volume, *English Professional Theatre 1530–1660*, by Glynne Wickham, Herbert Berry and William Ingram. Essays and books throwing light on particular aspects of the theatrical enterprise up to 1642 are listed in the Select Bibliography, where there is a fairly comprehensive selection of the more useful publications.

1. See George F. Reynolds, 'Hamlet at the Globe', *ShS* 9 (1956), 50.
2. This point is dealt with more extensively in Gurr, 'Headgear as a Paralinguistic Signifier in *King Lear*', *ShS* 55 (2002), 43–52.
3. M. W. Perkins, *The Works of that famous and worthie minister of Christ, in the universitie of Cambridge*, Cambridge, 1603, p. 120.
4. *The Letters and Epigrams of Sir John Harington*, ed. Norman Egbert McClure, Philadelphia, 1930, pp. 41–2.
5. *Dudley Carleton to John Chamberlain 1603–1624. Jacobean Letters*, ed. Maurice Lee Jr, Rutgers, New Brunswick, 1972, p. 51.
6. With one small change, I use Ernest Schanzer's translation here. See 'Thomas Platter's Observations on the Elizabethan Stage', *NQ* 201 (1956), 465–67.
7. For an account of the uses of the *locus* and *platea*, see Chapter 5, and especially Robert Weimann, *Author's Pen and Actor's Voice: Playing and Writing in Shakespeare's Theatre*, Cambridge, 2000, Chapter 7.
8. Stephen Greenblatt, *Shakespearean Negotiations: The Circulation of Social Energy in Renaissance England*, Berkeley, 1988, p. 119.
9. See Mark C. Pilkinton, 'The Playhouse in Wine Street, Bristol', *TN* 37 (1983), 14–21.
10. In the original Shakespeare company John Heminges, born in Droitwich, and William Shakespeare, born in Stratford, were the only non-Londoners.
11. *ES* IV, 269.
12. *JCS* VI, 49–50.
13. *ES* IV, 273–4.
14. *JCS* VI, 29.
15. *Shakespeare's Europe: A Survey of the Condition of Europe at the End of the 16th Century, Being Unpublished Chapters of Fynes Moryson's Itinerary (1617)*, ed. Charles Hughes, 2nd edn, New York, 1967, p. 476.
16. *Henslowe Papers*, p. 106. A facsimile is printed in R. A. Foakes (ed.) *The Henslowe Papers*, London, 1978, II.2.41.
17. John Burnett, *A History of the Cost of Living*, London, 1969, p. 71.
18. L. C. Knights, *Drama and Society in the Age of Jonson*, London, 1937, p. 174.
19. See Laurence Stone, *The Crisis of the Aristocracy 1558–1641*, Oxford, 1964, pp. 386–403.
20. *JCS* VI, 54.
21. This question is discussed more fully in Gurr, *Playgoing in Shakespeare's London*, 3rd edn, Cambridge, 2004, pp. 176–84.
22. See C. C. Mish, 'Comparative Popularity of Early Fiction and Drama', *NQ* 197 (1952), 269–70.

23. Michael Neill, '"Wits most accomplished Senate": The Audience of the Caroline Private Theatres', *SEL* 18 (1978), 359.
24. Alfred Harbage's *Shakespeare and the Rival Traditions*, New York, 1952, analyses the differences between hall and amphitheatre plays, though he overstates his case about the different audiences. See R. Ornstein, *The Moral Vision of Jacobean Tragedy*, Madison, 1962, p. 12, and Gurr, *Playgoing in Shakespeare's London*, pp. 170–76.
25. *ES* IV, 332.
26. Valerie Pearl, *London and the Outbreak of the Puritan Revolution*, London 1961, p. 41.
27. *JCS* IV, 555.
28. G. E. Bentley, *The Profession of Dramatist in Shakespeare's Time, 1590–1642*, Princeton, 1971, p. 30.
29. Ann Haaker, 'The Plague, the Theater and the Poet', *RD* n.s. 1 (1968), 283–306. See also Eleanor Collins, 'Richard Brome's Contract and the Relationship of Dramatist to Company in the Early Modern Period', *Early Theatre* 10 (2007), 116–28.
30. Bentley, *The Profession of Dramatist*, p. 131.
31. Ibid., p. 270.
32. The idea that Shakespeare sought publication of his plays, or at least that the printed texts were designed for reading rather than staging, has been promoted by Lukas Erne, *Shakespeare as a Literary Dramatist*, Cambridge, 2003. Given the often theatrical nature of the printed texts and the fact that half never got into print in their author's lifetime, I think this unlikely.
33. Richard Hosley, *Revels History*, p. 207. Hosley's view of the use of hall screens for acting has been challenged on the grounds that student players at Cambridge colleges did not use them.
34. The two traditions have been studied separately. Glynne Wickham (*EES*) emphasises Court influence on staging, while Robert Weimann (*Shakespeare and the Popular Tradition in the Theater*, ed. and trans. Robert Schwartz, London and Baltimore, 1978) emphasises the transfer of popular traditions into the London theatres.
35. Jonson, *Works*, VII, 735.
36. M. C. Bradbrook, 'Shakespeare and the Multiple Theatres of Jacobean London', *ET* 6 (1978), 94.
37. James P. Bednarz has an entertaining and fairly scrupulous if inevitably conjectural account of the contest in *Shakespeare and the Poets' War*, New York, 2001.
38. See Jonson, *Works*, I, 24–31, and David Bevington, *Tudor Drama and Politics*, Cambridge, Mass., 1968, pp. 262–88.
39. Marie Axton, *The Queen's Two Bodies*, London, 1978, makes a strong case for the Inns-of-Court lawyers using their entertainments as opportunities for political comment in allegorical form. The concept of allegorising, or the 'application' of fictional or historical instances to contemporary events, Jonson declared in the dedication to *Volpone* in 1607 had by then 'grown a trade'.

CHAPTER 2: THE COMPANIES (pp. 38–99)

Several studies of companies have appeared in the last few years, although the only general one is Gurr's *The Shakespearian Playing Companies*. Scott McMillin and Sally-Beth MacLean have produced a strikingly thorough study of the first company to get royal patronage, *The Queen's Men and their Plays*. Lucy Munro has a study of the Blackfriars boy company and Mary Bly has one on the Whitefriars company of 'youths' of 1609–10. Gurr has also written books about the Shakespeare company and its peer the Admiral's. The Foakes and Rickert edition of *Henslowe's Diary* has been reissued, and facsimiles of the Henslowe papers have appeared too. Much has been done to explain the process of Revels Office censorship in books by Bawcutt, Clare, Clegg, Dutton and others. Above all, the records of each playing company are slowly being augmented and clarified by listing the entries about them in various archives that survive for towns and villages in England's many counties, including now London and Westminster, as well as Scotland, Wales and Ireland. These appear in immaculate formulations in the many volumes of Toronto's *Records of Early English Drama*.

1. *ES* IV, 270.
2. *ES* IV, 324 and 337.
3. See note on playhouse origins, Chapter 4.
4. *ES* II, 86.
5. *ES* II, 87–8.
6. See Janet S. Leongard, 'An Elizabethan Lawsuit: John Brayne, His Carpenter, and the Building of the Red Lion Theatre', *SQ* 35 (1984), 298–310. For a comprehensive survey of early playhouse building, see John Orrell, *The Human Stage: English Theatre Design 1567–1640*, Cambridge, 1988.
7. *ES* IV, 200.
8. *ES* II, 462.
9. *ES* II, 104–5.
10. *ES* IV, 302.
11. *ES* IV, 202.
12. See Michael Shapiro, *Children of the Revels. The Boy Companies of Shakespeare's Time and their Plays*, New York, 1977, pp. 10–29.
13. *ES* II, 36.
14. *Dramatic Documents*, p. 19. The attribution has been contested, but see Gurr, 'The Work of Elizabethan Plotters and *2 Seven Deadly Sins*', *Early Theatre* 10 (2007), 67–88.
15. *ES* II, 123.
16. *Dramatic Documents*, p. 12.
17. *WS* I, 42.
18. For a more detailed account of the changes, see p. 156, and John Orrell and Andrew Gurr, 'What the Rose Can Tell Us', *Times Literary Supplement* 9 (15 June 1989), 636, 649; reprinted with additions in *Antiquity* 63 (1989), 421–9.
19. *Playhouse Wills, 1558–1642*, eds. E. A. J. Honigmann and Susan Brock, Manchester, 1993, pp. 58–60.

20. *Dramatic Documents*, p. 47.

21. See above, note 17.

22. See for instance Scott McMillin, 'Casting for Pembroke's Men: The Henry VI Quartos and *The Taming of A Shrew*', *SQ* 23 (1972), 141–59; G. M. Pinciss, 'Shakespeare, Her Majesty's Players, and Pembroke's Men', *ShS* 27 (1974), 129–36; David George, 'Shakespeare and Pembroke's Men', *SQ* 32 (1981), 305–23; and Karl P. Wentersdorf, 'The Origin and Personnel of the Pembroke Company', *TRI* 5 (1979), 45–68. The case for Shakespeare having belonged either to the Queen's Men or Pembroke's seems evenly divided.

23. *ES* IV, 311–12.

24. The only comprehensive study of the players' travels is John Tucker Murray's erratic *English Dramatic Companies 1558–1642*, 2 vols., London, 1910. His work is now being thoroughly corrected and supplemented by the many volumes in the *Records of Early English Drama* series.

25. The appearance of players' names in playtexts does not necessarily mean that they were members of the company for whom the play was originally written. Generally the minor rather than the principal players were named in playscripts, along with any changes made later. Will Kemp must have been added to the Second Quarto text of *Romeo and Juliet*, for instance. He was in Strange's before the middle of 1594 while the play was being performed by Pembroke's to judge from the echoes of it that appear in the Pembroke play texts. See Pinciss, 'Shakespeare, Her Majesty's Players, and Pembroke's Men', pp. 135–6.

26. Possibly their '*harey the vj*' staged in 1594 was Shakespeare's *1 Henry VI*.

27. In October 1594 the Chamberlain's Men are recorded as asking for leave to play at the Cross Keys Inn in Gracechurch Street in the City. They must have wanted it as a winter house to supplement their outdoor Theatre. See Gurr, 'Henry Carey's Peculiar Letter', *SQ* 56 (2005), 51–75.

28. See William Ingram, 'The Closing of the Theaters in 1597: A Dissenting View', *MP* 69 (1971–2), 105–15.

29. *ES* II, 152.

30. But see *Henslowe's Diary*, p. xxxix, and Neil Carson, *A Companion to Henslowe's Diary*, Cambridge, 1988, pp. 34–9.

31. *ES* II, 158.

32. T. W. Baldwin, *Organisation and Personnel of the Shakespearean Company*, Princeton, 1927, p. 52.

33. See Gurr, 'Money or Audiences: The Impact of Shakespeare's Globe', *TN* 42 (1988), 3–14.

34. Theodore B. Leinwand, in an 'Afterword' to *Theatre, Finance and Society in Early Modern England*, Cambridge, 1999, pp. 140–2, identifies a number of possible factors besides nostalgia as the company's reasons for setting up two playhouses for the one company in 1608 and renewing the deal in 1614 at considerable cost to themselves.

35. *ES* II, 173.

36. *ES* II, 225.

37. *ES* II, 231.

38. Shapiro, *Children of the Revels*, p. 21. See also Lucy Munro, *Children of the Queen's Revels: A Jacobean Theatre Repertory*, Cambridge, 2005.

39. Reavley Gair, *The Children of Paul's: The Story of a Theatre Company, 1553–1608*, Cambridge, 1982, pp. 118–27.

40. *ES* II, 44, 52.

41. In a letter by Sir Thomas Edmondes, in *Court and Times of James I*, ed. Thomas Birch, 2 vols., London, 1848, I, 60–1.

42. Mark Eccles, 'Martin Peerson and the Blackfriars', *ShS* 11 (1958), 101.

43. Richard Dutton, *Licensing, Censorship and Authorship in Early Modern England*, Basingstoke, 2000, p. 10, makes some pointed comments on the licensing of the boy companies.

44. See *Byron*, ed. John Margeson, Manchester, 1988, p. 276.

45. *ES* II, 258.

46. A concise account of the war is given in Jonson, *Works*, I, chapter on *Poetaster*. A more adventurous version is in James P. Bednarz, *Shakespeare and the Poets' War*, New York, 2001.

47. *JCS* I, 151. The loss of their playbooks and apparel in the fire was the first of a series of disasters that eclipsed them by 1625.

48. C. J. Sisson, 'Notes on Early Stuart Stage History', *MLR* 37 (1942), 34. Sisson gives the records of the Red Bull litigation on pp. 30–6. They are also summarised in *ES* II, 236–40.

49. *ES* II, 238.

50. See Gurr, 'Intertextuality in Henslowe', *SQ* 39 (1988), 394–8.

51. Neil Carson's examination of Henslowe's dealings with his playing companies gives the best detail. See *A Companion to Henslowe's Diary*, Chap. 2.

52. *Herbert*, p. 65.

53. *JCS* I, 201.

54. *JCS* I, 4–5.

55. *JCS* I, 328.

56. Bawcutt, p. 201.

57. *JCS* II, 684.

58. *JCS* I, 234.

59. G. E. Bentley, 'The Salisbury Court Theater and Its Boy Players', *HLQ* 49 (1977), 137.

60. Ibid., p. 143.

61. Ibid., p. 141.

62. *Herbert*, p. 67.

63. *JCS* I, 332–3. See also Martin Butler, *Theatre and Crisis 1632–1642*, Cambridge, 1984, Chap. 5.

64. See Arthur H. Nethercot, *Sir William Davenant*, New York, 1938, rev. edn 1967, Chap. 11.

65. *JCS* VI, 104–5.

66. Sisson, 'Early Stuart Stage History', 33.

67. *ES* I, 352; *JCS* I, 43,

68. *ES* II, 256–7.

69. *ES* I, 356n.
70. *ES* I, 372.
71. Burnett, *Cost of Living*, p. 71.
72. Irwin Smith, *Shakespeare's Blackfriars Playhouse*, New York, 1964, p 265; *JCS* I, 32–3.
73. *ES* I, 369.
74. Sisson, 'Early Stuart Stage History', 33.
75. *JCS* VI, 243.
76. *ES* I, 373 and note; Bentley, *The Profession of Dramatist*, p. 131.
77. *ES* I, 71.
78. See *ES* IV, 263.
79. *Herbert*, pp. 5–6.
80. W. R. Streitberger (ed.), *Jacobean and Caroline Revels Accounts 1603–1642*, Oxford, 1986, pp. x, xviii.
81. Ibid., p. 78.
82. *JCS* I, 178.
83. *Herbert*, pp. 44–5.
84. *ES* IV, 263.
85. *ES* IV, 338–9.
86. Bawcutt, p. 186.
87. Ibid., pp. 142, 148, 177.
88. Ibid., pp. 203–4.
89. *ES* IV, 267.
90. Leeds Barroll has appendices in *Politics, Plague, and Shakespeare's Theater: The Stuart Years*, Ithaca, 1991, on the effects both of plague and of Lenten closures. I find his account of the plague closures to be exaggerated, but the material about Lent is wholly reliable.
91. G. E. Bentley, 'Lenten Performances in the Jacobean and Caroline Theaters', in *Essays on Shakespeare and Elizabethan Drama*, ed. R. Hosley, New York, 1963, pp. 351–60; and J. Leeds Barroll, 'The Chronology of Shakespeare's Jacobean Plays and the Dating of *Antony and Cleopatra*', in *Essays on Shakespeare*, ed. Gordon Ross Brown, Philadelphia, 1965, pp. 122–4.
92. *JCS* II, 690.
93. *Salisbury Manuscripts*, Historical Manuscripts Commission, London, 1933, XVI.339. It reports Say and Sele claiming 'All interludes and common play-houses are as unnecessary [as tobacco], and yield no penny to the King: although for every comer in, 3d, 6d, or 9d before they come to the best places: if the King may not have 1d for every comer in, he thinks the players worse worthy of the rest.' These prices seem to fit equally the indoor playhouses or the best places at the outdoor.

CHAPTER 3: THE PLAYERS (pp. 100–38)

The best general account of Elizabethan players is still M. C. Bradbrook's *The Rise of the Common Player*. Nungezer's work on the lives of individual players has been augmented and corrected chiefly by Mark Eccles in a series of articles. David Kathman has worked on the system whereby senior sharers who happen to be freemen of the City such as John Heminges of the Chamberlain's Men enlisted youths to work in the playing companies. Numbers of boys were formally apprenticed in this way, although the law for London specified seventeen as the youngest that could be contracted in this way, an age when most boys' voices would have broken, so that they could not take the women's parts. Michael Shapiro supplements work on the boy company actors in Chap. 1 of *Children of the Revels*. A valuable indication of the status of the different companies at Court is in John H. Astington, *English Court Theatre, 1558–1642*, Cambridge, 1999.

1. The social origins of some players are described in detail by M. C. Bradbrook, *The Rise of the Common Player* London, 1962.
2. J. Stephens, *Essayes and Characters* (1615), V6–X1. Cocke revised his essay for the second edition of Stephens's collection, which was also printed in 1615. See *ES* IV, 255–7.
3. J. Overbury, *New Characters* (1615), M5v–M6v. See *ES* IV, 258–9.
4. The Dulwich Gallery has a painting allegedly done by Burbage. See Nungezer, p. 77.
5. Bradbrook, *Rise of the Common Player*, p. 203.
6. Alexandra Mason, 'The Social Status of Theatrical People', *SQ* 18 (1967) 429–30.
7. Nungezer, p. 73.
8. *ES* IV, 319–20.
9. Nungezer, p. 219.
10. Ibid., pp. 347–54.
11. Ibid., p. 360.
12. Ibid., p. 363.
13. *Thalia's Banquet* (1620), quoted in ibid., pp. 362–1.
14. Quoted in ibid., pp. 356–7.
15. A reference to Wilson by Thomas Lodge in his *Defence of Poetry, Musick, and Stage Plays* (1580) has been taken as a compliment to his learning.
16. David Wiles, *Shakespeare's Clown: Actor and Text in the Elizabethan Playhouse*, Cambridge, 1987, argues that Kemp played Falstaff. See also R. C. Bald, 'Will, My Lord of Leicester's Jesting Player', *NQ* 204 (1959), 112; and J. A. Bryant Jr, 'Shakespeare's Falstaff and the Mantle of Dick Tarlton', *SP* 51 (1954), 149–62.
17. H. D. Gray, 'The Roles of William Kemp', *MLR* 25 (1930), 261–73.
18. C. S. Felver, *Robert Armin, Shakespeare's Fool*, Kent State University Bulletin Research Series 5, Kent, 1961.
19. Nungezer, p. 8.
20. Bradbrook, *Rise of the Common Player*, p. 196.
21. Nungezer, p. 6.
22. Nungezer, p. 11. The most up-to-date information about Burbage is collected in Mark Eccles 'Elizabethan Actors i: A–D', *NQ* 236 (1991), 38–49. See especially p. 43.
23. Nungezer, pp. 67–8.
24. See above p. 55.
25. Nungezer, p. 70.

26. Ibid., pp. 140–1.
27. Ibid., p. 140.
28. *JCS* II, 401.
29. *JCS* II, 541.
30. See J. B. Streett, 'The Durability of Boy Actors', *NQ* 218 (1973), 461–5. David Kathman has accumulated a mass of evidence for players like John Heminges who were freemen of one of the great London livery companies taking up youths as apprentices to be players. One of the youths they apprenticed, Thomas Belte, who is named as a boy in the 'plot' of 2 *Seven Deadly Sins* (1591–2) when he was twelve, was not apprenticed to Heminges until 1595, when he was sixteen and a half. See Laurence Manley, 'Thomas Belte, Elizabethan Boy Actor', *NQ* 252 (2007), 310–13.
31. Nungezer, p. 68.
32. Bradbrook, *Rise of the Common Player*, p. 238; and see Shapiro, *Children of the Revels*, p. 4.
33. See B. L. Joseph, *Elizabethan Acting* (London, 1951; rev. edn 1964), and Gurr, 'Elizabethan Action', *SP* 63 (1966), 144–56.
34. For an indication of the pressure put on the boy-company managers to prove their respectability by maintaining the educational and chorister functions, see Bradbrook, *Rise of the Common Player*, p. 238.
35. Compare Shakespeare's Latin in the Folio texts of 2 and 3 *Henry VI* with the versions as transcribed in the Quarto and Octavo texts.
36. Bradbrook, *Rise of the Common Player*, p. 205.
37. We cannot understand the following passage in Chapman's *Gentleman Usher* (1601) unless we have some idea of the niceties of academic theory and the theoretical need for the orator to stir up in himself the actual passion he is to convey. Sarpego, a 'fustian lord', first ventures to display his talents:

> when I in Padua schoolde it,
> I plaid in one of *Plautus* Comedies,
> Namely *Curculo*, where his part I acted,
> Projecting from the poore summe of foure lines,
> Forty faire actions ....
> *Alp.* How like you Lords, this stirring action?
> *Stro.* In a cold morning it were good my Lord ....
> *Med.* My Lord, away with these scholastique wits,
> Lay the invention of your speech on me,
> And the performance too; ile play my parte,
> That you shall say, Nature yeelds more than Art.
> *Alp.* Bee't so resolv'd; unartificiall truth
> An unfaind passion can decipher best.

38. Gurr, 'Elizabethan Action', p. 144.
39. The important development is the noun, which signals a new concept of character-impersonation. There is a reference to 'personated' devils in 1594, but Marston seems to have neologised 'personation'.

40. The following passage, in the anonymous play *Nero* of 1623, is typical in its terminology:

> *Nero.* Come, Sirs, I faith, how did you like my acting?
> What? wast not as you lookt for?
> *Epaph.* Yes my Lord, and much beyond.
> *Nero.* Did I not doe it to the life?
> *Epaph.* The very doing never was so lively
> As now this counterfeyting.

41. BM. MS. Sloane 3709, fol. 8r.
42. See also Joseph, *Elizabethan Acting*, pp. 47–71.
43. See M. C. Bradbrook, *Themes and Conventions in Elizabethan Tragedy*, Cambridge, 1936.
44. See Lawrence Babb, 'Sorrow and Love on the Elizabethan Stage', *ShAB* 18 (1943), 140.
45. Richard Brome, *The Antipodes* (1638), 2.2, describing what in 1638 was thought of as antiquated.
46. S. L. Bethell, *Shakespeare and the Popular Dramatic Tradition*, London, 1944, pp. 87–9.
47. Bernard Beckerman, *Shakespeare at the Globe 1599–1609*, New York, 1962, p. 130.
48. The event is reported in detail by Bawcutt.
49. A modern edition of Puttenham's *Arte of English Poesie* is (eds.) Gladys Doidge Willcock and Alice Walker, Cambridge, 1936. David Crystal, in '*Think on my Words.' Exploring Shakespeare's Language*, Cambridge, 2008, despite quoting Puttenham several times, ignores this statement and claims that early modern England had nothing like a received pronunciation (p. 127). I think that Puttenham's point about using 'goode Southerne' argues strongly for a concept of rp.
50. Baldwin, *Organisation and Personnel*. The most substantial questioning of his theory is in Skiles Howard, 'A Re-examination of Baldwin's Theory of Acting Lines', *ThS* 26 (1985), 1–20.
51. Some of his earlier parts are noted by Baldwin Maxwell, *Studies in Beaumont, Fletcher and Massinger*, Chapel Hill, 1939, pp. 74–83.
52. See Skiles Howard, 'Re-examination', and Tiffany Stern, *Rehearsal from Shakespeare to Sheridan*, Oxford, 2000.
53. *ES* IV, 258.
54. Gurr, *The Shakespeare Company 1594–1642*, Cambridge, 2004, p. 243.
55. David Bradley, *From Text to Performance in the Elizabethan Theatre: Preparing the Play for the Stage*, Cambridge, 1992.
56. W. W. Greg, *Two Elizabethan Stage Abridgements*, Oxford, 1923.
57. Ibid., pp. 133–4.
58. See Harold Jenkins, 'Playhouse Interpolations in the Folio Text of *Hamlet*', *SB* 13 (1960), 31–47. Jenkins subsequently produced the Arden 2 edition of *Hamlet*, repeating his observation. The recent Arden 3 editors note his view

and do not counter it with any alternative theory based on more recent conclusions about the nature of the Folio text.

59. The contrast between 'maximal' texts, those submitted for approval by the Master of the Revels, and 'minimal' or shorter texts trimmed for performance, along with the argument for companies confining the length of performance to little more than two hours, is given in Gurr, 'Maximal and Minimal Texts: Shakespeare v. the Globe', *ShS* 52 (1999), 68–87.

60. For a full account of the case for the two versions, see *The First Quarto of King Henry V*, ed. Gurr, Cambridge, 2000. The form of the company's revision is described in Gurr, 'The Transforming of *Henry V*', *Shakespeare International Yearbook* 3 (2005), 303–13.

61. Nungezer, p. 32.

62. See for instance Gurr, 'Who Strutted and Bellowed?', *ShS* 16 (1963), 95–102.

63. Nungezer, p. 74.

64. See Jenkins, 'Interpolations in the Folio *Hamlet*', p. 32.

CHAPTER 4: THE PLAYHOUSES (pp. 139–208)

The discovery of the foundations of the Rose and some of the Globe in 1989 came at a time when scholars of early theatre design were beginning to recognise the substantial differences that existed between one outdoor playhouse and another. Julian Bowsher, chief archaeologist at the Rose dig, is currently producing a book about the findings. For what was built above ground, John Orrell in *The Quest for Shakespeare's Globe*, an account of his preliminary analysis of the evidence for Sam Wanamaker's replica Globe, completed in 1997, established the basic accuracy of Wenceslas Hollar's drawings for his 'Long View' of London made in the 1630s from the tower of what is now Southwark Cathedral. The case for the framing of each playhouse being made polygonal from timber frames was well established, though it surprised everyone that the Rose should turn out to have fourteen sides, and the Globe probably twenty, instead of the sixteen or twenty-four that simple mathematics suggested would be most likely. Jon Greenfield subsequently worked out how the outline of the Rose's fourteen sides could be laid out with nothing more substantial than a surveyor's rod (sixteen feet six inches) and a length of cord. Careful study went into the replica of the Globe built at the turn of the century on the riverside at Southwark and of the Blackfriars at Staunton in the Shenandoah Valley. Much of this evidence is still being argued over, as is the less substantial evidence about the shape of the indoor playhouses.

1. Orrell, *The Human Stage*, gives a good short history of the evolution of early playhouse design.

2. The lawsuit is quoted and studied in Loengard, 'An Elizabethan Lawsuit'.

3. *JCS* VI, 183.

4. On taprooms located by the playhouses, see Gabriel Egan, 'John Heminges's Tap-House at the Globe', *TN* 55 (2001), 72–7. John Cholmley's house found next to the Rose in 1989 was more the size of a storeroom than a tavern, and

must have been used for storage when they took food and drink round the playhouse audience.

5. See Gurr, 'Henry Carey's Peculiar Letter'.
6. Ibid., and see O. L. Brownstein, 'A Record of London Inn Play-houses from *c.* 1565–1590', *SQ* 22 (1971), 17–24.
7. See Herbert Berry, *The Boar's Head Playhouse*, Washington, 1986, Chap. 2.
8. The date of the Worcester College drawings, reproduced as illustrations 33 and 34, is in dispute. Gordon Higgott thinks they were done by John Webb, and dates them at 1660, which is odd since they reproduce all that we know about Jacobean indoor playhouses with some precision, including boxes flanking the stage and give plenty of room for spectators on the balcony behind the stage, alongside the music room, neither of which could be features of the proscenium-arch staging introduced at the Restoration. Webb may have been copying an earlier design by Jones.
9. *ES* II, 373.
10. *ES* II, 358.
11. *ES* II, 359.
12. The playhouses could not have been perfectly circular structures, unless they were built of brick and stone. Elizabethans did not have the technology to bend large timbers.
13. The Swan and the *Roxana* drawing, both illustrated in this book, show audience seated on the stage balcony.
14. See, for instance, Richard Southern, 'Colour in the Elizabethan Theatre', *TN* 6 (1951), 57–8.
15. *ES* II, 529–30, 545–6.
16. I spent much of that twenty years chairing the debates over the limited evidence for a multitude of details of the final structure of the Wanamaker Globe. Architecture is in large part a problem-solving exercise, and particular solutions helped to explain many of the unknowns whenever the design raised practical issues. The outcome is still conjectural.
17. See the archaeological diagrams and Orrell and Gurr, 'What the Rose Can Tell Us'.
18. How the Rose's groundplan was laid down was brilliantly identified by Jon Greenfield of the Rose Theatre Trust. The way he did it is explained in Jon Greenfield and Andrew Gurr, 'The Rose Theatre, London: The State of Knowledge and What We Still Need to Know", *Antiquity* 78 (2004), 330–40.
19. Henslowe was meticulous in paying his dues, unlike the Burbages, whom Tilney took to court in 1604 for a decade of non-payments. See Mary Edmond, 'On Licensing Playhouses', *RES* 46 (1995), 373–4.
20. Peter Thomson, *Shakespeare's Theatre*, London, 1985, p. 30.
21. A thoroughly detailed account of the remains found at the Rose is in Julian Bowsher and Patricia Miller, *The Rose and the Globe – Playhouses of Tudor Bankside, Southwark: Excavations 1988–91*, London, 2009. In addition, more information about the Rose can be found in Gurr, *Shakespeare's Opposites: The Admiral's Men 1594–1625*, Cambridge, 2009.
22. A transcription of the accompanying text is in *TN* 10 (1965–6), 57–8.

23. D. F. Rowan, 'The "Swan" Revisited', *Research Opportunities in Renaissance Drama* 10 (1965), reckoned that the roofing was thatch. Richard Hosley, *Revels History*, p. 150, however, interprets de Witt's drawing as showing a tiled roof. John Orrell sees the stage cover as tiled, but with curved pantiles, a Dutch feature not used in England for another fifty years.
24. T. J. King, *Shakespearean Staging*, p. 2.
25. Richard Hosley, 'The Gallery over the Stage in the Public Playhouse of Shakespeare's Time', *SQ* 8 (1957), 31.
26. The plot of *England's Joy* at the Swan promised 'beneath under the Stage set forth with strange fireworkes, divers blacke and damned Soules' (*ES* III, 501).
27. *ES* II, 436–9.
28. Richard Hosley 'A Reconstruction of the Fortune Playhouse: Part I', *ET* 6, 1978, pp. 15–18.
29. *JCS* VI, 154.
30. Berry quotes them in the appendices of *The Boar's Head Playhouse*.
31. Everard Guilpin, *Skialetheia*, 1598, Satire 5.
32. Berry, *The Boar's Head*, p. 31.
33. Ibid., Chap. 3.
34. *ES* II, 393. See also Herbert Berry (ed.) *The First Public Playhouse: The Theatre in Shoreditch 1576–1598*, Montreal, 1979.
35. Evidence of Tudor prefabrication techniques can be found in many buildings. See Nicholas Wood, 'Fifteenth-Century Prefab', *Architectural Review* 144 (1968), 140–1, which discusses Tyrell's End Farm in Bedfordshire.
36. The groundplans for the Rose and the Globe uncovered by recent archaeology give us little more than two of the three dimensions for each building. That nonetheless is more tangible than the pictorial evidence available up to 1989. For overviews of the Rose remains see Orrell and Gurr, 'What the Rose Can Tell Us', and Gurr, 'The Rose Repertory: What the Plays Might Tell Us about the Stage', in Franklin J. Hildy (ed.), *New Issues in the Reconstruction of Shakespeare's Theatre*, New York, 1991.
37. The initial dig which found a small section of the Globe's remains in October 1989 was only intended to find the exact location and the condition of what survives.
38. John Orrell, *The Quest for Shakespeare's Globe*, Cambridge, 1983, p. 154.
39. Guilpin, *Skialetheia*, Epigram 53, 'Of Cornelius'.
40. Bernard Beckerman, *Shakespeare at the Globe*, p. 92; Richard Hosley, 'The Gallery over the Stage', 27; and T. J. King, *Shakespearean Staging 1599–1642*, Cambridge, Mass., 1971, p. 2. A very helpful analysis of stage directions and their suggestive values is Alan C. Dessen and Leslie Thomson, *A Dictionary of Stage Directions in English Drama, 1580–1642*, Cambridge, 1999.
41. Beckerman, *Shakespeare at the Globe*, p. 90; Hosley, 'Shakespeare's Use of a Gallery over the Stage', *ShS* 10 (1957), 78.
42. Ibid., 78, 85.
43. See Richard Hosley, 'Was There a Music-Room in Shakespeare's Globe?', *ShS* 13 (1960), 113.

44. *ES* II, 47.

45. Hosley, 'Was There a Music-Room?', 113–14, 115–16.

46. *ES* III, 96.

47. Hosley, 'The Discovery-Space in Shakespeare's Globe', *ShS* 12 (1959), 36. For a reconsideration of the stage entrances, see Gurr, 'Stage Doors at the Globe', *TN* 53 (1999), 8–18, 'Doors at the Globe: The Gulf between Page and Stage', *TN* 55 (2001), 59–71, and Mariko Ichikawa, 'Were the Doors Open or Closed? The Use of Stage Doors in the Shakespearean Theatre', *TN* 60 (2006), 5–29.

48. See Beckerman, *Shakespeare at the Globe*, pp. 82–4.

49. See p. 279.

50. Beckerman, *Shakespeare at the Globe*, pp. 85–7; Hosley, 'The Discovery-Space', 36.

51. See John H. Astington, 'The Origins of the *Roxana* and *Messallina* Illustrations', *ShS* 43 (1991), 149–69.

52. G. F. Reynolds, *The Staging of Elizabethan Plays at the Red Bull Theater, 1605– 1625* (London, 1940), p. 188. Elsewhere (p. 109) Reynolds suggests that the third entry might have been through the hangings concealing the discovery-space.

53. *JCS* VI, 215.

54. King, *Shakespearean Staging*, p. 2.

55. See Lupold von Wedel, quoted in *ES* II, 455. But see also Gurr, 'Bears and Players. Philip Henslowe's Double Acts', *Shakespeare Bulletin* 30 (2004), 31–41.

56. *ES* II, 466–8.

57. *ES* II, 434.

58. *ES* II, 477–81.

59. *ES* II, 503.

60. *ES* IV, 319–20.

61. *JCS* VI, 5.

62. *JCS* VI, 6.

63. *ES* II, 513.

64. John Orrell, 'The Private Theatre Auditorium', *TRI* 9 (1984), 79–94.

65. Herbert Berry, 'The Stage and Boxes at Blackfriars', *SP* 63 (1966), 163–86.

66. See the discussion of this prologue in Gurr, *Playgoing in Shakespeare's London*, pp. 188–90.

67. Orrell deduces from a reference by Jonson that the Blackfriars auditorium had curved galleries. See 'The Private Theatre Auditorium', 79–84.

68. *JCS* VI, 7. The prices quoted are not supported by all the evidence, and there may well have been some variation in the standard charges through the forty or so years of the playhouse's existence. See Smith, *Shakespeare's Blackfriars Playhouse*, pp. 299–301. That stool-sitters reached the stage through the tiring-house and not by clambering over the stage rails is indicated by references in *The Gull's Hornbook* and Fitzgeoffery to gallants emerging through the hangings, and by the difficulty the Citizen's Wife in *The Knight of the Burning Pestle* has climbing onto the stage from the pit. There cannot have been any stairs from pit to stage.

69. The drawings were discovered by the Canadian scholar Don Rowan in 1971. They were identified as most likely being made for the Cockpit by Iain Mackintosh and John Orrell. Orrell's book *The Theatres of Inigo Jones and John Webb*, Cambridge, 1985, devotes Chapter 3 to the drawings. Gordon Higgott, however, a leading student of the large stock of Jones-Webb drawings, considers they must be by Webb and drawn after the Restoration. They are too clean to have ever been used by a builder. Since they clearly depict a Jacobean structure with all the features known to have been at the Blackfriars, it may be that Webb copied a set of old drawings that Jones made in his middle years.

70. *ES* III, 144. Analysis of the Paul's likely structure is Roger Bowers, 'The Playhouse of the Choristers of Paul's, *c.*1575–1608', *TN* 54 (2000), 70–85, and Herbert Berry, 'Where was the Playhouse in which the Boy Choristers of St. Paul's Cathedral Performed Plays?' *MRDE* 13 (2001), 101–16.

71. John Orrell sets out the case in Chapter 3 of *The Theatres of Inigo Jones and John Webb*.

72. D. F. Rowan, 'The English Playhouse: 1595–1630', *RD* n.s.4 (1971), 43.

73. *JCS* VI, 54.

74. See T. J. King, 'Staging of Plays at the Phoenix in Drury Lane, 1617–42', *TN* 19 (1965), 146–66.

75. Bentley, 'The Salisbury Court Theater and Its Boy Players', *HLQ* 40 (1977), 129–49.

76. *JCS* VI, 269.

77. *EES* II.2, 52.

78. Such information as exists is collected in *JCS* VI, 255–8.

79. *JCS* VI, 264; Per Palme, *Triumph of Peace*, London, 1957, p. 143.

80. *JCS* VI, 266–7.

81. *JCS* VI, 285.

82. The drawings are held at Worcester College Oxford. For an analysis of the designs see John Orrell, *The Theatres of Inigo Jones and John Webb*, Chap. 5. Unfortunately his depiction of Jones's plan was reversed in the printing, so his description of it has to be read with left for right and vice versa.

83. *JCS* VI, 272–3.

CHAPTER 5: THE STAGING (pp. 209–57)

Following in the steps of Bernard Beckerman, performance analysis has gained a lot of force recently, and valuable attention has been paid by Alan C. Dessen and others to features of the original staging so far as it can be deduced from the extant texts of the plays. Most of the work has gone into particular features of early staging, most notably stage directions, exits and entrances, costume, make-up, and properties, as well as set-piece shows such as banquets and battles. A comprehensive 'dictionary' of stage directions, with explanations of the terminology and full listings of examples, has been compiled by Alan C. Dessen and Leslie Thomson. The traditions of rehearsing have been analysed by Tiffany Stern, while Mariko

Ichikawa has studied the use of the stage doors for exits and entrances. Fran Teague and others have studied the properties used, while Peter Stallybrass and Annie Jones have studied the history of clothing on stage, and Jean MacIntyre has produced a book on the use of costume ('apparel') on stage. Virginia Mason Vaughan and others have written on the use of blacked-up faces. R. B. Graves has meticulously analysed the use of lighting in the early playhouses, especially the use of sunlight in the open-air theatres and candles at the indoor theatres. A dictionary of weapons and Shakespeare's military language has been produced by Charles Edelman, and one on music and musical language in Shakespeare by Christopher Wilson.

1. Kenneth R. Richards, 'Changeable Scenery for Plays on the Caroline Stage', *TN* 23 (1968), 20. See also John Freehafer, 'Perspective Scenery and the Caroline Play-houses', *TN* 27 (1973), 102–4, and T. J. King, '*Hannibal* and *Scipio* (1637): How "The Places Sometimes Changed"', *TN* 29 (1975), 20–2.
2. King, 'Staging of Plays at the Phoenix', p. 166.
3. Gurr, 'Hearers and Beholders in Shakespearean Drama', *Essays in Theatre* 3 (1984), 30–45.
4. A more detailed account of the trends in theatre fashion and changing tastes is in *Playgoing in Shakespeare's London*, Chap. 5.
5. Quoted in C. R. Baskervill, *The Elizabethan Jig*, Chicago, 1929, p. 102.
6. Ibid., p. 99.
7. 'Attewell's Jig' is reprinted in ibid., pp. 450–64, and 'Singing Simkin' on pp. 444–9.
8. *ES* IV, 340–1.
9. Baskervill, *The Elizabethan Jig*, p. 115.
10. 'Turners dish of Lenten stuffe' (1613?), in H. E. Rollins (ed.), *A Pepysian Garland* (Cambridge, 1922), p. 35.
11. John Scott Colley, 'Music in the Elizabethan Private Theatres', *Yearbook of English Studies* 4 (1974), 69.
12. *JCS* II, 354.
13. R. B. Graves, *Lighting the Shakespearean Stage, 1567–1642*, Carbondale, Ill., 1999, p. 156. See also Chapters 6 and 8.
14. Beaumont's *Knight of the Burning Pestle* has inter-act performances of music with a boy dancing after Acts 1 and 3, music (fiddlers) after Act 2, and a burlesque May lord speech after Act 4.
15. Warren D. Smith, 'New Light on Stage Directions in Shakespeare', *SP* 47 (1950), 173.
16. Rafe's Maylord speech in the last Interact of *The Knight of the Burning Pestle* has thirty-six lines of poulter's rhyme.
17. Jonson, *Works*, VI, 15. See David Klein, 'Time Allotted for an Elizabethan Performance', *SQ* 18 (1967), 434–8.
18. *ES* IV, 316.
19. See n.1. King refutes Freehafer's claim that Nabbes is referring to a physical 'scene'.
20. Hosley, 'Gallery over the Stage', p. 78; King, 'Staging of Plays at the Phoenix', p. 166.

21. For a history of the recognition of the open stage and the slow destruction of the 'inner stage' concept see George F. Reynolds, 'The Return of the Open Stage', in *Essays on Shakespeare and Elizabethan Drama in Honor of Hardin Craig*, London and New York, 1963, pp. 361–8.

22. Quoted in *ES* III, 40–1.

23. Inga-Stina Ewbank, '"The Eloquence of Masques": A Retrospective View of Masque Criticism', *RD* n.s. 1 (1968), 322.

24. Quoted in Orrell, *The Theatres of Inigo Jones and John Webb*, p. 157.

25. W. J. Lawrence, *Pre-Restoration Stage Studies*, Cambridge Mass., 1927, p. 221.

26. Ibid., p. 204.

27. Noted by Reynolds, *The Staging of Elizabethan Plays*, p. 13.

28. Quoted in *ES* III, 72. For an analysis of the Wagner Book, see Gurr, 'What the Plays Might Tell Us'.

29. John Melton, *Astrologaster* (1620), E4.

30. *ES* II, 455.

31. Other references to black hangings are listed in *ES* III, 79, n. 3.

32. See *EES* II.1, 206–44.

33. King, 'Staging of Plays at the Phoenix', p. 162. Alan C. Dessen and Leslie Thomson, *A Dictionary of Stage Directions in English Drama, 1580–1642*, Cambridge, 1999, provides an admirable coverage of the plays with such ambiguous directions and their likely meaning.

34. See Werner Habicht, 'Tree Properties and Tree Scenes in Elizabethan Theater', *RD* n.s. 4 (1971), 91.

35. *EES* II.1, 315.

36. Allardyce Nicoll, 'Passing over the Stage', *ShS* 12 (1959), 47–55. J. L. Simmons, 'Elizabethan Stage Practice and Marlowe's *Jew of Malta*', *RD* n.s. 4 (1971), 93–104, proposes that Barabbas is thrown off the stage in Act 5 in a similarly spacious use of the stage environs. I do not find the suggestion plausible.

37. Interact 4. There are two other similar dumb-shows in the play.

38. Beckerman, *Shakespeare at the Globe*, p. 106.

39. A comment on the original staging of the opening scene and the tricks it plays on its Blackfriars audience is in Gurr, '*The Tempest's* Tempest at Blackfriars', *ShS* 41 (1988), 91–102.

40. Lawrence, *Pre-Restoration Stage Studies*, p. 314; and Gurr, The "State" of Shakespeare's Audiences', in *Shakespeare and the Sense of Performance*, ed. Marvin and Ruth Thompson (Newark, 1989), pp. 162–79.

41. Lawrence cites the second of these passages in a text that provides only one man to carry the scaffold.

42. Magett's activities are regularly noted in *Henslowe's Diary*, pp. 37, 180 and elsewhere.

43. *Thomas Platter's Travels in England*, 1599, trans. Clare Williams, London, 1959, p. 167.

44. The best overview of the Elizabethan clothing industry and its concern with 'fripperies' is Peter Stallybrass and Annie Jones, *Renaissance Clothing and the Materials of Memory*, Cambridge, 2000.

45. M. Channing Linthicum, *Costume in the Drama of Shakespeare and his Contemporaries*, Oxford, 1936, p. 14.
46. Quoted in Curt Breight, '"Treason doth never prosper": *The Tempest* and the Discourse of Treason', *SQ* 41 (1990), 13.
47. Eldred D. Jones, 'The Physical Representation of African Characters on the English Stage during the 16th and 17th Centuries', *TN* 17 (1962), 18.
48. Ralph Winwood, *Memorials of Affairs of State*, quoted by ibid., p. 20.
49. Quoted by Richards, 'Changeable Scenery', p. 11.
50. *JCS* VI, 107–9; and see King, 'Staging of Plays at the Phoenix', pp. 147–8.
51. William E. Miller, '*Periaktoi* in the Old Blackfriars', *MLN* 74 (1959), 1–3; and '*Periaktoi*: Around Again', *SQ* 15 (1964), 61–5.
52. *JCS* VI, 283.
53. Quoted in Stephen Orgel and Roy Strong, *Inigo Jones: The Theatre of the Stuart Court*, 2 vols., Berkeley, 1973, I, 281–4.
54. Richards, 'Changeable Scenery', p. 18.
55. For an exhaustive study of the minuscule evidence about rehearsals, see Stern, *Rehearsal from Shakespeare to Sheridan*.
56. Neil Carson, *A Companion to Henslowe's Diary*, p. 56, calculates that between 5 June 1594 and 28 July 1597, the first three years of the Admiral's Company after its separation from Strange's, the company took in fifty-four new plays, an average of seventeen per year.
57. The rehearsal process is discussed in Stern, *Rehearsal from Shakespeare to Sheridan*. On the language of the 'plots' see Michela Calore, "Elizabethan Plots: A Shared Code of Theatrical and Fictional Language", *ThS* 44 (2003), 249–61. For a note about one particular book-holder working on the 'plots' of the Admiral's Men's plays see Gurr, 'The Work of Elizabethan Plotters'.
58. Dekker wrote about rushes on the stage in *The Gull's Hornbook*, cited here in Chapter 6. Other references appear in *1 Henry IV*, 3.1.207, played at the Theatre and Curtain, when Glendower translates his daughter's Welsh to her husband Mortimer: 'She bids you on the wanton rushes lay you down.' In Chapman's *The Gentleman Usher*, 2.1, at the Blackfriars (for a special masque to be staged in the play) he ordered '*Enter* Bassiolo *with servants, with rushes and a carpet. /* … lay me 'em thus, / In fine smooth threaves; look you, sir, thus, in threaves.' At the Globe when *Henry VIII* burned the playhouse down, Sir Henry Wotton wrote of 'the matting of the stage', but that suggests carpeting rather than rushes.
59. Holinshed, *Chronicles* III (1578), 760. See also p. 735: 'Where he went abroad, his eies whirled about, his bodie privilie fenced, his hand ever upon his dagger.'

CHAPTER 6: THE AUDIENCES (pp. 258–85)

Studies of Shakespearean audiences have fluctuated in ways that will be familiar to cultural materialists and most students of critical theory. Alfred Harbage produced a book in 1940 assuming that the typical playgoer was from the lowest social stratum, the artisan. Ann Jennalie Cook forty years later produced one arguing that all playgoers were members of the more privileged section of the London community. My own study, now in its third edition as the evidence strengthens and the numbers of identifiable playgoers increase, accepts that playgoers came from the widest range of society, emphasising the difference between outdoor and indoor playgoers. Charles Whitney has built on this work with a sound new study of individual audience reactions to the plays from the time.

1. Quoted in Alfred B. Harbage, *Shakespeare's Audience*, New York, 1941, p. 71.
2. Ibid., pp. 22–34.
3. Ibid., p. 30.
4. Irwin Smith, *Shakespeare's Globe Playhouse*, New York, 1956, p. 65.
5. Quoted in Harbage, *Shakespeare's Audience*, p. 91.
6. *Thomas Platter's Travels in England*, pp. 166–7.
7. W. A. Armstrong, 'The Audience of the Elizabethan Private Theatres', *RES* n.s. 10 (1959), 240–1.
8. A longer version of Nim's story and its context is given in Gurr, *The Shakespeare Company 1594–1642*, pp. 37–40.
9. Harbage, *Shakespeare's Audience*, p. 56. See also his table of comparative prices, p. 59.
10. *JCS* II, 673–81.
11. John Taylor, *The praise, antiquity, and commodity of beggary, beggars and begging*, London, 1628.
12. See Gurr, *Playgoing in Shakespeare's London* (2004), and 'More Shakespearean Playgoers', *NQ* 253 (2008), 219–21. Richard Levin, 'Women in the Renaissance Theatre Audience', *SQ* 40 (1989), 165–74, has some sound comments on their presence, as has David A. Mann in *Shakespeare's Women: Performance and Conception*, Cambridge, 2008.
13. *Historia Histrionica* (1699), p. 5.
14. A well-balanced view of the failure of *Burning Pestle* at Blackfriars n 1607 is by Alexander Leggat, 'The Audience as Patron: *The Knight of the Burning Pestle*', in *Shakespeare and Theatrical Patronage in Early Modern England*, ed. Paul Whitfield White and Suzanne R. Westfall, Cambridge, 2002, pp. 295–315, esp. pp. 312–14.
15. Epigrammes 17, 'In Cosmum', *The Poems of Sir John Davies*, ed. Robert Kruger (Oxford, 1975), p. 136.
16. John Chamberlain to Dudley Carleton, 21 August 1624, quoted in T. H. Howard-Hill (ed.), *A Game at Chess*, Manchester, 1993, p. 205.
17. *C. S. P. Venetian 1611–19*, pp. 67–8.
18. John Earle, *Microcosmographie* (1628), H3.
19. Verses by Thomas Craford. For a more detailed account of this quarrel, see Gurr, 'Singing through the Chatter: Ford and Contemporary Theatrical Fashion', in *John Ford: Critical Re-Visions*, ed. Michael Neill, Cambridge, 1988, pp. 81–96.
20. Ibid., and *Playgoing in Shakespeare's London*, pp. 202–8.
21. See ibid., pp. 135–7.
22. Harbage, *Shakespeare's Audience*, p. 17.

23. S. P. Zitner, 'Gosson, Ovid, and the Elizabethan Audience', *SQ* 9 (1958), 206–8.

24. *ES* I, 264–5.

25. Berry, 'Stage and Boxes', pp. 163–86.

26. Harbage, *Shakespeare's Audience*, p. 93.

27. William Ingram, '"Neere the Playe House": The Swan Theater and Community Blight', *RD* n.s. 4 (1972), 53.

28. *JCS* VI, 147. For the idea that the play in which Moll sang her song was the one Dekker and Middleton wrote about her, see P. A. Mulholland, 'The Date of *The Roaring Girl*', *RES* n.s. 28 (1977), 18–31.

29. *Pleasant Notes upon Don Quixot* (1654), p. 272.

30. See W. J. Lawrence, *Those Nut-cracking Elizabethans*, London, 1926, pp. 1–9.

31. *The Works of Michael Drayton*, ed. J. William Hebel, 5 vols., Oxford, 1934–41, II, p. 334.

32. Quoted by G. Tillotson, *Times Literary Supplement* (20 July 1933), 494.

33. Jonson, *Works*, VI, 283.

34. *The Gull's Hornbook* (1609), Chap. 6: 'How a Gallant should behave himself in a Play-house'.

35. Jonson *Works*, VI, 527–8.

36. The Fortune and Red Bull companies were both charged with misdemeanours on stage in the last few years. It seems they both staged plays, one mocking certain aldermen of the City, and another using Popish aspects of church ceremony. See Gurr, *The Shakespearian Playing Companies*, Oxford, 1996, pp. 444–5.

37. An. Sc., *Diaphantus* (1604), A2r. For the likelihood that this unknown author, thought by some quite improbably to be Anthony Scoloker, wrote not in 1604 but in 1600, when *Hamlet* was first on the stage: see *Hamlet*, ed. Ann Thompson and Neil Taylor, p. 49.

Select Bibliography

Adams, J. Q. (ed.), *The Dramatic Records of Sir Henry Herbert*, New Haven, 1917.

Armstrong, W. A., *The Elizabethan Private Theatres: Facts and Problems*, London, 1958.

'"Canopy" in Elizabethan Theatrical Terminology', *NQ* n.s. 4 (1957), 433–4.

'Shakespeare and the Acting of Edward Alleyn', *ShS* 7 (1954), 82–9.

Ashton, Robert, *The City and the Court 1603–1643*, Cambridge, 1979.

Astington, John H., 'Inigo Jones and the Whitehall Cockpit', in *ET* 7, ed. G. R. Hibbard, Port Credit, 1980, 46–64.

'The Whitehall Cockpit: the Building and the Theater', *ELR* 12 (1982), 301–18.

'Gallow Scenes on the Elizabethan Stage', *TN* 37 (1983), 3–9.

'Descent Machinery in the Playhouse', *MRDE* 11 (1985), 119–34.

'The Red Lion Playhouse: Two Notes', *SQ* 36 (1985), 456–7.

'The Origins of the *Roxana* and *Messallina* Illustrations' *ShS* 43 (1991), 149–69.

English Court Theatre 1558–1642, Cambridge, 1999.

Axton, Marie, *The Queen's Two Bodies*, London, 1977.

Bald, R. C, 'Will, My Lord of Leicester's Jesting Player', *NQ* 204 (1959), 112.

Baldwin, T. W., *Organisation and Personnel of the Shakespearean Company*, Princeton, 1927.

Barish, Jonas, *The Anti-Theatrical Prejudice*, Berkeley, 1981.

Barroll, J. Leeds, *Politics, Plague, and Shakespeare's Theater: The Stuart Years*, Ithaca, 1991.

Barroll, J. Leeds, Leggatt, Alexander, Hosley, Richard, and Kernan, Alvin, *The Revels History of Drama in English*, Vol. III: *1576–1613*, London, 1975.

Barthelemy, Anthony Gerard, *Black Face Maligned Race: The Representation of Blacks in English Drama from Shakespeare to Southerne*, Baton Rouge, 1987.

Baskervill, C. R., *The Elizabethan Jig*, Chicago, 1929.

Bawcutt, N. W., *The Control and Censorship of Caroline Drama: The Records of Sir Henry Herbert, Master of the Revels 1623–73*, Oxford, 1996.

Beckerman, Bernard, *Shakespeare at the Globe 1599–1609*, New York, 1962.

'Philip Henslowe', in *The Theatrical Manager in England and America*, ed. Joseph W. Donohue Jr, Princeton, 1971, pp. 19–62.

'Theatrical Plots and Elizabethan Stage Practice', in *Shakespeare and Dramatic Tradition: Essays in Honor of S. F. Johnson*, ed. W. R. Elton and William B. Long, Newark, 1989, pp. 109–24.

Bednarz, James P., *Shakespeare and the Poets' War*, New York, 2001.
Beier, A. L., 'Social Problems in Elizabethan London', *Journal of Interdisciplinary History* 9 (1978), 205–18.
Bentley, G. E., *The Jacobean and Caroline Stage*, 7 vols., Oxford, 1941–68.
   The Profession of Dramatist in Shakespeare's Time, 1590–1642, Princeton, 1971.
   'The Salisbury Court Theater and Its Boy Players', *HLQ* 40 (1977), 129–49
   The Profession of Player in Shakespeare's Time, 1590–1642, Princeton, 1984.
Bergeron, David M., *English Civic Pageantry, 1558–1642*, Columbia, 1971.
   (ed.), *Pageantry in the Shakespearean Theater*, Columbia, 1985.
Berry, Herbert, 'The Stage and Boxes at Blackfriars', *SP* 63 (1966), 163–86.
   (ed.), *The First Public Playhouse: The Theatre in Shoreditch 1576–1598*, Montreal, 1979.
   'The Player's Apprentice', *Essays in Theatre 1* (1983), 73–80.
   The Boar's Head Playhouse, Washington, D.C., 1986.
   Shakespeare's Playhouses, New York, 1987.
   'The First Public Playhouses, Especially the Red Lion', *SQ* 40 (1989), 133–45.
   'Where was the Playhouse in which the Boy Choristers of St. Paul's Cathedral Performed Plays?' *MRDE* 13 (2001), 101–16.
Bevington, David, *From 'Mankind' to Marlowe: Growth and Structure in the Popular Drama of Tudor England*, Cambridge, Mass., 1962.
   Tudor Drama and Politics, Cambridge, Mass., 1968.
   Action is Eloquence: Shakespeare's Language of Gesture, Cambridge, Mass., 1984.
Billington, Sandra, *A Social History of the Fool*, Brighton, 1984.
Bly, Mary, *Queer Virgins and Virgin Queans on the Early Modern Stage*, Oxford, 2000.
Boswell, Jackson Campbell, 'Seven Actors in Search of a Biographer', *MRDE* 2 (1985), 51–6.
Bowers, Roger, 'The Playhouse of the Choristers of Paul's, c.1575–1608', *TN* 54 (2000), 70–85.
Bowsher, Julian M. C., and Miller, Patricia, *The Rose and the Globe – Playhouses of Tudor Bankside, Southwark: Excavations 1988–91*, London, 2009.
Bradbrook, Muriel, *Themes and Conventions in Elizabethan Tragedy*, Cambridge, 1936.
   The Rise of the Common Player, London, 1962
   The Collected Papers, 4 vols., Brighton, 1982–9.
Bradley, David, *From Text to Performance in the Elizabethan Theatre: Preparing the Play for the Stage*, Cambridge, 1992.
Briley, John, 'Of Stake and Stage', *ShS* 8 (1955), 106–8.
   'Edward Alleyn and Henslowe's Will', *SQ* 9 (1958), 321–30.
Bristol, Michael D., *Carnival and Theater: Plebeian Culture and the Structure of Authority in Renaissance England*, New York, 1985.
Bromberg, Murray, 'Theatrical Wagers: A Sidelight on the Elizabethan Drama', *NQ* 196 (1951), 533–5.
Brooks, Douglas A., *From Playhouse to Printing House: Drama and Authorship in Early Modern England*, Cambridge, 2000.

Brownstein, O. L., 'A Record of London Inn Playhouses from *c.* 1565–1590', *SQ* 22 (1971), 17–24.

'Why Didn't Burbage Lease the Beargarden? A Conjecture in Comparative Architecture', in *The First Public Playhouse: The Theatre in Shoreditch 1576–1598*, ed. Herbert Berry, Montreal, 1979, 81–96.

Bruster, Douglas, *Drama and the Market in the Age of Shakespeare*, Cambridge, 1992.

Burnett, Mark Thornton, *Masters and Servants in English Renaissance Drama and Culture: Authority and Obedience*, Basingstoke, 1997.

Butler, Martin, *Theatre and Crisis 1632–1642*, Cambridge, 1984.

Butterworth, Philip, *Magic on the Early English Stage*, Cambridge, 2005.

Campbell, Lily B., *Scenes and Machines on the English Stage during the Renaissance*, Cambridge, 1923.

Carson, Neil, 'The Staircases of the Frame: New Light on the Structure of the Globe', *ShS* 29 (1976), 127–31.

A Companion to Henslowe's Diary, Cambridge, 1988.

Cerasano, S. P., 'Revising Philip Henslowe's Biography', *NQ* n.s. 32 (1985), 66–72.

'New Renaissance Players' Wills', *MP* 82 (1985), 299–304.

'The "Business" of Shareholding, the Fortune Playhouse, and Francis Grace's Will', *MRDE* 2 (1985), 231–52.

'Edward Alleyn's Early Years: His Life and Family', *NQ* n.s. 34 (1987), 237–43.

Chambers, E. K., *The Elizabethan Stage*, 4 vols., Oxford, 1923.

Clare, Janet, *'Art made Tongue-tied by Authority': Elizabethan and Jacobean Censorship*, Manchester, 1990.

Clegg, Cyndia Susan, *Press Censorship in Elizabethan England*, Cambridge, 1997.

Cole, Maja Jansson, 'A New Account of the Burning of the Globe', *SQ* 32 (1981), 352.

Colley, John Scott, 'Music in the Elizabethan Private Theatres', *Yearbook of English Studies* 4 (1974), 62–9.

Collins, Eleanor, 'Richard Brome's Contract and the Relationship of Dramatist to Company in the Early Modern Period', *Early Theatre* 10 (2007), 116–26.

Cook, Ann Jennalie, *The Privileged Playgoers of Shakespeare's London, 1576–1642*, Princeton, 1981.

Cope, Jackson J., 'Tourneur's *Atheist's Tragedy* and the Jig of "Singing Simkin"', *MLN* 70 (1955), 571–3.

Cox, John D., and Kastan, David Scott, ed. *A New History of Early English Drama*, New York, 1997.

Cox, John D., *The Devil and the Sacred in English Drama, 1350–1642*, Cambridge, 2000.

Craik, T. W., *The Tudor Interlude*, Leicester, 1958.

'The Reconstruction of Stage Action from Early Dramatic Texts', *ET* 5, ed. G. R. Hibbard, Don Mills, 1975, 76–91.

Darlington, Ida, and Howgego, James L., *Printed Maps of London circa 1553–1850*, London, 1964.

Dessen, Alan C, *Elizabethan Drama and the Viewer's Eye*, Chapel Hill, 1977.

Elizabethan Stage Conventions and Modern Interpreters, Cambridge, 1984.

Recovering Shakespeare's Theatrical Vocabulary, Cambridge, 1995.

Dessen, Alan C., and Thomson, Leslie, *A Dictionary of Stage Directions in English Drama, 1580–1642*, Cambridge, 1999.

Diehl, Huston, *Staging Reform, Reforming the Stage: Protestantism and Popular Theater in Early Modern England*, Ithaca, 1997.

Dillon, Janette, *Theatre, Court and City, 1595–1610: Drama and Social Space in London*, Cambridge, 2000.

Donawerth, Jane L., 'Shakespeare and Acting Theory in the English Renaissance', in *Shakespeare and the Arts*, ed. Cecile Williamson Cary and Henry S. Limouze, Ohio, 1983, pp. 165–78.

Duffin, Ross W., *Shakespeare's Songbook*, New York, 2004.

Dutton, Richard, '*Hamlet, An Apology for Actors*, and the Sign of the Globe', *ShS* 41 (1989), 35–43.

Mastering the Revels: The Regulation and Censorship of English Renaissance Drama, London, 1991.

Licensing, Censorship and Authorship in Early Modern England, Basingstoke, 2000.

'The Revels Office and the Boy Companies, 1600–1613: New Perspectives', *ELR* 32 (2002), 324–51.

Eccles, Mark, 'Martin Peerson and the Blackfriars', *ShS* 11 (1958), 100–6.

'Brief Lives: Tudor and Stuart Authors', *SP* 79 (1982), special numbers.

'Elizabethan Actors i: A–D', *NQ* 236 (1991), 38–49.

'Elizabethan Actors ii: E–K', *NQ* 236 (1991), 454–63.

'Elizabethan Actors iii: K–R', *NQ* 237 (1992), 293–303.

'Elizabethan Actors iv: S to end', *NQ* 238 (1993), 165–76.

Edelman, Charles, *Shakespeare's Military Language: A Dictionary*, London, 2000.

Edmond, Mary, 'Pembroke's Men', *RES* n.s. 25 (1974), 129–36.

Rare Sir William Davenant, Manchester, 1987.

Lukas Erne, *Shakespeare as a Literary Dramatist*, Cambridge, 2003.

Escolme, Bridget. *Talking to the Audience: Shakespeare, Performance, Self*, Abingdon, 2005.

Evans, G. Blakemore, 'An Elizabethan Theatrical Stocklist', *Harvard Library Bulletin* 21 (1973), pp. 254–70.

Ewbank, Inga-Stina, '"The Eloquence of Masques": A Retrospective View of Masque Criticism', *RD* n.s. 1 (1968), 307–27.

'"What words, what looks, what wonders?": Language and Spectacle in the Theatre of George Peele', *ET* 5, ed. G. R. Hibbard, Don Mills, 1975 124–54.

Feather, John, 'Robert Armin and the Chamberlain's Men', *NQ* 19 (1972), 448–50.

Felver, C. S., *Robert Armin, Shakespeare's Fool*, Kent State University Bulletin Research Series 5, Kent, 1961.

Finkelpearl, Philip J., '"The Comedians' Liberty": Censorship of the Jacobean Stage Reconsidered', *ELR* 16 (1986), 138–58.

Finlay, Roger, *Population and Metropolis: The Demography of London 1580–1650*, Cambridge, 1982.

Foakes, R. A., 'The Player's Passion: Some Notes on Elizabethan Psychology and Acting', *Essays and Studies* n.s. 7 (1954), 62–77.

(ed.) *The Henslowe Papers*, 2 vols., London, 1978.

Illustrations of the London Stage, 1580–1642, London, 1985.

and Rickert, R. T., (eds.), *Henslowe's Diary*, 1961, Cambridge, 1961.

Fotheringham, Richard, 'The Doubling of Roles on the Jacobean Stage', *TR 10* (1985), 18–32.

Freehafer, John, 'Perspective Scenery and the Caroline Playhouses', *TN* 27 (1973), 102–4.

Gair, W. Reavley, *The Children of Paul's: The Story of a Theatre Company, 1553–1608*, Cambridge, 1982.

George, David, 'Shakespeare and Pembroke's Men', *SQ* 32 (1981), 305–23.

Gerritsen, Johan, 'De Witt, Van Buchell, The Swan and the Globe: Some Notes', in *Essays in Honour of Kristian Smidt*, ed. Peter Bilton *et al.*, Oslo, 1986, 29–46.

Gibson, Colin A., 'Another Shot in the War of the Theatres (1630)', *NQ* n.s. 34 (1987), 308–9.

Gleason, John B., 'The Dutch Humanist Origins of the De Witt Drawing of the Swan Theatre', *SQ* 32 (1981), 324–8.

Goldsmith, R. B., *Wise Fools in Shakespeare*, Liverpool, 1958.

Graves, R. B., '*The Duchess of Malfi* at the Globe and Blackfriars', *RD* n.s. 9 (1978), 193–209.

Lighting the Shakespearean Stage, 1567–1642, Carbondale, 1999.

Graves, T. S., 'Some Aspects of Extemporall Acting', *SP* 19 (1922), 317–27.

Gray, H. D., 'The Roles of William Kemp', *MLR* 25 (1930), 261–73.

Greenblatt, Stephen, *Shakespearean Negotiations: The Circulation of Social Energy in Renaissance England*, Berkeley, 1988.

Greenfield, Jon, 'Reconstructing the Rose: Development of the Playhouse Building between 1587 and 1592', *ShS* 60 (2007), 23–35.

Greenfield, Jon, and Gurr, Andrew. 'The Rose Theatre, London: The State of Knowledge and What We Still Need to Know', *Antiquity* 78 (2004), 330–40.

Greg, W. W., (ed.), *The Henslowe Papers*, London, 1907.

Two Elizabethan Stage Abridgements, Oxford, 1923.

Dramatic Documents from the Elizabethan Playhouses, 2 vols., Oxford, 1931.

Grivelet, Michel, 'Note sur Thomas Heywood et le théâtre sous Charles I', *Etudes Anglaises* 7 (1954), 101–6.

Gurr, Andrew, 'Who Strutted and Bellowed?', *ShS* 16 (1963), 95–102.

'Elizabethan Action', *SP* 63 (1966), 144–56.

'Money or Audiences: The Impact of Shakespeare's Globe', *TN* 42 (1988), 3–14.

'The "State" of Shakespeare's Audiences', in *Shakespeare and the Sense of Performance*, ed. Marvin and Ruth Thompson, Newark, 1989, pp. 162–80.

'The Rose Repertory: What the Plays Might Tell us about the Stage', in *New Issues in the Reconstruction of Shakespeare's Theatre*, ed. Franklin J. Hildy, New York, 1991, pp. 119–35.

The Shakespearian Playing Companies, Oxford, 1996.

Playgoing in Shakespeare's London, Cambridge, 3rd edn, 2004.

The Shakespeare Company 1594–1642, Cambridge, 2004.

'Henry Carey's Peculiar Letter', *SQ* 56 (2005), 51–75.

'The Work of Elizabethan Plotters, and 2 *The Seven Deadly Sins*', *Early Theatre* 10 (2006), 67–87.

Shakespeare's Opposites: The Admiral's Company 1594–1625, Cambridge, 2008.

Haaker, Ann, 'The Plague, the Theater and the Poet', *RD* n.s. 1 (1968), 283–306.

Habicht, Werner, 'Tree Properties and Tree Scenes in Elizabethan Theater', *RD* n. s. 4 (1971), 69–92.

Harbage, Alfred B., *Annals of English Drama, 975–1700*, Philadelphia, 1940; revised by S. Schoenbaum, 1964, 1970; 3rd edn, ed. Sylvia S. Wagenheim, New York, 1989.

Shakespeare's Audience, New York, 1941.

Shakespeare and the Rival Traditions, New York, 1952.

Harris, Jonathan Gill, and Korda, Natasha (eds.), *Staged Properties in Early Modern Drama*, Cambridge, 2002.

Hart, A., 'The Length of Elizabethan and Jacobean Plays', *RES* 8 (1932), 139–54

'The Time Allotted for Representation of Elizabethan and Jacobean Plays', *RES* 8 (1932), 395–413.

Hattaway, Michael, *Elizabethan Popular Theatre*, London, 1982.

Heinemann, Margot, *Puritanism and Theatre*, Cambridge, 1980.

Hildy, Franklin J. (ed.) *New Issues in the Reconstruction of Shakespeare's Theatre*, New York, 1991.

Hillebrand, H. N., *The Child Actors: A Chapter in Elizabethan Stage History*, Urbana, 1926.

Hodges, C. Walter, *The Globe Restored*, London, 1953; 2nd edn 1968.

Shakespeare's Second Globe: The Missing Monument, London, 1973.

and Schoenbaum, S., and Leone, Leonard (eds.), *The Third Globe: Symposium for the Reconstruction of the Globe Playhouse*, Detroit, 1981.

Hoeniger, F. David, *Medicine and Shakespeare in the English Renaissance*, Newark, 1992.

Homan, Sidney (ed.), *Shakespeare's 'More than Words Can Witness': Essays on Visual and Nonverbal Enactment in the Plays*, Lewisburg, 1980.

Honigmann, E. A. J., and Brock, Susan (eds.), *Playhouse Wills, 1558–1642: An Edition of Wills by Shakespeare and His Contemporaries in the London Theatre*, Manchester, 1993.

Hosking, G. L., *The Life and Times of Edward Alleyn*, London, 1952.

Hosley, Richard, 'The Gallery over the Stage in the Public Playhouse of Shakespeare's Time', *SQ* 8 (1957), 16–31.

'Shakespeare's Use of a Gallery over the Stage', *ShS* 10 (1957), 77–89.

'The Discovery-Space in Shakespeare's Globe', *ShS* 12 (1959), 35–46.

'Was There a Music-Room in Shakespeare's Globe?', *ShS* 13 (1960), 113–23.

'Elizabethan Theatres and Audiences', *RORD* 10 (1967), 9–15.

'A Reconstruction of the Second Blackfriars', *ET* 1, Toronto, 1969, 74–88.

'Three Renaissance English Indoor Playhouses', *ELR* 3 (1973), 166–82.

'The Second Globe', *TN* 29 (1975), 140–5.

'A Reconstruction of the Fortune Playhouse: Part I', *ET* 6, 1978, 1–20.

'A Reconstruction of the Fortune Playhouse: Part II', *ET* 7, 1–20.

Howard, Jean E., *Shakespeare's Art of Orchestration*, Urbana, 1984.

The Stage and Social Struggle in Early Modern England, London, 1994.

Howard, Skiles, 'A Re-Examination of Baldwin's Theory of Acting Lines', *ThS* 26 (1985), 1–20.

Howgego, James L., *Printed Maps of London circa 1553–1850*, Folkestone, 1978.

Hunter, G. K., 'Flatcaps and Bluecoats: Visual Signals on the Elizabethan Stage', *Essays and Studies* 33 (1980), 16–47.

Hunter, Lynette, and Lichtenfels, Peter, *Shakespeare, Language and the Stage*, London, 2005.

Ichikawa, Mariko, 'A Note on Shakespeare's Stage Direction', *ShStud* 22 (1983), 31–56.

Shakespearean Entrances, Basingstoke, 2002.

Ingram, William, 'The Theatre at Newington Butts', *SQ* 21 (1970), 385–98.

'The Closing of the Theatres in 1597: A Dissenting View', *MP* 69 (1971–2), 105–15.

A London Life in the Brazen Age, Cambridge, Mass., 1978.

'Henry Laneman', *TN* 36 (1982), 118–19.

'The Playhouse as an Investment, 1607–1614; Thomas Woodford and Whitefriars', *MRDE* 2 (1985), 209–30.

'Robert Keysar, Playhouse Speculator', *SQ* 37 (1986), 476–85.

'The Early Career of James Burbage', in *ET* 10, 1988, 18–36.

Ioppolo, Grace, *Dramatists and their Manuscripts in the Age of Shakespeare, Jonson, Middleton and Heywood: Authorship, Authority and the Playhouse*, London, 2006.

Jensen, Ejner J., 'A New Allusion to the Sign of the Globe Theater', *SQ* 21 (1970), 95–7.

Jewkes, W. T., *Act Division in Elizabethan and Jacobean Plays, 1583–1616*, New York, 1958.

Johnston, Alexandra, *et al.* (eds.), *Records of Early English Drama*, Toronto, 1978–.

Jones, Eldred Durosimi, *Othello's Countrymen*, London, 1965.

Joseph, B. L., *Elizabethan Acting*, London, 1951; rev. edn 1964.

Jowett, John, *Shakespeare and Text*, Oxford, 2007.

Karim-Cooper, Farah, *Cosmetics in Shakespearean and Renaissance Drama*, Edinburgh, 2006.

Kastan, David Scott, and Stallybrass, Peter (eds.), *Staging the Renaissance: Reinterpretations of Elizabethan and Jacobean Drama*, London, 1991.

Kennedy, Edward D., 'James I and Chapman's Byron Plays', *JEGP* 64 (1965), 677–90.

King, T. J., 'Staging of Plays at the Phoenix in Drury Lane, 1617–42', *TN* 19 (1965), 146–66.

Shakespearean Staging 1599–1642, Cambridge, Mass., 1971.

'*Hannibal and Scipio* (1637): How "The Places Sometimes Changed"', *TN* 29 (1975), 20–2.

Casting Shakespeare's Plays: London Actors and Their Roles, 1590–1642, Cambridge, 1992.

Klein, David, 'Did Shakespeare Produce his own Plays?' *MLR* 57 (1962), 556–60.

'Time Allotted for an Elizabethan Performance', *SQ* 18 (1967), 434–8.

Knutson, Roslyn Lander, *The Repertory of Shakespeare's Company 1594–1613*, Fayetteville, 1991.

Playing Companies and Commerce in Shakespeare's Time, Cambridge, 2001.

'What if there wasn't a "Blackfriars Repertory"?', in *Inside Shakespeare: Essays on the Blackfriars Stage*, Selinsgrove, 2006, pp. 54–60.

Lancaster, Marjorie S., 'Middleton's Use of the Upper Stage in *Women Beware Women*', *Tulane Studies in English* 22 (1977), 69–85.

Lavin, J. A., 'Shakespeare and the Second Blackfriars', *ET* 3, 1973, 66–81.

Lawrence, W. J., 'John Kirke, the Caroline Actor-Dramatist', *SP* 21 (1924), 586–93.

Pre-Restoration Stage Studies, Cambridge, Mass., 1927.

Speeding Up Shakespeare, London, 1937.

Leggatt, Alexander, *Jacobean Public Theatre*, London, 1992.

Leinwand, Theodore, *Theatre, Finance and Society in Early Modern England*, Cambridge, 1999.

Levin, Richard, 'Women in the Renaissance Theatre Audience', *SQ* 40 (1989), 165–74.

Linthicum, M. Channing, *Costume in the Drama of Shakespeare and his Contemporaries*, Oxford, 1936.

Loengard, Janet, 'An Elizabethan Lawsuit: John Brayne, His Carpenter, and the Building of the Red Lion Theatre', *SQ* 35 (1984), 298–310.

Long, John H., *Shakespeare's Use of Music: A Study .... of Seven Comedies*, Miami, 1955.

Shakespeare's Use of Music: The Histories and Tragedies, Miami, 1972.

Long, William B., '"A Bed for Woodstock": A Warning for the Unwary', *MRDE* 2 (1985), 91–118.

'*John a Kent and John a Cumber*: An Elizabethan Playbook and Its Implications', in *Shakespeare and Dramatic Tradition: Essays in Honor of S. F. Johnson*, ed. W. R. Elton and William B. Long, Newark, 1989, pp. 125–43.

Lopez, Jeremy, *Theatrical Convention and Audience Response in Early Modern Drama*, Cambridge, 2003.

Macintyre, Jean, *Costumes and Scripts in the Elizabethan Theatre*, Edmonton, 1992.

McJannet, Linda, *The Voice of Elizabethan Stage Directions: The Evolution of a Theatrical Code*, Newark, 1999.

McMillin, Scott, 'Casting for Pembroke's Men: The *Henry VI* Quartos and *The Taming of a Shrew*', *SQ* 23 (1972), 141–59.

'Simon Jewell and the Queen's Men', *RES* 27 (1976), 174–7.

The Elizabethan Theatre and the Book of Sir Thomas More, Ithaca, 1987.

'Sussex's Men in 1594: The Evidence of *Titus Andronicus* and *The Jew of Malta*', *Theatre Studies* 32 (1991), 214–23.

'Professional Playwriting', in *A Companion to Shakespeare*, ed. David Scott Kastan, Oxford, 1999, pp. 225–38.

McMillin, Scott, and MacLean, Sally-Beth, *The Queen's Men and their Plays*, Cambridge, 1998.

Maguire, Laurie, *Shakespearean Suspect Texts: The 'Bad' Quartos and Their Contexts*, Cambridge, 1996.

McPherson, David, 'Three Charges against Sixteenth and Seventeenth Century Playwrights: Libel, Bawdy, and Blasphemy', *MRDE* 2 (1985), 269–82.

Manley, Lawrence, 'Thomas Belte, Elizabethan Boy Actor', *NQ* 252 (2007), 310–13.

Mann, David A., *Shakespeare's Women: Performance and Conception*, Cambridge, 2008.

Meads, Chris, *Banquets Set Forth: Banqueting in English Renaissance Drama*, Manchester, 2001.

Mehl, Dieter, *The Elizabethan Dumb Show*, London, 1965.

Merchant, W. Moelwyn, 'Classical Costume in Shakespearean Productions', *ShS* 10 (1957), 71–6.

Metz, G. Harold, 'The Early Staging of *Titus Andronicus*', *ShStud* 14 (1981), 99–109.

Miller, William E., '*Periaktoi* in the Old Blackfriars', *MLN* 74 (1959), 1–3.
  '*Periaktoi*: Around Again', *SQ* 15 (1964), 61–5.

Mowat, Barbara A., '"The Getting up of the Spectacle": The Role of the Visual on the Elizabethan Stage, 1576–1600', *ET* 9, 1983, 60–76.

Munro, Lucy, *Children of the Queen's Revels: A Jacobean Theatre Repertory*, Cambridge, 2005.

Murray, John Tucker, *English Dramatic Companies 1358–1642*, 2 vols., London 1910.

Neill, Michael, '"Wits most accomplished Senate": The Audience of the Caroline Private Theaters', *SEL* 18 (1978), 341–60.

Nethercot, Arthur H., *Sir William Davenant*, New York, 1938; rev. edn. 1967.

Newton, Stella Mary, *Renaissance Theatre Costume and the Sense of the Historic Past*, London, 1975.

Nicoll, Allardyce, *Stuart Masques and the Renaissance Stage*, London, 1938.
  'A Note on the Swan Theatre Drawing', *ShS* 1 (1948), 23–4.
  'Passing over the Stage', *ShS* 12 (1959), 47–55.

Nosworthy, J. M., 'A Note on John Heminge', *Library* 3 (1948), 287–8.

Nungezer, E., *A Dictionary of Actors and Other Persons Associated with the Public Representation of Plays in England before 1642*, New Haven, 1929.

Orgel, Stephen, *Impersonations: The Performance of Gender in Shakespeare's England*, Cambridge, 1996.

Orgel, Stephen, and Strong, Roy, *Inigo Jones: The Theatre of the Stuart Court*, 2 vols., Berkeley, 1973.

Orrell, John, *The Quest for Shakespeare's Globe*, Cambridge, 1983.
  'The Private Theatre Auditorium', *TRI* 9 (1984), 79–94.
  'Sunlight at the Globe', *TN* 38 (1984), 69–76.
  The Theatres of Inigo Jones and John Webb, Cambridge, 1985.
  The Human Stage: English Theatre Design, 1567–1640, Cambridge, 1988.
  (with Andrew Gurr) 'What the Rose Can Tell Us', *Antiquity* 63 (1989), 421–9.

Palfrey, Simon, and Stern, Tiffany, *Shakespeare in Parts*, Oxford, 2007.

Palme, Per, *Triumph of Peace*, London, 1957.

Peat, Derek, 'Looking Back to Front: The View from the Lords' Room', in *Shakespeare and the Sense of Performance*, ed. Marvin and Ruth Thompson, Newark, 1989, pp. 180–94.

Pilkinton, Mark C., 'The Playhouse in Wine Street, Bristol', *TN* 37 (1983), 14–21.

Pinciss, G. M., 'The Queen's Men, 1583–1592', *ThS* 11 (1970), 50–65.

   'Thomas Creede and the Repertory of the Queen's Men', *MP* 67 (1970), 321–30.

   'Shakespeare, Her Majesty's Players, and Pembroke's Men', *ShS* 27 (1974), 129–36.

Proudfoot, Richard, *Shakespeare: Text, Stage and Canon*, London, 2001.

Pugliatti, Paola, *Beggary and Theatre in Early Modern England*, Aldershot, 2003.

Rappaport, Steve, *Worlds within Worlds: Structures of Life in Sixteenth-Century London*, Cambridge, 1989.

Ravelhofer, Barbara, *The Early Stuart Masque: Dance, Costume, and Music*, Oxford, 2006.

Reynolds, George F., *The Staging of Elizabethan Plays at the Red Bull Theater, 1605–1625*, London, 1940.

   'Was There a "Tarras" in Shakespeare's Globe?' *ShS* 4 (1951), 97–100.

Richards, Kenneth R., 'Changeable Scenery for Plays on the Caroline Stage', *TN* 23 (1968), 7–20.

Riewald, J. G., 'Some Late Elizabethan and Early Stuart Actors and Musicians', *English Studies* 40 (1959), 33–41.

Righter, Anne, *Shakespeare and the Idea of the Play*, London, 1962.

Ringler, William A., Jr, 'The Number of Actors in Shakespeare's Early Plays', in *The Seventeenth-Century Stage*, ed. G. E. Bentley, Toronto, 1968.

Roach, Joseph R., *The Player's Passion, Studies in the Science of Acting*, Newark, 1985.

Rooney, Tom, 'Who "Plaid" the Bear in *Mucedorus*?', *NQ* 252 (2007), 259–62.

Rosenberg, Marvin, 'Elizabethan Actors, Men or Marionettes', *PMLA* 69 (1954), 915–27.

Rowan, D. F., 'The Cockpit-in-Court', *ET* 1, 1969, 89–102.

   'A Neglected Jones/Webb Theatre Project, Part II: A Theatrical Missing Link', *ET* 2, 1970, 60–73.

   'The Staging of *The Spanish Tragedy*', *ET* 5, 1976, 112–23.

Rutter, Carol Chillington, *Documents of the Rose Playhouse*, Manchester, 1984.

Salomon, Brownell, 'Visual and Aural Signs in the Performed English Renaissance Play', *RD* n.s. 5 (1972), 143–69.

Saunders, J. W., 'Vaulting the Rails', *ShS* 7 (1954), 69–81.

   'Staging at the Globe, 1599–1613', *SQ* 11 (1960), 401–25.

Schrickx, Willem, *Foreign Envoys and Travelling Players in the Age of Shakespeare and Jonson*, Wetteren, 1986.

Schoenbaum, Samuel, *William Shakespeare: A Compact Documentary Life*, Oxford, 1977.

Scouten, Arthur H., 'The Anti-Evolutionary Development of the London Theatres', in *British Theatre and the Other Arts*, ed. S. S. Kenny, Washington, D.C., 1984, 171–81.

Seltzer, Daniel, 'Elizabethan Acting in *Othello*', *SQ* 10 (1959), 201–10.

Shapiro, I. A., 'The Bankside Theatres: Early Engravings', *ShS* 1 (1948), 25–37.
  'An Original Drawing of the Globe Theatre', *ShS* 2 (1949), 21–3.

Shapiro, Michael, *Children of the Revels: The Boy Companies of Shakespeare's Time and their Plays*, New York, 1977.

Shirley, Frances Ann, *Shakespeare's Use of Off-Stage Sounds*, Lincoln, Nebr. 1963.

Simmons, J. L., 'Elizabethan Stage Practice and Marlowe's *The Jew of Malta*', *RD* n.s. 4 (1971), 93–104.

Sisson, C. J., 'The Red Bull Company and the Importunate Widow', *ShS* 7 (1954), 57–68.

Smith, Hal H., 'Some Principles of Elizabethan Stage Costume', *Journal of the Warburg and Courtauld Institutes* 25 (1962), 240–57.

Smith, Irwin, '"Gates" on Shakespeare's Stage', *SQ* 7 (1956), 159–76.
  Shakespeare's Blackfriars Playhouse, New York, 1964.

Smith, Warren D., *Shakespeare's Playhouse Practice: A Handbook*, Hanover, N.H., 1975.

Sofer, Andrew, *The Stage Life of Props*, Ann Arbor, 2003.

Somerset, Alan, 'Cultural Poetics or Historical Prose? The Places of the Stage', *MRDE* 11 (1999), 34–60.

Southern, Richard, 'Colour in the Elizabethan Theatre', *TN* 6 (1951), 57–8.
  Changeable Scenery: Its Origin and Development in the British Theatre, London, 1952.
  The Staging of Plays before Shakespeare, London, 1973.

Stallybrass, Peter, and Jones, Annie, *Renaissance Clothing and the Materials of Memory*, Cambridge, 2000.

Stern, Tiffany, *Rehearsal from Shakespeare to Sheridan*, Oxford, 2000.
  'Taking Part: Actors and Audience on the Stage at Blackfriars', in *Inside Shakespeare: Essays on the Blackfriars Stage*, Selinsgrove, 2006, pp. 35–53.

Sternfeld, F. W., *Music in Shakespearean Tragedy*, London, 1963.

Stevens, David, 'The Staging of Plays at the Salisbury Court Theatre, 1630–1642', *Theatre Journal* 31 (1979), 511–25.

Streett, J. B., 'The Durability of Boy Actors', *NQ* 218 (1973), 461–5.

Streitberger, W. R. (ed.), *Jacobean and Caroline Revels Accounts, 1603–1642*, Malone Society Collections XIII, Oxford, 1986.
  'Chambers on the Revels Office and Elizabethan Theatre History', *SQ* 59 (2008), 185–209.

Teague, Frances, 'Ben Jonson's Stagecraft in *Epicoene*', *RD* n.s. 9 (1978), 175–92.
  Shakespeare's Speaking Properties, Lewisburg, 1991.

Thompson, Marvin and Ruth (eds.), *Shakespeare and the Sense of Performance*, Newark, 1989.

Thomson, Peter, *Shakespeare's Theatre*, London, 1985.
  Shakespeare's Professional Career, Cambridge, 1992.

Venezky, Alice, *Pageantry on the Shakespearean Stage*, New York, 1951.

Weimann, Robert, *Shakespeare and the Popular Tradition in the Theater*, ed. and trans. Robert Schwartz, London, 1978.

Author's Pen and Actor's Voice: Playing and Writing in Shakespeare's Theatre, Cambridge, 2000.

Welsford, Enid, *The Fool,* London, 1935.

Wentersdorf, Karl P., 'The Origin and Personnel of the Pembroke Company', *TRI* 5 (1979), 45–68.

White, Beatrice, *An Index to 'The Elizabethan Stage' and 'William Shakespeare: A Study of the Facts and Problems' by Sir Edmund Chambers,* Oxford, 1934.

White, Martin, *Renaissance Drama in Action,* London, 1998.

Whitney, Charles, *Early Responses to Renaissance Drama,* Cambridge, 2006.

Wickham, Glynne, *Early English Stages, 1300–1660,* 3 vols., London, 1959–81.

'"Heavens", Machinery, and Pillars in the Theatre and Other Early Playhouses', in *The First Public Playhouse: The Theatre in Shoreditch 1576–1598,* ed. Herbert Berry, Montreal, 1979, 1–15.

Wickham, Glynne, Berry, Herbert, and Ingram, William, *English Professional Theatre 1530–1660,* Cambridge, 2000.

Wiles, David, *Shakespeare's Clown: Actor and Text in the Elizabethan Playhouse,* Cambridge, 1987.

Wilson, Christopher, *Music in Shakespeare: A Dictionary,* London, 2005.

Wilson, F. P., *The Plague in Shakespeare's London,* Oxford, 1927.

Elizabethan and Jacobean, Oxford, 1948.

Wren, Robert M., 'Salisbury and the Blackfriars Theatre', *TN* 23 (1968), 103–9.

Wrightson, Keith, *English Society 1580–1680,* London, 1981.

Zitner, Sheldon P., 'Gosson, Ovid, and the Elizabethan Audience', *SQ* 9 (1958), 206–8.

Index